Ends of
Enlightenment

Ends of
Enlightenment

JOHN BENDER

STANFORD UNIVERSITY PRESS

Stanford, California

Stanford University Press
Stanford, California

Printed in the United States of America on acid-free, archival-quality paper

Library of Congress Cataloging-in-Publication Data

Bender, John B., author.
   Ends of Enlightenment / John Bender.
      page cm
   Includes bibliographical references and index.
   ISBN 978-0-8047-4211-5 (cloth : alk. paper) –
ISBN 978-0-8047-4212-2 (pbk. : alk. paper)
   1. European fiction–18th century–History and criticism. 2. Literature and
science–Europe–History–18th century. 3. Realism in literature. 4. Literature–
Philosophy. 5. Enlightenment–Influence. I. Title.
   PN3495.B46 2012
   809.3'033–dc23
                              2012004371

Typeset by Bruce Lundquist in 10/13 Galliard

To Ann Bender

Contents

Illustrations   ix

Acknowledgments   xi

I. Introduction

Ends of Enlightenment   3

II. Enlightenment Knowledge

1. Novel Knowledge: Judgment, Experience, Experiment   21

2. Enlightenment Fiction and the Scientific Hypothesis   38

3. Matters of Fact: Virtual Witnessing and the Public
   in Hogarth's Narratives   57

4. Hume's Learned and Conversible Worlds
   (with Robin Valenza)   79

III. Enlightenment Novels

5. The Novel as Modern Myth:
   Robinson Crusoe, Frankenstein, Dracula   95

6. *Tom Jones* and the Public   109

7. Prison Reform and the Sentence of Narration
   in *The Vicar of Wakefield*   133

8. Impersonal Violence: The Penetrating Gaze
   and the Field of Narration in *Caleb Williams*   154

   A Postscript on My Gross Anatomy Lab   180

9. Rational Choice in Love: *Les Liaisons dangereuses*   183

IV. Enlightenment Frameworks

10. Rhetoricality: On the Modernist Return of Rhetoric
    (with David E. Wellbery)   203

   Notes   237
   Index   279

Illustrations

1. William Hogarth, "Satire on False Perspective" (1754). The British Museum © The Trustees of the British Museum.   61

2. Anon., "Robert Boyle's Air-Pump," from Robert Boyle, *New Experiments Physico-Mechanicall, Touching the Spring of the Air, and its Effects* (1660). Courtesy Department of Special Collections, Stanford University Libraries.   62

3. William Hogarth, *A Harlot's Progress*, Plate 2 (1732). Harvard Art Museums/Fogg Museum, Gift of William Gray from the collection of Francis Calley Gray, G1809.   70

4. William Hogarth, *A Harlot's Progress*, Plate 5 (1732). Harvard Art Museums/Fogg Museum, Gift of William Gray from the collection of Francis Calley Gray, G1812.   72

5. William Hogarth, *A Rake's Progress*, Plate 8, 2nd State (1735). Harvard Art Museums/Fogg Museum, Gift of Belinda L. Randall from the collection of John Witt Randall, R5694.   74

6. L. Flameng after W. P. Frith, "The End," from *The Road to Ruin* (1889). The British Museum © The Trustees of the British Museum.   75

7. "Tom Jones's Journey through England and the Jacobite Invasion of 1745," from Henry Fielding, *Tom Jones*. By permission of Oxford University Press.   129

8. William Hunter, *Anatomy of the Human Gravid Uterus*, Table 4 (1774). Wellcome Images.   158

9. William Hunter, *Anatomy of the Human Gravid Uterus*, Table 6 (1774). Wellcome Images.   159

10. Gautier d'Agoty, *Myologie complette en couleur et grandeur naturelle*, Plate 4 (1746). Wellcome Images.   160

11. Gautier d'Agoty, *Myologie complette en couleur et grandeur naturelle*, Plate 7 (1746). Wellcome Images.   161

12. William Hogarth, *The Four Stages of Cruelty*, Plate 4 (1735). Harvard Art Museums/Fogg Museum, Gray Collection of Engravings Fund, G9035.   162

13. Anara Morandi Mazzolini, *Wax Female Figure with Parts Moveable to Reveal the Structure Beneath* (c. 1760). Wellcome Images.   174

14. Anara Morandi Mazzolini, *Wax Female Figure with First Part Removed to Show Superficial Layers, Ribs, and Structures of the Breast* (c. 1760). Wellcome Images.   176

15. Anara Morandi Mazzolini, *Wax Female Figure, Parts Removed to Show the Stomach, Kidneys, Bladder* (c. 1760). Wellcome Images.   177

16. Anara Morandi Mazzolini, *Wax Female Figure with Uterus Removed and the Structure of the Heart Revealed* (c. 1760). Wellcome Images.   178

17. Anara Morandi Mazzolini, *Wax Female Figure, Close-up of Heart* (c. 1760). Wellcome Images.   179

Acknowledgments

Ann Bender holds a unique place in my heart. Without her constant encouragement, criticism, and detailed editorial assistance, my every publication would lack more than I care to imagine. The dedication in her name is deeply felt, if hardly adequate.

The very character of this book, as a collection of essays written over some twenty-five years, implies incalculable indebtedness to colleagues, friends, and institutions. I can only hope to be naming most of them here or in footnotes recognizing their help with specific references and issues. Although permissions required by copyright appear in notes throughout or with the illustrations, I wish more broadly to thank the various owners of rights for their often liberal assistance.

Both the pleasures and the obligations that come with coauthorship deserve separate mention. My collaborations with Robin Valenza and David E. Wellbery remain signal moments in my life as a writer. I thank them warmly. A less specific but constantly inspiring form of collaboration has been with the marvelous students enrolled in my courses and, above all, with those who asked me to serve on their dissertation committees. I am proud that many of their theses have grown into fine books and that the authors are no longer my students but cherished colleagues.

Some of these essays might not exist without the requests of colleagues who formed edited collections. I am grateful that they published my work in their own volumes and that they often suggested valuable revisions. They include: Felicity Nussbaum and Laura Brown; Stephen Melville and the late Bill Readings; David Bindman, Frédéric Ogée, and Peter Wagner;

Teri Reynolds; Judith Butler, Jonathan Culler, and Kevin Lamb; Robert M. Maniquis and Carl Fisher; Clifford Siskin and William Warner; David Palumbo-Liu; and Yota Batsaki, Subha Mukerji, and Jan-Melissa Schramm. Likewise, Judith Luna of Oxford University Press commissioned the edition of *Tom Jones* (edited with Simon Stern) that contains my introduction—here published as Chapter 6.

෧

I attribute whatever accuracy may mark this book to the helpers who have checked the text and references. Kate Washington started the project. James Wood soldiered through the long quest for images and permissions. Stephen Osadetz gets extra helpings of appreciation for detailed work over the course of a year to bring the manuscript and notes into uniform spelling and citational consistency. Beyond this, he advised me continually on matters of style, and, with my introduction, the essay on Laclos, and the postscript on anatomy, he substantially influenced their final form. With similar shaping influence, Erik Johnson brought his concentrated attention to the edited manuscript and to the proofs.

A few close associates have persistently encouraged my work on this book and notably improved its quality. They include, especially, Clifford Siskin, who twice read manuscripts for the Stanford University Press. He joined H. U. Gumbrecht, Jonathan Kramnick, and William Warner in offering penetrating yet friendly criticisms of drafts of my introduction.

Many other colleagues and friends assisted in significant ways too varied to detail here. They are Dirk Bäcker, Keith Baker, Karl Heinz Bohrer, Alyce Boster, Bliss Carnochan, Dan Edelstein, Catherine Gallagher, Marjorie Garber, Stephen Greenblatt, Paul Hunter, Joan DeJean, Peter de Bolla, Werner Frick, Jocelyn Harris, Jürgen Kaube, Michael Marrinan, Loy Martin, Michael McKeon, Jesse Molesworth, Judith Norton, Nicholas Paige, Nelia Peralta, Robert Polhemus, John Richetti, Haun Saussy, and Helen Tartar.

Research underlies everything published in this book, and it became possible with the assistance of librarians and curators. I thank the Stanford University Libraries and specifically Michael Keller, Annette Keogh, and John Mustain. My anatomical research took place chiefly at the library of the Wellcome Institute and at the University of Glasgow in the institutions there that house William Hunter's varied collections of anatomical and anthropological specimens, paintings, drawings, and books. I am indebted to the unfailing generosity of the librarians and curators at the Wellcome and in Glasgow.

The Stanford University Press stood patiently in wait for this book, even while publishing two others with my name on the spine along with Michael Marrinan's. I am deeply obliged to the dedicated people there, including Geoffrey Burn, Alan Harvey, Emily-Jane Cohen, Judith Hibbard, Bruce Lundquist, Rob Ehle, Richard Gunde, David Luljak, Sarah Crane Newman, and Emma S. Harper. At Stanford, this project has been supported financially by the Division of Literatures, Cultures, and Languages, the Department of English, and the Dean of the School of Humanities and Sciences.

Readers will notice that the documentation of previously published essays generally remains as it was in the originals.

Ends of
Enlightenment

I. Introduction

Ends of Enlightenment

Critique defined the Enlightenment so strongly that the two terms approach tautology. We might now call this critical impulse reflexivity—whether as exemplified by Newtonian induction, by the restless skepticism of a David Hume, or by the *esprit philosophique* that for Denis Diderot and his colleagues proudly defined contemporaneity as such. In Immanuel Kant's article "What Is Enlightenment?" (1784), the *philosophe*, who had been sketched in a 1765 entry in the *Encyclopédie* as the model of independently balanced critical thinking, reemerges as the ideal subject to live under an enlightened monarch. In America, the Declaration of Independence and the United States Constitution assumed such an ideal new citizen. As Kant declared in the preface to his *Critique of Pure Reason* (1781): "Our age is the genuine age of criticism, to which everything must submit. Religion through its holiness and legislation through its majesty commonly seek to exempt themselves from it. But in this way they excite a just suspicion against themselves, and cannot lay claim to that unfeigned respect that reason grants only to that which has been able to withstand its free and public examination." Enlightenment critique delineated not only distinctive ideas but also idealized actors and institutional outcomes.[1] Enlightenment was a state of being, a personal stance, an orientation to the world, and a present moment in history. We live with residual versions of these ideas, actors, and institutions in today's world, even if most often in the modes of cultural unconsciousness and fragmentary recollection.

The essays collected here aim to be in the spirit of Enlightenment critique, though of our own time. I am concerned, that is, with the Enlightenment and its consequences, but always from today's perspective. I try to step outside of the framework of eighteenth-century ideas and not to let the objects of enquiry define my approach. We must conserve our own systems of reference and our own contemporaneity. Otherwise, as Anthony Giddens has remarked, the result approaches recapitulation. Without such distance, any period's historical character will remain elusive.[2] Thus, although my essays centrally engage the now remote period called the Enlightenment, I do not attempt strict reconstruction, even when my arguments depend upon historical understanding. Rather, I look back upon the past through analytic and interpretive lenses that crystallize around the armature of the Enlightenment and that stabilize our perceptions of its residual and fragmentary survival in the realms of philosophy, ethics, institutional formations, and in imaginative creation in literature and the arts. The Enlightenment ended long ago, and its initial ends are part of history, but its purposes return as new impulses that produce seemingly new endings. My title, *Ends of Enlightenment*, refers both to the past of a period long over and to the continuing presence of its purposes. Enlightenment repeated itself in the twentieth century and is doing so still today, but with the differences inevitably present in return and with the productive dissonance that belated repetition enables.

Critical distance allows me to redescribe the eighteenth-century novel as an Enlightenment knowledge system that overlapped with those of science and philosophy in a period before the modern disciplines were marked off from one another. I show how ways of probing experience in the novel were interleaved with methods of experimentation in science. My continuing discussion of realism and fictionality focuses on techniques of narration that emerged in novels of the period but that much later became apparent as such—techniques that in fact permeated social thought and interaction as well. Realism and its accompanying fictionality are, in my account, not so much literary practices as modes that attribute coherence to life as it is lived in the modern world—ways of imparting order and decipherability to the flux of data conferred by our perceptual faculties. Eighteenth-century realism, significantly, replaced the techniques of classical rhetoric, which, as David Wellbery and I maintain in "Rhetoricality," no longer had the power to organize experience within networks of social communication. Instead of formal oral persuasion, which had motivated classical rhetoric, one finds increasingly in the eighteenth century that socially motivated forms assumed dominance: conversation, conversationally actuated writing like letters and essays, and the informally structured exchange of ideas through public opinion.[3] Realism, with its systems of evidence and judgment—as well as its capacity to render thought and thus to foster the communal sense that our minds are interconnected—sustained the fiction that people could move collectively in the wake of the solipsistic, individual-centered faculty psychology that empiricism had brought with it. Such fictions still structure ordinary life in modern society. Ideas central to my analysis, such as literary "realism," "virtual witnessing," and "free indirect discourse," among others, did not exist in the eighteenth century. But, living as we do now at one of the ends of Enlightenment, later ideas allow us to reframe the period and to reinhabit it on our own terms.

In this introduction I interweave short accounts of the essays that follow with an overview of recurring central themes of the volume. The sections of my introduction mark out central concerns for the reader: "Novelistic Realism and the Forms of Knowledge"; "Debating Enlightenment"; "Verisimilitude and New Media"; "Ends and Persistence of Enlightenment"; and "Enlightenment Today?" The table of contents shows that the essays themselves are grouped into parts centered on knowledge, on the novel as a genre, and on the framework of rhetoric inherited from the past.

I. Novelistic Realism and the Forms of Knowledge

How did the novel of the eighteenth century embody knowledge? In my essays, this question lies sometimes at the surface, sometimes in the substrate. How do I place the novel in the epistemological field of the period? I consider the novel not merely as an aesthetic genre but as a force in thinking. In *Imagining the Penitentiary*, I claimed an enabling presence for the novel in the emergence of reformative conscience and thus in the cognitive system that justified, actuated, and shaped the new penitentiary prisons of the later eighteenth century. There, I sought to engage novelistic practice and narrative technique with reformist discourse and with social psychology of the period, especially with the ideas of Jeremy Bentham and of Adam Smith in his *Theory of Moral Sentiments* (1759). I found not only thematic conjunctures but also alignments between the narration of thought in the novel—especially with the technique now known as free indirect discourse—and the constitutive impersonality underlying individual mental states and social formations. Although Locke, Hume, Smith, and Bentham were strongly present, my story traced the confluence of diverse knowledge practices more than the specific arguments of philosophers themselves.[4]

Six essays in this volume strive explicitly to broaden the domain of practical philosophy to include the novel—more often as a genre that inquires into knowledge and knowing than as a site of philosophical argumentation itself. I am guided, always, by Hume's understanding that the ideal of philosophy is to bring together, in a "double existence," the examination of experience through reasoned reflection with the consideration of ordinary life in light of imagination and the moral sentiments. These essays refer often and centrally to Hume, who is for me a presiding point of reference.[5]

"Enlightenment Fiction and the Scientific Hypothesis," traces ways in which unease about fiction played out during the eighteenth century, both in the novel and in theories about the proper role of hypotheses in scientific inquiry. I argue that, as the century unfolded, the earlier discourse that integrated fictionality in narrative and science mutated into a proto-disciplinary division between manifest fictionality in the novel and the tacit, methodologically submerged fictionality that supported a new factuality in science—a fiction that is called "hypothesis." I maintain, further, that manifest fictionality in the realm of the novel came, over time, to certify scientific factuality.

"Matters of Fact: Virtual Witnessing and the Public in Hogarth's Narratives," shows how an ostentatious hyperrealism in Hogarth's early progresses, along with the sheer density of factual reference in these plates, calls objects to attention as physical facts—bringing them to focused awareness in ways analogous to Martin Heidegger's claims that philosophy makes the everyday available to reflective consciousness. I parallel Hogarth's realism with narrative and visual methods of persuasion that fostered consensus about scientific factuality in the period—"virtual witnessing" as Steven Shapin and Simon Schaffer call it.[6] Invitations to reflection opened by realism, I argue, demanded for their audience the traits Jürgen Habermas in his account of the public sphere assigned to the ideal disinterested actor.

With "Novel Knowledge," I again put the novel explicitly into the realm of epistemology and treat it alongside works of philosophy and natural science. Having observed that the words "experience" and "experiment" lie in the same semantic domain (explicitly in French, implicitly in English), I consider the novel side by side with the period's presentations of scientific findings using devices of surrogate witnessing, a topic I also explored in the essay on Hogarth. I compare the staging of experience in the novel with experimental contrivance in science and claim that fictionality is central to both. Finally, with reference to the debate about the validity of induction sparked by Hume, I turn to the problem of generalization from specific instances that lies at the heart of claims to knowledge both by the novel and by experimental culture during the Scientific Revolution.

In "The Novel as Modern Myth," the topic of verisimilitude recurs, along with questions about the nature of the "real." Here, again influenced by Hume, I maintain that our experience of the real as such is verisimilar and that realism is, thus, a way of proceeding in life, not merely a literary mode. I venture that the real operates in the modern world as myth and, further, that realism in the novel is not chiefly thematic and referential but rather deploys an arsenal of narrative techniques that permit language to mimic the experience of transparency through which we certify the real as such. The real, in this account, is phantasmatic and the realism that renders it is fundamentally Gothic. The Gothic novel is, then, not an aberrant sub-genre but the metagenre that exposes the nature of realism itself.

Realism, as it figures in the European novel from the seventeenth century to the present, has profound ideological implications. I explore these in the essays described above but also in "Prison Reform and the Sentence of Narration in *The Vicar of Wakefield*" and in "Impersonal Violence: The Penetrating Gaze and the Field of Narration in *Caleb Williams*." I accept many standard markers of realism: for instance, attention to detail, settings in a recognizable present or historical past, characters with everyday concerns, plots driven by probabilistic connections of cause and effect, and stylistic forms that echo plain, factual reporting. But I focus in particular on the interchange of first- and third-person narrative forms in free indirect discourse, where first-person thoughts appear impersonally in third-person grammar. External sociolinguistic usage interweaves with internal subjective states to form the structure of the modern human character and citizen as at once public and private. Adam Smith described this modern person in *The Theory of Moral Sentiments* and gave an account of the fusion of social norms with individual conscience. With Goldsmith, I explore the political placement of the impersonal within the personal in the 1760s and track the presence of implicit omniscient authority both in the vicar's ideas about prisons and in the covert third-person grammar concealed within his first-person narrative. These concerns lead me, especially in "The Novel as Modern Myth," to identify how the spectral effects of devices such as free indirect discourse reveal a crucial, if counterintuitive, kinship between classic realism and the Gothic in fiction. With Godwin, I uncover the violence which, overtly present in his account of Lord Falkland, is everywhere implicit in the narrative techniques Godwin employs to anatomize (his metaphor) the characters. As a personal aside, I may note that my fascination with the medical and anatomical imagery of the eighteenth century, which arose during my work on this piece, led me to participate fully for a term in the Stanford Medical School's course in gross anatomy. A postscript to the essay on Godwin offers a kind of anthropology of my experience of anatomizing a human body with a team of three other students.

Realism and verisimilitude crystallize important values that we associate with the Enlightenment, just as do other such characteristic phenomena of the eighteenth century: the consensus-building that yields scientific fact, free-floating conversation in coffeehouses and salons, and the rapid exchange of ideas in expeditiously available print media.

II. Debating Enlightenment

During the 1950s, while working within the Frankfurt School critique of Max Horkheimer and Theodor Adorno, and yet straining against boundaries drawn by its masters, Jürgen Habermas redescribed the Enlightenment as both a historical phenomenon and a model for public discourse in the present, whereas Horkheimer and Adorno's *Dialectic of Enlightenment* emerges, in typical abstracts, as an attack on eighteenth-century thought. For them, the example of Nazism became the horrifying endpoint of the will to master nature through scientific, technological, and governmental devices. In fact, they traced the rationalistic impetus toward mastery—seen as the elimination of uncertainty, doubt, and fear—back to the ancient Greeks, and, in doing so, they marked "enlightenment" as a philosophical and societal urge across Western history. Yet, in a real sense, the project to improve humankind through enlightenment had ended again with the antifascist construction of Horkheimer and Adorno.[7]

Habermas focused in *The Structural Transformation of the Public Sphere* on the eighteenth century itself and on social interaction more than on philosophical thought. He recast the Enlightenment as a historical moment that figured forth ideals worthy to guide public discourse in the present. His account of Enlightenment conversation and writing in the public sphere as models for rational discussion in contemporary society departed sharply from the characterization by his mentors of the Enlightenment's instrumental reason, which set the stage for twentieth-century atrocities. Similarly, Habermas rejected the negative stance of Reinhart Koselleck's *Critique and Crisis*—a work roughly contemporaneous with his own positive construction—although he acknowledged Koselleck's account of the destructive contradictions unleashed by Enlightenment critique.[8]

Habermas attempted to restart the Enlightenment by framing it as a constructive model. Referring to ideals about sociability promoted by

Joseph Addison's periodical *The Spectator* and to the representation of private subjectivity in Samuel Richardson's novel *Pamela*, as well as to the conversational practices that governed coffeehouses in eighteenth-century London and salons in Paris, Habermas constructed a history that reinforced his ideal of rationally driven, interest-free discussion by politically engaged but unofficial actors, as the basis for progress in modern democracy. He crucially designated the kind of speaker capable of participating in disinterested discourse as one in possession of a species of self-reflexive interiority shaped privately within the bourgeois family. This speaker's authority derived not from title or social rank but from reflective reason, emotional poise, and social responsiveness.

These ideas were widely recognized and disputed in Germany after Habermas's book appeared in 1962. But only in 1989—after almost thirty years of intervening work during which Habermas's emphasis had moved away from actual actors to the structure of discourse itself—did the English translation of *The Structural Transformation of the Public Sphere* set off powerful new waves of research into Enlightenment ideas and practices. Disputes about the historical accuracy of Habermas's account of the eighteenth century and about the validity of the ideals he defined for public discourse continue unabated. But the 1765 *philosophe*—historically concrete, possessed of *l'esprit philosophique*, and conversationally engaged—was transmuted in Habermas's later work into abstract language-functions defined by rules. What had been conversation recurred as motivated discourse. The historical Enlightenment, which in Habermas's critique had ended because of the domination of writing and discussion in print by commercial and political interests, had, in effect, been transformed by his thinking during the latter decades of the twentieth century into a debate about the nature and validity of debate.

Some of my essays join in the resurgence of attention to Habermas, and my thinking has been responsive to his ideas about the formation of knowledge and the roles of those involved in its construction and dissemination. Often, I consider readers and the nature of social actors in the eighteenth century. Although I cited Habermas in *Imagining the Penitentiary*, the real impact of his historical work on me and on the field of eighteenth-century studies came only after the English publication of *The Structural Transformation of the Public Sphere*. All of the essays in this volume were written after the appearance of this translation except those on Goldsmith and Godwin. Habermas is present especially in "Enlightenment Fiction and the Scientific Hypothesis" and in "Matters of Fact:

Virtual Witnessing and the Public in Hogarth's Narratives." In these pieces, I connect two tendencies: on one hand, Habermas's claim that consensus may be reached among disinterested actors in public discussion; and on the other, the derivation of scientific fact through surrogate witnessing in genres of publication that Shapin and Schaffer take as crucial to the constitution of *fact* in the period. In my introduction to *Tom Jones*, I align the audience that Henry Fielding defines and addresses in his introductory essays to the eighteen books of his novel with Habermas's public. Fielding's narratorial stance enables him to educate the reader as a judge of the complexities of human action—to lead the reader to judgments characteristic of the ideal citizen/speaker/writer in the public sphere: judgments that are rational, impartial, balanced, evidentiary, and subject to change through altered circumstance. Habermas took Richardson's *Pamela* as a test case revealing the formation of what he called "audience-oriented subjectivity," and thus defined the inner world and social orientation of the actor/citizen who speaks in public on the basis of traits formed in the private realm of the family. But Fielding, much more explicitly than Richardson, delineates the private/public symbiosis crucial to Habermas.[9]

Habermas insists that the ideal actor in the public sphere had to put rank and private interests aside in order to act ideally in the debates of the coffeehouse, the stock exchange, or the salon. In one of my essays, I raise an implicit challenge to his assumption. In "Rational Choice in Love," I consider the depiction in Choderlos de Laclos's *Les Liaisons dangereuses* (1782) of the limits of rational planning and gaming—activities specifically excluded from Habermas's definition of rational discourse. I pose the alternative discourse of interests so powerfully documented in Albert O. Hirschman's *The Passions and the Interests*.[10] In his account, during the first half of the eighteenth century and in prior decades, important intellectuals maintained that the exercise of self-interest—sometimes driven by reason but, more typically, by the passions—was beneficial to society. The countervailing forces of such interests, interacting with one another, brought the passions of men into balance and worked to the benefit of civilization. In this analysis, the traditional moral advocacy that placed reason over the passions had failed to control fundamental human drives and had not recognized their productive social dynamic. This view, in which an active tension among interests beneficially shapes society, is incompatible with Habermas's idealization of interest-free actors engaged in autonomous, free-flowing discussion as the essential basis for modern social and political structures. Hirschman accounts historically for a range of theories that justify the pursuit of self-interest by groups and individuals as valuable to society. Habermas, by contrast, poses a utopian ideal for communication that posits interest-free critical discussion as the route to consensus and rational action in modern society. My account of Laclos's novel implicitly casts doubt in both directions.

III. Verisimilitude and New Media

Since the first of these essays was published in 1987, the Enlightenment has returned in virtual guises and dispersed forms. My writings here are like recollections, at once capturing a past that has ended and holding it present in newly mediated forms. Knowledge systems, for example, have become digital and exhaustively indexable. Such indexing made a recent essay like "Novel Knowledge" possible. The Enlightenment ideal of universal, ever-expanding learning might seem at last to have been digitally realized, just as the technology of cross-referencing so vital to Diderot and d'Alembert's *Encyclopédie* might appear to have been fully achieved by multi-indexical data mining, and by the internet itself, where a search using Google yields the content I seek and silently cross-references my search with other searches. The internet's parallel to Diderot is Wikipedia, an online encyclopedia that notionally is unmoderated by any central authority, barring minor censorship and the prevention of vandalism. Anyone may contribute and anyone may modify the ever-transient entries. A listing of recent changes allows knowledge vigilantes to confirm the accuracy of newly added materials. Wikipedia's fundamental principles—its "five pillars"—interestingly include central markers of Enlightenment critique. Articles must assume a neutral stance and represent multiple points of view. Articles must "strive for verifiable accuracy," exclude personal experiences and opinions, and cite verifiable sources. Authors must be civil, respectful, act in good faith, and work toward consensus. All of this testifies to the durability of Enlightenment values.[11] But internet systems are vast on a scale that alters the nature of things. Wikipedia, for instance, approaches 4,000,000 articles in English. By contrast, Diderot and D'Alembert's *Encyclopédie* contained only about 74,000 articles. The earlier systems were scaled to the human being—a reader capable of grasping diverse fields of inquiry.

The present scale of knowledge is ungraspable—dispersed into modules of extreme specialization that are indexable, and thus superficially accessible, but that do not interlock. This dispersal arises not merely because of scale, but because the objects of knowledge are now organized into disciplinary domains, each with its own separate protocols. Such disciplinary segmentation had barely begun to take shape during the Enlightenment. It is now pervasive, even in digital media like Wikipedia. The essay in this volume on "Hume's Learned and Conversible Worlds," coauthored with Robin Valenza, traces this process and the consequences of the divergent cultures and expectations that were already emerging in the eighteenth century for the sciences and the humanities. We live still today with the assumption that difficult scientific ideas can be satisfactorily explained for general audiences, even as they remain technical and complex, whereas specialized arguments in the humanities are given bad-writing awards if they are not couched in everyday language immediately accessible to the common reader.[12]

Running parallel with the transformation of knowledge into data has been the mutation of conversation into social networks enabled by the internet. I may communicate with anyone at any time, anywhere, but at least on Twitter, only in isolated bursts of 140 characters. Under these conditions, the formation of individual personality in face-to-face socio-psychic interactions of the kind that Adam Smith described in *The Theory of Moral Sentiments*, his account of the "impartial spectator" as the ever-vigilant monitor in each of us, could become irrelevant. The basic mechanism that Smith delineated remained influential well into the twentieth century, whether in the psychic force of Freud's superego derived from one's personal past, in George Herbert Mead's literally Smithean inner person in *Mind, Self, and Society*, or in Alvin W. Gouldner's forces of cultural guilt and shame in *Enter Plato*. Current social-networking devices are too new for us to judge, and others will yet emerge, but with the enormous potential they allow for deceit—far beyond the possibilities of face-to-face interaction—they will open society to new personality formations. As early as 1959, in *The Presentation of Self in Everyday Life*, Erving Goffman launched a long series of studies that may anticipate the new person without personality—the situational and performative social human being. Recently, however, studies of consciousness and thought in cognitive science reveal new dimensions within which to consider social formation. So-called "mind reading" addresses issues similar to those Smith raised but with conceptual tools from today's cognitive science. More intriguing are findings about the ways "mirror neurons" link us to others through mutually reflexive responses at the brain's most detailed levels.[13]

Is verisimilitude the new truth? Are the new media not the new knowledge but rather verisimilar infrastructures in which truth-value is secondary?

Will the alert user confuse form and content? The skeptical, always critical *philosophe* of the *Encyclopédie*'s 1765 article had thought not:

> For the philosopher truth is not a mistress that corrupts his imagination. . . . He does not confuse it with verisimilitude: he accepts as true what is true, as false what is false, as doubtful what is doubtful, and as probable what is merely probable. He goes even further: when he does not have any proper basis, he knows how to suspend judgment, and this is the most perfect trait of the philosopher.[14]

In his *Treatise of Human Nature* (1739–40), Hume had been more rigorous about method and more reserved about the possibility of finding truth. Even the faculty of reason is contingent. I quote him at the end of my essay "Novel Knowledge."

> We must . . . in every reasoning form a new judgment, as a check or controul on our first judgment or belief; and must enlarge our view to comprehend a kind of history of all the instances, wherein our understanding has deceiv'd us, compar'd with those, wherein its testimony was just and true. Our reason must be consider'd as a kind of cause, of which truth is the natural effect; but such-a-one as by the irruption of other causes, and by the inconstancy of our mental powers, may frequently be prevented. By this means all knowledge degenerates into probability; and this probability is greater or less, according to our experience of the veracity or deceitfulness of our understanding, and according to the simplicity or intricacy of the question.[15]

When it comes to the search for knowledge and the conduct of human life, Hume cannot dismiss verisimilitude like the *philosophe*, but instead pragmatically assigns contingent value to it. Yet he and the *philosophe* crucially share confidence in the contingent power of judgment to sort out hierarchies of value.

The state of suspended judgment endorsed by the 1765 *philosophe* as one dimension of the quest to separate truth from the flux of verisimilitude has, in the postmodernist account, been supplanted by the media containing every form of life. Jean Baudrillard's simulacra are nothing if not verisimilar stand-ins for a real that had been guaranteed from the eighteenth century onward by the sensory faculties. Then, one might suspend judgment but also move toward probability by making critical observations and gathering facts. Veri-Similitude may seem now to be a permanent condition. Theories such as those of Baudrillard and Jean-François Lyotard point in this direction.[16] But, leaving out such extreme theories, the world around us actually does run on probabilistic procedures, which, for all of their vulnerability to failure, generally do allow lives to function and knowledge to be gained. Scientific findings that underlie cures to diseases and space-landings are, at their base, statistical in nature and therefore not absolutely certain. I believe that vigor yet remains in these Enlightenment practices, no less than in such real, if at times tremulous, values as those of rights, majority rule, compromise, judicial evidence, and even in the observation of trivial rules, such as stopping at stop signs, that let us get on without harm to ourselves and others.

IV. Ends and Persistence of Enlightenment

The Enlightenment as a cluster of writings and performative events already had been defined by the end of the 1780s, when the French Revolution bloodily refigured its crafted critical balances into stark oppositions. Although Enlightenment giants such as the Marquis de Condorcet played important roles after 1789, a brief but cataclysmic few years soon unleashed the reason-haunting demons of Francisco Goya's *Caprichos* (1799) in a Terror of Gothic extremity. The Enlightenment was now in the past—engulfed by the very emotions that it cherished but sought to moderate through the force of civil society. Whether challenged by revolution, by the Romantic embrace of the individual creative imagination, by the elevation of spirit in German idealist critique, by the vast social changes wrought by urbanism and industrialism, by nationalistic fervor, or by extreme rearticulations of its own intellectual productions such as Utilitarianism, or centrally inspected prisons and factories, the Enlightenment would recede during the nineteenth century into a topic for historians. Only aesthetic reminiscences could, nostalgically, recall the period's texture: Sir Walter Scott's novels; the writings of the Goncourt brothers on Rococo art; the Wallace Collection of eighteenth-century French painting, furniture, and art objects; reconstructions of eighteenth-century musical style in cameo moments by Tchaikovsky; and, most oddly, phantasmagoric reappearances of Marie Antoinette in memoirs and jeweled portraits.[17] Or, personal ironists might cast backward glances at eighteenth-century skeptical critique, echoing it in works such as Lord Byron's *Don Juan* (1819–24), Thomas Carlyle's *Sartor Resartus* (1833–34), or William Makepeace Thackeray's *Vanity Fair* (1847–48).

Critique had produced potent ideals such as the autonomy of the self and institutionalized freedom. But Kant's Horatian dictum "dare to know" could turn corrosive. Jean-Jacques Rousseau's condemnation that society's most basic institutions were fundamentally corrupting reversed the reigning assumption that the *philosophes* lived in an age of ever-increasing refinement and intellectual acumen. Even an idea such as the rights of man, positive in itself, produced ideological stresses that existing political institutions could not subsume. Neither Enlightenment systems nor the period's political and social order could remain whole in the presence of critique's acid environment of skepticism and paradox. Critique, by its very nature, according to Koselleck, was governed by internal contradictions of such profundity that they undermined even the regimes that attempted to assimilate them through reform. The ends—the very purposes—of Enlightenment shattered.[18]

Michel Foucault declared that Kant's "What Is Enlightenment?" posed a question that "modern philosophy has not been capable of answering but has never managed to get rid of either." Nor has the question remained quite the same as for Kant in 1784. This is because "criticism is no longer going to be practiced in the search for formal structures with universal value but, rather, as a historical investigation into the events that have led us to constitute ourselves and to recognize ourselves as subjects of what we are doing, thinking, saying."[19] To be for or against Enlightenment, for Foucault, is a burden—a false dichotomy—compared with an acceptance of the skeptical posture implicit in critique itself. This is the stance I strive to maintain. More explicitly, Foucault's words could well serve as an epigraph to the earlier essays in this collection, for the articles here on Goldsmith and Godwin, no less than my book *Imagining the Penitentiary*, were written under the sign of Foucault.[20]

V. Enlightenment Today?

What is the standing of Enlightenment today? Do its ends, in the sense of its purposes, remain vital through multiple endings? Is it still possible to experience Enlightenment, or are we bound by the postmodern condition merely to recollect it? In *The Culture of Diagram*, which Michael Marrinan and I coauthored, we concluded by suggesting that

> the descriptive regimes of our digital age, bound historically and philosophically to those of the *Encyclopedia*, are capable of producing working descriptions for living, despite—or even because of—their reliance on sampling, calculations, and probability. . . . Perceptual certainty has been sacrificed, but human beings are highly adaptable: our fascination with new media means that we have all become creatures of chance. Reality returns as virtual so that we might see.[21]

Can we move beyond critique to action staged pragmatically within the remnants of Enlightenment? Habermas's own thought about the public sphere has transmuted over the decades into a highly abstract set of theories defining the rules of disinterested rational discourse concerning society. But he seeks to grasp the essence of an ideal that continues to fascinate. The virtual domain of Wikipedia still attempts to govern itself within categories that survive from the Enlightenment. However great the stresses and strains, citizens of the United States and the countries of the European Economic Community, among many others across the world, live politically under constitutions built on Enlightenment principles defined by Locke and his successors. The legacy of equality, human rights, objective scientific inquiry, and open communication continues with normative force for countless citizens of the world. Functional differentiation among human beings has replaced hierarchy based on birth as an ideal in large sectors of the world, though class heritage and economic privilege constantly threaten to replace new forms of hierarchy with the old.[22]

In launching a project called "Re:Enlightenment," aimed both to grasp and change this ideal, Clifford Siskin, William Warner, Peter de Bolla, Kevin Brine and others, representing universities, libraries, museums, and academies, assert that

> The Enlightenment of the eighteenth century—the revolution in tools, methods, and institutions that recast inquiry and enterprise in the West—still shapes the ways in which knowledge is produced and disseminated today. . . . Now, more than two centuries later, gradual and sudden changes in technology, finance, and society have put that inheritance and its heirs under pressure—pressure not only to understand those changes but also to participate actively in shaping them.[23]

The very term "Re:Enlightenment" implies endings definitive enough to require the reformulation of basic premises. We may juxtapose a phenomenon from modern cognitive science such as the mirror neuron with Adam Smith's description of social interactivity, but the idea of the mirror neuron is not a return to Smith or a repetition. It occupies a parallel universe of thought and experience. While recalling eighteenth-century ideas about conversation, we may consider Facebook or Twitter without confusing social networking with face-to-face give-and-take. Yet, as Michael Marrinan and I suggest, we might still rediscover the real within the virtual. If so, Re:Enlightenment would represent not the new within the old, but rather a new that refabricated fragments of the old.

To present the essays collected here for publication together seems to imply a larger coherence of thought not present in any single piece standing alone. For me, such coherence resides more in an orientation to the past—and thus to the present—than in method alone. I consider Enlightenment thought to have been driven fundamentally by skepticism and the critiques it produced, but Enlightenment aspiration also was impelled by empiricism and pragmatism. The drive to make "working objects" in the mind—to engage in constant thought experiments as Marrinan and I insist—supplanted classic forms of philosophy.[24] The Enlightenment was built on paradox, for it yielded institutions and forms of knowledge-production like virtual witnessing and statistical thinking that are fundamental to modern knowledge, yet which retain a stance of critique through their very stylization as procedures that produce so-called facts, but are not themselves factual. The Enlightenment's legacy enfolds continual enactment of such paradox.

As I maintain such a bifocal view of the Enlightenment, I see myself echoing Hume's double posture when he closes book 1 of his *Treatise*. Hume there specifies critical distance as the orientation required of the learned—the capacity "knowingly" to "embrace a manifest contradiction." He declares that, "In all the incidents of life we ought still to preserve our skepticism." Yet he is driven "almost to despair" by skeptical philosophizing, which leaves him in "forelorn solitude" and beset by "the wretched condition, weakness, and disorder of the faculties." At the same time, thanks to the power of imagination to confer upon us memory, the senses, the understanding and even the substructure of reason itself, he can turn for consolation to the unreflective routines and habits of "common life." For Hume in 1739–40, these included not only dining, backgammon, and conversation but would, later on, embrace his scholarly authorship of *The History of England* (1754–62).[25]

Like Hume, "my only hope is, that I may contribute a little to the advancement of knowledge." I am a skeptical historicist who believes in evidence, in documentation, and in our capacity to grasp the past—even if in the manner of the vignette rather than of the grand narrative. I align myself with Hume and his double vision: there actually is one passage in the *Treatise* in which he manipulates his own eye to produce overlapping images.[26] Jean-François Marmontel's account of "demi-illusion" or mixed illusion in the theater also comes to mind, for he followed Diderot's theory of theatrical representation in imagining that we are capable of profound absorption in the actions of theater, but he insisted that viewers also mentally maintain a constant, shadowy awareness of the proscenium arch of the stage and of themselves as spectators. His account could well apply to the novel as I frame it:

> It was to furnish imitation with all the external appearances of reality that the genre of drama was invented, where not everything is illusion as in a painting, nor real as in the natural world, but where the mingling of fiction and truth produces this restrained illusion that constitutes the magic of theater. . . . The illusion exists only in my head.[27]

Marmontel's aesthetic points to the layered infrastructure of Enlightenment thought itself—a suspension of disbelief that enabled actions with profound force in the world of the eighteenth century and that may do so in our own day.

II. Enlightenment Knowledge

Novel Knowledge
Judgment, Experience, Experiment

I begin with Émile Zola's manifesto "Le roman expérimental" of 1880, although my own essay is concerned with the novel of the first half of the eighteenth century, and specifically with the place of the new novel of that time in the Scientific Revolution. Inspired by the writings of the physician Claude Bernard about contemporary medical research, Zola set forth a program for the novel, emphasizing its power to define the workings of the human machine in society. "What constitutes the experimental novel," Zola says, is "to possess a knowledge of the mechanism of the phenomena inherent in man, to show the machinery of his intellectual and sensory manifestations, under the influences of heredity and environment, such as physiology shall give them to us, and then finally to exhibit man living in social conditions produced by himself, which he modifies daily, and in the heart of which he himself experiences a continual transformation." Paraphrasing Bernard, Zola declares that "experiment is but provoked observation." He goes on to insist that "all experimental reasoning is based on doubt, for the experimentalist should have no preconceived idea, in the face of nature, and should always retain his liberty of thought. He simply accepts the phenomena that are produced, when they are proved."[1] Zola's novelist was heir to Sir Francis Bacon's skeptical natural philosopher.

It is something of a reach from Zola back to a Daniel Defoe, Henry Fielding, or Samuel Richardson. But the line of skeptical, experimental inquiry bridges across time from the earlier period to its later and exaggerated form in the positivist program of naturalist fiction—a program underpinned by Zola's insistence upon empirical observation governed by doubt. The long strand of invasive, fact-obsessed, even indecent realism was more obvious to the nineteenth-century American Oliver Wendell Holmes than it may be for us today. His critique of Henry David Thoreau linked *Robinson Crusoe* to *Walden*, and both in turn to Zola—that master "scavenger" with a "slop-pail"—as a "story of Nature in undress as only one who had hidden in her bedroom could have told it." Holmes explicitly understood the link of realism to scientific inquiry: "Happy were it for the world if M. Zola and his tribe would stop even there; but when they cross the borders of science into its infected districts, leaving behind them the reserve and delicacy which the genuine scientific observer never forgets to carry with him, they disgust even those to whom the worst scenes they describe are too wretchedly familiar."[2] Holmes traced the realist lineage from *Robinson Crusoe*, to *Walden*, to the poems of Walt Whitman, to the novels of Zola. The connection of Thoreau to scientific inquiry may seem surprising, yet he does reject received knowledge and insists from the early pages of *Walden* on the validity of experience based in experiment. "How could youths better learn to live," he says, "than by at once trying the experiment of living."[3] In Holmes's frame of reference, a statement like this participated in the dangerous social values he associated with extreme realism.

In a reversal of the usual scientistic expectations, Zola insisted that the novel is equal or superior to medical science. Like the physician, the novelist can engage in structured observation and description. But above all, the novelist can employ the experimental method to reveal the inner workings of living beings interacting in society, whereas analytic medicine has to deal with individuals, and largely with dead ones at that. Zola insists that the element of imagination no longer should find a place in the novelist's profession. In doing so, he merges novelistic fiction with the natural sciences and philosophy. He shares this proximity with earlier novelists and continues their ambition to communicate complex findings to their audiences. William Godwin in *Caleb Williams*, for instance, aimed to bring his own "refined and abstract" rationalist analysis to "persons whom books of philosophy and science are never likely to reach." The original title *Things as They Are* lets readers know that he wants to teach "a valuable lesson, without subtracting from . . . interest and passion."[4] Here, as with Fielding's insistence in *Tom Jones* upon the "probable" as the proper realm of action for the novel, the explicit purpose is to open wider experience to a large public by, as Fielding says, "showing many persons and things which may possibly have never fallen within the knowledge of great part of his readers."[5] Early critics often suggested that readers might best remain free of enlightenment.

My beginning with Zola throws into relief likenesses and differences between knowledge systems, including the novel, that are separated by two hundred years and more. The novel of the first half of the eighteenth century was indeed a novel of experiment, but not precisely in Zola's sense or with his explicitly programmatic demands. For Zola, doubt was a tool of inquiry. In the earlier period doubt more often had remained an implicit epistemological stance. Yet, as I consider here, the earlier novel did also participate in the aspirations and uncertainties about knowledge, experience, and experiment pervasive during the Scientific Revolution of which it was a part.

I

The place of the novel in the crosscurrents of experimental natural philosophy is the chief concern of this essay. My title reflects the central terms and ideas that I will be exploring, "judgment," "experience," and "experiment." These terms link into a broad range of concerns about the relationship of novelistic fictions in the eighteenth century to hypothesis- and knowledge-making. Novels often were criticized in the eighteenth century because they were licentious or excessively absorptive: their fictional diversion of readers from work, education, or constructive social exchange appeared to be a threat. But perhaps novels were both attractive and criticized because they were sites of experiment issuing into surrogate experience. Perhaps they produced not too much knowledge about vice but too many thought experiments and, with them, too great an expansion of experience and, with it, a potentially dangerous capacity for independent judgment.

The clergyman who instructs the heroine Arabella toward the end of *The Female Quixote* by Charlotte Lennox enters on both sides of the debate when he says, on the one hand, that the "Power of Prognostication, may, by Reading and Conversation, be extended beyond our own Knowledge: And the great Use of Books, is that of participating without Labour or Hazard [in] the Experience of others." On the other hand, he narrows the range of valid fiction to that of the empiricist novel when he attacks the kind of romance that

> disfigures the whole Appearance of the World, and represents every Thing in a Form different from that which Experience has shewn. It is the Fault of the best Fictions, that they teach young Minds to expect strange Adventures and sudden Vicissitudes, and therefore encourage them often to trust to Chance. A long life may be passed without a single Occurrence that can cause much Surprize,

or produce any unexpected Consequence. . . . the Order of the World is so established, that all human Affairs proceed in a regular Method, and very little Opportunity is left for Sallies or Hazards, for Assault or Rescue; but the Brave and the Coward, the Sprightly and the Dull, suffer themselves to be carried alike down the Stream of Custom.

Given the close connection between experiment and experience in the thought of the time, novels seem to have been feared because their experiments produced a surplus of experience. This same chapter of *The Female Quixote* contains a ringing endorsement of the newly defined novel of experience: "Truth is not always injured by Fiction. An admirable Writer of our own Time, has found the Way to convey the most solid Instructions, the noblest Sentiments, and the most exalted Piety, in the pleasing Dress of a Novel."[6] The reference to Richardson and a quotation from Samuel Johnson in the same paragraph solidly place Lennox in the latest line of thought about the new novel as a mode of fiction that dwells in the realm of fact.

II

At one level, this essay has to be an exercise in the history of concepts—*Begriffsgeschichte*—for research on this subject is served by understanding its central terms and the semantic fields they inhabit. These terms have meanings in English and French that resonate together in the context of thought about the novel. This is the level at which I began originally to project this inquiry.

English "judgment" and French *jugement* line up rather closely in senses like "to render judgment juridically" or "to form an opinion," and, after John Locke and David Hume, also "the human faculty that judges and compares ideas." French carries important additional senses that can shade over all but invisibly into English. I have in mind both Claude Adrien Helvétius's "To feel is to judge" ("Sentir est juger"), which appears in the context of his discussion of powerful imaginative or artistic imagery, and also, in parallel, the dictionary sense in French of "to understand in one's mind—to figure forth in the mind, to imagine." Here, the French meaning of *jugement* supplements English significantly with meanings that might be summed up with words like "apprehend" or even "conceive."[7]

English "experience" and French *expérience* line up with one another but also explicitly diverge: for the French term *expérience* means "experiment" as well as "experience." Even in English, the words "experience" and "experiment" intertwine so richly, as in Hume's discussions of judgment and probability in his *Treatise of Human Nature*, that they become elements in one conceptual domain. For instance, "we consider, that tho' we are here suppos'd to have only one experiment of a particular effect, yet we have many millions to convince us of this principle; that like objects, plac'd in like circumstances, will always produce like effects. . . . The connexion of ideas is not habitual after one experiment; but this connexion is comprehended under another principle, that is habitual. . . . In all cases we transfer our experience to instances, of which we have no experience, either expressly or tacitly, either directly or indirectly."[8] The domain is semantically continuous in French. It is divided in English but can flow easily with a contiguity approaching the continuous.

The word "experiment" also exists in French (*expériment*), of course, and with meanings that align with English. But French offers a fascinating extension of the word. For a person can be *expérimenté*, meaning "one who has benefited empirically from experience" in both of its French senses. I am suggesting here that novel readers in the eighteenth century became *expérimenté*. This is the condition that Thoreau defined in *Walden* when he ranged, like Crusoe, within the domain of experience governed by experiment.[9]

At another level of concern, as I have tracked these terms through dictionaries, novels, and philosophical texts, it has become clear that they bear on the large question at the heart of this essay: what kind of knowledge did novels make? And for whom? Or, perhaps more precisely, one might ask this: in the context of eighteenth-century thought, how can one characterize the knowledge novels were thought to produce?

Let us pause to ask what "knowledge" meant during the period. The answer is that knowledge forms had undergone profound change during the seventeenth century and continued to be under exacting scrutiny across the eighteenth. Broadly speaking, knowledge, which had been shaped by Aristotelian ideas for centuries before, was no longer an armature of accepted generalizations from which classifications, observations, and understandings of particulars could be derived. Interestingly, these generalizations were earlier called "experience," which in that older frame was considered to be of a general and received character, not the historical, situational, or personally specific information we now assign to the word. In the new paradigm, by contrast, experience was profuse, anecdotal, and scattered. Knowledge increasingly was formed when general principles were determined through controlled analysis of particulars as they emerged from the planned and specialized form of experience called the experiment. Knowledge became contextual, specific, and historical.

I am relying here on Peter Dear's book *Discipline and Experience*, where he declares that "a new kind of experience had become available to European philosophers: the experiment." He continues,

> At the beginning of the seventeenth century, a scientific "experience" was not an "experiment" in the sense of a historically reported experiential event. Instead, it was a statement about the world that, although known to be true thanks to the senses, did not rest on a historically specifiable instance—it was a statement such as "Heavy bodies fall" or "The sun rises in the east." Singular, unusual events were of course noticed and reported, but they were not, by definition, revealing of how nature behaves.

Dear might be placing Bacon's ideas in context when he continues,

> The new scientific experience of the seventeenth century was characterized by the singular historical event experiment, which acted as a surrogate for universal experience. The latter had routinely been regarded as the proper grounding for philosophically legitimate knowledge-statements about nature; the advent of event experiments was a practical response within the mixed mathematical science to a confrontation between such Aristotelian methodological demands and the practical exigencies of making knowledge that would be acceptable to all relevant judges.[10]

Dear does not quote Bacon's words in *The Advancement of Learning* but might well have noted Bacon's early designation of experiment as planned experience:

> There remains simple experience which, if taken as it comes, is called accident; if sought for, experiment. But this kind of experience is no better than a broom without its band, as the saying is—a mere groping, as of men in the dark, that feel all round them for the chance of finding their way, when they had much better wait for daylight, or light a candle, and then go. But the true method of experience, on the contrary, first lights the candle, and then by means of the candle shows the way; commencing as it does with experience duly ordered and digested, not bungling or erratic, and from it educing axioms, and from established axioms again new experiments; even as it was not without order and method that the divine word operated on the created mass.[11]

Bacon expounded the institutional form of his ideal in the account of the methodical experiments conducted in Salomon's house in *The New Atlantis*, passages that often are taken to describe the basic ideals of the modern scientific method. That he turned to narrative fiction, albeit in a form traditional since Sir Thomas More's *Utopia*, signals the organic connection between his ideas and emergent new genres of storytelling.

III

This new approach to knowledge raised any number of issues, and while we may in retrospect imagine the Scientific Revolution as a focal point, experimentalists of the time explored a huge range of procedures and formations and raged with debates about method that presented internal and external challenges to the emergent epistemology. Indeed, I would insist that questions about method and the nature of knowledge are intrinsic to modernity as it takes form during the seventeenth and eighteenth centuries. I am identifying the new novel of the eighteenth century as one of the strands in these debates and as one of the modes of experimentation. Indeed, in my view, the implicit ambitions of the new novel parallel those Hume voiced for a new human science in the introduction to *A Treatise of Human Nature*:

> Moral philosophy has . . . this peculiar disadvantage, which is not found in natural, that in collecting its experiments, it cannot make them purposely, with premeditation. . . . We must therefore glean up our experiments in this science from a cautious observation of human life, and take them as they appear in the common course of the world, by men's behaviour in company, in affairs, and in their pleasures. Where experiments of this kind are judiciously collected and compared, we may hope to establish on them a science which will not be inferior in certainty, and will be much superior in utility to any other of human comprehension.[12]

Tom Jones cannot but come to mind as a prime novelistic exhibit in this Humean frame of reference. Can the novel overcome the disadvantages of Hume's new science of the human?[13]

Fielding's continual presence in *Tom Jones*, especially in the opening chapters of each book, points to the work's organization of its characters' scattered experience into the focused and methodical order of experiment. *Tom Jones* explicitly puts its leading character into the laboratory and asks readers to observe his behavior side-by-side with the narrator. The theme is clear, for instance, when Mr. Allworthy refuses to allow Thwackum to continue a whipping that, "possibly fell little short of the torture with which confessions are in some countries extorted from criminals," in order to break young Tom's stalwart unwillingness to implicate Allworthy's gamekeeper in an episode of poaching: "But Mr. Allworthy absolutely refused to consent to the experiment. He said the boy had suffered enough already for concealing the truth, even if he was guilty, seeing that he could have no motive but a mistaken point of honour."[14] Mr. Allworthy draws the line at an experiment with a human subject that verges on torture.

The fictional flexibility of the novel as a genre opens a range of experimental possibilities that Hume does not consider when he writes, again in his introduction, "When I am at a loss to know the effects of one body upon another in any situation, I need only put them in that situation, and observe what results from it. But should I endeavour to clear up after the same manner any doubt in moral philosophy, by placing myself in the same case with that which I consider, 'tis evident this reflection and premeditation would so disturb the operation of my natural principles, as must render it impossible to form any just conclusion from the phaenomenon."[15] As Fielding's narrative experiment unfolds, his introductions encourage readers to become moral philosophers and active critical enquirers under his guidance. Readers must constantly judge evidence, probability, and the chain of cause and effect as he pushes them toward the inductive method of moral philosophy.

Concurrently, the very existence of a narrative frame and the internal logic of the plot, so strongly emphasized by Fielding as a clockwork device, guarantee that such induction will uncover patterns of cause and effect that underlie the action. Fielding, one might say, builds a novel on the very defect that Hume had identified in Newtonian induction: that its conclusions are prefigured in its premises and methodological rules. The circular character of induction so devastatingly criticized by Hume meshes in *Tom Jones* with a plot literally mapped across England in a circular pattern of error and return.

The halts, starts, and erroneous trials in *Tom Jones* call to mind the many false starts and failed attempts in Robert Boyle's published experiments. Boyle's form of presentation was structured, as Steven Shapin and Simon Schaffer show in *Leviathan and the Air-Pump*, to project a rhetorical formation that they name the "virtual witness" to the experiments—a witness who authenticates Boyle's findings for readers who, by definition, participate at a distance. This virtual witnessing parallels surrogate observation in novels by witnesses who stand in for readers or who, as with the narrator of *Tom Jones*, set the very terms of observation.[16]

And so, with this framework from Hume and Fielding in view, among the many interrelated questions germane to our consideration of the novel in this essay, and among the many circulating at the time, three strike me as central to inquiry about the place of the novel during the period.

The first, as I have been arguing, is that of surrogate witnessing. This is the practice in early modern science of placing a single experiment at the foundation of a generalizing inductive process even though this unique experiment could not have been witnessed by the wide audience required for assent to newly defined general principles, or indeed witnessed by anyone or any but a very small group present at the experimental site. What Robert Hooke called the *instantia crucis* and Sir Isaac Newton the *experimentum crucis* demands that we place our trust in accounts of the historical experience of others and use their accounts to extend our own experience to the point of assent—despite the potential for deceit or fictionalization.

The second question has to do with the contrived nature of these experiments. The methodological move was away from a Scholastic, formally mediated observation of a nature that was imagined as a book to be read, and toward experimental contrivances involving precision-manufactured devices like the telescope, the microscope, the refined glass prism, or the finely blown glass-globed air pump. Artificiality and contrivance all raised the specter of fictionality and trust. As knowledge became extrinsic rather than intrinsic, the concurrent insistence on replicability that was, for instance, so much a part of the reception of Newton's *Opticks*, emerged as a response to this specter. Replicability made possible a literal witnessing by further limited observers but did not eliminate the benefits of virtual witnessing as produced linguistically.[17]

My third question has to do with the challenge of moving from the unique historical particularity and contrivance of the *experimentum crucis* to truths of general validity. Baconian induction became, in Newton's hands, the device to resolve this challenge. Newton's "Rules of Reasoning in Philosophy" aimed to codify the method. The last of the four rules, added to the *Principia* in 1726, directly addressed the standing of inductive findings as knowledge: "In experimental philosophy we are to look upon propositions collected by general induction from phaenomena as accurately or very nearly true, notwithstanding any contrary hypotheses that may be imagined, till such time as other phaenomena occur, by which they may either be made more accurate, or liable to exceptions."[18] Hume, who originally aimed to follow Newton's example in his *Treatise*, delimited induction much more sharply. He found that induction, for all of its theoretical and practical benefits, crumbled under skeptical scrutiny, and lost its epistemological stability because it was at ground a device for filling in the gap between empirical, factually based sensory observation and mental constructs dependent on human memory and mental fictions of causality. For Hume, these fictions enabled provisional findings to be made and worked to stabilize our perception of the real, but they did not certify knowledge. I consider here that the manifest fictions of the new novel could work, paradoxically, to guarantee induction by framing it within tightly controlled narrative structures.

Thomas Reid's reassertion of Newtonian induction under the banner of his commonsense philosophy did not close the gap Hume had opened in his treatment of the problem of induction, and the so-called "problem of induction" remains an active philosophical topic even now.

My claim in this essay, at its core, then, is quite simple: that the early novel figures in specific ways in the discursive network now called the Scientific Revolution, and that our understanding of the novel as a genre is expanded by viewing it as a system that puts into play the three basic issues I have identified.

IV

The early novel in its many permutations, including works by Defoe, Richardson, and Fielding, depended crucially upon devices associated with surrogate observation of the kind described by Shapin and Schaffer under the heading "virtual witnessing." Let us recall here that these devices are largely those of a historically specific sort of verbal rhetoric. The novel depends fundamentally on a rhetoric that allows, even demands, that readers add to their stock of knowledge through assent to the truth of absent experience. Defoe early experimented with rhetoric of this kind in *A True Relation of the Apparition of One Mrs. Veal* (1706), a story of visitation from the dead that is attested in the manner of an affidavit with minute evidentiary particulars certified by a gentleman justice of the peace of Maidstone, Kent: "This relation is matter of fact, and attended with such circumstances as may induce any reasonable man to believe it." It ends with an assertion that might seem like a prefiguration of Hume through a glass darkly: "This thing has very much affected me, and I am as well satisfied as I am of the best grounded matter of fact. And why should we dispute matter of fact because we cannot solve things of which we can have no certain or demonstrative notions, seems strange to me."[19] The powerful frame of narration here works to certify the evidence and points to its factuality by simulating the effect not only of a legal document but also of a scientific report. Bacon's unbound broom of experience is shaped into an account resembling that of an *experimentum crucis*.

Richardson's definition of the precisely balanced mental posture he hoped for in readers of Clarissa's fictional letters remarkably mirrors Newton's fourth rule, albeit from the inversely parallel realm of the novel:

> I could wish that the *Air* of Genuineness had been kept up, tho' I want not the letters to be *thought* genuine; only so far kept up, I mean, as they should not prefatically be owned *not* to be genuine: and this for fear of weakening their

Influence where any of them are aimed to be exemplary; as well as to avoid hurting that kind of Historical Faith which Fiction itself is generally read with, tho' we know it to be Fiction.[20]

In other words, Richardson wants readers to be poised on a skeptical knife-edge between acceptance of his novelistic letters as real and awareness that they are fictions. Catherine Gallagher embraces the term "ironic credulity" to account for this posture in fiction more broadly.[21]

In parallel to my second question about contrivance in experiments, the novel also contrives situations—often extreme and counterintuitive—that transform fictional experience into decisive experiments in the course of their action. A contrivance of this kind is what Arabella's clergyman instructor notes in *The Female Quixote*. Indeed, Arabella's own awakening to reality comes after a contrivance, within the plot of the novel, of what she takes to be a life-threatening attack on her. And, in tandem with my third question about the standing of the unique event, the quasi-inductive leap from particulars to general principles that Defoe, Richardson, and Fielding aspired to actuate in readers of their novels operates in these books through the causal sequences we call narratives. In a reverse system, cause and effect frame induction and even stand in for it rather than being its outcome. The precise operation of machinery contrived by the novelist—as Fielding continually informs his readers—replaces the clockmaker God's precision. Novels of this kind suspend the limitations of induction for their duration.

V

Modern theory of the novel includes a concept that assists my thinking in this essay. It is Ian Watt's "realism of assessment" as he applied it to the novel—especially the novels of Henry Fielding and Jane Austen. "Realism of assessment," in the context of Watt's central category of "realism of presentation," means something like judgment founded on experiment and experience. The experience in question for Watt is that of the represented narrator, or so it seems to me, though of course such assessment has the reader as its audience.[22]

Assessment is at the heart of both Locke's and Hume's accounts of judgment but for them this judgment does not attain the status of knowledge. Locke observes of this limit that, "I must apply my self to *Experience*; as far as that reaches, I may have certain Knowledge, but not farther." He continues, "I deny not, but a Man accustomed to rational and regular Experiments shall be able to see farther into the Nature of Bodies, and guess righter at their yet unknown Properties, than one, that is a Stranger to them: But yet, as I have said, this is but Judgment and Opinion, not Knowledge and Certainty."[23] Hume asserts that "since it is not from knowledge or any scientific reasoning that we derive the opinion of the necessity of a cause to every new production, that opinion must necessarily arise from observation and experience." And he goes on to insist that, "'Tis therefore by experience only that we can infer the existence of one object from that of another. The nature of experience is this."[24] Clarissa claims as much when she writes to Miss Howe—herself impersonating an elderly lady giving advice to a younger mother:

> Nothing but experience can give us a strong and efficacious conviction . . . and when we would inculcate the fruits of *that* upon the minds of those we love, who have not lived long enough to find those fruits, and would hope that our *advice* should have as much force upon *them* as *experience* has upon *us*; and which, perhaps *our* parents' advice had not upon *ourselves* at our daughters' time of life; should we not proceed by patient reasoning and gentleness, that we may not harden where we would convince?[25]

We should not be deceived by Richardson's post-facto moralistic explications of *Clarissa* or by his pietism, for he appears to have been quite attuned to the problematics with which I am concerned here.

Robinson Crusoe illustrates the theory of experiment-based experience when he describes his acquisition of knowledge about the strategy of planting crops:

> The rainy season, and the dry season, began now to appear regular to me, and I learn'd to divide them so, as to provide for them accordingly. But I bought all by experience before I had it; and this I am going to relate, was one of the most discouraging experiments that I made at all: I have mention'd that I had sav'd the few ears of barley and rice which I had so surprisingly found spring up, as I thought, of themselves, and believe there were about thirty stalks of rice, and about twenty of barley; and now I thought it a proper time to sow it after the rains, the sun being in its *southern* position going from me.
>
> Accordingly I dug up a Piece of Ground, as well as I could with my wooden spade, and dividing it into two parts, I sow'd my grain; but as I was sowing, it casually occur'd to my thoughts, that I would not sow it all at first, because I did not know when was the proper time for it; so I sow'd about two thirds of the seed, leaving about a handful of each.[26]

Crusoe forms his judgment through ongoing experimental assessment based on observation and probability. He makes a prudential decision founded on experience, and he emerges with knowledge as Hume later will characterize it. His repertory of knowledge grows across the action, developing into a virtuoso expertise, not just in natural processes but, as Zola says, in the capacity "to exhibit man living in social conditions produced by himself, which he modifies daily, and in the heart of which he himself experiences a continual transformation." Significant here is the reach of Crusoe's experience across time, for the concept of experience would mean little without memory of the past and projection into the future. The reach of remembered experience as history is crucial when, a few pages before his story about the crops, Crusoe recounts having found abundant fruit, especially grapes, in his island's highland woods: "I was exceeding glad of them; but I was warn'd by my experience to eat sparingly of them, remembering, that when I was ashore in *Barbary*, the eating of Grapes kill'd several of our *English* Men who were slaves there, by throwing them into fluxes and fevers."[27] With expertise gained by experience at Crusoe's command, he is able to stage the episode toward the end of his island stay in which he entraps the mutineers. His expertise now comprehends not only experience and its special variant, experiment, but also the power to make the narrative fictions with which he lures his prey.[28]

What other approach might Defoe have written for Crusoe to take as a character? It is hard to imagine Crusoe as a master of received knowledge and deduction rather than of sense observation and induction, but we may speculate that he could have employed the opposite of his experiential experimentalism, which was called "theory" in his own time. Clarissa's own Lovelace, for instance, declares of one Miss Rawlins that she is, "an agreeable young Lady enough; but not beautiful. She has sense, and would be thought *to know the world*, as it is called; but, for her knowledge, is more indebted to *theory* than *experience*. A mere whipped-syllabub knowledge this, Jack, that always fails the person who trusts to it, when it should hold to do her service. . . . But, for Miss Rawlins, if I can add *experience* to her *theory*, what an accomplished person will she be!"[29] Although Lovelace gives the idea of experience a salacious twist here, he is operating within the epistemology of his day. Did *Clarissa* protect the Miss Rawlinses of the world by expanding their experience? Richardson seems sincerely to have believed that it would.

Jonathan Swift's Gulliver has experiment forced upon him, and vows that it confirms both what he has heard and his own past experience when confronted with a gigantic domestic cat in the phantasmatically huge realm of Brobdingnag:

> I heard a Noise behind me like that of a Dozen Stocking-Weavers at work; and turning my Head, I found it proceeded from the Purring of this Animal, who

seemed to be three Times larger than an Ox, as I computed by the View of her Head, and one of her Paws. . . . The Fierceness of this Creature's Countenance altogether discomposed me; although I stood . . . above fifty Foot off. . . . But it happened there was no Danger; for the Cat took not the least Notice of me when my Master placed me within three Yards of her. And as I have been always told, and found true by Experience in my Travels, that flying, or discovering Fear before a fierce Animal, is a certain Way to make it pursue or attack you; so I resolved in this dangerous Juncture to shew no Manner of Concern. I walked with Intrepidity five or six Times before the very Head of the Cat, and came within half a Yard of her; whereupon she drew her self back, as if she were more afraid of me.[30]

Gulliver's senses deceive him into thinking about stocking weavers, but his experience, and what he has been told, secure his safety despite the doubtful analogy between wild and domestic animals. Crusoe's assessments based on experience are confirmed by experiment, and Gulliver's prove at least in part to be. But their actions do not both constitute realism of assessment in Watt's sense. Rather, the narrations in which the two appear as characters frame their assessments in ways that produce quite diverse effects. The implicit ironic asides of Swift's narration, as it presents Gulliver's alternate cowering and swaggering, guide the reader to a specific stance. And one wonders in Swift how integral Gulliver's narration is supposed to be when it is possible that the metaphor of the stocking weavers may be a retrospective ornament on the hero's part. Close readers also may question Gulliver's judgment if they recall the episode when huge Brobdingnagian field workers bear down on him and he decrees that everyone knows animals to be more savage the larger they are. This is precisely the opposite of what he could have observed in Lilliput where he himself is a gentle giant and the Lilliputians are, on the whole, vicious.

Swift's critique of scientific inquiry run amok in book 3 of *Gulliver's Travels* could seem to diminish the probability that his narratives in the other books would intersect with the rhetoric of the Scientific Revolution. But his satire of excess in that one book does not rule out what one might call "normal science" in the others—books that are often treated as part of the history of the new novel. Swift's generic choice of the travel story as the armature of his accounts also worked in the 1720s, after the enormous impact of *Robinson Crusoe*, to embed devices of the empiricist novel in his narrative. Even as he satirizes such narratives, he is swept into their technical vortex. Another dimension of *Gulliver's Travels* that may seem to cut against any association of it with the new novel is the element of fantasy at the core of each book's action. Yet, fantastic stories are not necessarily incompatible with the narrative techniques of realism, as the linguistic practices of the Gothic novel reveal in Horace Walpole's *The Castle of Otranto* and its heirs. Indeed, many works in the canon of the nineteenth-century British and American novel have powerful Gothic aspects and yet are narrated in the modes of realism.[31]

Swift's ironic signposts, which become so massive in book 3 of *Gulliver's Travels* that they move away from implication and indirect statement to manifesto, define possible responses. The much more neutral presentation of Crusoe by Defoe opens the potential for readers to make judgments of their own—that is, to the weighing of evidence, experience, and experiment in order to arrive at judgments of the kind characteristic of Fielding's or Austen's realism of assessment.

VI

Realism of assessment implicitly includes the consideration of probability. Locke devoted an entire chapter to the topic in book 4 of his *Essay Concerning Human Understanding*. Knowledge being, in his account, "nothing but the perception of connexion and agreement, or disagreement and repugnancy of any of our ideas," probability "is nothing but the appearance of such an Agreement, or Disagreement, by the intervention of Proofs, whose connexion is not constant and immutable, or at least is not perceived to be so, but is, or appears for the most part to be so, and is enough to induce the Mind to *judge* the Proposition to be true, or false, rather than the contrary." He continues, "*Probability* is likeliness to be true, the very notation of the Word signifying such a Proposition, for which there be Arguments or Proofs, to make it pass or to be received for true. The entertainment the Mind gives this sort of Propositions, is called *Belief, Assent*, or *Opinion*."[32] In such a context, as Peter Dear notes, citing Ian Hacking, the "probable" means "worthy of approbation" rather than simply "likely."[33] We should not hurry, then, to bring the modernist rise of mathematical probabilities too quickly into the picture in thinking about novelistic knowledge during the first half of the century or even later.

Although many speculations about probabilistic understanding in moral, ethical, and judicial affairs were undertaken in the eighteenth century, and the Marquis de Condorcet, for instance, tried to apply mathematical probabilistic thinking to aspects of society including judicial practice, the sense that the calculus of probability might govern practical human decisions was not widespread.[34] Even in the realm of games of chance, where Edmond Hoyle's work was very broadly disseminated beginning in the 1740s and 1750s, the practical effects were few.[35] Insurance brokers and annuity writers, for instance, were slow to bring into practice the findings of mathematicians—even findings that were specifically about the field of business.[36] In addition, and in general harmony with Locke's approach to probability, which includes an element of intuition, the very modern assumption that the rational, probabilistic projection of circumstance is at odds with common sense does not reflect eighteenth-century practice, in which, according to Lorraine Daston and her colleagues, the mathematicians studying probability actively sought to align their findings with those of commonsense reasoning—even sometimes adjusting their math to conform to common sense.

The Female Quixote is the novelistic *locus classicus* defining the kind of judgment that Watt calls "realism of assessment" and that he assigns to narrators. This novel also includes a debate on the issues of concern here. At the end of this work, as noted earlier, the clergyman who appears in order to set the heroine, Arabella, to rights and to correct her uncritical belief in fantastical romance fictions asserts that, "when the Sailor in certain Latitudes sees the Clouds rise, Experience bids him expect a Storm. When any Monarch levies Armies, his Neighbours prepare to repel any Invasion." And then, "The only Excellence of Falshood . . . is its Resemblance to Truth; as therefore any Narrative is more liable to be confuted by its Inconsistency with known Facts, it is at a greater Distance from the Perfection of Fiction; for there can be no Difficulty in framing a Tale, if we are left at Liberty to invert all History and Nature for our own Conveniency."[37] The good divine is functioning as a hybrid of narrator and character when he works Arabella through a series of empirical tests of her faith in romance. He is, from the point of view I take here, framing a distinction, on the one hand, between fictions that enhance the powers of readers as they form the probabilistic judgments with which they must make their way through he world, and on the other hand, fictions that diminish these powers or, at worst, foster delusion. He is framing a method for using experience to distinguish between fiction and reality. For this purpose, the broad expansion of experience that the empiricist novel made possible functioned as knowledge.

Do the fictions that the divine implicitly endorses—the ones we now call realist novels—actually make knowledge for readers? Or for science? Certainly, they can provide templates for practical reason or judgment based in experiment, experience, and—to invoke that French sense of *jugement*—intuitive apprehension of the world. As John Richetti says of Locke's *Essay*,

"Within the dramatizations of Book II at least, 'reality' itself is an ultimate hypothesis, an extrapolation from the data experience provides."[38]

I would suggest in closing that novelistic knowledge resides not only in the new novel's expansion of experience but also in the genre's staging of the act of assessment as ongoing probabilistic judgment. And is this knowledge? Let us recall, as I give Hume the last word in this essay, that his arguments come down to this astonishing finding—one that in itself could be described as a theory of the novel:

> We must . . . in every reasoning form a new judgment, as a check or controul on our first judgment or belief; and must enlarge our view to comprehend a kind of history of all the instances, wherein our understanding has deceiv'd us, compar'd with those, wherein its testimony was just and true. Our reason must be consider'd as a kind of cause, of which truth is the natural effect; but such-a-one as by the irruption of other causes, and by the inconstancy of our mental powers, may frequently be prevented. By this means all knowledge degenerates into probability; and this probability is greater or less, according to our experience of the veracity or deceitfulness of our understanding, and according to the simplicity or intricacy of the question.[39]

Perhaps this is the best we can do, useful as the discipline of what we now call the scientific method has proven to be. But the new novel of Hume's own time was experimenting with methods to improve the odds.

CHAPTER 2

Enlightenment Fiction and the Scientific Hypothesis

The eighteenth-century novel was part of a cultural system that worked to validate Enlightenment canons of knowledge by dynamically linking the realms of science and fiction in the very process of setting them in opposition. In contemplating the historical particulars of this always mobile counterpoise, this essay focuses on a realignment that occurred around 1750, when the guarantee of factuality in science increasingly required the presence of its opposite, a manifest yet verisimilar fictionality in the novel. My method is purposely to erase boundaries among specialized senses of words that, even today, remain central to our protocols of knowledge in order to suggest how freely the problematics they engage jostled with one another during a period when the modern disciplines and professions were emerging in correlation with new divisions of knowledge. I have ignored the tiny parentheses that followed headings—for example, "HYPOTHESE (Métaphysiq.)"—in the dictionaries and encyclopedias that played a crucial role in marking out these divisions and in linking words to disciplines. Parenthetical allocations in Denis Diderot and Jean le Rond d'Alembert's *Encyclopédie*—for instance, dividing "VERISIMILITUDE" into three specialized articles marked "metaphysics," "poetry," and "painting," or designating "PROBABILITY" to "philosophy," "logic," and "mathematics" while treating related issues in the mimetic arts under a selection by a poet about "FICTION"—block the cross talk that I study here. These tiny parenthetical marks in the semantic domain are traces of fierce struggles in which different *meanings* were assigned to fields as part of the process that defined and maintained their disciplinary autonomy. Watching words in this way lets me propose an affinity in difference between Enlightenment science and the novel.[1]

The eighteenth-century trends described here need to be understood as elements in a set of long-term transactions concerning the maintenance and ownership of impartial discourse, because public exchange aiming toward consensus was the medium that enabled the modern sense of objectivity and constructed and stabilized its terminologies. These terminologies include not only the concepts of hypothesis and fiction that this essay explores, but also related ones like verisimilitude, probability, fact, history, and even truth, which remain vital to present-day philosophy of science.[2] For only through public discussion and contestation in open conversation and printed exchange did the array of terms treated here come to signify differently than they had before the Scientific Revolution and to assume different interrelationships. The article in the *Encyclopédie* on "Hypothesis" (1765), for instance, at once impartially reflected a positive consensus about the value of hypotheses in science emerging at midcentury and defined an arena of debate by cordoning off *both* Cartesians and Newtonians as extremists in a manner reminiscent of Diderot's attack on both schools as abstractionist and anti-empirical in his pornographic novel *The Indiscreet Jewels* (1748). In doing so, the article also implicitly engaged the sharp division that opened up around midcentury between two forms of science. The first was a speculative science theorized by Diderot, for whom hypotheses were a guiding value and function when anchored empirically in experiments that provided continual feedback from observation. The second was an aggressive hyperinductivism typified in England by the work of Thomas Reid, which was similarly experimentalist but neo-Newtonian in its absolute rejection of hypotheses and its ridicule of them as dangerous fictions.[3]

The *Encyclopédie* was a symptom of the Enlightenment's embrace of new ways of formulating knowledge based on empirically oriented critical communication, which opposed itself to the abstract system-making characteristic of late medieval Scholasticism and early modern metaphysics.[4] Consensus, the essential yet mobile reference point that defined critical discussion aimed at the progressive improvement of knowledge, is the hallmark of modern inquiry as epitomized in Immanuel Kant's essay, "What Is Enlightenment?" (1784). Here, of course, I also have in mind Jürgen Habermas's description of the eighteenth-century public sphere as a scene of communication freed from the constraints of courtly hierarchy and a priori thinking: within this arena a public science could thrive in which lectures and demonstrations in coffeehouses and other sites would take place on a continuum with formal proceedings and in which descriptive techniques for making scientific experiments vividly present in published form could develop.[5] Empiricism, the experimental method, and an emergent sense of science as progressing through accumulation and refinement, all fostered the ideal of impartial knowledge as a product of rationally moderated interactions among such problematics as (1) theories of observation; (2) the derivation of "facts" from nature directly via the senses and indirectly through their extension with instruments; and (3) the practice of inductive thought, which arrived at synthesis by methodically breaking problems down into sequential, empirically definable parts and judging validity or "truth" according to coherence and completeness of sequence and probabilistic weighing of evidence. Although derived from mathematics, such methods extended as far as rules of evidence in law and even to proofs of God's nature in theology.[6]

The "new" novel of the earlier eighteenth century may be described as an institution of the Enlightenment not only because it partook, to greater or lesser degrees, in what Webster's dictionary calls "a philosophic movement . . . marked by questioning of traditional doctrines and values, a tendency toward individualism, and an emphasis on the idea of universal human progress, the empirical method in science, and the free use of reason" but also, more significantly, because the novel operated within the Enlightenment model of critical communication. Not only do the novels of Daniel Defoe, Samuel Richardson, and Henry Fielding, for example, pretend to offer densely particular, virtually evidentiary accounts of the physical and mental circumstances that actuate their characters and motivate the causal sequences of their plots, but they also attempt to frame the subjectivity of their characters within editorial objectivity, as in Defoe and Richardson, or narratorial objectivity, as in Fielding. These novels share a way of representing the world and kind of verisimilitude that Steven Shapin and Simon Schaffer in *Leviathan and the Air-Pump* call "virtual witnessing," by which they mean the rhetorical and visual apparatus for communicating scientific experiments to a public and convincing that public of their authenticity. Shapin and Schaffer cite, for instance, the hyperrealism of diagrams in which additions of fine detail and unneeded illusionism work to satisfy and convince an audience.[7]

Samuel Johnson defined "verisimilitude" simply as "probability."[8] These synonyms are not directly the subject of this essay, but they are constant referents of the concepts that are, and they recur continually in discussions of both scientific method and novelistic practice. These terminological axes are not accidental. From a philosophical perspective, all hypotheses are fictional, but the most serviceable (those that appear to yield scientific truth) are the ones most probable given the evidence and the prevailing rules of verification—which is to say, the ones most veri-similar. Paradoxically, the best hypotheses are those that *seem* the most like truth. Yet their very plausibility also renders them suspect because they are products of imagination that are logically indistinguishable from po-etic fictions. David Hume held that "vivacity" in poetry "never has the same *feeling* with that which arises in the mind, when we reason, tho' even upon the lowest species of probability" because ideas in manifest fictions rely on imagination rather than on distinct impressions.[9] He cannot say the same of hypotheses, which early fall victim to his deconstruction of most causal connections as fictional. Hume struggles valiantly to *feel* the difference between fiction and reality, but, in his own skeptical account, verisimilitude is essential to our apprehension of both because both rest upon probable inference and upon the fiction of causal continuity.[10] As Hume says, "All knowledge resolves itself into probability, and becomes at last of the same nature with that evidence, which we employ in common life. . . . In every judgment, which we can form concerning probability, as well as concerning knowledge, we ought always to correct the first judg-ment, deriv'd from the nature of the object, by another judgment, deriv'd from the nature of the understanding. . . . As demonstration is subject to the control of probability, so is probability liable to a new correction by a reflex act of the mind, wherein the nature of our understanding, and our reasoning from the first probability become our objects."[11] Unlikely as the pairing may at first appear, Hume's simultaneously skeptical and com-monsensical now-you-see-it-now-you-don't position about reality and fic-tion shows an affinity with Samuel Richardson's position on the kind of conviction he wished readers to experience in the letters that make up *Clarissa* (1747–48): "I could wish that the *Air* of Genuineness had been kept up, tho' I want not the letters to be *thought* genuine; only so far kept up, I mean, as that they would not prefatically be owned *not* to be genu-ine: and this for fear of weakening their Influence where any of them are aimed to be exemplary; as well as to avoid hurting that kind of Historical Faith which Fiction itself is generally read with, tho' we know it to be Fic-tion."[12] Fictions, be they hypotheses or novels, yield a provisional reality, an "as if," that possesses an explanatory power lacking in ordinary experi-ence. Science needs separation of its findings and procedures from the ordinary, and explanatory hypotheses have compelling power as stories that approximate truth, but the scientific disciplines cannot tolerate the imputation of fictionality. Hence induction emerges as the opposite of hypothesis in scientific method because it attains or seems to attain independence from the fictional.[13]

Even the novel shares the impulse toward formal proof so strongly voiced in the embrace of induction by scientific theorists inspired by Isaac Newton. Fielding declares, for instance, "In reality, there are many little circumstances too often omitted by injudicious historians, from which events of the utmost importance arise. The world may indeed be considered as a vast machine, in which the great wheels are originally set in motion by those which are very minute, and almost imperceptible to any but the strongest eyes."[14] But while novels may present attributes of inductive proof, they cannot attain such status and find themselves recurring to other models such as the juridical. Thus Richardson directly linked circumstantiality, probability, and legal proof when he wrote (after the 1749 publication of Fielding's *Tom Jones*), that "the Probability of all Stories told, or of Narrations given, depends upon small Circumstances; as may be observed, that in all Tryals for Life and Property, the Merits of the Cause are more determinable by such [details], than by the greater Facts; which usually are so laid, and taken care of, as to seem to authenticate themselves."[15] In point of both thematic exposition and narrative strategy, these novels force readers into the position of neutral observers arriving, probabilistically, at judgments based upon the weight of available facts and reasonable inferences. Although these works continue to echo plot forms and incidents traditional to the fantastical seventeenth-century romances their prefaces ritually condemn, the concern expressed by their authors to distinguish their enterprise from that of earlier prose fiction signals the reformulation of generic traits and cultural function that transformed the novel during the eighteenth century. Richardson was tacitly acknowledging that *Tom Jones* decisively marked the success of Fielding's effort to find formal means to legitimate novels as objects of and forums for critical discussion by bringing to the foreground issues of evidence and probability. Yet, given the moment of its publication in 1749, *Tom Jones* must also be viewed as a monument to a fading ideal of apparent historical factuality as the basis for impartiality in the genre of the novel, because, at the same time that Fielding's work relied on this historical factuality, it also embodied a turn, characteristic of midcentury, toward a manifest fictionality that tends to undercut the novel's own claim to simple factuality as a basis for its truth. Thus Michael McKeon can argue in *The Origins of the English Novel* that the novel at midcentury was giving up claims to embodying literal, historical truth in favor of claims to manifesting higher truths through the transparently fictional construction of specialized versions of the "real" world within strict canons of physical, temporal, and psychological probability.[16]

I

Questions about fictionality are crucial to the period's theories of both literature and science, yet a certain denial of fictionality marks both the earlier eighteenth-century novel and early science. Two famous, nearly concurrent instances from Isaac Newton and Daniel Defoe can serve as launching points for this discussion.

Newton, in the "General Scholium" added to the second edition of his *Principia* in 1713, wrote the much disputed words "hypotheses non fingo," which early were translated as "I do not frame hypotheses" and, more recently, have been accepted as meaning "I do not feign hypotheses." The context includes an attack on Cartesian celestial mechanics and an assertion of Newton's sincere if unprovable belief in God as all-present cause:

> Hitherto we have explained the phenomena of the heavens and of our sea by the power of gravity, but have not yet assigned the cause of this power. . . . I have not been able to discover the cause of those properties of gravity from phenomena, and I frame [feign] no hypotheses; for whatever is not deduced from the phenomena is to be called an hypothesis; and hypotheses, whether metaphysical or physical, whether of occult qualities or mechanical, have no place in experimental philosophy. In this philosophy, particular propositions are inferred from the phenomena, and afterward rendered general by induction.[17]

The opposite of "hypothesis" for Newton was inductive proof, which found its basis in his natural philosophy on observational and experimental fact and yielded valid generalities about nature. Newton's disputed phrase is oriented both to the issue of hypothesis versus fact or truth, thus defined, and to the issue of feigning—for the Latin root of the word "fiction" is *fingo*, and, as we shall see, it is no accident, given sound ancient precedent, that Newton linked this concept with that of hypothesis. Defoe, who like Newton believed his representations embodied the higher truth of God's being, took on the role of Editor in the preface to *Robinson Crusoe* of 1719 in order to assert the standing of his text as "a just history of fact." He instantly defined the opposite of "fact" by declaring that his story is without "any appearance of fiction in it." That same year, he maintained this stance in the preface to *The Farther Adventures of Robinson Crusoe*, with the slight concession that the "just application of every incident, the religious and useful inferences drawn from every part . . . must legitimate all the part that may be called invention or parable." The critic Charles Gildon shortly attacked both works for their implausibility not only as "fact" but even as "fable," cataloging one implausibility after another and in the process revealing criteria for verisimilitude so stringent that he would have required the character Xury to speak Arabic rather than English. Though from different realms, both Gildon's literalist response to *Robinson Crusoe* and Newton's ever more intransigent statements against hypotheses added to the *Principia* during the 1720s may be viewed as indices of a crisis concerning the nature of factuality and verisimilitude that Defoe tried to bridge using terms like "parable" and "allegory." Another symptom of this crisis was the furious debate over whether physical laws were factual manifestations of God's literal nature—as opposed to representations in the mind of God or in mere human consciousness—that was published under the sponsorship of Princess Caroline in the technical but widely circulated correspondence between Gottfried Wilhelm Leibniz and Samuel Clarke on the consequences of Newtonianism for religion.[18]

Both Newton and Defoe in their different ways are forced to back away from the absolute stance. Newton, in a 1726 addition to his "Rules of Reasoning in Philosophy" in the *Principia*, said,

> In experimental philosophy we are to look upon propositions inferred by general induction from phenomena as accurately or very nearly true, notwithstanding any contrary hypothesis that may be imagined, till such time as other phenomena occur by which they may either be made more accurate, or liable to exceptions. . . . This rule we must follow, that the argument of induction may not be evaded by hypotheses.[19]

Truth, it turns out, is a matter of approximation. Speaking as the supposed editor, Defoe retreats also—even within his own sentence—asserting that *Robinson Crusoe*'s power of "improvement . . . will be the same," whether fact or fiction, since in either case it works "as well as to the diversion, as to the instruction of the reader." Analogously, Defoe questions the factuality of "fact" in Robinson Crusoe's *Serious Reflections* (1720), his defensive sequel justifying the original novel as true in the larger sense of parable or allegory, declaring that "nothing is more common than to have two men tell the same story quite differing one from another, yet both of them eye-witnesses to the fact related." In a strange kind of consonance with Newton's "hypotheses non fingo," Defoe declares that "this supplying a story by invention . . . is a sort of lying that makes a great hole in the heart."[20] Newton's propositions, it seems, must withstand hypotheses while partaking in the partiality of being "very nearly true"—and Defoe's facts slide easily, through the process of narration, into untruths that erode self-certainty. In both cases, narration symptomizes the disease of fictionality. Narration bears with it the infection of fictionality. Newton sets the feigning of hypotheses, which spring from the imagination, opposite the accuracy of propositions, yet these too are only relatively accurate, very nearly true, and liable to exceptions. Their epistemological standing is different from hypotheses, yet they share the extension in time fundamental to narrative and are threatened by its tendency toward fictionality—even, as Defoe pointed out, in eyewitness accounts. Newton's denial of hypothesis in the "General Scholium" immediately follows a discussion of the assignment of human passions and agency to God "by way of allegory": "For all our notions of God are taken from the ways of mankind by a certain similitude, which, though not perfect, has some likeness."[21] In context, his refusal of hypotheses is specifically a rejection of fictional "similitude" and its substitution of stories for the vexingly unattainable truth about first causes.

Hans Vaihinger argues in *The Philosophy of "As if"* that "the Greeks made no clear-cut distinction between hypothetical and fictional assumptions."[22] Indeed, the very concept of hypothesis, though urged toward a different status by Copernicus and others during the Scientific Revolution, in antiquity traditionally referred to the narration of specific facts and particular cases treated by rhetoricians or to a plot outline. According to Wesley Trimpi, citing Aristotle's *Nicomachean Ethics* (3.3.9–13), "The philosophical-scientific function of 'hypothesis' in a mathematical construction begins simultaneously with the choice of an 'hypothesis' in the dramatic sense of a plot outline."[23] In Quintilian, too, the relationship between hypothesis and fictional argumentation and narration remains intimate: "When I speak of fictitious arguments I mean the proposition of something which, if true, would either solve a problem or contribute to its solution." Finally, as Trimpi shows, "The use of 'hypothesis' in a literary context [was] not restricted to summary or outline, but [gradually came] to refer to fiction itself or rather to [that] historically important type of fictional narrative, the verisimilar." Newton's theoretical condemnation took as a premise these associations of hypothesis with fiction and narrative found in the rhetorical tradition (a tradition central to grammar school education and to the first-year curriculum at Cambridge). The powerfully antirhetorical bias of the new science is one facet of his attempt to disentangle himself from imputations of hypothetical thinking.[24]

Despite Newton's late theoretical declarations, his attitude toward hypothesis turns out to have been remarkably unstable across his career. In practice, Newton himself did form hypotheses and often in his works went so far as to call them just that. Historically, as the context of the 1713 "General Scholium" makes clear, his condemnation was aimed at the extravagant use of explanatory hypotheses without experimental reference that marked Cartesianism and Leibnizianism as he viewed them. With this context in mind, then, the key word in Newton's phrase becomes "fingo," rather than "hypotheses," and his statement is reoriented away from the issue of fact or truth versus hypothesis to the issue of feigning; that is, to the issue of manifest, empirically unanchored, fictionality. This Newtonian tendency to suspend or erase the speculative function—including its uncomfortable associations with verisimilar narrative, as opposed to the factual truth of demonstration in both its analytic and physical senses—continues with surprising strength in both English and French science. Joseph Priestley declared, for instance, in a lecture of 1761 at the Warrington Academy that "all true history has a capital advantage over every work of fiction" because "works of fiction resemble those machines which we contrive to illustrate the principles of philosophy, such as globes and orreries, the use of which extend no further than the views of human ingenuity; whereas real history resembles the experiments by the air pump, condensing engine and electrical machine, which exhibit the operations of nature, and the God of nature himself."[25] Fiction for Priestley can never be more than representation, and even "real history" can do no more than resemble physical experiments, which are the thing itself. His assertions parallel Newton's about allegory in the "General Scholium" while extending them to fiction in general and establishing a contrast with science in which history is the middle term. This contrast of fiction with real science became codified in eighteenth-century French usage of the term for the novel, *roman*. Voltaire styled Père Louis-Bertrand Castel, a Jesuit popularizer of mathematics and science whom he loved to hate, as "the Don Quixote of mathematics," while the 1739 revision to his essay in the *Philosophical Letters*, "On the System of Attraction," condemned René Descartes because, in his desire "to create a universe, he made a philosophy the way one makes a good novel: everything seems verisimilar, and nothing is true."[26]

Questions about fictionality are crucial not only to the period's theorization of literature and science but also to its general epistemology. The *Encyclopédie* devotes more than three folio pages to an article on poetic "fiction" by the poet Jean-François Marmontel (1756). The more technical aspects of the topic "Fiction" are managed chiefly through cross-references and in other articles, but Marmontel allows himself a paragraph praising the new "esprit philosophique" as condemning "extravagant fictions," while embracing poetic fictions that respect probability and verisimilitude because the new philosophy, which "observes, penetrates, and unfolds nature . . . alone is capable of appreciating imitation because it alone knows the model." Discussions dealing with the matter of fiction appear in the main text and supplements on topics such as "Fact" (by Diderot), "Experiment," "Induction," "Unbelievability" (by Diderot), "Observation," "Phenomenon" (by d'Alembert), "Probability," and "Verisimilitude" (possibly by Diderot). The *Encyclopédie* article on "Hypothesis," by the mathematics teacher Abbé de La Chapelle, also deals centrally with the question of fiction.[27] It is a virtual panegyric about the centrality of hypotheses to scientific progress and specifically contrasts the orderly, empirically oriented usage of hypotheses in the scientific method with their fabulous employment by the followers of Descartes. He presents Newton's condemnation as an overreaction to the abuse of hypotheses and urges what we may take as the commonsense view of the mid-eighteenth century: namely, that the process of hypothesis is necessary to scientific research, which, by its nature, must stretch over long periods and must be conducted by many different people "before attaining a certain perfection." Hypotheses, he says, need to have a place in science because they "give us new points of view," an idea that seems to point to something like Nelson Goodman's "worldmaking."[28] And yet he confidently asserts that hypotheses can be falsified and recognized as fictions if they are "made up of empty terms or ones that lack fixed and determinate ideas, if they explain nothing, [or] if more difficulties follow from them than they resolve, and so forth." Throughout the article, La Chapelle assumes the validity of what amounts to a proto-Kantian notion of the perfection of knowledge through public circulation and, interestingly, considers hypothesis as a medium of critical communication.

The *Encyclopédie* article epitomizes in everyday language a practical yet theoretically treacherous understanding of the relationship among fictions, hypotheses, and verifiable findings that has informed countless more technical discussions by "realists" from Newton to Vaihinger.[29] Diderot expressed it metaphorically in his *Thoughts on the Interpretation of Nature* (1754):

> As long as things are only in our understanding, they are opinions—notions that may be true or false, agreed upon or contradicted. They assume solidity only in relation to externally existing things. This connection comes about

either through an uninterrupted chain of experience or through an uninterrupted chain of reasoning anchored at one end to observation and at the other to experience—or, alternatively, through a chain of experiments spread at intervals between deductions like weights along a line suspended by its two ends. Without these weights, the line would become the sport of the least movement of air.[30]

Throughout this work, Diderot strives to define the practice of objectivity as a dialectical fusion of observation and creative speculation, which yields probable, verisimilar representations of nature. As Diderot's metaphor implies, such a fusion transcends the tendency of individual subjectivity to fantasy or fiction by employing sensory feedback—an effect that is amplified by critical communication. Even Hume, whose far more skeptical account of causality as entirely mental has devastating consequences for the distinction between fictions and hypotheses, remained convinced that he could *feel* the difference between manifest fictions, such as those of literature, and logically fictional real entities because manifest fictions rely on imagination rather than on distinct impressions, which Hume says are physically closer to reality.[31] But even for Hume, facts, unless of the most rudimentary physical or historical kinds, are verisimilar representations based on consensus. Madame du Châtelet, a Leibnizian and an ardent defender of hypothesis-making in science, reveals with perfect clarity the groundless grounding that was usually hidden in defenses of hypothesizing as the path to truth—that is, the subjectivity underlying the "objectivity" of science:

> Hypotheses are not merely probable propositions that have a greater or lesser degree of certitude when they conform to a greater or lesser number of those circumstances accompanying the phenomenon that one wants to explain by means of hypotheses; since a very large degree of probability commands our assent and has nearly the same effect on us as certainty, hypotheses at last become truths when their probability mounts to such a point that, *morally,* one can let them pass for certitude. This is what came to pass with Copernicus's system.[32]

At the end of Madame du Châtelet's statement, the divergent ideas of scientific and moral certainty suddenly converge paradoxically and peep slyly through the standard disguise of probabilistic rhetoric. Another way of thinking about "moral certainty" in science would be to redescribe it as the end point of a long process of informed public exchange yielding consensus.

What I want to consider here in thinking about the novel together with the debate over the fictionality of hypotheses is not the merit of eighteenth-century arguments about the scientific validity of hypothesis but rather the significance of the debate's persistence over such a long period from the seventeenth century onward. This period coincides with the development of the modern novel, and eighteenth-century proponents of the genre and its critics alike, obsessed with questions about its standing as a form of knowledge, recurred again and again to concepts that haunt both the scientific discussion and debates like Defoe's with Gildon: "fact," "fiction," "probability," "verisimilitude," and "truth" are the common terms.[33] I suggest that the novel, in tandem with the Enlightenment debate under review here, partook of a crisis precipitated when the Scientific Revolution disrupted the old continuity between the hypothetical and the fictional, a continuity that Vaihinger and Trimpi document. Yet even rigorous experimentation and theorizing could not guarantee or ultimately underwrite the difference between the scientific hypothesis and fiction because both are based in "cases"—that is, in causal and narrative sequences—and both share basic technologies of world-making and sense-making: they are not just features of logic and science or of fantasy and literature, but of both. Yet in the emergent discipline of science, hypotheses, which were central to the experimental method, had to be vaccinated against fictionality. The novel, while in the main sharing verisimilar reference with empiricist science, responded to the crisis by abandoning claims to literal, historical fact of the kind Defoe had worked so strenuously to maintain and, by asserting its own manifest fictionality, strove, as Michael McKeon and Catherine Gallagher suggest, toward the representation of higher truths and toward a more intense emotional identification between readers and novelistic fictions. This novelistic occupation of the terrain of fiction then could ground the factuality of experimental science, oddly freeing it to encompass double tendencies of which the literalist inductionism of a Reid and the more imaginative versions of fact in Georges-Louis Buffon are extreme instances.

II

I want to propose, then, that the new novel of the eighteenth century can be regarded as a guarantee of difference. It shares such attributes with the hypothetical as narrativity and verisimilitude, yet its fictionality is manifest—even paradoxically underlined through the insistence upon factuality that we have noticed in the early novel. By midcentury, however, as Catherine Gallagher shows—especially with regard to Charlotte Lennox's novel *The*

Female Quixote (1752) — the novel's attraction was increasingly based upon the readerly identification that manifest fictionality strangely enabled.[34] As Anna Laetitia Barbauld and her brother John Aikin wrote in 1773,

> To the writer of fiction alone, every ear is open . . . and every bosom is throbbing with concern.
>
> It is . . . easy to account for this enchantment. To follow the chain of perplexed ratiocination, to view with critical skill the airy architecture of systems, to unravel the web of sophistry, or weigh the merits of opposite hypotheses, requires perspicacity, and presupposes learning. Works of this kind, therefore, are not so well adapted to the generality of readers as familiar and colloquial composition; for few can reason, but all can feel, and many who cannot enter into an argument, may yet listen to a tale.[35]

What had happened by this juncture in the eighteenth century was a specialization (running in tandem with the period's great division of knowledge) whereby manifest fictionality underwrote the factuality of science. Just before midcentury, Fielding had been poised strangely between the old world of the novel as fact and the new world of the novel as fiction: his essay about verisimilitude, which makes up the introductory chapter to book 8 of *Tom Jones*, attempts theoretically to protect the new novel against charges of unbelievability. These charges would arise from what Defoe called "falling into fiction." Fielding insists that the novel must not deal in the "possible" but must limit itself strictly to the "probable." As his chief modern editor, Martin Battestin, notes, he was the first author consistently to have defined the genre of the novel, with reference to Aristotle, as centrally concerned with probability.[36] Yet in practice he was already of the avant-garde in his wholesale abandonment, in the actual telling of the story by an intrusive narrator, of the apparatus of apparent factuality that surrounds Defoe's and Richardson's novels. By 1773, the trend toward viewing novels as fictional appeals to subjectivity had become fully articulate.

By 1759, at the end of the first installment of *Tristram Shandy*, Laurence Sterne could declare that "it is in the nature of an hypothesis, when once a man has conceived it, that it assimilates every thing to itself." He goes on to challenge the reader to "conjecture upon it, if you please. . . . Raise a system to account for the loss of my nose by marriage articles, — and shew the world how it could happen, that I should have the misfortune to be called TRISTRAM, in opposition to my father's hypothesis, and the wish of the whole family. . . . But I tell you before-hand it will be in vain."[37] Sterne is purposely dealing in the improbable everyday world where fact is stranger than hypothesis or fiction. Sterne's is the world of the "possible," a terrain that Fielding tried to forbid novelists. Following classical literary theory, Fielding allotted the "possible" to historians relating proven, thoroughly witnessed fact (which can compel belief through incontrovertible evidence), while ceding the "marvelous" to poets as tellers of miraculous events that are credible only to audiences already convinced of their truth through belief in myth or religion. For Fielding, the "probable" had been the only domain in which a novelist could move with assurance because he sought to engage readers in an economy of rational exchange, which he summed up with the word "judgment."

Five years after *Tristram's* debut, Horace Walpole, the inventor of the Gothic novel, could formalize the turn toward manifest fictionality in the first preface to *The Castle of Otranto* (1764): "If this *air* of the *miraculous* is excused, the reader will find nothing else unworthy of his perusal. Allow the possibility of the facts, and all the actors comport themselves as [real] persons would do in their situation." Interestingly, in the anonymous first edition where he poses as editor and translator of an old manuscript, Walpole also echoes previous novelistic convention when he declares, "Though the machinery is invention, and the names of the actors imaginary, I cannot but believe that the groundwork of the story is founded on truth. The scene is undoubtedly laid in some real castle." The wildly paradoxical program that Walpole outlines in his preface to the second edition, where his initials give away his authorship, says much about the midcentury emergence of the novel as the simultaneous site of manifest fictionality and ostensible probability. *Otranto*, he says,

> was an attempt to blend the two kinds of romance, the ancient and the modern [that is, the new novel]. In the former, all was imagination and improbability: in the latter, nature is always intended to be, and sometimes has been, copied with success. Invention has not been wanting; but the great resources of fancy have been dammed up, by a strict adherence to common life. . . .
>
> The author of the following pages thought it possible to reconcile the two kinds. Desirous of leaving the powers of fancy at liberty to expatiate through the boundless realms of invention, and thence of creating more interesting situations, he wished to conduct the mortal agents in his drama according to the rules of probability; in short to make them think, speak, and act, as it might be supposed mere men and women would do in extraordinary positions.[38]

Walpole aspires to a kind of novel unmistakably fictional in its premises yet tethered to experienced reality by psychological realism and by the canons of probability. The common ground with science is, of course, that of the probable. The probable is the ground where scientific hypothesis meets fictionality; the probable is the point around which science and the novel rotate in complementary orbit, the meeting point at which fact can, apparently, be separated from fiction. Yet Walpole's words also point to the duplicity of the probable—to its instability as a ground. For "the rules of probability" in fact leave "the powers of fancy at liberty to expatiate through the boundless realms of invention"—which is to say, fiction. We return, then, to Newton's objection to feigning and to his attempt to refuse both hypothesis and fiction. For, following Friedrich Kittler, I might call the system I am describing an "Aufschreibesysteme" or "discourse network," in which all parts are systemically interconnected.[39] Scientific truth may be guaranteed by the cultural elaboration of a domain like the novel that shares certain of its protocols yet is manifestly fictional, but then science cannot fully escape implication in that very fictionality.

Corresponding to the specialization in which the novel's fictionality worked to underwrite the factuality of science, whether in the *Encyclopédie* or in the culture at large, we find a profound relativization of narrative in science—through the insistence upon hypotheses as necessary catalysts that structure inquiry but theoretically are not part of knowledge. This trend was accompanied by what Alexander Welsh has recently designated "strong representations." From the mid-eighteenth century, as Welsh says, "Narrative consisting of carefully managed circumstantial evidence, highly conclusive in itself and often scornful of direct testimony, flourished nearly everywhere—not only in literature but in criminal jurisprudence, . . . natural religion, and history writing itself."[40] One thinks in this regard of Jean-Jacques Rousseau, though Welsh does not cite him. Early in the *Discourse on the Origin and Foundation of Inequality* (1755), Rousseau declares, "Let us begin, therefore, by laying aside all facts, for they do not affect the question. The researches in which we may engage on this occasion are not to be taken for historical truths, but merely as hypothetical and conditional reasonings better suited to illustrate the nature of things than to show their true origin, like those systems that our naturalists daily make of the formation of the world."[41] According to Welsh, the powerful causal narrative structures characteristic of strong representation, "claiming to encompass more than can ever be experienced at first hand," invaded even natural science itself—suggesting afresh the instability of the very edifice of scientific factuality that the novel may be seen as underwriting.

III

I conclude by reflecting on the emergent current of speculation that occurred doubly in the novel and science in England and France just past midcentury. I already have noted that Lennox, Sterne, and Walpole are crucial for an understanding of this turn. An analogous figure in French science was the great midcentury naturalist Georges-Louis Buffon, a friend of Diderot who was attacked from every quarter for elaborating theories without the support of facts and for shaping "facts" to support his speculations. Probably he was Rousseau's target in the passage quoted above. Buffon's work in natural history, biology, and geology, as described by modern historians of science like Virginia Dawson, does epitomize a burgeoning of speculative science at midcentury.[42] It would be easy to link Buffon to the turn toward manifest fictionality that I have pointed to in the novel by suggesting, for instance, that the discourse network in which the novel becomes a domain of striking fictionality supporting the factuality of science and concealing its fictionality by something like relative contrast also produces discursive space for scientific speculation. Probably this linkage is apposite, but, contrary to Buffon's practice as viewed by contemporary critics and later historians, his own framing of arguments against hypothesis-making shows instead, or in addition, that he followed the classic strategy of attempting to maintain the scientificity of his work by associating hypotheses with fictionality and limiting their relevance to his findings, which he stringently contrasted with hypotheses and called "theories." Bowing to Leibnizians like Christian Wolff and Madame du Châtelet, but also thinking as the translator of Newton that he was, Buffon categorically rejects hypotheses that operate as abstractions: abstractions may be useful heuristically, but science ought instead to be founded on the observation of concrete physical fact. Such observation yields real knowledge in the form of "*théories physiques*":

> We hope to make the reader more able to articulate the large difference between . . . a hypothesis, which merely opens possibilities, and a theory built on facts — between a system such as we are offering in this essay on the formation and first state of the earth and a physical history of its present condition such as we have just given in the previous work.[43]

Although Buffon allows hypotheses, he refuses those that disguise statements of belief or imply answers about cause and effect — cause and effect being regarded, in the spirit of Hume, as fictional constructs. As he says, introducing his vast *Natural History* (whose publication began in 1749) in words that could as well come from Diderot or, indeed, constitute a theory of verisimilitude in the novel:

> The word truth gives rise to only a vague idea; it never has had a precise definition. And the definition itself, taken in a general and absolute sense, is but an abstraction which exists only by virtue of some supposition. Instead of trying to form a definition of truth, let us rather try to make an enumeration of truths. . . . Physical truths . . . are in no way arbitrary, and in no way depend on us. Instead of being founded on suppositions which we have made, they depend only on facts. A sequence of similar facts, or, if you prefer, a frequent repetition and an uninterrupted succession of the same occurrences constitute the essence of this sort of truth. What is called physical truth is thus only a probability, but a probability so great that it is equivalent to certitude. In mathematics, one supposes. In the physical sciences, one sets down a claim and establishes it. There one has definitions; here, there are facts. In the first case one arrives at evidence, while in the latter the result is certitude.[44]

Later in the *Natural History*, he allows hypotheses that answer the question "how" but never those that answer the question "why."[45] Only hypotheses answering the question "how" can point to "*théories physiques*," the buried treasure of Buffon's science. In trying to stake out factual ground for his "*théories physiques*" by pushing hypothesis toward fiction, Buffon serves as the mirror reverse of Walpole's attempt to free a space for fancy by hewing to strict probability of action, characters, and psychology within initially fantastic fictional premises. Buffon is rejecting fantastic premises—which for him are concealed in hypotheses that function as abstractions or that attempt to answer the question "why"—and insisting upon exact analysis of observable physical fact in order to free a space for strictly controlled speculation in the form of hypotheses that answer the question "how." Fantasy opens space for circumstantial and psychological realism in Walpole's novel—the space within which he develops techniques for the first sustained third-person (impartial) narration of thought in English fiction. Fact opens a space for speculative thought experiment in Buffon's *Natural History*.

IV

This essay has concerned ways in which eighteenth-century science worked to assume the mantle of factuality as the novel became increasingly the domain of manifest fictionality. Yet while moving toward the positions of absolute opposition they occupy today, both joined in the larger project—seen so clearly in my quotation from the introduction to Buffon's *Natural History*—of defining truth in terms of verisimilitude or probability.

Another way of putting this would be to say that they defined the most accurate representations of reality as those that contextualized empirical, sense-based facts by arraying them in probable explanatory networks—be these experimental cases and reports or manifest fictional narratives. Hypotheses were crucial to this mode of representation but they were also sites of crisis in the theory of verisimilitude because, while they were fictitious in essence, they could *become* true if verified through the assimilation of enough empirical data. The contradictory nature of hypotheses produced paradoxical symptoms across the period I have described. For against the backdrop of a commitment shared by the two realms to the system of verisimilitude, the novel began to ground science's claim to be nonfiction by becoming increasingly the domain of manifest though probable fictionality. Then, in a doubly paradoxical twist at midcentury, as I propose, the move toward verisimilar yet "possible" fiction that occurred with Lennox, Sterne, and Walpole participated (relationally, not causally) in a turn toward the more imaginative or speculative variant of "truth" advocated by Diderot and Buffon.[46]

What is the long-term import of the phenomena I have been describing? The guarantee of scientific factuality through the manifest yet verisimilar fictionality that I have been discussing finds a counterpart in the emergence across the nineteenth century of broader cultural forms in which probabilistic thinking dominates, such as Welsh's "strong representations" in legal rules of evidence and in religious thought. The rise of modern disciplines in the social sciences was well underway by the 1830s. Terminological change during the same period suggests completion of the process of polarization that I describe above, since, according to the *Oxford English Dictionary*, the term "novel" became synonymous in English with "fiction" in 1871. In fact, the first major instance of this usage may well have been in John Dunlop's *The History of Fiction*, whose subtitle suggests that the new mapping of the terrain already had been accomplished: *Being a Critical Account of the Most Celebrated Prose Works of Fiction, from the Earliest Greek Romances to the Novels of the Present Age*.[47]

The conclusion that fictionality plays a role in certifying reality is hard to avoid even today, when long dead "real" stars like Humphrey Bogart or Marilyn Monroe can sell products of our moment on television. And when, despite infinite permutations and sophistications over the past three hundred years, debates about the truth status of scientific representation are still being fought out within polarities built around terms like "realism," "verisimilitude," and even "approximate truth." Whether one notices the persistence of realism in popular and pulp fiction—and this despite any number of twentieth-century avant-garde deconstructions—or constant accounts in the *New York Times* about the rampant interfoliation of reality and virtuality, fact and fiction, past and present on the contemporary scene, the questions remain similar to those raised in my contemplation of the novel and the Enlightenment. At least in the Western cultural system, are not fact and fiction, reality and verisimilitude, proposition and hypothesis, truth and narrative, inseparably bound functions of each other?

CHAPTER 3

Matters of Fact

Virtual Witnessing and the Public in Hogarth's Narratives

The circumstantial rendering of the facts of London life in Hogarth's earlier cycles or progresses is noticed by his every commentator and has been from the beginning. Jean Rouquet's inaugural commentary of 1746, which sought to help French audiences decipher details at once striking but obscure in significance, codified a tradition of factual reference that remains unbroken. Hogarth criticism has thrived on the detection of such facts and their denotation since the initial publication of *A Harlot's Progress* (1732) and *A Rake's Progress* (1735). This effort found its monumental outcome in Ronald Paulson's *Hogarth: His Life, Art and Times* (1971) and *Hogarth's Graphic Works* (1965), both later rewritten and enhanced by his further decades of research.[1] But why do the cycles provoke such activity? What is the meaning of their facticity?

This chapter revolves around senses of "facticity" that lie in constellation with, but differ subtly from, the most contemporary usages in the *Oxford English Dictionary*, which defines the term as "the quality or condition of being a fact; factuality." Its examples are inconsistent. The dictionary's first context lies close to my meaning and occurs in a legal work of 1945, which defines "facticity" as "the efficacy of the idea of the law." The other contexts are theological, contrasting or comparing physical and divine fact. One sits uneasily with mine and is psychological: "Suddenly in the excitement of the battle the soldier loses his self, his 'facticity,' his consciousness of himself as a human being and becomes an anonymous machine" (1960). Crucial in this constellation, though not in the *OED*, is the word's relation to the German, *Faktizität*, a philosophical term important to Martin Heidegger and signifying everyday, unreflective experience of the world. I both refer to this sense and crucially depart from it.[2]

Most basically, I intend by "facticity" not just a certain reality effect involving the rendering of material elements in visual or verbal form but a self-reflexive, self-referential, self-indexical rendering of material elements. This definition is not strictly philosophical. Rather, it represents my condensation of two elements in Heidegger's thinking. The first is his sense of facticity as the everydayness of familiar objects, including the body and even ideas themselves, which, through their very familiarity exist, unreflected upon, as unexamined yet always already preinterpreted factors of experience. The second element is a rather down-to-earth version of Heidegger's insistence that the job of philosophy is to bring forth such objects to reflective consciousness. Hogarth produces the effect of bringing the everyday to awareness through his self-reflexive visual staging of ordinary objects and bodily forms. Later, I will suggest ways in which this essentially reflective conception of facticity that I am deriving from Heidegger—whose rather passive ethics in *Being and Time* are so inimical to the ideal of rational consensus in the public sphere advanced in the writings of Jürgen Habermas— may clarify retrospectively, through its application to Hogarth's cycles, our sense of how Hogarth's series may have consolidated a "public" in England in the 1730s.[3]

I

Neither realism nor its canonical power to reform through the vivid depiction of abuses is strictly the issue here, for what I call "facticity" stages everyday objects and actions in a self-aware fashion that tends to undercut illusionism. In *Imagining the Penitentiary*, I previously joined others in linking Hogarth's cycles to the formal attributes of the early English novel by describing them as "realistic," a classically articulated category that, in this more stringent context, cannot be explanatory because it is tautologically defined as the presence of real or pretended factuality. Facticity, rather, disrupts both the mere factuality of the everyday and also the convention of realistic representation by suspending objects between two different ways of apprehending them. Facticity is, to paraphrase the *OED*'s instance above, about the efficacy of the idea of the fact. For this reason, facticity acknowledges (even exploits) visual or textual ruptures in the densely specific realist fabric and requires us to look differently at objects. Such ruptures in Hogarth's plates work, at one level, as part of illusion but, at another, they call attention to the means of illusion (perspective, for instance) and tend to fly to the pictorial surface in collage-like ways. Nor is the specificity of satire the question. Paulson and David Bindman have persuasively connected Hogarth to the Augustan tradition of moral satire, a genre whose effect, in the carefully elaborated views of early eighteenth-century literary practitioners like Alexander Pope and Jonathan Swift, required recognizable specificity of reference in order to gain its moral impact. The cycles are indeed moral satires—more on the tough Juvenalian side than the Horatian in my view. Yet, while the reformative power of the satire in *A Harlot's Progress* and *A Rake's Progress* may have depended upon factual reference, their facticity cannot be said to derive from their satiric effect or to be explained by it.[4]

The objects represented in these plates have demanded and received both historical explication as satires and also allegoresis moral and iconological. This demand depends upon their facticity, but the visual provocations that launch such exegesis remain largely unanalyzed. These provocations include the odd positionings of objects and of bodily parts everywhere present in Hogarth's plates, as well as disruptions of the visual field by distortions of scale or perspective.[5] These aspects of Hogarth's earlier cycles are, I believe, the very ones to which Rouquet referred when he said of the later *March to Finchley* that "the first and greatest fault that I find in Mr. Hogarth's painting is that it is totally new." The idea is not ironic, which Paulson suggests, but a "paradox," as Rouquet immediately says, for he claims Hogarth's work to be "new" in the sense not of novelty but of its raw, unprocessed immediacy: "quite brilliant with that low freshness one finds in nature but never in the best collections." He means "new" in the sense of "new-mown hay." Rouquet had looked intently and had seen something quite specific, for he has just declared that Hogarth's vision "corresponds too closely to the objects it represents."[6] What Rouquet saw was Hogarth's visual insistence that his audience witness the commonplace in a certain particular way that brings the everyday world to consciousness, reframing it and calling attention to its visual oddities—a step necessary to ethical awareness yet prior to it. I believe that Rouquet intuited this aspect of Hogarth's achievement, for, at the start of his brief volume, he recognizes the artist's place in the tradition of satire while denying the genre's power to correct. This chapter considers, then, not what objects mean in Hogarth but the meaning of how they look.

Hogarth's "Satire on False Perspective" (1754) takes the visual provocation of perspective distortion to such an extreme that its drawing appears to be different in kind from that of the early cycles. Yet they share the use of visual distortion to provoke thought (Figure 1). The "Satire" introduced a treatise on the nature of accurate draftsmanship, but, as Paulson says, "the perspective errors (characteristic of signboards) are used to engender puns, to show not only how *not* to draw but, in a sense, *how* to draw—how to suggest a different set of relationships by using a different set of rules." Paulson gets at just part of the problem because of his linkage of this plate to the later (1762) exhibition of signboards in which Hogarth was involved. He sees the plate as a celebration of the "naïve." Yet illustrations and diagrams in didactic treatises and in natural-science publications also employed distorted or naively simple-looking images—among them both treatises on perspective and that most exhaustive of compilations, the volumes of plates that accompanied the *Encyclopédie*. While the relationship of Hogarth's plate to illustrations and diagrams in works on natural science is not causal, the use of a "different set of rules" to instruct the viewer is a point of contact. Robert Boyle may have to apologize for the engravings in which he presents diagrams and quasi-illusionistic drawings to persuade readers of the accuracy and veracity of his experiments with the air pump, but they in fact combine illusionism and naïveté (in ways analogous to Hogarth's) in order to underline their truthfulness and their instructive force (Figure 2).[7] Their lack of precise, strictly illusionistic alignment with their denotation and with that of his written text provokes us both to believe in them and to think about the truth they represent. They are both illusionistic and diagrammatic in character. Viewed in this way, Hogarth's "Satire" becomes a regionalized or fragmented diagram of options within the perspective system. Hogarth's use of perspective distortions to underline comic points in his satiric progresses of the 1730s and 1740s, considered both retrospectively through the lens of the 1754 "Satire on False Perspective" and also in light of the importance of multiple scales and points of view to the new methods of presentation in natural science, suggests a Hogarthian analytic in which both alignment and failure of alignment with the real are meaningful.[8] This "double existence," to use a phrase from Hume's *Treatise of Human Nature* (1739–40), lies at the heart of facticity as I employ the term in this essay.[9]

Hogarth's cycles and early experimental science—as well as the novels of Daniel Defoe and others during the earlier eighteenth century—were marked by a certain denial of fictionality of which the claim to factuality is the obverse and facticity the effect. In stressing their factuality, all three of these discourses partook in technologies aimed at the construction of

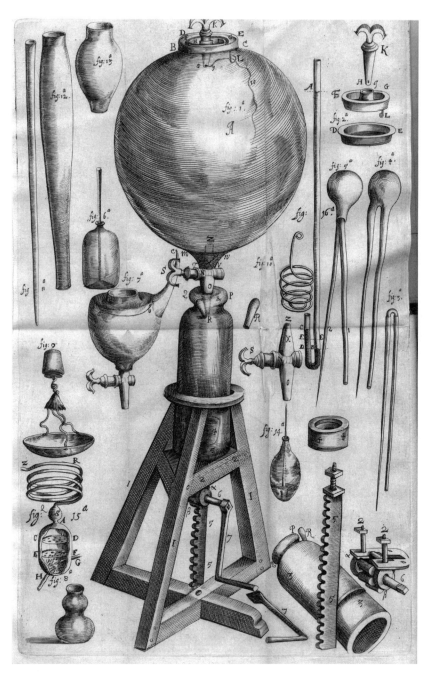

FIGURE 2. Anon., "Robert Boyle's Air-Pump," from Robert Boyle, *New Experiments Physico-Mechanicall, Touching the Spring of the Air, and its Effects* (1660). Courtesy Department of Special Collections, Stanford University Libraries.

an imagined public that shared certain intellectual and ethical values and that both established and promulgated these values through open, impersonal, empirically grounded discussion. This public used fact and evidence as points of departure for conversation aimed at, if not always necessarily achieving, consensus. Such conversation required reflection and, as Habermas suggests, depended, therefore, upon an easy flow between private consciousness and public exchange. Because of the importance of print culture and private reflection, not just conversation, to communication within this public, it was more of a working fiction than an actual aggregation of people. Although the English novel after about 1740 tended to abandon the pretense of literal historical factuality along with specific reference to the casuistical weighing of conscience, it continued to impel readers to consider the "cases" of characters juridically in light of fictive factual evidence about them presented through narration. Similarly, "facts" in the account of Steven Shapin and Simon Schaffer in *Leviathan and the Air-Pump* could be constituted through a rhetoric of verbal and visual appearances in print. I should hardly need to stress in this context that Hogarth's cycles were *prints* made for and circulated in a new world of publication whose chief media were the printed word *and* the printed *image*. Such images served a public that used "factual" evidence as the ground both for consciousness and for consensus. All of these media forms could serve the easy flow between inwardness and open exchange among the informed public that Habermas describes, but, like novels, they also worked pedagogically to recruit a broadening circle of the population. In the 1740s Hogarth's friend Henry Fielding found a novelistic analogue of this easy flow in bestselling works where openly fictive narratives were both framed by and shot through with the reflective awareness of a conversational narrator of apparent factual solidity.[10] Fielding, like Hogarth in my account, quite purposively put the techniques of realism in the service of organizing an audience's perceptions with a view to its developing independent critical standards. The implicit audience shaped within the tutelage of Hogarth's fractured illusionism and Fielding's intrusively self-aware narrator may, historically, have been more of a notional function than a concrete body of individuals—just as Boyle's "facts" as Shapin and Schaffer analyze them were at once experimentally founded and sociomedia constructions—but this system of exchange produced potent effects that went beyond ideology to its embodiment, for instance, in a burgeoning commercial market purveying the clothing, images, books, furniture, objects of use, and even the taste that marked membership in its domain.[11]

The ethical aspect—what is both prior to and beyond satire—in Hogarth's cycles was achieved in part by the pressure exerted by an idealized public that was itself projected by the machinery of appearance in the prints Hogarth made, not merely by the existence of some heterogeneous mass of people who lived actual lives in eighteenth-century London. Hogarth was, in many ways, on a cusp between two publics: one that did share the values of the ideal constructed audience he was trying to project visually in the prints, and the other, a public he was trying to educate. He sought to bring the latter group into his audience and to bestow on them ideal forms of reflexivity. A productive tension, if not actual warfare, exists in the plates between the values of these two audiences.

Certainly, the initial customers for *A Harlot's Progress* and *A Rake's Progress* were drawn from among "persons of fashion and artists" as George Vertue suggested, but the ideal public that Hogarth engraved into his prints was far wider—as the cycle of piracy and his own involvement in the wider publication of inexpensive versions during the 1730s shows.[12] This public was not so much an aggregation of concrete individuals as an ideal. It resembled more closely the "impartial spectator" of Adam Smith's later *Theory of Moral Sentiments* than it did the specific individuals who visited Hogarth's studio or appeared in his painted conversations. These individuals were, of course, important, and the role they played in the making of an ideal of public behavior and public ideas that served both private and community interests was crucial, as David Solkin has shown in his book *Painting for Money*; but as a group their collective power far exceeded the influence they exerted individually. As Solkin argues, these ideals were powerfully ideological and were not shared by all, but their force depended upon the illusion that they were shared by everyone.[13]

II

I am focusing upon this apparent illusion in thinking about facticity. What I want to argue, most generally, is that the self-reflexive "factness" of Hogarth's realism is an effect crucial to its functioning in the public sphere of the first half of the eighteenth century, because reflexivity and self-contemplation are basic to the kind of moral and ethical consciousness Hogarth's and his contemporaries in the novel sought.[14] Such a public represents ideals and employs modes of communication and interpretation that are fundamentally different from those assumed by the composite popular/polite public described in Paulson's works on Hogarth. Without doubt these and many other subcultures ranging along the popular/polite spectrum existed in eighteenth-century England, and their various performative domains from fairs, riots, traditional "liberties" or "rules," to the judicial, masterly and courtly theaters of cultural hegemony so brilliantly described by the late E. P. Thompson certainly existed too. This aggregate society continued, also, to use forms of communication that were histrionic, rhetorical, and emotionally demonstrative on the theatrical model—forms accompanied by corresponding, allegorically derived modes of interpretation, which, like Paulson's own, correlated different "levels" of historical reference and cognitive complexity in a given communication or piece of art with different strata of social class, education, and sophistication in the audience. I believe, however, that this essentially allegorical form of "reading" visual signs iconologically was not the crucial outcome of Hogarth's visual strategies. Although the peculiar visuality of the cycles reinvigorated traditional iconographies, which, as Paulson shows, Hogarth employed in sophisticated abundance, these signs are among the objects of his visuality, not its means. The iconological approach, while not mistaken, has tended to efface the impact of Hogarthian looking so accurately identified by Rouquet.[15]

At least at some levels, Paulson cannot be faulted for structuring his analysis of Hogarth around this armature. Paulson, stressing the "high and low" in Hogarth's art, focuses in the main on myriad social groups reflected in the prints and on "reading" them from distinctive educational and social vantage points. Yet, while still concerned chiefly with actual customers, Paulson does gesture toward the implicit, idealized audience function imagined here when he observes that "an alternative space . . . was opened by the . . . enterprising artist like Hogarth who sought to develop a *new* product that corresponded to (and caught) the expanding audience on its own terms, especially those who wished to maintain their identity and *not* merely emulate their betters."[16] But what I mean to suggest in moving now to consider Hogarth's facticity in light of communicational practices employed in English experimental science is that the old vision of society as a jostling aggregation of the common and the courtly, the popular and the genteel, the tolerated and the legal, had increasingly to compete, from the Restoration onward, with a liberal ideal of society as a scene of experimentation and discussion which, while endlessly tolerant of good-faith disagreement and counterevidence, aimed at the production of consensus about matters of fact. "Consensus" in this context does not necessarily mean agreement about every aspect of content but, rather, consensus about how to move toward agreement and how to manage disagreement. The communications that characterized this scene were antitheatrical, plain in style, and, at least overtly, unrhetorical in manner as well as emotionally detached and unallegorical. Thus, I am asking what happens if we try to account for the pattern of overdetermined factual reference in Hogarth's cycles and, by extension, in the early novel, by viewing them as partaking in the new ideal and, by implication, as working to establish consensus about moral issues in the way experimental science sought consensus about empirical fact.

"Matters of fact," as Shapin and Schaffer have argued with reference to the experimental and literary projects of Robert Boyle, are a crucial product of the new forms of experimentation and discussion, whether in the technically public but actually rather exclusive experimental theaters of the Royal Society or in the larger domains where descriptions of experimental work were disseminated, debated, and popularized in print as well as through lectures and demonstrations in coffeehouses and salons. This domain, though smaller than Addison and Steele's public, would, by the earlier eighteenth century, have overlapped to a considerable extent with the approximately 60,000 readers having daily access to *The Spectator*. Shapin and Schaffer describe the operative technologies of the new forms as those literary and, to a lesser extent, visual devices that create "virtual witnesses"—that is, surrogate observers created out of readers who could not be present at an actual experiment but can come to lend credence to it and to participate in discussion of it through representation. "Matters of fact," in this account, are beliefs constituted through verbal and visual formations of "circumstantiality," "plenitude," or even "prolixity." Thus, "the matter of fact is to be seen as both an epistemological and a social category. The foundational item of experimental knowledge . . . generally, was an artifact of communication and whatever social forms were deemed necessary to sustain and enhance communication" (25).

Description and verisimilitude, then, are formations that, though seemingly empirical and antirhetorical and, in Shapin and Schaffer's account, "modest" in their emphasis on a plain, unassuming style, in truth become part of a machinery of persuasion that is covert, antitheatrical, and antiallegorical. The aim is to produce in "a *reader's* mind . . . such an image of an experimental scene as obviates the necessity for either direct witness or replication" (60). Shapin and Schaffer argue that these effects of hyperreality work, through a kind of nonrhetorical rhetoric of representation (whether it is visual or verbal), to convince an audience that never saw the experiment and never can see the experiment that it really took place, that it was done honestly, that the account represents what really happened and that the outcome of the experiment is "true" *as if* the person who reads and sees this printed account were the nominally modest witness (in fact privileged and powerful) who actually was present in Boyle's laboratory and actually did see the air pump in operation. Overdetermination in the manner of presentation may actually be said to constitute factuality for the public. Residing only in notebooks, Boyle's findings might point to truths but they would not be formulated as facts. Thus, in this account, over-determination itself becomes the efficient force: Boyle's flood of detail supports facts but does not constitute them as much as does their presentation in the mode of virtual witnessing. In reality it was exceedingly hard to make the air pump operate accurately. And, therefore, in a way these representations (verbal and visual) are more real than real because there is in them an implicit teleology in which (although Boyle was very meticulous about noting when the pump did not work) the outcome is going to be that it does work and that we will see it perform through his account. In this way, an impetus toward narrative and temporal development hovers covertly within virtual witnessing.

Now we may return to the troubling elision between Heidegger's "facticity" and Habermas's ideal of rational consensus under the contradictory aegis of which I have proceeded thus far. Heidegger's facticity is the point of departure for a process of philosophical reflection that brings to light the always already interpreted nature of the everyday as we normally experience it. The outcome of such reflection is the rather passive stance of "letting be" (*Gelassenheit*). For Habermas, however, the outcome of inward reflection is rational exchange aimed at consensus and, therefore, at action. His system treats "facts" as products—as markers of the consensus yielded by rational inquiry on the road to action—whereas Heidegger's facticity is the point of departure for private reflection leading to acceptance.

From the vantage point of late modernity, these positions are irreconcilable. But, whatever the validity of Habermas's philosophy, his idealization of the earlier eighteenth century in *The Structural Transformation of the Public Sphere* is significant. His nostalgia for this period yearns implicitly for a time when the use of factual evidence to produce consensus and modify behavior was possible because the tensions between reflection and action represented by the opposition between his own thought and Heidegger's were not experienced as antitheses. Rather, factuality could then be a basis both for a private stance toward the world and for action in it. Even the radical skeptic, David Hume, whose *Treatise of Human Nature* was composed and published during the decade of Hogarth's first cycles, introduced his book with this assertion:

> And as the science of man is the only solid foundation for the other sciences, so the only solid foundation we can give to this science itself must be laid on experience and observation. 'Tis no astonishing reflection to consider, that the application of experimental philosophy to moral subjects should come after that to natural at the distance of above a whole century . . . [since] my Lord Bacon. (xvi–xvii)

Hume's experimental method remains unitary even as he moves, far more radically than others espousing the scientific model, to divide knowledge according to its objects. The realm of reason, where "truth or falshood consists in an agreement or disagreement either to the *real* relations of ideas, or to *real* existence and matter of fact," is separate from that of "our passions, volitions, and actions," because these are "original facts and realities, compleat in themselves" (458). But even within the limitations imposed by this skepticism (and I have chosen Hume as the least congenial illustration of my argument), reason can work practically in both domains:

> Thus upon the whole, 'tis impossible, that the distinction betwixt moral good and evil, can be made by reason; since that distinction has an influence upon our actions, of which reason alone is incapable. Reason and judgment may, indeed, be the mediate cause of an action, by prompting, or by directing a passion: But it is not pretended, that a judgment of this kind, either in its truth or falshood, is attended with virtue or vice. (462)

Although Hume similarly divided the strict thinking of philosophy, governed on the whole by reason, from the impulses of ordinary life, governed on the whole by the moral sentiment, the method for understanding each remained that of experimental inquiry and its capacity to intervene in, if not to dominate, our lives. As Donald Livingston has powerfully shown, Hume's ideal of the "common life" represented a continuing attempt to synthesize both ways of viewing the world.[17] Hume sums up this split-focused existence as one in which we "endeavour to set ourselves at ease . . . by feigning a double existence" (215). Earlier in this same passage, Hume asks readers to reflect on the relativity of perception and its dependence upon "our organs and the disposition of our nerves and animal spirits," by instructing them to press one eye with a finger to observe the multiplication of images (210–11). Hogarth's facticity provokes analogous experimentation and, with it, stages the reflexivity that founds moral consciousness.

Thus, I have been using the term "facticity" for a reason. For I consider the ostentatious density of factual reference and the crowded texture of minutely represented objects in Hogarth's earlier cycles as markers or signals indicating that the technologies of virtual witnessing are at work. This superfluity or prolixity functions much as did the illusionism of the plates showing Boyle's experiments with air pressure (Figure 2). The point here, although Boyle's are not the most sophisticated engravings imaginable, is that many illusionistic details are added in the rendering of this machine that would not be necessary for the strict reproduction of this scientific experiment by another scientist. I am suggesting that one finds a similar prolixity or superfluity of detail that calls attention to itself in the Hogarth plate. I have in mind, specifically, the overturning table in the foreground of *A Harlot's Progress*, plate 2 (Figure 3). Here is an example of an ostentatious or hyperrealism since, if anyone were actually kicking over such a table, it would look quite like this but slow-motion photography would be necessary to capture the sight. In the perspective frame of Hogarth's plate, this table looks quite provocatively immediate, with three legs suspended in midair and bits of crockery and silver frozen in transit from its top to the floor. The scene is at once precise in detail and unlike real-world vision, in which stopped time is more of a retrospective intuition ("it seemed to hover in the air") than a mode of sight in clock-time. This is exactly the point about facticity: this sense of something so real that we pause to think about its realness. This coming to awareness, this matter of factness produced by effects of hyperreality, works through a nonrhetorical rhetoric of representation (whether visual or verbal in Shapin and Schaffer's account) to convince an audience that never saw a given experiment that it really took place, that it was done honestly, that the account represents what really happened and that the outcome is true—as if the person who reads and sees the printed account were a modest witness who actually was present in Boyle's garage and actually did see the air pump functioning as described. Facticity lies in the "as if," in the gap between represented and firsthand experience to which Hogarth calls attention.

The documentary purpose of Boyle's image—its usefulness, for instance, in assisting other scientists attempting to replicate the experiment—could have been served equally well by a line etching but the expensive engraved plate's crucial role in producing a compelling, consensus-building image of the experimental scene for a wider public required the startling use of light and shade that one sees in his illustration. Similarly, the conviction on the part of Hogarth's audience that matters of fact are indeed tangibly,

FIGURE 3. William Hogarth, *A Harlot's Progress*, Plate 2 (1732). Harvard Art Museums/Fogg Museum, Gift of William Gray from the collection of Francis Calley Gray, G1809.

circumstantially, and opulently set forth in the plates works to build consensus—if not about specific ethical values the plates advance (the commentaries show that these are not always perfectly clear), then about experiential engagement with the evidentiary and factual bases of ethical judgment. In this sense, although Hogarth and his public were not necessarily engaged in science or scientific consensus-making, his hyperrealism worked similarly to novel scientific instruments, which, as Shapin and Schaffer say, constituted "new perceptual objects" and generated "matters of fact that were objects of perceptual experience" (36).

III

The facticity of the cycles works to persuade the viewer to be not so much part of a consensus about moral values and judgments as part of a consensus about how to judge moral values on the basis of evidence—in short to be part of an enlightened community or public. This kind of representation differs decisively from the vividness of description that had been thought, in traditional rhetorical analysis, to direct an audience toward action, because those classical forms of what was called *descriptio* in the rhetorical tradition were selective and local whereas the technology of virtual witnessing requires not merely circumstantiality but what I have called overdetermination and what Shapin and Schaffer call "prolixity." Ultimately, the goal of this kind of representation, in contrast to *descriptio*, is not action but self-reflection.[18]

Other plates from the progresses can illustrate further what I mean by facticity. One example might be the broken dish and spilled writing materials in the foreground of the plate showing Moll's death. These may be read allegorically, though their rendering with a prolixity of detail that calls marked attention to itself commands visual as well as intellectual explication (Figure 4). Even more to the point is the overturned table in this plate, referring back visually to the earlier tea table and oddly drawn as if it were both falling toward and resting on the floor. Although supposedly at rest, it recalls the caught-in-midair quality of its predecessor and, more immediately, of the falling chair just abandoned by one of the two quarrelling quacks in the middle ground. The plate's firmly drawn framing perspective points up the anomalies here, just as the strong perspective frame of plate 2 enables the visual joke in which Moll's lover's sword and cane almost seem to stab the Jew in the back (Figure 3). Further examples would include the Rake's protruding foot in plate 7 of *A Rake's Progress* or the very

FIGURE 4. William Hogarth, *A Harlot's Progress*, Plate 5 (1732). Harvard Art Museums/Fogg Museum, Gift of William Gray from the collection of Francis Calley Gray, G1812.

interesting earlier states of the last plate, "The Rake in Bedlam" (Figure 5). Visual prolixity is more evident and more effectual earlier than in the third state, where an illusion-breaking medallion of the mad Britannia appears, demanding interpretation and calling our attention to a specific discursive interpretation among the many possible prior to the medal's insertion. The earlier states allow us to contemplate the visual immediacy of the scene—for instance in the shimmering dress of the lady visitor, which almost seems like a collage fragment out of a French or Dutch painting, and her awkwardly drawn right arm. Awkwardly drawn or exaggerated bodily parts, which seem deliberate in the cycles, often push viewers toward the kind of visual awareness I am describing. Proportional exaggeration or misdrawing of limbs occurs, for instance, in plates 4, 5, and 6 of *Harlot* and in *Rake*, plates 1, 7, and 8. So trenchant is the character of these stylistic features that they largely survive the coarsening of copies like those of the *Harlot* by Giles King. Some remain even in the homogeneously photographic engravings of *The Road to Ruin*, a cycle by Hogarth's nineteenth-century admirer, W. P. Frith—especially in the plate titled "The End," showing the hero of the series preparing to commit suicide in a garret (Figure 6).

Hogarth's cycles project an observer consonant with the mode of virtual witnessing I am describing and with the kind of public assent through which it constitutes matters of fact. This observer neither requires overt signs of histrionic performance nor responds to demonstrative rhetorical communication. In this way, the objects Hogarth describes exist in a closed world possessing distinct features of the "absorptive" mode in pictorial representation that Michael Fried has described in French painting from the 1760s onward. Such plates as "The Death of the Harlot" or "The Rake in Bedlam" illustrate the internal focus and refusal of address to the beholder of absorptivity *avant la lettre*. This way of organizing pictures in Hogarth, whether one calls it "absorptive" or some other name, creates a conditional kind of observation, an engaged disengagement in which we are asked to respond to the situations depicted but not to participate directly in them. The characters, with rare exceptions, turn not to the viewer but to one another, communicating with others or with themselves alone in the represented world they occupy but eschewing direct address to the observer. Such direct address would constitute, using Fried's terms, a theatrical, openly rhetorical kind of suasion contrary to the understated precision required to move the modest witness to assent. The allegorical and satiric impulses in Hogarth's cycles preserve aspects of such traditional forms of address.

FIGURE 5. William Hogarth, *A Rake's Progress*, Plate 8, 2nd State (1735). Harvard Art Museums/Fogg Museum, Gift of Belinda L. Randall from the collection of John Witt Randall, R5694.

FIGURE 6. L. Flameng after W. P. Frith, "The End," from *The Road to Ruin* (1889). The British Museum © The Trustees of the British Museum.

Paradoxically, as I believe Fried shows, such forced disengagement of the beholder from the representational scene of the tableau, when intensified in paintings that minimize traditional symbolism and allegory, while allowing the beholder none of the entry points I am grouping under the heading of Hogarth's facticity, produces not detachment, objectivity, and conversation leading to consensus, but overwhelming emotion.[19] Modest presentation, paradoxically, increases the effect of hyperreality, which in turn compels the virtual witness to conviction. Hogarth's series of the 1730s are not, strictly, absorptive in Fried's sense. Yet, the intense and widespread response they provoked may in some measure be traceable to contradictions inherent in their visual technology. The effect of impartiality, as Smith was to show in *The Theory of Moral Sentiments*, is grounded in imaginative engagement.

Be that as it may, "absorptive" techniques, though already evident in scenes such as "The Death of the Harlot" or "The Rake in Bedlam" (Figures 4 and 5) tend toward their apogee in *Industry and Idleness*—as "The Fellow 'Prentices at Their Looms" and "The Idle 'Prentice at Play in the Church Yard, During Divine Service" may illustrate. In this regard, it is no accident that some of the prime exhibits in Fried's argument are paintings by Jean-Baptiste Greuze, an artist profoundly influenced by Hogarth's cycles, whether at his own or Diderot's instigation.[20] The modest narrator or primary witness with his plain, impersonal style and unobtrusive, even antirhetorical presence was an essential part of the technology used by experimental science for gaining the kind of conviction that obviated the need for direct witness or replication. Such impersonality eventually would contribute crucially to illusionism in the novel as third-person forms—especially free indirect discourse—became dominant.[21] The modest narrator/observer, the represented world that refers absorptively to itself (not histrionically to an audience), and the illusionism produced by impersonality can be seen as working to yield consensus about moral and ethical matters of fact by positioning an ideal, impartial judgment and spectatorial detachment in an imagined realm of audience observation and discussion. And finally, in Hogarth's cycles, as with the actually hard-to-witness experiments described in the works of Boyle and other empirical scientists, the devices of modest or impersonal representation are at their most compelling when opening to public view those detailed, extended, hard-to-replicate experiments. Even if one were physically there, it was not easy to witness some of these experiments, and therefore the illusion of witnessing in the engravings is all the more instrumental. Similarly, those exclusive, intimate scenes of London life that in truth never could have been directly witnessed by a public assumed a raw immediacy in the framing Hogarth's cycles gave them. The intimacy of many of the scenes in Hogarth is crucial. Obviously, however, some plates are of public sites. Sightseers could actually go to Bedlam or to see the whores at work in Bridewell, but in general we are privileged observers in Hogarth's progresses to scenes that could not easily be witnessed, just as scientific experiments could not be directly witnessed because they were too small in scale, too microscopic, too privately conducted to be part of a physically public world. Even in the demonstrations in salons and coffeehouses and lecture sites where, as Larry Stewart suggests in his book *The Rise of Public Science*, science was purveyed to a larger public in eighteenth-century England, one is dealing with small aggregations of people where conversation and debate over the experiment represented could be conducted.[22]

Thus, the kind of public I am linking to Hogarth's facticity, in contrast with Paulson's multitiered audience, is defined not by its diversity but by a unity gained through consensus about acceptable methods of fact production. In this regard, if not in the actual circumstances of life, this public is discursively constructed as classless because all of its members have equal status as witnesses: equal status because the densely textured technologies of virtual witnessing are supposed to put the direct witness and the surrogate witness on an equal footing. No doubt this imagined community was in fact exclusive in many ways and certainly, as Solkin and others observe, it was ideological. Whether this public was ideal or actual is a matter of debate but, either way, the perception of its viability could alter.[23] In Hogarth's case such an alteration certainly appears to have occurred when, during the 1740s, he purposely divided his audience according to class. With *Marriage A-la-Mode* he proudly embraced not only aristocratic subject matter but expensive, sensuous French engraving. He specifically refused to authorize cheaper copies, choosing instead to address *Industry and Idleness* and *The Four Stages of Cruelty* to apprentices at the opposite end of the social spectrum. Indeed, as early as *A Midnight Modern Conversation* (1733), he may be seen to point scathingly at the limits of "conversation" as a medium of social coherence. In any case, by 1763 he had inserted into the final plate of *A Rake's Progress* that large medallion of Britannia as mad woman: in this form, the print delivers a univocal message rather than provoking self-reflexive discussion.[24]

Paulson allows for the kind of public of the 1730s that I have been describing when he cites Vertue's statement that *A Harlot's Progress* "captivated the Minds of most People[,] persons of all ranks & conditions from the greatest Quality to the meanest" and then goes on to add up the cumulative audience of the original subscription and the various authorized and unauthorized copies—observing finally that Hogarth's audience may well have come to approximate the 60,000 of *The Spectator*. Paulson is following Vertue's lead in depicting this different ideal or ideology of the public. The 60,000 in truth must surely have been as diverse in their ways of life as Paulson indicates in enumerating them, but the operative fiction that Vertue understood was that they, as surrogate witnesses with "Minds" (and I am repeating Vertue's word), occupied one world—a world of fact.[25]

Locke opens his *Essay Concerning Human Understanding* with the observation that "the Understanding, like the Eye, whilst it makes us see, and perceive all other Things, takes no notice of it self: And it requires Art and Pains to set it at a distance, and make it its own Object." Hogarth accomplished precisely this impartial vision in his cycles of the 1730s, though by his own visual means rather than Locke's verbal ones. Interestingly, Hume suggested in his *Treatise* during the same decade a simple experiment with the eye to convince his readers of the relativity of visual perception (210). Later in Locke's *Essay*, invoking the images that fall from a pinpoint upon the walls of a chamber darkened to form the camera obscura, he proposes that "external and internal Sensation" are "the Windows by which light is let into this *dark Room*" of the understanding, which "is not much unlike a Closet wholly shut from light, with only some little openings left, to let in external visible Resemblances, or *Ideas* of things without; would the Pictures coming into such a dark Room but stay there, and lie so orderly as to be found upon occasion, it would very much resemble the Understanding of a Man." Locke's metaphor is double-edged. Paulson reads this passage quite bleakly, stressing Locke's initial invocation of darkness, as an analogue to Moll's entrapment in the world of *A Harlot's Progress*. Yet, the room-sized camera obscura Locke summons to mind is flooded with the subdued light that sustains magical images of the world outside. Such a room seems an astonishing magic chamber, not a prison. The room is dark only when its apertures are closed; otherwise, it is filled with the images that constitute understanding. Hogarth emphasized this bright side of the coin during the 1730s. By 1763 its somber obverse guided his rereading of *A Rake's Progress* almost thirty years after its publication.[26]

CHAPTER 4

Hume's Learned and Conversible Worlds

With Robin Valenza

They that content themselves with general ideas may rest in general terms;
but those whose studies or employments force . . . closer inspection must
have names for particular parts, and words by which they may express various
modes of combination, such as none but themselves have occasion to consider.
— Samuel Johnson, *The Idler* (1759)[1]

Samuel Johnson denied the possibility that the language of common life
could be sufficient to provide all the "terms of art," the expert terminologies, necessary for specialized studies and employments. In the *Idler* essays
and the preface to his *Dictionary* (1755) he describes this lexical divide as a
consequence of the pursuit of advanced knowledge, accepting with regret
the professional isolation that inevitably results. Although Johnson con-
fronts the issues concerning specialized language that we address in this
essay, the degree to which general languages could speak to expert needs
seems more settled for him than for other writers, whether before or after.

British philosopher, historian, and essayist David Hume characterized
the conflict between specialized and public languages as a split between
the "learned" and the "conversible" worlds. "Learned," for Hume, signified
the idiom of university-trained specialists, "conversible" the conversational
vernacular of a broadly educated public. In his 1742 *Essays, Moral and Political*, Hume imagined himself as an ambassador moving between these
worlds. Such an emissary was needed, Hume noted, because philosophy
in particular had suffered much from its disengagement from common life,
losing any claims to "Liberty and Facility of Thought and Expression" and

becoming "chimerical in her Conclusions as she was unintelligible in her Stile and Manner of Delivery."[2] Hume's advocacy of a more conversational style in philosophical writing came in the wake of the popular failure of both his own, highly learned *Treatise of Human Nature* (1739–40) and John Locke's earlier efforts to make philosophy better suited to "well-bred Company" and "polite conversation."[3] Locke's push to conjoin the expert pursuit of knowledge with rational conversation in society, here reiterated by Hume, resembles concerns raised in our own time about the accessibility of academic writing. And, as Hume shows, although questions about the intelligibility of a discourse are, on one hand, about linguistic choice, they are, on the other, about the values we attach to technical humanistic studies. Then as now, they are loaded questions.

Our chief subject here is neither the role of the modern university in the heritage of these debates nor the debates' genesis in the eighteenth century. Rather, we examine how the ideal of conversational language endorsed by Locke and his successors was differently deployed in scientific and humanistic contexts in the eighteenth century. In so doing we speak genealogically across time to the methodological divides facing today's academic writers. We treat the case of David Hume because his career, although unusual in its trajectory, crystallizes our concerns: in response to the mistakes he perceived in earlier metaphysical systems, he began life as a professional philosopher looking for a scientific method, one that would allow him to achieve a revolution in morality and epistemology analogous to the one Newton achieved in physics. However, in publishing the *Treatise* he ran up against the fundamental difference between disciplines that do their work on and in natural languages and those that work on physical objects or through mathematical representations.

The precondition of describing the findings of physical science in ordinary languages is that such formulations inevitably will be incomplete: the essence of the work is given up in the transition from mathematical to linguistic representation. The vernacular description of the work is acknowledged as a series of metaphors that can be shaped to conform to the level of understanding of the projected audience without affecting the original results. Thinking in language comes after the mathematical or experimental fact and is, or is presumed to be, radically autonomous from science itself.

By contrast, in the humanities and social sciences findings and their representations to an audience are bound up together in one and the same language. This entanglement between the work itself and its linguistic presentation gives rise to the assumption that because one can understand a vernacular language, one should be able to understand all things written in it. But the problem with this assumption is that it discounts the histories, traditions, and methods that develop in expert discourses and their constituent terminologies. Although specialized vocabularies are intertwined with the language of common life (if indeed a common-life language exists as such), they are not identical to it. The oft-voiced prejudice against disciplinary jargons likewise adumbrates a host of suspicions. Such wariness is founded on a hazy but nonetheless powerful anxiety that texts written in expert idioms are hiding important knowledge from the vernacular culture for diabolical or at least potentially exploitative purposes. The widespread distrust of legal language is the paradigmatic example, but other disciplines have likewise contended against similar misgivings.

The sciences and humanities thus have long displayed asymmetrical relationships to natural languages. This asymmetry confounds modern readers no less than it confounded Hume when he assumed in his early work that the audience for philosophical prose was coextensive with the generally educated reading public. When his early effort at a scientific philosophy in the *Treatise* was met with general incomprehension and was largely ignored, he moved toward a more sociable, collegial style, adopting the language of coffeehouse periodicals for metaphysical ends. He simultaneously discarded the technical, epistemological pursuits that could not be represented in nonexpert languages.

I. Language and Specialization

We frame our own investigation with a polemical question: why does the claim that science can only be incompletely represented by ordinary-language descriptions make the work done by scientists seem all the more important because all the more incomprehensible to the lay reader?[4] And why does the pressure work in the opposite direction in the humanistic disciplines: the more specialized humanistic language becomes, the readier the reading public is to discount or suspect its value? Ordinary, or conversational, language figures centrally here because the eighteenth century witnessed the movement of specialized, disciplinary knowledge into the public sphere through demonstrations and expositions couched in language readily available to an ever-broadening, nontechnical readership. But why was there a felt need for such knowledge to move into the public sphere, the world of everyday language? If we begin with the case of science, we can find answers in recent scholarship. The new, experimental scientists (Newton, Boyle) differentiated themselves from their rationalist counterparts (Descartes) by conducting their work on and with nonlinguistic materials—prisms, air pumps, telescopes—and through the highly specialized language of mathematics. They fostered a new epistemology based on experimental objects and mathematical symbols. This innovation required justification. Scientists made the empiricist epistemology credible by staging their work in public demonstrations and describing it in publications written in ordinary language. Popular exhibitions of scientific instruments served to show how natural and mechanical objects could be made to speak.[5]

Laboratory work made its way into common parlance through lecture tours and written exegeses that glossed mathematical reasoning in everyday terms. Popularizations of works such as Newton's *Principia* (1687) made their basic claims, if not always their methods, accessible to the lay reader.[6] The fiction guiding these scientists was that their laboratory experiments and mathematical expressions made the facts of nature available to them, and that their public demonstrations—when they differed from what was done in the lab or the study—were only secondary representations meant to convince an untrained audience. They were not the thing itself.

In a 1761 lecture chemist Joseph Priestley compared this relationship between fact and representation to the difference between history and fiction. "All true history has a capital advantage [over] every work of fiction," he wrote, because "works of fiction resemble those machines which we contrive to illustrate the principles of philosophy, such as globes and orreries, the use of which extend no further than the views of human ingenuity; whereas real history resembles the experiments by the air pump, condensing engine and electrical machine, which exhibit the operations of nature, and the God of nature himself."[7] Priestley's facts of nature—made available through experimental mechanical devices—were constructed in the belief that "facts were theory-free and value-free."[8] The eighteenth-century scientist's insistence on the separation of the scientific fact from the capriciousness and imprecision of language was crucial. Experimental scientists became publicly credible because they emphasized the limits of the authority of language and the dominance of specialized modes of knowing. Paradoxically, they leaned heavily on visual and linguistic rhetoric to make this distinction clear. Over time the perceived remoteness of science from the world of rhetoric gave it independence and power. The burgeoning realm of vernacular print culture both expanded audiences and confronted the emerging disciplines with unforeseen demands.

If the public sphere was where rational, factual knowledge could be tested and deemed credible, it would seem to be the ideal place to try the claims of any new epistemology. There was thus a parallel impetus for new methods in humanistic studies to make the same move into the public sphere. David Hume thought along these lines, calling his 1739–40 *Treatise of Human Nature* an "Attempt to introduce the experimental Method of Reasoning INTO Moral Subjects."[9] In it Hume railed against the narrow, technical logic of his metaphysical predecessors who would cavil endlessly over concepts such as "the self," inventing entities without seeking empirical evidence for their existence. Rather than beginning with general principles, he founded his work on observation, the evidence of his senses, taken individually and collectively. He called his method inductive, directing attention to his procedural distinctions from the deductive techniques of earlier moral philosophers.

Hume thus embarked on a project with the same set of assumptions that Newton or Priestley did: that experiment could make fact—the real thing—available to him through sensory observation. His chosen method obliged him to proceed as if his analysis would produce objective certainty. But following his process through to its logical extreme, he undermined his own operating assumptions. His prima facie privileging of our sensorium—our best source of empirical information—was itself deconstructed. He demonstrated that we have no way to prove that our sense organs give us facts about the world. Inquiring into the basis of our notion of what is real, he instead discovered he could not show that what our senses give us are facts; they only offer grounds for strongly held beliefs. He showed that we work from our beliefs in our representations of nature without any assurance that this *is* nature itself. In so doing he revealed that the inductive method, when applied to consciousness, increases our sense of the contingency of our knowledge and thus delimits the claims of the method. Hume did not entirely discredit our ways of knowing; rather he pointed to their susceptibilities and qualifications and to the inability of any observation-based procedure to stabilize its object of knowledge.

But Hume presented his struggle with the nature of knowledge through a method difficult enough to keep most readers from grasping what he had done. To Hume's consternation the reading public failed to follow—or to want to follow—him through his own involved reasoning. This outcome should not have surprised him as much as it did, considering the complexity of his analytic procedures and the idiosyncratic precision with which he uses ordinary vocabulary. Almost from the beginning, in letters and published commentary, he attributed his readers' difficulties to their misunderstanding his use of language. When the third volume of the *Treatise* was published in 1740, he annexed this remark: "I have not yet been so fortunate as to discover any very considerable mistakes in the reasonings deliver'd in the preceding volumes. . . . But I have found by experience, that *some of my expressions have not been so well chosen, as to guard against all mistakes in the readers*."[10] Hume follows the footsteps of Locke, who had similarly found that his writing was subject to misunderstandings and miscommunications and had likewise blamed insufficiently attentive readers for the communication gap.

In an effort to untangle his work for the inexpert reader, Hume took it upon himself to imitate the scientists by becoming his own expositor and adopting a second, more public language. He wrote in 1748 the more accessible and considerably shorter *Enquiry Concerning Human Understanding* and in 1751 the *Enquiry Concerning the Principles of Morals*. Even taken together, these two works leave out many of the most technical aspects of the *Treatise*. Over the course of his career Hume moved toward increasingly approachable, essayistic forms and left off writing more technical works altogether. Here is where the correspondence we have been tracing between moral philosophers and natural philosophers, between humanists and scientists, ends. In moving from philosophical discourse to more readily available language, Hume eventually abandoned wholesale the most difficult, most technical aspects of his philosophical writing. With it, he also cast aside the set of ideas not responsive to treatment in the language of the essay, the genre of the public sphere.

But even after the successes of Hume's later writings, his *Treatise* did not, at least in the public sphere, follow the trajectory of Newton's *Principia* by becoming more valued because more inaccessible. The difference seems to lie in some combination of their respective disciplinary practices themselves and the rhetoric they used to present their own work. Shortly before he died, Hume penned an advertisement that would be prefaced to his posthumous collected works:

> Most of the principles, and reasonings, contained in this volume, were published in . . . *A Treatise of Human Nature*. . . . But not finding it successful, he was sensible of his error in going to the press too early, and he cast the whole anew in the following pieces, where some negligences in his former reasoning *and more in the expression*, are, he hopes, corrected. . . . Henceforth, the Author desires, that the following Pieces may alone be regarded as containing his philosophical sentiments and principles.[11]

Hume locates the difference between the two kinds of writing not in their reasoning, although he says he did rectify a few errors there; rather, he finds it "in the[ir] expression." That is, he represents the two works as differing primarily in their linguistic style. He proceeds as if the difference happened only in the manner and not in the matter. Here Hume's concerns intersect with our own: Hume performs the same critical maneuver on his writings that more recent critics are quick to perform on academic writing when they confer bad-writing awards and the like. They insist that difficult writing is a marker of muddled or lazy thinking. They share the splenetic and delusional perspective of the dying Hume who held the wishful sentiment that all reasoning, however strenuous, could be embodied in ordinary language.[12] Critiques (including Hume's self-critique) that consider difficult writing to be by definition bad writing mask deeper, structural divergences that such thinking refuses to acknowledge.

Although untrained readers may not have grasped much of Hume's *Treatise*, what they did comprehend were reviewers who suggested they should not read Hume's work at all because it was so pockmarked by the unpleasantness of skepticism. One of the few published reviews of Hume's *Treatise* takes him to task for the difficulties to which he puts his readers:

> I should have taken no notice of what he has wrote, if I had not thought his book, in several parts, so very abstruse and perplex'd, that, I am convinced, no Man can comprehend what he means; and as one of the greatest Wits of this Age has justly observed, this may impose upon weak Readers, and make them imagine, there is a Great Deal of deep Learning in it, because they do not understand it.[13]

This review's unnamed author exhibits a keen awareness of the power the recondite text may hold over its readership, suggesting itself as holding secrets unavailable to the casual reader. He dismisses such an interpretation of Hume's *Treatise* as a red herring. The *Treatise*'s rhetorical complexity is not caused by the immense learnedness of its author—as the weak reader might assume—but rather by its author's linguistic inexactness and faulty reasoning. But as another critic has observed, this anonymous reader was himself not a very careful one, refusing or failing to evaluate Hume's system on its own terms and, instead, holding it accountable to the very rationalist doctrines Hume sought to undercut.[14]

Hume's critical reader would have agreed in part with the more perceptive reviewer of the *Bibliothèque raisonnée*: "Perhaps it will be found that in wishing to investigate the inmost nature of things, [Hume] sometimes uses a language a little unintelligible to his readers. . . . Metaphysics has its stumbling blocks as well as the other sciences. When it passes certain limits, it obscures the objects that it searches out. Under pretence of yielding only to evidence, it finds difficulties in everything."[15] Hume himself worried over this: if clarity of understanding is the goal, certain philosophical or rhetorical procedures ought not to be employed under any circumstances because they inevitably muddy the water, impeding the view of the very objects they wished to expose. Much of the *Treatise* is devoted to leading its readers into philosophical dead ends, to showing the limits both of received epistemologies that argue for nonempirical sources of knowledge and of experimental methods that rely on experience alone to explain human understanding. Such a procedure is by its very nature difficult to follow. What later academic philosophers have found most compelling about Hume's method lies in these very mazes. It is in the nature of his philosophical maneuverings to leave more questions than answers. However, an appreciation of such a method runs counter to the prejudices of a wider reading public, who tended (and still tend) to believe that what is possible at all in language is possible in commonsensical formulations.

The belief in the power of common language to address philosophical questions was and is still bolstered by a host of eighteenth-century writings on the topic. Authors from John Locke to Hugh Blair have averred that when language is held strictly accountable to the ideas underlying it, both language and ideas will be transparent to their readers. That is to say, critical investigations into subjects not easily made tractable to straightforward (or straightforwardly worded) solutions ran counter to the stated aims of enlightenment. For at least this brief moment in history, popular pressure and philosophical epistemology coincided—in theory. Rhetorical clarity was the hallmark of the way empiricist philosophers thought of themselves. When clarity was not possible, inquiry was inadvisable.

But alongside this belief ran another, perhaps articulated best by philosopher George Berkeley (1685–1753), about the difficulty that the nonscientific disciplines faced in sharing the vocabulary of everyday life:

> Herein Mathematiques have the advantage over Metaphysiques & Morality. Their Definitions being of words not yet known to [th]e Learner are not Disputed, but words in Metaphysiques & Morality being mostly known to all[,] the definitions of them may chance to be controverted. . . . The short jejune way in Mathematiques will not do in Metaphysiques & Ethiques, for y[e]t about Mathematical propositions men have no prejudices, no anticipated opinions to be encounter'd, they not having yet thought on such matters. [T]is not so in the other 2 mention'd sciences, a Man must not onely demonstrate the truth, he must also vindicate it against scruples & establish'd opinions w[hi]ch contradict it. In short the dry strigose rigid way will not suffice.[16]

That is, mathematicians do not have to contend with their audience's preconceptions about their terms because such terms are expressly set apart from and defined in contradistinction to everyday language. In contrast, metaphysicians must defend their language from the claims of common sense. Practitioners of nonmathematical, technical disciplines must contend with the commonplace notion—in Berkeley's time and our own—that language is language is language. The operative belief here is that common speech embodies common sense and that anything worth saying can and should be said in broadly accessible terms. This is the heart of the critique of Hume's *Treatise* by Thomas Reid, the eighteenth-century commonsense philosopher: knowledge is not knowledge if it cannot be comprehended in commonsensical terms.[17] Twentieth-century ordinary-language philosophers have leveled a similar critique at technical disciplines more generally: technical work must have been ultimately—at its origin—based on ordinary understandings of the world.[18] This search for intuitive origins or even a consistent language of common sense entails problems very much like the ones Berkeley spells out, namely that expert languages often operate differently from commonplace usages, even if they had at one time overlapped.[19] Indeed, one of post-Lockean philosophy's—as well as post-Newtonian science's—tasks has long been to point out the assumptions and presumptions lying behind common sense and its unilateral advocates.

Hume confers great value on common sense and habit because they allow us to get on with the business of everyday life. He does not, however, see common sense as the solution to epistemological problems. Hume's achievement in the *Treatise* is to illustrate that our faith in the alignment between fact and its representations is itself a problem, riddled with difficulties implicit in the act of representing. Hume's *Treatise* opens up the fundamental mistake in the insistence on the rhetorical transparency of common sense embodied in ordinary language.

We can thus recognize that reducing the difference between Hume's two kinds of writing to "stylistics" is itself a rhetorical move on Hume's part. Much of his readers' trouble in parsing the *Treatise* did not stem from Hume's language as such (as many critics have demonstrated, his sentences are generally very lucid), but rather from the philosophical method bound up in the language. Hume responds to this level of difficulty by banishing many of the parts of the *Treatise* he had explicitly marked as abstruse to his first *Enquiry*'s appendix and eliminating others altogether. He also provides his readers with suggestions on which sections of his *Enquiries* they ought to skip if looking for light entertainment. In writing the *Enquiries* he both implicitly and explicitly denies the possibility of translating the *Treatise*. Hume hovers between on the one hand admitting that philosophical abstraction cannot be explained without resort to a highly learned approach necessarily difficult to read, and on the other asserting that he will manage it anyway by dismissing much of what he had to say altogether.[20]

II. Lost in Translation

Reading Hume thus raises for us a question: is it possible for nothing to be lost in such a "translation"? Literary scholar Gerald Graff has argued, "Good academic writing . . . tends to be 'bilingual,' making its point in the complicated language of academese and then restating it in the vernacular (which, interestingly, alters the meaning)."[21] This is a version of Hume's point about the transfer of knowledge between learned and conversible worlds. But, although Graff ostensibly maintains that specialized writings have a certain, if limited, right to exist, his remarks belie a basic suspicion of the value of specialized, "difficult" language. The neologistic denomination "academese" tends to mock the language in which many academics write. The fundamental problem, though, is the metaphor of translation that Graff applies to the process of moving from disciplinary language to everyday language. "Translation" is misleading because it suggests that the operative fiction here is that as little as possible is lost in the move. This is not to disregard recent work in translation theory but rather to suggest that the process of transmutation may be described better by "representation" than "translation." Graff's own parenthetical remark—"which, interestingly, alters the meaning"—is a recovery effort, an acknowledgment that "translation" may be inadequate to describe what is accomplished and what is forfeited in moving between two methodologies.

In fact, the alteration of meaning lies at the heart of the move from expert to general language. Simplification has its value. As admirers of Hume have observed, few people might have ever read the *Treatise* if the better-reviewed *Enquiries* had not called attention to it. In his own time Hume gained widespread approval for his efforts to focus on the aspects of philosophy more compliant to vernacular treatment. His *Enquiry Concerning the Principles of Morals* was the best received of his philosophical works; not coincidentally he also called it his favorite. The January 1752 *Monthly Review* recommended this *Enquiry* for its congeniality to the taste and abilities of the general reader:

> The reputation this ingenious author has acquir'd as a fine and elegant writer, renders it unnecessary for us to say any thing in his praise. We shall only observe

in general, that clearness and precision of ideas on abstracted and metaphysical subjects, and at the same time propriety, elegance and spirit, are seldom found united in any writings in a more eminent degree than in those of Mr. *Hume*. The work now before us will, as far as we are able to judge, considerably raise his reputation; and, being free from that sceptical turn which appears in his other pieces, will be more agreeable to the generality of Readers. His subject is important and interesting, and the manner of treating it easy and natural[.][22]

On the one hand, Hume's sacrifice of complexity as he moved from the *Treatise* to the *Enquiries* was rewarded by reviewers who found grounds for praise in both the easy flow of Hume's language and the absence of philosophical difficulty. On the other, critics have remarked almost since Hume's own time that in order to fit the *Treatise*'s ideas into the more conversational *Enquiries*, he left out much of what has most interested professional philosophers in his own time and ours. Far from being stylistic residue, certain methods of inquiry were abandoned because they were not directly amenable to linear expository presentation.

We can easily see how the impulse not to differentiate between philosophical and customary uses of words arises—both technical terminologies and general usage are embodied in one and the same words. An ordinary-language philosopher of the twentieth century might well agree that Hume was on the right track in abandoning problems that did not exist in ordinary language. Hume says as much himself. However, such abandonment still begs the question: is it possible to talk about the range of difficulties we find in ordinary-language constructions of the world without a technical language? Hume's explicit answer to this question might have been a qualified "yes," but the course of his career after the *Treatise* suggests that the answer is "no." That is, Hume's later writings indicate that when he turned to popular forms, he gave up pursuits deemed impossible for a general reading audience to understand.

Hume's rhetorical strategy differed fundamentally from the techniques of self-presentation used in science, where the scientific experiment itself was put forward as essentially different in nature, not simply in style, from the ordinary language later used to represent it. Science was able to find an epistemology that lay outside ordinary linguistic norms while also receiving public approval for the existence of such ways of knowing. We do not want to suggest that scientists can avoid vernacular language in their writing; scientists today must as a matter of course describe their research for nonspecialists when applying for grants in ways similar to those that the early experimentalists did to gain approval for their labors.[23] Instead, we want to point out that the separation between the work scientists do and the ways they represent it has, from an early point, been clearly demarcated as an act of representation. Vernacular formulations are considered fundamentally different from the work itself because the experiments and calculations were neither conducted in nor reliant on the same language used in everyday life. Such thinking persists in our own time. Indeed, in 1988 Stephen Hawking could write that "if we do discover a [unified] theory [of physics], it should in time be understandable in broad principle by everyone, not just a few scientists. Then we shall all, philosophers, scientists, and just ordinary people, be able to take part in the discussion of the question of why it is that we and the universe exist."[24] According to Hawking, public conversation about such findings can and will happen only after the scientific facts are determined and then only in broadly metaphoric terms.

What remains for those of us whose work and the language used to represent it are indistinguishable?[25] The case of David Hume lets us see that attempts to insist that specialized knowledge can be translated into "everyday language" with minimal loss are incorrectly formulated. If we accept the modern point of view that facts, formulae, and statistics are themselves representations, the gap between those representations and ordinary language is the same rift that opens up when one makes a representation of a representation. There is an axiomatic difference between the fiction of translation (what Graff urges) and an acknowledgment of the process of representation (the lesson we take away from David Hume).

Historians have shown that the rhetoric surrounding early empirical science established in the popular consciousness the idea that experimental practice has a claim on a reality not subject to the accidents and ambiguities of conversational languages. We have tried to suggest a backward look at how and why practitioners of what would become the humanistic disciplines sought—unlike the scientists—to avoid marking themselves off into a separate realm of specialized knowledge apart from the public sphere. In the case of Hume we hypothesize that he succumbed to his own reasoning, which called into question all claims to any separate, factual spheres of knowledge that were not contingent on habit and common sense. In the *Treatise* he sought truth and found only belief; in his later writings he stopped looking for shared truth and worked instead from commonly held beliefs. Hume's radical linguistic shift seems thus to have resulted from some combination of his own skepticism about the claims to factuality of any epistemology, including his own, and of the social and marketplace pressures influencing the reception of his writing. Print culture and

Hume's own love affair with it disallowed this insulating divide between specialist and ordinary uses of language because it elided multiple audiences into a single one.

In retreating from the *Treatise* Hume's technicality suggested he was making a decision about a way of life as much as about a philosophical method. Indeed, in the *Treatise* Hume dramatizes the difficulties of pursuing such a methodology. He portrays the problem as a split between a life in society and a life of the mind, a divide between conversational and philosophical ways of regarding the world. In philosophical mode he finds himself "affrighted and confounded with that forelorn solitude" to which his thoughts subject him, imagining himself "some strange uncouth monster, who not being able to mingle and unite in society, has been expell'd [from] all human commerce, and left utterly abandon'd and disconsolate." Hume runs himself ever deeper into his solitary, abandoned realm until his senses call him back into a convivial, social world of "blind submission": "I dine, I play a game of back-gammon, I converse, and am merry with my friends; and when after three or four hour's amusement, I wou'd return to these speculations, they appear so cold, and strain'd, and ridiculous, that I cannot find in my heart to enter into them any farther."[26] The choice is sentimentalized, allegorized, made into a decision between fear and despair, on the one hand, and sweetness and light, on the other. With such a value-laden choice, who could wonder at Hume's eventual adoption of the latter? Hume preferred ultimately to follow in the capacious train of Joseph Addison, the eighteenth-century master of essayistic language, in exerting himself to bring philosophy "out of closets and libraries, schools and colleges, to dwell in clubs and assemblies, at tea tables, and in coffee houses."[27] This decision pushed Hume's philosophy away from an emerging intellectual disciplinarity, away from the difficulties of questions that required special exertion, broad and deep reading, and perhaps some suffering. Whatever may be gained herein, it also entails a substantial loss.

III. Enlightenment Novels

The Novel as Modern Myth

Robinson Crusoe, Frankenstein, Dracula

Three novels in English have entered the vernacular of myth so fully that the authors themselves tend to be effaced and surface features of the stories tend to drop away just as myths undergo multiple permutations and become cultural icons. The three works are *Robinson Crusoe*, *Frankenstein*, and *Dracula*. This essay is a thought experiment about the ways these three iconic novels may interrelate as myth, about axes that intersect in them and that have allowed them to develop the remarkable power they seem to possess over the *longue durée* of cultural time. I propose that they have the permeability of myth, the surface transparency of myth, and the structural permanence of myth.

I have often imagined that it would be provocative to link these three books. Of course, they share certain superficial traits, one of which could be more deeply significant. *Robinson Crusoe* (1719) was Daniel Defoe's first extended work of fiction, or novel. *Frankenstein* (1818) was Mary Shelley's first novel. *Dracula* (1897) was Bram Stoker's first fully conceived novel, though previously he had published a few short stories in the thriller vein and some serialized fictions reflecting his experiences as an Inspector of Petty Sessions that came out as an episodic collection. Among candidates for mythic status, one might think of another first "novel," *Gulliver's Travels*, but it is actually three stories and some fragments, not one novel, while its crisply pointed style hardly suggests literary initiation. And *Dr. Jekyll and Mr. Hyde*, though a work that originated with a dream, really is a long short story produced deep in its author's literary career. Does *Alice in Wonderland* have the mythic reach of my big three? It qualifies on some counts but, for now, I will leave it aside because I do not see it as having the metamorphic dimension of the others—perhaps because its own subject is metamorphosis and its surface effects so compelling.

The three novels I am considering seem to me to have a certain rustic or rough-hewn quality that may arise in part because of their firstness, though one can name other first novels, apart from Swift's, of immense stylistic polish. For instance, *Les Liaisons dangereuses* of Choderlos de Laclos. I would not claim that firstness alone defines my three novels but I believe that some of the immediacy and stark energy they project does somehow go to their firstness: above all that the kind of simplicity or directness or immediacy of style that I want to present as crucial to all three does connect with firstness. This is not a naïve simplicity in writing. Indeed, we now know that Defoe habitually revised, despite his earlier reputation as a hack journalist. Certainly, Shelley and Stoker rewrote. So I do not suggest that the air of rusticity derives from carelessness. On the contrary, I would say that it springs from an *orientation* to the world (to use a term from phenomenology)—an orientation that produces an aura of initiation, beginnings, or, as I am calling it, "firstness." Martin Heidegger's term, "the unconcealment of being" (*Entbergung des Seins*), which concerns emergence into substantial form, can make a bridge between the quality of firstness pointed to here and the sense of the apparitional that becomes important later on. Firstness, like the appearance of an apparition, could be called the archetypal *event*—the event per se, an emergence that assumes significance in light of what has been and will be known—like Heidegger's "unconcealment of being." Firstness has the effect of revelation but it also drains substance from what was previously experienced as vivid, in the sense that revelation or unconcealment at the same time obscures and partly conceals or "ghosts" the margins around it, just as a spotlight reveals some things and throws others into shade. Myths, of course, are all but defined by firstness, by our sense that they possess a primal originality.

Although two of my three books were extremely popular from the outset—*Crusoe* and *Dracula*—all three achieved, within a certain period of time, a truly remarkable popularity, so great in fact that they became standards for ordinary readers including young people, if not always for critics. In the case of *Frankenstein*, this process stretched out somewhat, for the book does not seem to have been a best seller until after various dramatic adaptations in the 1820s, and its inclusion in Bentley's Standard Novels series of 1831 launched a growing popularity throughout the nineteenth century. By contrast, *Crusoe* took off fast and had a flood of editions and translations during its first fifty years. The work achieved enormous popularity in eighteenth- and nineteenth-century England. Its popularity in later eighteenth-century America almost approached that of the Bible. In keeping with this history, *Crusoe*'s early canonization seems to have been more because of its inspirational spirituality or as a children's work than as a classic of Literature with a capital "L."

The three novels share attributes of Shakespeare's reception, for while extremely popular and admired by some critics and literary figures, all three were patronized by the literati and were slow to come to canonization as works of Literature with a capital "L." Alexander Pope's *Dunciad* early set the snobbish pace against Defoe, and even his private praise of *Crusoe* to his friend Joseph Spence was grudging. Both *Dracula* and *Frankenstein* were canonized as Literature with a capital "L" quite recently—indeed, just during the last forty years, to judge from the reception history I have found. This time frame, of course, coincides with the rise of feminist critique. A search of the Stanford University Library catalog shows little scholarly attention to either novel before 1970. Indeed, it is far from clear that *Frankenstein* and *Dracula* could have been thought about critically as novels *qua* novel any sooner because, at least superficially, they defy a classic criterion for the novel that Ian Watt voiced with the term "realism of assessment" in *The Rise of the Novel*.[1]

I

One can certainly find numerous thematic parallels among these books. *Frankenstein* and *Dracula* show strong affinities of theme. The vampire stories that those in the Shelley circle were reading at the time *Frankenstein*'s composition began also are works read by Stoker prior to composing *Dracula*. The two books commonly have been discussed together, and audiotapes and CDs advertised on Amazon.com link them in sets even now. Adding *Crusoe* points toward a rather different range of issues that will come up later. But here is a list of some themes and features that do mark all three:

- the super- and supranatural
- the inhuman
- terror
- the making of things and machines (in *Frankenstein*, a being)
- education
- frame stories.

Dracula in its published form lacks a frame, but Stoker seems to have cut a significant chunk of a frame story from his original manuscript, which could be seen prior to its sale at Christie's as recently as 2002. The theme of what one might call science and technology is present in all three, along with that of the technology of writing per se—the question of how one writes, what one writes, the tools of writing, and how one tells a story. The theme of travel is crucial, of course, along with overreaching, monstrosity, and survivorship. All are features around which one *could* construct critical essays.

But then of course, many other masterworks and lesser pieces of writing share these themes. In fact, I am not trying to make the claim that the themes in and of themselves define the unique mythic iconicity of these novels. It seems likely, indeed, that the emergence of these three as books of an extraordinary vigor in the popular, the critical, and even the scholarly imagination has to do with the convergence of a number of different factors. I suspect that in this history affinity of theme is no more significant than chance.

Instead of theme, the factor stressed here is *style* in the largest sense. I mentioned before that the firstness of these books could have a role to play in their relative lack of stylistic polish. We know with *Frankenstein* that, for better or worse, prior to the 1818 publication, Percy Shelley heavily edited the prose—altering some 4,000 words—and that Mary Shelley herself made large editorial changes and substantive additions in the interval leading up to the 1831 edition, which presented a polished, revised, and in many ways sophisticated text. The Charles Robinson edition of the *Frankenstein Notebooks* reveals that the rustic or naïve stylistic energy of the first version was considerably submerged.[2] Still, some of that rough-hewn quality, some of that sense of raw vigor, does come through the sophistications to which the book was subjected. Its firstness survived its rewritings. Indeed, even the higher-style phrases and literary references in *Frankenstein* often have a rustic or appliquéd aspect themselves—like an education not yet fully assimilated.

Edgar Allan Poe declared of *Crusoe*:

> It has become a household thing in nearly every family in Christendom. Yet never was admiration of any work—universal admiration—more indiscriminately or more inappropriately bestowed. Not one person in ten—nay, not one person in five hundred—has during the perusal of "Robinson Crusoe," the most remote conception that any particle of genius, or even common talent, has been employed in its creation! Men do not look upon it in the light of a literary performance. Defoe has none of their thoughts—Robinson all. The powers which have wrought the wonder have been thrown into obscurity by the very

stupendousness of the wonder they have wrought! We read, and become perfect abstractions in the intensity of our interest; we close the book, and are quite satisfied that we could have written as well ourselves. All this is effected by the potent magic of verisimilitude.[3]

So says Poe, suggesting in "abstraction" that readers became detached from reality *through realism* and that they, or indeed the text of *Robinson Crusoe* itself, became a kind of apparition by virtue of its supreme realistic transparency—its capacity to disappear as writing.

Poe and other critics note that the features one might call Defoe's "style" tend to disappear into a vernacular English that assumes transparency simply by virtue of its plainness, its everydayness, and even its awkwardness. We all know that in ordinary speech even the most sophisticated users of a language make awkward utterances. Much of the point of what we might call "educated" or "high" or "literary" style traditionally has been to efface awkwardness in order to arrive at a perspicacity that is associated with more concentrated and potent forms of expression than can be achieved in common language.

This very quality of disappearance that the rough-hewn novelistic style can produce parallels the tendency of style to disappear in mythic or iconic stories. Claude Lévi-Strauss and other structuralists such as Vladimir Propp have effaced the element of style in their treatment of the fundamentals of myth. Lévi-Strauss says, for example, that a myth is "felt as myth by any reader anywhere in the world. Its substance does not lie in its style, in its original music, or its syntax, but in the *story* which it tells."[4] The identities of the authors and the framing features of our three books tend to drop away when the core stories are translated or adapted to other media. In Shelley's case, even the name "Frankenstein" has migrated in popular culture from the hero of the novel to the monster himself. These are signs of a stylistic vaporization that can happen with archetypal stories.

The Literary with a capital "L" has traditionally been associated with finely or highly wrought individual styles. For this reason alone, the three books I am considering slid under the radar of the canon—in the sense of the literary canon—for protracted periods. Shakespeare slid under that radar for the first hundred years or more after his death, for rather different reasons having to do with the literary standing of drama and, given a rising neoclassicism, possibly overwroughtness of style rather than underwroughtness. But the extreme adaptation—even mutilation—of his works for staging during the seventeenth and early eighteenth centuries must have had a role, along with a certain suspicion of drama as literature. Similarly, the novel as an entire genre slid under the radar and was not perceived as high literature until rather recently.

Plainness of style is a definitive aspect of realism's power to give an impression of the real "thing." As John Richetti says in a recent introduction, "things," in the sense of *res* in Latin, are rendered in realist texts in general and overwhelmingly so in *Crusoe*.[5] But *things* also hold tremendous importance in *Frankenstein* and certainly in *Dracula*. Stoker powerfully places material objects in the foreground, whether they be the earth covering the vampires or the many different dictaphones, typewriters, steamships, railroads, and other machinery embedded in the plot. In his hands, even the innovative technique of blood transfusion becomes starkly physical.

The very quality of realism depends, as Poe indicated, on the capacity of its language to disappear into things and into thought. This is a paradox built into the genre of the realist novel: writing, and therefore style, defines objects as if real in the realm of the novel because they can exist *only* through the medium of language and style, but the reader's awareness of style per se is expected to drop away as it does in news reportage. The illusion is of objects per se. Yet these objects, in fact, have no tangibility, no applicability, no dimensional shape. I will explore this paradox later with regard to the notion of realism as itself an apparitional form or mode of writing.

Plainness of language has also allowed an extraordinary degree of translatability in our three novels. This rough-hewn style has led to translatability not only in the sense that versions in other languages work well, but also in the sense that the stories can be transmuted from one medium to another with great facility. One of the curious aspects of English high literary culture is that some of its finest, most esteemed writings—by Geoffrey Chaucer, Edmund Spenser, John Milton, for instance—have not translated well in the way Shakespeare did when August Wilhelm von Schlegel assumed his writings into German, whereas masterpieces such as the *Divine Comedy*, the *Decameron*, *Don Quixote*, and *Faust* have moved freely into many languages.

II

Let us turn now to my claim about the archetypical or mythic status of our three books. One might say, as Bronislaw Malinowski did in *Myth and Primitive Psychology*, that myth "is not of the nature of fiction, such as we read today in a novel, but it is a living reality, believed to have once happened in primeval times, and continuing ever since to influence the world and human destinies."[6] Novelistic fiction and myth lie at opposite poles from one another for Malinowski.

It has been a commonplace in myth studies since Émile Durkheim, James Frazer, Sigmund Freud, and Ernst Cassirer to view myth as prior to or more fundamental than any literary manifestations it may have in point of social organization, ritual, or psychology. One way or another, myth is considered deeply symbolic or structural. In a real way, myth and literature—even epic and novelistic ideologies in the case of Georg Lukács—have been set in opposition. In Northrop Frye, along with Roland Barthes the most powerfully literary critic of myth in the twentieth century, the scale of value goes from ancient myth at one end to recent, and lesser, "ironic" forms at the other: forms of writing that share both their modernity and their novelistic potential with prose fiction rather than with early tragedy or epic poetry. Again and again, we encounter the sense that the mythic or archetypal is somehow antithetic to literature, though literature is seen as feeding on or embodying or preserving the power of myth. Myth is seen as having the tangibility—the vividness or immediacy—that more finely wrought forms may lack. Malinowski seems to imply, for instance, that the novel attempts to resuscitate or replace the sense of lived reality or experience that is part of everyday life to peoples immersed in myth. Folktales were imagined in this fashion during their reception following Johann Gottfried von Herder and the brothers Jacob and Wilhelm Grimm during the German Romantic period. The notion extends in our own day even to "urban legends," which somehow have a remarkable grip on our imaginations for all their factual absurdity.

Raymond Williams points out that the use of the root term "myth" as a word on its own in English, its present meanings shaped by Romantic thinking about the folk imagination, itself is a product of nineteenth-century modernity. It first appeared in 1830. The modern meanings attribute to myth, according to Williams, "a truer (deeper) version of reality than (secular) history or realistic description or scientific explanation."[7] Older words based on this root, going back to the fifteenth century, like the word "mythology" and its variants, bear no relation to our sense of myth as some kind of primal, enduring, culturally profound story. Instead, the words built on the root "myth" used to refer to "fabulous narration," to the fictional and unbelievable. One could say, then, that the word itself, and with it the growth of the modern idea of myth, goes hand in hand with the emergence of the realist novel.

In general, myth is idealized in these discussions, whether through Frye's opposition of myth to the ironic modes of modernity, or through

Lévi-Strauss's treatment of tribal myths as having unique structures that can survive enormous surface permutations while continuing to serve profound cultural needs over long periods of time. In Frazer's more rationalistic version, myth is seen as primitive, deeply rooted human knowledge. The one critic who has framed myth in largely questioning or even negative ways is Barthes, who shows how semiotic structures work in cultural formations that he designates as "mythologies." Using examples like the image of a French soldier saluting the flag, he reveals how these formations assume the rigidity of linguistic usage, and how they are drained of their deeper metaphorical significance, just as are habitual linguistic formations. Myths become naturalized as ideology and block the critical faculty, just as our ordinary use of language requires us to pass over profound etymological or metaphorical resonances and contradictions. Naturalized usage causes words, like the myths that Barthes describes, to become unconscious gestures or automaton-like mechanisms.[8] Barthes probably was inspired by Durkheim's treatment of myth and religion as maintaining secular values by projecting them into realms of divinity.

The indifference of mythic tales to surface plays out in the realist novel as that plainness of style I have stressed earlier. This way of telling stories finds early analogues in newspapers, in Baconian claims for the accuracy of unornamented writing, and in the kind of transparent scientific reportage that Steven Shapin and Simon Schaffer have called "virtual witnessing."[9] The implications for technique in novelistic fiction are far-reaching. For plainness of style enables the illusory, even apparitional effects of realism, including free indirect discourse (*style indirect libre* or *erlebte Rede*). Free indirect discourse is a grammar within which first-person thoughts are rendered impersonally in third-person linguistic forms in ways that exist only in writing. Neutrality of style is no longer a matter of simple diction and syntax but a vehicle for rendering the *entrelacement* of external sociolinguistic forms with internal subjective states that characterize modernity. Adam Smith, in his *Theory of Moral Sentiments* (1759), was one of the first to give a generalized account of the psychosocial mental state that the impersonal narration of thought crystallizes in novelistic fiction. This kind of narration heightens in the extreme the readerly absorption that has been thought to characterize realist fiction generally and that is often considered to make it dangerous to a public vulnerable to apparitions. Delusional belief in myths, including their ritual reenactment, may have been socially constructive or mentally therapeutic for primitive peoples. Moderns must beware of similar forcefulness in novels.

III

I turn now to a final attribute of *Crusoe, Frankenstein*, and *Dracula* as myth. It enfolds the others as definitive. This is the aspect of the three novels as apparitions. I suggest here that what becomes iconic or mythic in modernity is an *experience* of a certain psychosocial kind, whether individual or collective. I suggest that, in modernity, the content per se of the story—and here I may to some extent be inspired by Malinowski and Lévi-Strauss—becomes less important in works that assume mythic status than the experience of the fiction itself as real or compelling. The solitary experience of silent novel reading, in which a text becomes alive to a single individual *as if* the real were fully present, is a specifically modern experience compared with earlier recitations of tales. The fusion of novelistic texts with the reader's own emotional and physical experiences from moment to moment was a power commonly remarked in the eighteenth century and was the one most admired by the Chevalier Jaucourt in his articles on "*Roman*" and "*Description*" in Diderot's *Encyclopédie*. Jaucourt insisted, above all, on the revelation of "secret emotion" in the trajectory of the new novel that he traced from Madame de La Fayette through Samuel Richardson and Henry Fielding. Jean-Jacques Rousseau reveled in this power as a reader of *Crusoe* and *Clarissa* and as author of his own *Julie*, though in the *Confessions* he scorned novels that one reads with one hand. One could say that eighteenth-century claims about the dangers of absorption in novels are pointing to the capacity of realist prose fiction to subject and enthrall readers with apparitional presences privately experienced and inaccessible to society.

All three of our novels are apparitional. They present apparitions enacted within the real. Just at the center of *Robinson Crusoe*, when Crusoe first encounters the single footprint, he says: "I stood like one Thunderstruck, or as if I had seen an Apparition; I listen'd, I look'd round me, I could hear nothing, nor see any Thing, I went up to a rising Ground to look farther, I went up the Shore and down the Shore, but it was all one, I could see no other Impression but that one, I went to it again to see if there were any more, and to observe if it might not be my Fancy; but there was no Room for that, for there was exactly the very Print of a Foot, Toes, Heel, and every Part of a Foot."[10] The story shows Crusoe's witnessing not only the apparition of the footprint but the apparition of cannibalism, and, in the end, shows his turning himself into an apparition for others when he appears as Governor of the island. Even earlier, he assumes such qualities in his own imagination because of his bizarre dress. It is clear that the monster in *Frankenstein* becomes an apparition, particularly as he disappears over Mont Blanc or across the Arctic ice to immolate *himself*—or not—for there is always the possibility he will return, apparition-like. Other characters, too, are or become wraith-like in *Frankenstein*. Dracula is an apparition if ever there was one: he materializes mysteriously, can move over great spaces, and lives on the very essence of human life: blood. Several characters in the novel take on his qualities and, in the case of Lucy, even become vampires themselves.

Yet the issue here is not chiefly that these three works thematically involve apparitions in the story, or plot, or events, or characters, but that the apparitional is deeply written into the very fiber of their technique as realist novels. It may seem surprising that I group *Frankenstein* and *Dracula* with *Crusoe* as realist novels, but technically and procedurally they are. They also are metarealistic because they bring the apparitional quality of realism itself to the surface: the capacity of realism to give us the impression of real things—to use means other than the direct, sensory apprehension of the real in order to project a reality. In this sense, realism, the genre of the realist novel in itself, is apparitional. The mode of these works connects profoundly with their thematics—with the thematics of apparition—but this is a symptom not a cause. An analog would be William Nestrick's analysis of early film as obsessed, like Shelley's *Frankenstein*, with the magic of "coming to life" through the illusion of apparent movement produced mechanically.[11] The thematic of zombies, vampires, and ghosts moving between life and death is found everywhere in early film, and is a symptom of the grip held on viewers by its own ghostly technology. The thematics are secondary not primary, though their presence may bring to awareness imagery and editing that, in Walter Benjamin's terms, enact the constitutive character of film illusion as a mode of "mechanical reproduction."[12]

More needs to be said about the apparitional core of realist fiction. I am inspired here by Terry Castle's use of the term "apparition" to describe the arc beginning in the eighteenth century and culminating in Freud's theories. Castle describes a historical complex of psychosocial developments in which ghosts and apparitions, which in prior times had been conceived as agents existing outside the human body, were progressively introjected imaginatively as psychic phenomena, ultimately as symptoms of psychoanalytically accessible conditions. The merger of ghosts, phantasms, landscapes, and inner states that characterizes the haunted experience of heroines in eighteenth-century Gothic novels is a literary crystallization of one stage in the process. The quest for phantasmagoric experience of the supernatural that permeates nineteenth-century culture is another. Psychoanalysis, with its theory of curative apparitions in the analytic chamber, known as "transference" experiences, both exploits and works to contain the apparitional in a modern psychocultural form. The haunted heroine and the Gothic genre manifest the modern life of apparitions as internal to the psyche rather than as external agents.[13]

My sense of the apparitional, in contrast to Castle's, is linked not to subject matter—to ghosts external or internal—but rather to the technical attributes of realism itself. Crucial here is the long discussion of probability in its traditional commonsensical aspect, not in the modern mathematical sense. Whether in Aristotle or Fielding, the theory of fiction did not admit the vagaries of everyday life, though Fielding pushed the boundaries by articulating a thematics of coincidence in the voice of his narrators. Every newspaper contains events that no one would believe in a novel. Every reflective modern person, not just David Hume as he manipulated his eyeballs to produce double vision, knows how unstable and multiple perception is. As Alexander Welsh has shown, eighteenth- and nineteenth-century law courts in England progressively abandoned eyewitness testimony in favor of forensic evidence precisely because the real is impossible to stabilize juridically except through probabilistic inference.[14] But realist fiction does stabilize the real *qua* reality. Through its neutrality of style, its profusion of detail, and its causal sequences of action, realism produces a coherent linguistic version of the real that never has been, is, or will be. Expect the principles of realist fiction to apply in everyday life and you get delusion at best, madness at worst. This is the sense in which I mean that realist fiction is apparitional: it is apparitional not with regard to thematic content or specific characters or actions but with regard to its very technical procedures.

Myth can have the realness of apparition, the vividness that only transient things seem to have, the vividness of dreams and phantasms. And in the three novels under discussion here one finds a sense of the transience that underlies the real in everyday life, the apparitional quality of sensory perception that preoccupied Hume and other eighteenth-century philosophers and supernaturalists who juxtaposed the real with the counterintuitive. Even when, like Hume, they debunked spiritual interventions in the world, they evoked the apparitional quality of the very experience we call the real.

Our three works are metanovels—modern myths—in their revelation of unreality within the real. Their phenomenology is analogous to the "coming to life" in early horror films inspired by *Frankenstein* and *Dracula* or to the revelation of the footprint's spectral presence to Robinson Crusoe. In modernity, especially the kind of industrial urban modernity that *Dracula* addresses and in a fashion predicts, the real becomes indistinguishable from media simulations of it. The process already had begun in the eighteenth century with the insane popularity of Richardson's *Pamela* (1740), clearly a media phenomenon in the modern sense according to William Warner.[15] The realist novel is part of a long-term history of the invasion of the real by media that enable us to assume, through surrogate projection, the illusion of sharing the firsthand experience of others. The membrane of the real in novels may be stretched gossamer-thin over its linguistic and grammatical structures—even ruptured—just as film can maintain effects of illusion while flirting with the viewer's awareness of the mechanical demons that bring it to life. One glimpses the ghost in the machine.

The medium or genre that institutionalized this mode of flirtation within the realist novel is called the "Gothic." Indeed, the Gothic is in many ways *the* mode of modern fiction, though invented by Horace Walpole only in 1764. Walpole tapped into crucial aspects of realism as the defining features of the Gothic in his prefaces to *The Castle of Otranto*. "Allow the possibility of the facts," he declared, "and all the actors comport themselves as persons would do in their situation." Walpole "wished to conduct the mortal agents in his drama according to the rules of probability; in short, to make them think, speak and act, as it might be supposed mere men and women would do in extraordinary positions." In disavowing "similies, flowers, digressions, or unnecesary descriptions," he stresses, in particular, the conscious choice of an unadorned, unmetaphoric simplicity of style that has been noted by critics from Sir Walter Scott onward.[16] Looking carefully at *Otranto*, one sees that, plot and setting notwithstanding, its forms of narration are fundamentally those of the realist novel, including free indirect discourse. Indeed, *Otranto* arguably contains the first sustained use of free indirect discourse in English fiction. The events are extraordinary but the way the story is told is straightforward, simple, and transparent. Although the psychology of characters may not be complex by the standards of a Richardson or a Laurence Sterne, one finds crucial passages of mental reflection under stress in the text of *Otranto*. One finds the rendering of first-person thought in third-person grammar that defines free indirect discourse and that, later, will support the astonishing psychological transparency of Austen's novels. Paula Backscheider points to Walpole's strategy in her biography of Defoe, when she says that eighteenth-century novelists in general often put ordinary people in extraordinary situations.[17] Walpole simply took a basic strategy of realist fiction and pushed it to the Gothic extreme.

Is the Gothic so very improbable after all? Jesse Molesworth has shown, for example, that eighteenth-century gamblers were steadfast in behaving contrary to the new laws of mathematical probability easily accessible in the period's omnipresent publications of works about gaming by Edmond Hoyle.[18] Real gambling behavior did not follow mathematical probability any more than everyday life follows the rules of realist fiction. In such a context, the delusional embrace of the Gothic novel's supernaturalism can seem like a symbolic recognition of the absurdity of the everyday as we experience it in the flow of existence: of the real that newspapers try to capture in all of its bizarre immediacy. Probability is all well and good, but can it predict the next second of my life or the next card dealt? No, it can predict only the long-term, the average, the outcome of countless coin tosses. On the other hand, the underlying realist structure of the Gothic novel, in context with its thematics and romantic plot structure, can be described as a mere vehicle for managing the unpredictability of the everyday—the madness of real life. The submerged but omnipresent realistic technique so characteristic of the Gothic novel is in this sense spectral or ghost-like. The technique works rather as a digital sorting program might work to contain and corral a flood of data too large to be comprehended by mere human agency. This realist program is, as Flaubert noted in a famous letter to Louise Colet, everywhere felt but never seen.

The three books that I am discussing here combine that sense of the *extraordinary* within the forms of the ordinary that we associate with the Gothic novel's production of terror and panic. Such forms are fundamental to the apprehension of culture and its values in modernity. So in this sense there may not be a Gothic novel but rather a Gothic mode marked by its way of pointing up traits that define the realist novel per se. It is commonplace to say that the core of the American novel is Gothic, when we think of Charles Brockden Brown in the late eighteenth century or of Nathaniel Hawthorne, Herman Melville, or William Faulkner. Perhaps, in fact, the Gothic is not best considered a subset of the modern novel. Rather, the modern novel is best understood in its essence as apparitional, that is as Gothic. After all, even newspapers, those bastions of "fact" from which the novel is said to have evolved, easily spin into the realm of fantasy and factual fiction that we associate with today's tabloids.[19]

What I suggest is that these three most compellingly mythic English novels in the modern period are also the most metanovelistic. Ian Watt exclaims as follows: "Almost universally known, almost universally thought of as at least half real," Robinson Crusoe "cannot be refused the status of myth." "But," asks Watt, "a myth of what?"[20] He goes on to expose his thesis about the *homo economicus* and the myth of individualism. Yet, Watt's essay, like countless others on Defoe's novel, on Shelley's, and on Stoker's, is fundamentally thematic. It is no more than an allegorical exegesis. These works, so it goes, are mythic because they are about individualism, science, motherhood, education, sexual initiation, or what have you.

What I would say instead is that the mythic standing of these three books is not thematic but rather structurally experiential. Their very apparitional quality of disappearing as books makes them icons of the modern sense of the paradoxical concreteness and evanescence of reality itself. They are myths about the myth of the real. They are not allegorical but direct, demonstrative revelations. They let us glimpse the workings of the novel much as the illusions projected by film, for Benjamin, are animations that both conceal and reveal the machinery that produces them. Thus, Malinowski got it wrong when he put novelistic fiction against "a living reality, believed to have once happened in primeval times, and continuing ever since to influence the world and human destinies." What is being memorialized in *Robinson Crusoe*, *Frankenstein*, and *Dracula* is the modern belief in the firstness, originality, and continuing workability of what we call "reality" itself in the face of overwhelming evidence of the ungraspability of the real in our experience.

CHAPTER 6

Tom Jones and the Public

Although Henry Fielding's comic novel, *The History of Tom Jones, A Found-ling*, was not formally published until February of 1749, favored readers already possessed its first volumes by December 1748 when the final part of Samuel Richardson's tragedy, *Clarissa*, appeared. These two large novels, opposite in their every aspect, together map out the technical and spiritual terrain of fiction-writing in England for the rest of the century and even beyond. Fielding's literary talent was comedic to the core yet, for all his devastating attacks on Richardson's epistolary comedy, *Pamela* (1740), he reviewed the first installment of *Clarissa* with unreserved enthusiasm a month after its appearance late in 1747 when *Tom Jones* was too far along to have been influenced. After the next installment, with his own novel in press, he wrote a letter to the author brimming with praise and offering friendship. The thin-skinned Richardson, possibly alert to double-dealing tendencies in Fielding's rhetoric, reciprocated first with silence and, later, with contemptuous remarks about *Tom Jones* and its author. Fielding's last novel, *Amelia* (1751), dark in atmosphere and concerned with the trials of an ideal wife, pays further tribute to Richardson. Still, their two masterworks are poles apart.[1]

In *Clarissa*, Richardson had perfected the technique he called "writing to the moment," by which the thoughts and emotions of the four chief characters are minutely reflected in letters composed immediately after, or even during, the course of events. The letters become physically part of the action not only because they purport to be written in the real time of the novel but because they are intercepted, redirected, delayed, copied, and forged. Clarissa's deathbed epistles even affect the paths of others after she is gone. Although Richardson later loaded the text with notes and commentary in order to guide readers toward a "correct" understanding of the novel (right down to a moral for each of the more than five hundred letters), in the first edition he presented the heroine's fate at the hands of Lovelace—her would-be lover, possible husband, and ultimate rapist—almost exclusively through the ebb and flow of the letters themselves, with a minimum of intervention by their supposed "editor." *Tom Jones*, on the other hand, is written almost exclusively in the third person. Both through the commentaries that begin each of the eighteen books and through countless interventions during the telling, its "author" emerges in many ways as its chief protagonist. This narrator is usually called "Fielding," both for the sake of convenience and because his voice rings true as the historical author's ideal self-depiction. We rarely glimpse the thoughts of characters without Fielding's mediation and his byplay moves in ongoing counterpoint with the action.

Like earlier English novelists such as Aphra Behn, Delarivier Manley, Daniel Defoe, or Eliza Haywood, Richardson and Fielding both laid claim to a wide, socially varied audience. They strove, however, to guide readers toward conclusions about personal virtue in much more authoritative ways than had been characteristic of the hairsplitting pros and cons weighed by Defoe's rather common protagonists or the amorous and courtly intrigues that dominate the concerns of Behn's and Manley's more uppish characters. Though choosing opposite methods and embracing quite different values, Fielding and Richardson, like contemporaries who joined the debate over their respective merits, saw themselves as raising the moral stakes of novel-writing and -reading. They shifted the focus away from the topical referentiality of *romans à clef* like Behn's and Manley's, and from the questions about literal factuality that Defoe and his critics considered crucial in judging the effect of his novels. They devised differently compelling new techniques for engaging their readers in the predicaments of fictional characters. Richardson worked to increase the moral capital of his readers through the overwhelmingly detailed representation of model subjects under conditions of extreme stress. Fielding worked to the same end through direct intervention in the experience of the story and through virtual conversation with the reader about the complexities involved in knowing and judging. Both saw their books as fully consonant with Christianity in both precept and spirit, though Richardson loaded *Clarissa* with specifically religious themes and symbolism—even allegory—whereas Fielding concerned himself with issues largely in the domain of ethics.

I

Fielding was the first among the still widely read trio of early masters of the English novel, including Defoe and Richardson, to have been born in the eighteenth century (1707); the first to have a classical education, at Eton (1719–24); and the first to come from a genteel, even obliquely aristocratic, family. His important connections yielded few assets apart from schooling, which quite early helped him to live as a writer, but family probably did help later to speed his certification as a lawyer and to pave his way to office. Pride in his social background and education had its snobbish aspect given Fielding's proximity to the Grub Street milieu. All the same, he could truly claim that his own firsthand experience with the full range of life from high to low lent a veracity to his writing that few of his rivals, especially Richardson, could match.

Fielding turned late to fiction, like Defoe, the journalist, political spy, and failed businessman who published *Robinson Crusoe* (1719) at the age of 59, and like Richardson, the prosperous printer whose *Pamela* appeared when he was 51. From 1728 until a crackdown on the theaters by Robert Walpole's government through censorship instituted by the Licensing Act of 1737, he authored a brilliant succession of satiric plays, including the heroic burlesque, *The Tragedy of Tragedies; or the Life and Death of Tom Thumb the Great* (1731). Put out of work as a political dramatist by the Licensing Act, he fell back on family tradition and began legal training at the Middle Temple in order to support Charlotte, his wife of three years, and their two children. Admitted to the bar in 1740 after only three years of study, he regularly rode the Western Circuit as a barrister and later, during the autumn and winter when *Tom Jones* appeared, took the bench as magistrate in the courts of Westminster and Middlesex. While sitting in the Bow Street court, Covent Garden, Fielding devised new methods that would become models of future law enforcement. He introduced strategies for identifying evidence through systematic advertisements, assembling facts, and running down criminals through the use of a quasi-official police force called the Bow Street Runners. He and his half-brother John, who continued this work after Fielding's health failed in 1754, are usually considered the founders of London's Metropolitan Police, an institution that was to wait until 1829 for parliamentary sanction.

The Licensing Act by no means stopped the flow of Fielding's pen. Inclination and talent must have played a part. More compelling still were lifelong habits of personal extravagance and generosity to others that left him continually in need of money and often on the edge of financial collapse. Just two years after his 1737 entry to the Middle Temple, Fielding again took up the cry against Walpole as frequent author of leading articles in a new paper called *The Champion*. In form, as well as in the use of a distinctive character to voice much of its commentary, the paper resembled Joseph Addison and Richard Steele's *Spectator* (initial run, 1711–12). In content it differed sharply from *The Spectator*, which eschewed politics and articulated a conversational, seemingly artless, yet meticulously balanced style of writing that soon became the gold standard for English prose. Samuel Johnson wrote, in his *Lives of the English Poets* (1779–81), that Addison's "prose is the model of the middle stile; on grave subjects not formal, on light occasions not grovelling; pure without scrupulosity, and exact without apparent elaboration; always equable, and always easy, without glowing words or pointed sentences."[2] Fielding, though at first comparably gentle in his *Champion* pieces, soon shifted to a keen satiric tone, embraced political controversy, and wrote an edgy prose in keeping with his adoption of the character of Captain Hercules Vinegar. Indeed, it is true of Fielding's writing more generally that, while he typically hews to the Addisonian stylistic virtues, his capacity for moral indignation, rapier wit, and sly irony spice his easy style with a bite reminiscent of Alexander Pope's or Jonathan Swift's brilliant diction and pointed sentences.

Writing continued to supplement Fielding's income from the law during the pre-novelistic years, as it would in one form or another through the rest of his life. Around 1740 he was ranging from journalistic work to verse satires, from Grub Street tasks like translation to the beginning, most probably, of his acerbic anti-Walpole narrative *Jonathan Wild* (published in the *Miscellanies* of 1743). In November 1740, however, just as Fielding was producing his last significant contributions to *The Champion*, an advertisement appeared in the paper for the first part of a book that would occasion his transformation into the novelist we remember today. It was a technically and socially revolutionary anonymous novel called *Pamela: or, Virtue Rewarded*. The story is simple. A lady's maid—a girl of some accomplishment thanks to tutelage in the household—upon the mistress's death finds her virtue under siege by the son and heir, Mr. B——. We witness her plight through a long series of breathless, enormously detailed letters that are interrupted but occasionally by those from other correspondents or by third-person narration. At first, Mr. B—— assails Pamela verbally, becoming ever more threatening physically until, having imprisoned her on a remote estate in the care of a housekeeper who lacks only fangs to scare young girls to death, he attempts rape. After Pamela talks him out of it, Mr. B—— turns into a devotee of her virtue, largely through his reading of her letters and journals. He proposes marriage and the fairy-tale dream comes true with Pamela's transformation into a great lady. To Fielding and some others, the moral was all too clear: chastity is a commodity that can be exchanged for wealth and social position.

Since Richardson, a tradesman working in the City of London far from the court, the government, and the newly developed West End, was not a recognized writer, his authorship of *Pamela* remained hidden for some while. But his heroine's name was on every lip. The popularity of her story went far beyond anything literary England had witnessed before. Fake continuations, poems to Pamela's glory, stage versions including an opera, high-class paintings, and cheaper decorative objects like fans flooded England and turned the novel into something akin to a modern media event. Although the chorus of praise for *Pamela*'s compelling combination of moral seriousness and stunning immediacy was deafening, Fielding was not to be alone in satirizing the heroine's sanctimonious verbosity, her at times less than innocent scheming, her covert attraction to Mr. B——, the greedy materialism of her inventories, and her conflation of moral virtue and material goods. But his *Shamela* (1741) was the first parody and his abilities were uniquely suited to expose these defects through devastatingly precise imitation of the febrile immediacy of *Pamela*'s moment-to-moment epistolary manner. Given this mastery, he needed only to reverse Pamela's pious character into a conniving and rapacious wench narrating the success of her scheme to trap Squire Booby into marriage with the lure of sex. Fielding's authorship was recognized at once and has never been doubted even though he never acknowledged the work.

Shamela laid the groundwork for Fielding's hugely successful first novel, *Joseph Andrews* (1742), which presents Pamela's sincerely chaste, comically straight-faced brother as a footman working in the house of Mr. B——'s uncle. The novel's Shamelesque aspect fades quickly once Joseph takes to the road after being fired for refusing to service Lady Booby's lust. He soon joins the wonderfully preoccupied Parson Abraham Adams—scholar of Greek, idealist, and true Christian—on a series of adventures overtly modeled on those of Don Quixote and Sancho Panza in Cervantes's paradigmatic novel from the preceding century. Ironic distance, often reinforced by the ridicule that had figured in *Shamela*, accompanies a heavy schematization of characters in *Joseph Andrews*, but this was Fielding's first novel to attempt the narrative stance combining detachment, an appearance of disinterested inquiry into factual detail, and a good-natured conversational alliance with the reader that he would bring to perfection in *Tom Jones*. Cervantes inspired both Fielding's narrative stance and his use of the mock-heroic and the mock-romantic to mark off boundaries for the novel as he conceived it.

In *Joseph Andrews* Fielding sought to raise the literary standing of the novel (not to mention increasing the stakes on Richardson) both by imitating the prestigious and popular *Don Quixote* (1604–14) and by importing classical generic categories and narrative devices into the novel. The preface, like a number of passages in *Tom Jones*, ingeniously finds a place for Fielding's kind of novel in the traditional hierarchy of genres or literary types, where tragedy and the serious epic ranked above comedy. He declares this new work to be a "comic Epic-Poem in Prose," alluding to the lost comic epic by Homer. Although mock diction will sometimes find admission to this new way of writing, says Fielding, the burlesque of sentiments and characters will be rigorously excluded along with all forms of the grotesque associated with low satire but often confused with comedy. True comedy must be founded in the observation of nature and thus cannot admit bizarre extremes. It deals, instead, with the ridiculous, which in turn arises from the discovery of affectation, the most notable forms of which are vanity and hypocrisy: "Great Vices are the proper Objects of our Detestation, smaller Faults of our Pity: but Affectation appears to me the only true Source of the Ridiculous."[3] Ideas such as these are more fully explored in the essays prefatory to each book of *Tom Jones*, which stands as Fielding's fullest illustration of the possibilities open to the new genre he was defining. Mock diction recalling the great classical epics of Homer and Virgil, as well as John Milton's *Paradise Lost* (1667), also appears in many parts of *Tom Jones*, for instance in scenes such as the battle outside the church over Molly Seagrim's borrowed fancy dress (4.8) or the introduction of Sophia Western in language suitable to a classical heroine (4.2). Given Fielding's redefinition of the comic novel in *Joseph Andrews*, it is possible to understand Richardson's turn to tragedy in *Clarissa* as a riposte to Fielding's elevation of the novel to comic-epic status. For tragedy was above comedy in the traditional literary pecking order and, while for want of a classical education Richardson could not link his tragic story to the serious epic, he could and did saturate it with the language of the Bible—a work of divine inspiration occupying the very pinnacle of the hierarchy of literary types. In any case, it is clear that Fielding's epic send-ups in *Joseph Andrews* and in *Tom Jones*, as well as his echoes of *Don Quixote*, are part and parcel of a program to define a new kind of novel that is strongly marked as part of "literature," and thus morally—even stylistically—serious in ways that novels of adventure and of amorous intrigue by his immediate predecessors in England had not been.

Fielding appears to have started *Tom Jones* in the winter or spring of 1745 after a break in literary activity of well over a year following the considerable successes of *Joseph Andrews* in 1742 and the *Miscellanies* in 1743. There are signs that he may have possessed a draft of about six books when the forces of the Young Pretender, Prince Charles Edward Stuart, invaded Britain in the summer of 1745. This invasion, which had succeeded brilliantly in a feudal Scotland disaffected ever since the Act of Union of 1707, faltered as it advanced into England despite having set London in panic by penetrating as far as Derby (Figure 7). Although hindsight allows us to see the invasion as an evanescent affair, doomed from the start, in the eighteenth-century perspective and indeed in that of Sir Walter Scott writing in the earlier nineteenth, it was experienced as one of the signal events of British history. Fielding, like the majority of his contemporaries, saw this Jacobite uprising as a profound threat to legitimate government. One sign of the importance of 1745 to Fielding was his six-month editorship of *The True Patriot*, a journal in which he wrote with fervor defending the constitutionalist position and the Hanoverian monarchy. Given his topical approach to writing, it would have seemed entirely natural to Fielding to weave the momentous events of the "Forty-Five," as it was called, into the texture of his novel, making Tom take up with troops fighting for the Hanoverian King George II and letting Sophia's identity be confused with that of the Pretender's mistress. No doubt, Fielding also had in mind the historical dimension obligatory to the classical epic when he involved the action of *Tom Jones* with these great events.

The leader of the invasion, called Bonnie Prince Charlie by his supporters in Scotland, was the grandson of the Catholic James II, who had been exiled after a brief and disastrous reign that ended in 1688 with the bloodless election to the throne of his daughter Mary and her Dutch husband William of Orange. They were both Protestants. Mary's sister, Anne, took the throne in 1702 but since her many children died before her, it passed in 1714 to George I of the German house of Hanover, which was distantly connected to the English royal line through Princess Sophia, the granddaughter of James II and the nearest Protestant heir. The ultimate outcome of the "Glorious Revolution" of 1688 was the Settlement Act of 1701, which reacted both to the absolutist, crypto-Catholic rule of the Stuarts and to the moralistic militarism of William by placing the king in a contractual relationship with Parliament. The Settlement imposed constitutional limits on the throne, which henceforth was to be Anglican, vastly broadened Parliament's powers, and set the stage for toleration of religious dissent. Ideological conflict over the succession and the place of the Church of England continued, however, ultimately enabling the alarms of 1745. The dominant Whig faction, in general, consisted of urban, professional, and mercantile interests reinforced by a number of aristocratic magnates and country gentlemen of the politically independent and commercially minded sort. The lesser Tory faction, still strong enough at times to control the government, could count on numbers of conservative aristocrats and landed gentry, country clergy and craftsmen, for whom tradition and loyalty to the hereditary monarch were paramount and who believed in the absolute right of the Church of England. Still, only a few Tories continued actively to fight the Settlement and, while many among them might sentimentally toast the "King over the water," few were ready to take up arms either for the Old Pretender, James Edward, around whom there had been a Scottish uprising in 1715, or for his son in 1745. We can see with this background that Squire Western's support of the "King over the water" fits his character perfectly and that the incorporation of urgent current events into the novel lent a public weight to *Tom Jones* that it might otherwise have lacked. More importantly, the world as Fielding imagined it, not to mention life as he led it, depended crucially upon the relative freedom from social hierarchy and the comparatively open communication that had prevailed in England since the Settlement that immediately preceded his birth.

II

Tom Jones is governed by an ideal of intelligent, broadly educated sociability that lies at the heart of Fielding's achievement as an author no less than of the eighteenth century itself. In this novel Fielding fused the all-but-sensual pleasure wrought by intricate, tightly structured storytelling with the indomitable, yet thoroughly problematic, human compulsion to judge the conduct of others. This fusion took place under the aegis of commercial, social, and cultural institutions that mark the period's turn toward modernity and that link its concerns to ours today. In particular, the explosion of printed materials was a significant feature of the eighteenth century's expanding marketplace and a sign of the increasing economic, educational, and class mobility of urban society. Fielding was far from alone in viewing these phenomena with considerable ambivalence. Publications ranged from ephemeral political pamphlets and newspapers like Fielding's *Champion* or *True Patriot*, through business manuals and conduct books like Richardson's own *Familiar Letters* (1741), to the elegantly written treatises and compendia on philosophic, scientific, moral, and historical topics produced by famous Enlightenment figures such as Denis Diderot, David Hume, Jean-Jacques Rousseau, and Adam Smith.

In the midst of this outpouring of print, popular novels—whether by Manley, Haywood, Defoe, Richardson, or Fielding himself—appeared as a new and rather threatening permutation of literary culture because they represented the conditions of society in graphic, unidealized, even shocking, terms and gave priority to the thoughts, feelings, moral dilemmas, and practical experience of autonomous individuals as over and against traditional wisdom and established authority. In part because of their wide distribution, novels often were condemned as dangerous amusements that kept youths, women, and servants from their proper occupations. Johnson trenchantly voiced this attitude in a *Rambler* essay of 1750:

> These books are written chiefly to the young, the ignorant, and the idle, to whom they serve as lectures of conduct, and introductions into life. They are the entertainment of minds unfurnished with ideas, and therefore easily susceptible of impressions; not fixed by principles, and therefore easily following the current of fancy; not informed by experience and consequently open to every false suggestion and partial account.

Johnson elsewhere showed his appreciation of *Clarissa* but it is not far to seek why a book like *Tom Jones* would be disliked by the stern moralist who rejected novels because they "confound the colours of right and wrong, and instead of helping to settle their boundaries, mix them with so much art that no common mind is able to disunite them."[4]

Yet novels were such successful consumer products that criticism could not stem the tide. Richardson's *Pamela* went through five editions in its first year. *Joseph Andrews*, Fielding's parodic antidote to Pamela's sanctimonious, highly profitable chastity, quickly sold 6,500 copies and *Tom Jones* 10,000 copies at a time when the population of London numbered something over 600,000. It is easily plausible that a tenth of that population had substantial knowledge of Fielding's book. Frequent comments about reading aloud tell us something of the broad audience for novels, and we know, for example, from William Shenstone's having borrowed and then loaned out Lady Henrietta Luxborough's volumes of Fielding's masterpiece shortly after their publication, that each copy could well have served several families even apart from sets circulated by lending libraries. Novels were popular, in part because they proffered unauthorized pleasure and found value in unsanctioned stories of thieves and courtesans like Defoe's Moll Flanders and Roxana, social-climbing servants like Pamela, or, in the case of Tom Jones, an illegitimate ladies' man. But novels were popular, too, because they partook in a broad public exchange about the basic values of the society they depicted—a discussion occurring, largely outside the official channels of church and state, in newspapers, popular accounts of law cases, conduct books, privately circulated correspondence, literary circles, and clubs.

Although the early reception of *The History of Tom Jones, A Foundling* included frequent comments debating its truth to life, as well as the *Monthly Review*'s identification with readers who chose to give themselves "pleasure by the perusal of a work chiefly calculated for entertainment," most comments focused on questions about the moral worthiness of the hero (not to mention the author); on the validity of Fielding's inclusion of "low" and "vulgar" characters, diction, and behavior; or, in Johnson's case, on the dangerous influence of such novels on the ideas and behavior of young people. During the late spring following publication, for instance, Elizabeth Carter wrote as an educated woman and balanced observer of the world—in reply to a dismissal by Catherine Talbot, a fellow admirer of Richardson—declaring that "Fielding's book is the most natural representation of what passes in the world, and of the bizarreries which arise from the mixture of good and bad." Richardson, imbued with the high seriousness of *Clarissa*, fussed in his letters about the "coarse-titled *Tom Jones*" and, surprisingly, given his steadfast claim not to have read more than a few passages, made disparaging remarks about its hero and heroine. The title was "coarse" because of the hero's generic name and because "foundling" could be experienced as synonymous with "bastard," the lowest of social categories. Members of Richardson's circle, who timorously defended aspects of the novel in correspondence with the master, wished that it had as much "heart" as "head," found that it had "bold shocking pictures," and finished judiciously with the complaint that although "in every part it has humanity for its intention, in too many it *seems* wantoner that it was meant to be." One anonymous critic, styled Orbilius, felt compelled late in 1749 to publish a substantial pamphlet of chapter-by-chapter commentary, condemning *Tom Jones*'s "incredibilities," its "bad morals," and its "counterfeit wit." But in a pamphlet titled *An Essay on the New Species of Writing Founded by Mr. Fielding* (1751), another critic (probably Francis Coventry) lavished praise on the author's originality and his ability to see "all the little movements by which human nature is actuated." With it all, *Tom Jones* decisively marked the success of Fielding's effort to legitimate novels as objects of and forums for critical discussion.[5]

Critical discussion is a vital term here—with its implication of a reach toward rational consensus through sociable commerce. For none of the eighteenth century's cultural institutions was more characteristic than that of critical exchange. Whether in print, in conversation in dining- and drawing-rooms, or in debate at any of the more than five hundred coffee-houses that graced London in the 1740s, the idea recurs that informed discussion leads to understanding and then to cogent action, first by individuals and then by society as a whole. Fielding acknowledged the centrality of conversation in the essay that begins one of the two books at the symmetrical heart of *Tom Jones*:

> There is another sort of knowledge, beyond the power of learning to bestow, and this is to be had by conversation. So necessary is this to the understanding the characters of men, that none are more ignorant of them than those learned pedants whose lives have been entirely consumed in colleges and among books; for however exquisitely human nature may have been described by writers, the true practical system can be learnt only in the world. (9.1)

Here, Fielding mirrored his age, for the ideal of impartial inquiry, tested through critical discussion among equals, emerged in the eighteenth century first in settings now associated with the "public sphere" such as coffee-houses, clubs, lodges, exchanges, and salons and much later as a theoretical conception memorably crystallized in Kant's brief essay "What Is Enlightenment?" (1784). Medical and experimental sciences during the same period adopted impersonal forms of observation and presentation, while thinkers like David Hume and Adam Smith theorized the ways the moral order of society functioned by inhabiting individual, first-person awareness with an "impartial spectator" or third-person conscience founded on the sympathetic bond among human beings. Real character, like scientific knowledge and legitimate government, was recognizable only when tested against public consensus. In every area of knowledge, the assumed model of communication was of a flow from private contingency to public affirmation through critical investigation and discussion outside the framework of the state. For this reason, though personal conversation was paradigmatic, and remained of signal importance, printing—with its capacity to involve a far-flung community of readers—was a crucial medium. Critical conversation and the commerce in print went hand in hand. In addition to authors and presses, this commerce required not only widespread literacy but also technical innovations that enabled communication such as above-grade road-building and a systematic postal service. Fielding was attuned to these developments as a writer supported by paying readers, as an innovative law-enforcement official who used promptly circulated advertisements to apprehend criminals, and as an author who counted as a loyal patron Ralph Allen—the man who grew rich and famous through his reorganization of the public post.

Addison and Steele's continually reprinted and obsessively imitated periodical, *The Spectator*, served as a virtual handbook for sociable conduct and literary practice in the new public sphere where, for purposes of critical discussion, and in contrast to exchange within the traditional courtly milieu, external marks of rank were laid aside. Especially in the earlier phases, aristocratic privilege everywhere penetrated the new intellectual institutions, and the kind of education necessary for entry into the realm of critical discussion was available to few beneath what were called the "middling sort." But this is not the point. A powerful convention had come into being: the convention that ideas are equally accessible to educated men and that, in the realm of public discussion, men are judged by the degree of their information and the quality of their ideas, not by rank, office, or wealth. Aristocratic patronage of literature, which had fostered relatively formal, classically inspired writing, was progressively displaced by a paying, literate public that favored the informality and utilitarian clarity of prose like Addison's or Fielding's and the flexibility of literary forms such as the familiar letter, the essay, the lecture, the experimental report, and, of course, the novel.[6]

In the tenth issue of *The Spectator*, Addison estimated his daily audience at 60,000—more than ten percent of London's current population—and expressed his aspirations for readers in words that we have seen Fielding echo at the core of *Tom Jones*:

> to the End that their Virtue and Discretion may not be short transient intermitting Starts of Thought, I have resolved to refresh their Memories from Day to Day, till I have recovered them out of that desperate State of Vice and Folly into which the Age is fallen. The Mind that lies fallow but a single Day, sprouts up in Follies that are only to be killed by constant and assiduous Culture. It was said of *Socrates*, that he brought Philosophy down from Heaven to inhabit among Men; and I shall be ambitious to have it said of me that I have brought Philosophy out of Closets and Libraries, Schools and Colleges, to dwell in Clubs and Assemblies, at Tea-Tables, and in Coffee-Houses.

The mention of assemblies and tea tables makes it clear that women were certainly part of the ideal public sphere projected by *The Spectator*. Addison may have typified men of his age in patronizing women and tending to exclude them from serious discussion but, later in the same issue, hoping that his paper will increase their number, he welcomes as readers the "Multitudes" of women who "join all the Beauties of Mind to the Ornaments of Dress and inspire a kind of Awe and Respect, as well as Love."[7]

Fielding, who often patronized women too (think of Miss Western's flaunted reading), still decisively included them in satiric legislation governing critics that appeared over the name of Sir Alexander Drawcansir in issue three of his *Covent-Garden Journal* (1752), a periodical paper formally reminiscent of *The Spectator* if, typically for Fielding, rather more jagged in style:

> But as it is reasonable to extend this Power of judging for themselves, no farther in this Case of Criticism, than it is allowed to Men in some others, I do here declare, that I shall not, for the future, admit any Males to the Office of Criticism till they be of the full age of 18, that being the age when the Laws allow them to have a Capacity of disposing personal Chattles: for, before that Time, they have only the Power of disposing of themselves in the trifling Articles of Marriage. Females, perhaps, I shall admit somewhat earlier, provided they be either witty or handsome.[8]

The air of condescension remains even though Fielding's reasoned judgments about women often echoed those of feminists of his time—and despite his stalwart support of his talented literary sister, Sarah, whose novel *David Simple* (1744) is recognized as part of today's literary canon. Certainly, these facts, along with the numerous gender reversals and episodes of cross-dressing in his plays and novels, suggest that he was no orthodox misogynist.

In this same number of the *Covent-Garden Journal*, Fielding interestingly excluded from the domain of criticism "Officers of State, and wou'd-be Officers of State (honest Men only excepted)." In so doing, he made a point vital to an understanding—as defined by Jürgen Habermas in *The Structural Transformation of the Public Sphere*—of impartial discussion in the eighteenth century as a realm free of special interests. For the public sphere does not include the state. Instead, though it is defined by rational exchange of statements subject to open criticism by all comers and in this sense is public, it adopts the form of free commerce among equals like the discourse of adults in a private household. Politics may be a subject of discussion in the public sphere but officeholders and agents of the state—"their Attendants, and Dependents, their Placemen, and wou'd-be Placemen, Pimps, Spies, Parasites, Informers, and Agents"—cannot be proper participants because they are self-interested actors who "are forbidden" by Fielding "to give their Opinions of any Work in which the Good of the

Kingdom, in general, is designed to be advanced." Otherwise, the qualifications for participation are simple, if seldom met by the scribblers he is
attacking with the announced aim of limiting the number of self-appointed
critics to fewer than 276,302:

> The only Learning, therefore, that I must insist upon, is, That my Critic BE
> ABLE TO READ. . . . Nor do I only require the Capacity of Reading, but the
> actual Exercise of that Capacity. . . . Thirdly, all Critics who from and after the
> First Day of February next, shall condemn any Book, shall be ready to give some
> Reason for their Judgment.

Having thus opened the field of criticism to a wide public with well-
grounded opinions, Fielding goes on to establish a special Order of Critics
for those who understand Aristotle, Horace, and Longinus in the original.
But whether he uses the term "critic" in the narrower sense of a person
qualified to judge writing in relation to the best performances of antiquity
or more broadly to mean a member of the community of informed readers and conversationalists, his aim of fostering rationally informed public
discussion is unmistakable. As he says of critics, introducing book 8 of *Tom
Jones*, "By this word here, and in most other parts of our work, we mean
every reader in the world."

III

Henry Fielding the author assumes numerous roles as narrator of *Tom
Jones*. First among them is that of the host at an open table: "one who keeps
a public ordinary, at which all persons are welcome for their money." They
may choose what they please and receive it as they like. In their freedom "to
censure, to abuse and to d--n their dinner without control," they differ fundamentally from invited guests at a gentleman's "eleemosynary treat," who,
though the fare be "very indifferent, and utterly disagreeable," must suspend critical exchange and "not find any fault; nay, on the contrary, good
breeding forces them outwardly to approve and to commend whatever is
set before them" (1.1). Thus Fielding announces in the first paragraph that
his novel exists, like it or not, as a communication for consumption in the
public sphere. He calls it "mental entertainment," using the word "entertainment" to mean not only an amusement but "conversation," the primary sense recorded in Johnson's *Dictionary of the English Language* (1755).
At Fielding's novelistic feast, the medium will be discussion (another old
meaning of the word "entertainment") and "human nature" the subject.
While Fielding's book is not theoretical like *A Treatise of Human Nature*

by Hume (1739–40), he would have agreed with the philosopher's introductory statement that those engaged on the subject must "glean up" their "experiments in this science from a cautious observation of human life, and take them as they appear in the common course of the world, by men's behaviour in company, in affairs, and in their pleasures."[9] This is the sense in which Fielding's novel assumes active readers who are far more than the objects of simple moralizing. They are virtually obliged, contrary to Johnson's complaint, to separate "the colours of right and wrong" and to "settle their boundaries," while learning the required skills and coming to a forbearant understanding of the difficulties.

Although Fielding's narrator displays moods ranging from the skeptical to the sentimental, and appears by turns as learned man, teacher, judge, literary critic, moral philosopher, dramatist, and novelist at work, as well as an actuary accounting for the probabilities of human life and a person with firsthand experience of the spectrum from low life to high, he is above all an interlocutor—a figure engaged in familiar exchange with readers. Indeed, this narrator speaks in so many voices that he can seem more a repertoire of conversational gambits than a cohesive person. At the beginning of *Tom Jones*, book 7, Fielding says that everyone likens life in "this vast theatre of time" to the stage but "None, as I remember, have at all considered the audience of this great drama." He insists that no performance, certainly not his own, exists independent of its multifarious audience. His survey of this audience—ranging across upper gallery, pit, and boxes—reveals a range of superficial, starkly polarized responses to Black George's "running away with £500 from his friend and benefactor." By contrast, the "man of candour and true understanding is never hasty to condemn" but recognizes that "A single bad act no more constitutes a villain in life than a single bad part on the stage." Such a man is the narrator of *Tom Jones* and Fielding appears in many ways to define his object as the education of readers into such "candour" and "true understanding." These qualities, founded in turn on the primary capacity to take in sensory data as an impartial spectator (4.13), leave such a reader at only one crucial disadvantage compared with the author himself, namely the lack of behind-the-scenes knowledge of plot and motive enjoyed by the inventor of a story who is virtually in the position of God himself. No doubt Fielding flaunts this superiority and, finally, can no more be our equal than could the great Doctor in James Boswell's *Life of Samuel Johnson* (1791) exist quite on the same plane with the interlocutors who approached him in conversation. Yet again and again, in calling attention to the manifest fictionality of his

novel, in asking readers to approach it with eyes open and rational faculties at work, Fielding offers them a boost toward ideal public citizenship
as envisioned by Addison.

Fielding's ideal reader is imbued with good nature, like Tom Jones, or
perhaps the more observant souls from Sophia Western to Mrs. Miller,
who recognize his qualities and possess "that solid inward comfort of
mind, which is the sure companion of innocence and virtue" (Dedication).
Comedy, the governing genius invoked at the beginning of book 13, possesses the magic to instill such comfort in author and reader alike:

> Teach me, which to thee is no difficult task, to know mankind better than they
> know themselves. Remove that mist which dims the intellects of mortals, and
> causes them to adore men for their art, or to detest them for their cunning,
> in deceiving others, when they are, in reality, the objects only of ridicule, for
> deceiving themselves. . . . [F]ill my pages with humour, till mankind learn the
> good nature to laugh only at the follies of others, and the humility to grieve at
> their own. (13.1)

Without the perspective afforded by comedy, one risks vanity and hypocrisy at best and, at worst, the solitary misanthropy that leads the Man of
the Hill to question why a benevolent God would create "so foolish and
so vile an animal." Later, during the novel's climactic episodes, when Tom
falls into despair in prison and the story brushes closest to tragedy, he forgets his own earlier response: "If there was, indeed, much more wicked-
ness in the world than there is, it would not prove such general assertions
against human nature, since much of this arrives by mere accident, and
many a man who commits evil is not totally bad and corrupt in his heart"
(8.15). Such a man, of course, is Tom himself. Tom's heart anchors Fielding's comic world, for it is the constant against which are measured both
the harmless failings of humanity and its crimes. We are asked to hold Tom
and his fellow characters to a variety of prudential standards that rely on
reason and on educated judgment but Tom's heart—the life-affirming ebul-
lience with which he faces the world—represents an essential acceptance of
the human animal without which judgment becomes sterile and punitive in
Thwackum's manner. Tom is the living embodiment of life's comic essence.
He has to have the commonest of names and, as a bastard, to be a legal nobody, for his defining trait precedes social forms. He is, paradoxically, the
least and the most of men. By telling a tale that allows us to maintain faith
in Tom's goodness of heart, even during his disgraceful London entanglement with Lady Bellaston, Fielding habituates us, through experience, into
well-tempered, self-reflective judgment.

Concepts like habit and experience are perhaps more apt in this context than that of education, for they specify concrete forms of knowledge that must be acquired over time in order to lend substance to goodness. As Fielding says in issue 66 of the *Covent-Garden Journal*, "Habit hath been often called a second Nature. . . . I am much deceived (and so was Mr. Locke too) if from our earliest Habits we do not in a great Measure derive those Dispositions, which are commonly called our Nature, and which afterwards constitute our Characters."[10] In opening the fourth book of his *Treatise*, Hume observes of experience that:

> 'Tis certain a man of solid sense and long experience ought to have, and usually has, a greater assurance in his opinions, than one that is foolish and ignorant, and that our sentiments have different degrees of authority, even with ourselves, in proportion to the degrees of our reason and experience. [But even] in the man of the best sense and longest experience, this authority is never quite entire; since even such-a-one must be conscious of many errors in the past, and must still dread the like for the future.[11]

Hume's stress on fallibility is entirely consonant with Fielding's resilient representation of good nature and with his sense that in life, as in reading, one must be prepared to accept error as a defining feature of the human.

Indeed, Fielding goes even further. Mr. Allworthy, though one of the novel's truly good-natured figures, makes constant errors of judgment and falls short of Fielding's ideal because of an apparent incapacity to learn from experience. Allworthy remains a good man even as his gullibility and precipitate verdicts bring real grief to others, for his failings, like Tom's graver errors, are of an entirely different species from Blifil's willful malevolence. One reason that *Tom Jones* stands as a masterpiece of comedy—a work that stretches the limits of discord and social confusion yet in the end, without sentimentality, affirms order and the value of human bonds—is that Fielding acknowledges, especially through the personification of Blifil, a presence of irrecuperable bad nature in the world. Just as experience raises in good judgment an awareness of potential error, so the comprehensive good nature, like complete comedy, must accept a presence of the bad. Such acceptance is why Tom Jones, comically yet seriously propelled at the end into the prospect of becoming a justice of the peace, will be a superior judge to Allworthy. Fielding shows readers how to think skeptically and ironically about humanity without losing heart, and habituates them through exercise to such thinking.

For Fielding, private habits and public values, personal awareness and factual evidence, individual experience and legal judgment are inseparable parts of the puzzle. The sorts of discourse within which Fielding casts *Tom Jones* (public conversation, journalistic account, forensic debate, evidentiary consideration, factual chronicle), like the character types and plot forms he takes as points of departure (caricatures from stage comedy, standard protagonists from heroic prose romances or low picaresque tales of the preceding century, larger-than-life epic adventure as originated in the *Odyssey*), all serve his public, historically referenced conception of the novel in contrast to Richardson's predominant focus on transient mental states. In particular, as Fielding's chief modern editor, Martin Battestin, notes, he was the first consistently to have defined the genre of the novel, with reference to Aristotle, as centrally concerned with "probability." To Fielding, the "probable" was the only legitimate domain of the novel. His arguments appear in the essay that opens book 8, where he allots the "possible" to historians relating proven, thoroughly witnessed fact (they can compel belief in the improbable through incontrovertible evidence) while ceding the "marvelous" to poets as tellers of miraculous events that are credible only to audiences already convinced of their truth through belief in myth or religion. He may not have been as much the skeptic as Hume, but he would have agreed with the statement in the section of the *Treatise* quoted above that "all knowledge resolves itself into probability, and becomes at last of the same nature with that evidence which we employ in common life" and that "as demonstration is subject to the controul of probability, so is probability liable to a new correction by a reflex act of the mind, wherein the nature of our understanding, and our reasoning from the first probability become our objects."[12] Fielding's stress on probability as the novel's operative domain is part and parcel of the economy of rational exchange that he sums up with the word "judgment."

Even one of the more touching expressions of Tom's love of Sophia is couched in terms of inference and calculation that mark it as quite different from the seemingly direct thoughts and emotions elaborated in Richardson's "writing to the moment." After leaving an inn at Gloucester in the middle of the night, Tom, showing himself the literary man, gains the narrator's approval for quoting Milton on the beauty of the moon because he "hath certainly excelled all other poets in his description of the heavenly luminaries." Then, with a reluctant, freezing-cold Partridge as his audience, Tom tells the story from *The Spectator* of "two lovers who had agreed to entertain themselves when they were at a great distance from each other, by repairing, at a certain fixed hour, to look at the moon; thus pleasing themselves with the thought that they were both employed in contemplating the same object at the same time. 'Those lovers' added [Tom], 'must have had souls truly capable of feeling all the tenderness of the sublimest of all human passions'" (8.9). Here, Fielding's reference to epic is lighter of touch than usual, and more layered thanks to the oblique allusion to Addison's famous critical essays on Milton in *The Spectator*. Fielding underscores in this way that his innovations as "founder of a new province of writing" (2.1) open up specific forms of interlocution that bridge the private world of fantasy and pleasure specific to earlier novels of amorous intrigue with the intelligent comprehension and the shared activity of critical evaluation evoked by epic, the most public of forms. Tom's own sincere love is expressed as an inference (and as an implicit hope that Sophia might be looking at the very same moon at the very same moment). Tom emerges—rather surprisingly, given what we have learned of his education under Thwackum and Square, and rather absurdly, given the time, the place, and his companionship—as a modern conversationalist ready to talk upon any subject at any time, supplying relevant allusions that authenticate private, uncommunicable emotion, paradoxically making it available yet serving as a membrane shielding it from direct public view. Yet, important though they be, such moments of reflection—typically lying, like this one, between phases of action—are comparatively uncommon in *Tom Jones*. Other such moments include a notable passage of third-person interior monologue showing Tom's "debate with himself" after his expulsion from Allworthy's house (7.2) and another following his extrication from dependence upon Lady Bellaston (15.9). Fielding's chosen medium was, rather, a grandly shaped yet enormously involved plot that offers the reader countless exercises in understanding the actions characters take in response to the deeds of others and to the quirks of fortune.

IV

Ever since Fielding's first biographer, Arthur Murphy, praised the plot of *Tom Jones* in the collected works of 1762, critics have marveled at the intricate perfection of the action. James Beattie, writing in 1783, declared that,

> Since the days of Homer, the world has not seen a more artful Epick fable. The characters and adventures are wonderfully diversified: yet the circumstances are all so natural, and rise so easily from one another, and co-operate with so much regularity in bringing on, even while they seem to retard, the catastrophe, that the curiosity of the reader . . . grows more and more impatient as the story advances, till at last it becomes downright anxiety. And when we get to the end . . . we are amazed to find, that of so many incidents there should be so few

superfluous; that in such variety of fiction there should be so great probability; and that so complex a tale should be so perspicuously conducted, with perfect unity of design.[13]

Samuel Taylor Coleridge put it most succinctly when he exclaimed in 1834, "What a master of composition Fielding was! Upon my word, I think the *Oedipus Tyrannus*, *The Alchemist*, and *Tom Jones* the three most perfect plots ever planned."[14] The novel, most obviously, is built around such contrasting pairs of characters as Tom and Blifil, Allworthy and Western, Square and Thwackum, and Sophia and Lady Bellaston. But the critics have more than this in mind. Think, crucially, both of the geometry that ultimately returns Tom, via a circular odyssey, to the home county of Squires Allworthy and Western, where the action started (Figure 7), and also of the symmetrical structure laid out around the hilarious farcical episode at Upton in which, at the novel's center, virtually every character is at cross-purposes with every other. Upton anchors the middle section of the story, which takes place on the road, and is flanked on one side by the early books set in Somerset county and on the other side by those set in London. Lesser elements, too, are symmetrically arrayed. In book 6, Tom loses to the dishonest, if needy, Black George a pocketbook containing £500 granted by Allworthy on his expulsion, while in book 12, Tom finds the purse that holds Sophia's bank bill, which he lovingly keeps intact despite financial desperation, and then in book 18 the £500 returns, via Nightingale, from a still treacherous Black George. Even substantial digressions, in the form of cautionary tales told first by the Man of the Hill and then by Mrs. Fitzpatrick, find formally marked places on either side of the two books containing the Upton contretemps.

These symmetries, however, remain superficial compared with the deeper structure of motivation whereby circumstances, as Beattie says, "rise so easily from one another, and co-operate with so much regularity." Sophia, for instance, flees an impending forced marriage to Blifil and pursues Tom on the road to Upton. But then, she storms away from a near meeting there, more infuriated at Tom's supposed misuse of her name than at his infidelity with Mrs. Waters, and leaves their love token (her muff) as a message of rejection, which, in turn, sets in motion Tom's pursuit of her to London. Similarly, unbeknownst to him or to the first-time reader, Tom's tryst with Mrs. Waters at Upton ties back to the beginning of the novel and will bring him to his lowest point at the crisis near the end. Fielding, who is quite proud about his design of the plot, sometimes points explicitly to its niceties, as when he calls upon the reader near the novel's end "to refresh

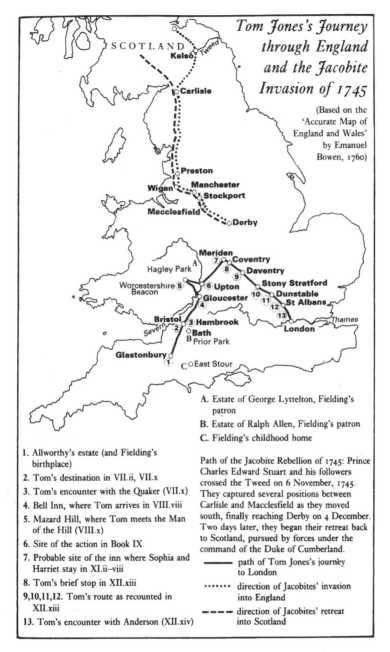

Tom Jones's Journey through England and the Jacobite Invasion of 1745

(Based on the 'Accurate Map of England and Wales' by Emanuel Bowen, 1760)

SCOTLAND
Kelso
Tweed
Carlisle
Preston
Wigan
Manchester
Stockport
Macclesfield
Derby
Meriden
Coventry
Hagley Park A
Daventry
Worcestershire Beacon 5
Upton 6
Stony Stratford
Gloucester 4
Dunstable
St Albans
Bristol 3 Hambrook
Bath
Prior Park B
London
Thames
Severn
Glastonbury 1
C East Stour

A. Estate of George Lyttelton, Fielding's patron
B. Estate of Ralph Allen, Fielding's patron
C. Fielding's childhood home

1. Allworthy's estate (and Fielding's birthplace)
2. Tom's destination in VII.ii, VII.x
3. Tom's encounter with the Quaker (VII.x)
4. Bell Inn, where Tom arrives in VIII.viii
5. Mazard Hill, where Tom meets the Man of the Hill (VIII.x)
6. Site of the action in Book IX
7. Probable site of the inn where Sophia and Harriet stay in XI.ii–viii
8. Tom's brief stop in XII.xiii
9,10,11,12. Tom's route as recounted in XII.xiii
13. Tom's encounter with Anderson (XII.xiv)

Path of the Jacobite Rebellion of 1745: Prince Charles Edward Stuart and his followers crossed the Tweed on 6 November, 1745. They captured several positions between Carlisle and Macclesfield as they moved south, finally reaching Derby on 4 December. Two days later, they began their retreat back to Scotland, pursued by forces under the command of the Duke of Cumberland.

——— path of Tom Jones's journey to London

••••••• direction of Jacobites' invasion into England

– – – direction of Jacobites' retreat into Scotland

FIGURE 7. "Tom Jones's Journey through England and the Jacobite Invasion of 1745," from Henry Fielding, *Tom Jones*. By permission of Oxford University Press.

his memory, by turning to the scene at Upton, [where] he will be apt to admire the many strange accidents which unfortunately prevented any interview between Partridge and Mrs. Waters. . . . Instances of this kind we may frequently observe in life, where the greatest events are produced by a nice train of little circumstances" (18.2). The theory is sophisticated here since a meeting that did not happen is recognized as a defining event.

Fielding's godlike machinations as author seem intended to guarantee the providential order in which we know he believed. Tom's firm asseveration of providence in opposition to the Man of the Hill's corrosive doubt (8.10) is a sure sign that we must take seriously the idea of an ordering force. As Fielding says of the overwhelming effect on Jones's affections when he saves Sophia's muff from the fire, "there are many little circumstances too often omitted by injudicious historians, from which events of the utmost importance arise. The world may indeed be considered as a vast machine, in which the great wheels are originally set in motion by those which are very minute, and almost imperceptible to any but the strongest eyes" (5.4). Thanks to the fictionality of his novel, Fielding can have it both ways in *Tom Jones*, whether or not we can do so in actual life, for the action bristles with contingencies, unpredictable twists, and chance events that can only be understood as the work of pagan fortune or fate not of Christian providence. That "a nasty hawk" carries away the thirteen-year-old Sophia's little bird Tommy after Blifil maliciously turns it loose is an accident of fortune, but it is providential that the incident as a whole allows Sophia's emotional comprehension of the two young boys' real characters, predisposing her to love the one and hate the other. Some accidents are just accidents, while others set great wheels in motion. In the novel, a patient reader or an author with advance knowledge can judge the difference by outcomes. Up to a point this is true in life as well, but there, in important regards, a simple religious faith such as Tom's has to suffice since so many outcomes in actual life must remain unknown. Hapless first-time readers have similarly to live on faith. In the midst of the chaos at Upton Fielding sternly warns readers that they must not "hastily . . . condemn any of the incidents in this our history as impertinent and foreign to our main design." Insisting that "this work may, indeed, be considered as a great creation of our own," he takes a sardonic swipe at any "little reptile of a critic" who might "presume to find fault with any of its parts, without knowing the manner in which the whole is connected, and before he comes to the final catastrophe" (10.1). However fragile its illusion, the symmetry of the plot and its appearance of total internal logic proffers the assurance, if not of ultimate knowability, at least that we may proceed on the belief that stable general conditions govern our attempts to decode human affairs.

Character and plot, though often discussed independently by critics, are inseparable in *Tom Jones*, because the actions of characters are so much the occasion of judgments about their motives. Fielding's usual strategy is to stage the actions that form the plot in a context of debate about their merit by the characters themselves, by the narrator, and (in anticipation) by the reader. In "An Essay on the Knowledge of the Characters of Men," Fielding says that "the Actions of Men are the best Index to their Thoughts, as they do, if well attended to and understood, with the utmost Certainty demonstrate the Character." Having traced the mistakes in analysis that disguise and hypocrisy in others can induce, he concludes that the best rule is "carefully to observe the Actions of Men with others, and especially with those to whom they are allied in Blood, Marriage, Friendship, Profession, Neighbourhood, or any other Connection."[15] This is precisely the kind of information Fielding profusely offers in *Tom Jones*, where interlocking, comparative, and contrastive episodes of the plot form the medium within which he defines and projects the complexities of his chief characters. In following Tom through dozens of episodes from his stubbornly principled protection of Black George early in the novel, through his affairs with Molly and with Mrs. Waters, to the painful recognition that his affair with Lady Bellaston has brought him to "a distressful situation" in which he is "obliged to be guilty of some dishonour" to her or to Sophia (15.9), we come to see him in exactly these intimate ways. The layered complexity that makes him believable as a person is achieved by a process of sedimentation. We learn in like manner that the goddess Sophia, who has the untamed country spunk to defy her father by fleeing at night with no more company than her maid, is also capable of sophisticated conversational equivocation when Lady Bellaston walks in on her interview with Tom in London. We see that Allworthy really is a good man despite his impetuosity as a judge and that, authentic though Western's brutishness may be, it is redeemed at least partially by genuine love of his daughter. Even minor figures like Sophia's maid Honour can emerge vividly as individuals through the kind of debate over action that Fielding repeatedly stages (7.8). These and so many of his other characters possess a self-justifying immediacy that escapes explanation except by reference to the immanence of action in every one of them. Fielding links every character, no matter how small, into the huge totality of his plot and in the process gives each of them a life beyond simple individuality. This understood, one easily grasps why Fielding's brilliant literary cousin, Lady Mary Wortley Montagu, could write in her copy of *Tom Jones*: *ne plus ultra*—none better.[16]

Fielding offers a fictional world where we can know others only by circumstantial inference from the variable appearances of words and actions. For in actual life we cannot see the minds of others at first hand like characters in Richardson's novels. Thus Johnson seriously missed the point in his famous comparison of Richardson and Fielding, when he said in 1768, "that there was as great a difference between them as between a man who knew how a watch was made, and a man who could tell the hour by looking on the dial-plate."[17] Fielding shows how we may bring reason, experience, and good temper to bear on inferences about the inner working of the human heart but he is too much the doubter to foster any illusion that, finally, we can know how the watch is made. Surface when viewed repeatedly under the widest possible array of circumstances offers us the only access to depth we can realistically expect to gain in life as Fielding understands it. Such an acceptance of human limitation need not be a counsel of despair for, as he says in "An Essay on the Knowledge of the Characters of Men," "however cunning the Disguise be which a Masquerader wears: however foreign to his Age, Degree, or Circumstance, yet if closely attended to, he very rarely escapes the Discovery of an accurate Observer; for Nature, which unwillingly submits to the Imposture, is ever endeavouring to peep forth and shew herself."[18] The essential qualities of the "accurate observer" specified in *Tom Jones* include empathy untainted by sentimentality and ironic distance free of corrosive or cynical skepticism. Fielding achieves his aim in leading readers of *Tom Jones* to appreciate and, ideally, to maintain such a delicate, paradoxical wisdom.

CHAPTER 7

Prison Reform and the Sentence of Narration in *The Vicar of Wakefield*

Now that particular psychology, in the name of which you can very well today have your head cut off, comes straight from our traditional literature, that which one calls in bourgeois style literature of the Human Document. . . . Justice and literature have made an alliance, they have exchanged their old techniques, thus revealing their basic identity.

—Roland Barthes, Mythologies[1]

The Vicar of Wakefield is not often described as a political novel. Ordinarily it is treated as a fable, a parable, or a fairy tale without meaningful reference to the actual social realm that produced it. But in order to purchase such timeless coherence for the work, readers have tended to blink at some remarkable ruptures in fictional continuity and oddities of narrative technique. Once noticed, these discontinuities are apt to be passed off as generic conventions, read as ironic, or judged as faults arising from carelessness or ineptitude, not to be analyzed as significant. In this essay I attempt to uncover the import of one such rupture. I move from a discussion of the apparently disruptive arguments for prison reform in chapters 26 and 27 to suggestions about the place of *The Vicar of Wakefield* in the history of the novel and about its significance in the framework of post-Enlightenment culture. Goldsmith may have sought to transcend petty faction, even to "dispel the prejudice of party," as he claimed to have attempted in his first *History of England*, but his novel's form and technique, no less than its contentiousness, are profoundly ideological.[2]

I am interested here not only in Goldsmith's articulate political stance but also in unforeseen consequences—in the meaning of his textual practice. Essentially tactical government of the kind England experienced during this period tended to conceal deeper motivations, broad societal movements, and long-term innovation. I call this government "tactical" because its political programs were shaped more by the maneuvers necessary to maintain the working entities of day-to-day rule—especially ministerial coalitions—than by sustained or coherent principles or even by articulate party allegiances. Under such government, any specific issue such as prison reform could be appropriated for transient political ends that obscured its larger import. Of course tactics play a role in every government; but in England during the third quarter of the eighteenth century they were dominant. Tactical government during the period of Goldsmith's novel both represented a fundamentally contradictory social structure and established conditions under which an emergent ideology could come into focus. I associate this ideology with the illusionistic aesthetic of transparent discourse in the realist novel; with the moral idea of character governed by conscience; and with modern governmental procedures that disperse authority into depersonalized rules, systems, bureaucracies, and institutions—most especially the penitentiary. I discuss the ways in which incongruent methods of narration and exposition in *The Vicar of Wakefield* at once mask this ideology and make it accessible—ways in which the novel is poised between speaking out and acting out reformist thought. Since, as Mikhail Bakhtin maintains, the novel

> is constructed in a zone of contact with the incomplete events of a particular present, [it] often crosses the boundary of what we strictly call fictional literature—making use first of a moral confession, then of a philosophical tract, then of manifestos that are openly political, then degenerating into the raw spirituality of a confession, a "cry of the soul" that has not yet found its formal contours.[3]

Novels not only reveal ideology through their registration of contradictory voices, they *must* do so in order to maintain their generic identity. They make visible the means of production of the social text. They have the dual structure that Anthony Giddens finds in other cultural formations and social institutions: they are both the medium and the outcome of the practices that constitute social systems.[4]

By "ideology" I intend not merely all articulate frameworks of belief, but the symbolic practices through which we manifest our social presence, or subjectivity. Such practices produce material institutions but also structures of domination, as well as the imagery through which emergent social and cultural formulations come into focus and gain conceptual status. A primary medium of these symbolic practices is linguistic behavior, which produces kinds of discourse ranging from everyday speech, through argumentation and exposition, to literary representation in the technically discrete language of written narrative fiction. Through the analysis of discourse we can understand how articulate belief operates and also how its dysfunctions mark out the terrain of future social and institutional structures. As Raymond Williams suggests, "What matters, finally, in understanding emergent culture, as distinct from both the dominant and residual, is that it is never only a matter of immediate practice; indeed it depends crucially on finding new forms or adaptations of form."[5] Such forms anticipate forthcoming organizational principles and master narratives.

I

Certainly the reformist dimension of *The Vicar of Wakefield* occupied the press when Goldsmith's novel first appeared in 1766. London newspapers and magazines often excerpted the work during the year of its publication, and chapter 27 was by far the most frequent selection.[6] In this chapter (and that just previous) Dr. Primrose is jailed under a warrant of arrest for unpaid rent because he has resisted his landlord, Squire Thornhill, the unscrupulous seducer of his eldest daughter. Primrose seeks to reform the prison in which he is held with the remnants of his family. He sums up the contemporary view of jails as licentious spawning places where debtors and petty criminals learned the arts of felony. He preaches to the common prisoners and goes among them with a series of precepts, rules, and regulations which, under his enforcement, reform the prison into a prototype that anticipates the penitentiary as later delineated by the Penitentiary Act of 1779. Chapter 27 was warmly discussed in the press on the same footing with essays and letters from correspondents. Why were Dr. Primrose's thoughts on prison so timely? What were these ideas? Where do they stand in the history of reform? What have they to do with politics? Why, above all, should an essay on prison reform be lodged in a novelistic context?

Dr. Primrose's ideas about imprisonment may have struck the editors of journals as topical because Cesare Beccaria's book *On Crimes and Punishments*, which took intellectual circles in Europe by storm upon its publication in July of 1764, had gained wide currency when the French translation appeared in January of 1766. Beccaria praised the "immortal Montesquieu" as the guiding light of his treatise,[7] and more than a trace of the *Persian Letters* (1721) and *The Spirit of the Laws* (1748) also appears in Goldsmith. In fact, Goldsmith had been engaged with questions of legal reform at least since 1760–61, when he composed *The Citizen of the World*, a series of periodical pieces in imitation of the *Persian Letters*. By the early 1760s, when Goldsmith was writing these essays and *The Vicar of Wakefield*, it had become commonplace to argue, in Montesquieu's vein, that punishments ought to be proportional to crimes and that excessively severe punishments for moderate offenses inspired indiscriminate criminal behavior. For example, when robbery and murder are both capital crimes, the law encourages highwaymen to kill their victims (as Samuel Johnson maintained in *The Rambler* 114, [1751]). These and other ideas in chapter 27 recall both the matter of *The Spirit of the Laws*, as well as its anecdotal manner, which Goldsmith declared to be more that of a "poet than a philosopher" (*Works*, 1.301).[8]

The French connection was important to Goldsmith, but his ideas also figure in a line of English thought about prison discipline that dates, most memorably and consistently, from the activist years of Fielding's magistracy during midcentury. The case for reformative imprisonment involving supervised labor and reflective solitude set forth in chapter 27 reads like an abstract of Fielding's plan for a Middlesex County House in *A Proposal for Making all Effectual Provision for the Poor* (1753). These ideas do not appear in works by Montesquieu or Beccaria; rather, they are presentiments of a consensus that would emerge among English intellectuals, philanthropists, and legislators of the 1770s, a consensus that eventually led to the replacement of prisons like the one in which Primrose is confined with newly designed and constructed penitentiaries.[9]

This is part of the story, but in addition Goldsmith associated with men at the center of contemporary British legal thinking. The famous jurist William Blackstone authoritatively brought together continental and English strands of thought about legal reform and prison discipline in his *Commentaries on the Laws of England* (1765–69), the fourth volume of which concerns criminal law and was written, explicitly, under the influence of Beccaria. The *Commentaries* were based in large part upon Blackstone's lectures as the first Vinerian Professor of Law at Oxford, a position he held from 1758 until his resignation in 1766. Robert Chambers, Blackstone's leading student and eventual successor to the Vinerian Chair, was a longstanding friend of Samuel Johnson's. Such a friend, indeed, that Johnson assisted him as a collaborator when he proved incapable of composing the lectures required of him as Vinerian Professor. When Goldsmith received the Bachelor of Medicine at Oxford in 1769, he stayed four days as a guest of Chambers, who had recently been elected a member of the Reynolds-Johnson Club.[10] Goldsmith, as a friend who shared Johnson's interest in law, had ample opportunity to know about the ideas Blackstone presented in his lectures, which were in progress during *The Vicar of Wakefield's* composition and revision. Although any similarly acquired knowledge of *On Crimes and Punishments* probably would have come too late to affect his revision of the novel, Goldsmith could have known quite early about Beccaria.[11]

It is worth pausing to describe the kind of imprisonment under attack by the reformers of this period. The typical residents of eighteenth-century prisons were debtors and people awaiting trial, often joined by their families, as is Goldsmith's vicar. Their society might include convicts awaiting transportation or execution as well as innocent witnesses held by the court. The old prisons were not intended, in themselves, as penal instruments but as places of detention prior to judgment or disposition. Death was the common penalty, though often commuted to transportation abroad. Prisons were temporary lodgings for all but a few, and the jailer collected fees from prisoners for room, board, and services like a lord of the manor collecting rents from tenants. As Smollett observed, these prisons microcosmically condensed the society that created them.[12]

The reformers rejected these old, domestically ordered prisons, conceiving instead the penitentiaries later perfected by industrial society. This reconception occurred in several stages. As impulses to reform became intellectually focused during the 1760s, prison *exteriors* were reimagined, although their *interiors* actually remained much as before. While the old contract system based on jailors' fees sturdily resisted change, prisons during this decade outwardly assumed a fearful, awesome, sublimely intimidating aspect—imagery envisioned in the graphic arts by Piranesi and in architecture by George Dance's 1768 design for London Newgate. *The Vicar of Wakefield* went beyond this early stage of reformist reconception by presenting the old prison interiors as the sites of a new kind of regime.

Following the Penitentiary Act of 1779, newly designed English prisons displayed revolutionary changes in interior plan. Governmental authorities began to pay all expenses and to dictate every detail of penitentiary architecture along with every movement in the prisoner's carefully specified daily regime. Each structure was contrived as the physical setting implied by a narrative—or series of narratives—of criminal reformation. Often inspired by a religious fervor that proved remarkably compatible with Beccaria's utilitarian analysis of human nature, the reformers aimed to reshape the life story of each criminal by the measured application of pleasure and pain within a planned framework. Upon entering one of the new penitentiaries, each convict would be assigned to live out a program or scenario that took as its point of departure a generic classification based upon age, sex, type of offense, and social background. Confinement itself became the punishment, and by the mid-nineteenth century penitentiary sentences had virtually supplanted other criminal punishments except execution for murder or treason.

II

What did the old prisons mean to Goldsmith? And what did the issue of prison reform have to do with politics in the narrower sense? These questions may be condensed into another: how could a writer ordinarily described as something of a backward-looking traditionalist find himself on the side of reform?

In eighteenth-century England, reformist arguments concerning criminal law and prisons, at least in their earlier manifestations, are more accurately understood as aspects of the politics of opposition than as elements in a sharply defined program. When Goldsmith was drafting *The Vicar of Wakefield* in the early 1760s, soon after George III's accession, the old oligarchy of court Whigs that had ruled the country for most of the century was thought, by diverse factions with very little in common besides their opposition to those in office, to have imposed ever-harsher criminal laws—especially capital punishment—as a means of enforcing its power. Thus Goldsmith, whose secular politics may be fairly if broadly characterized as those of a nostalgic country conservative, could have views on prisons and the criminal law generally consonant with those of a man as different in other respects as Jonas Hanway. Hanway, like a number of philanthropists of the time, came from an essentially disenfranchised category of traders and manufacturers whose reformism was consciously motivated by powerful, very often dissenting, religious belief. By the same token, reformist argumentation and the introduction of parliamentary bills during the later 1760s and the 1770s helped the Rockingham group define its political opposition to the king and his ministers, even though significant members of their party had figured in the old corps of Whigs earlier responsible for the rapid increase in the number of crimes designated as capital offenses. Party relations in this world were positional, not absolute. Indeed, modern ideas of party and class were not yet sharply defined, though the forces that would delineate them were already powerfully at work.[13]

Goldsmith's opposition to rule by "aristocratical" plutocrats is vehemently set forth in "The Revolution in Low Life" (1762; *Works*, 3.195–98). His repeated references to "the Great" unmistakably place this essay in a long tradition of attacks on the Whig oligarchy reaching back through Fielding and Gay. He sees foreign commerce as enabling the accumulation of "immense property," which leads in turn to government by numerous petty tyrants. In the country, as landlords and magistrates, these magnates abrogate ancient rights and push small farmers—the virtuous "middle order of mankind"—off the land. In the city, the "Great" indulge in luxurious entertainments that set a disastrous example for shopkeepers and craftsmen of the "middling class of people."[14] This view of contemporary history, along with the theory of government that justifies it, is voiced most trenchantly in *The Traveller* (1764):

> But when contending chiefs blockade the throne
> Contracting regal power to stretch their own,
> When I behold a factious band agree
> To call it freedom, when themselves are free;
> Each wanton judge new penal statutes draw,
> Laws grind the poor, and rich men rule the law;
> The wealth of climes, where savage nations roam,
> Pillag'd from slaves, to purchase slaves at home;
> Fear, pity, justice, indignation start,
> Tear off reserve, and bare my swelling heart;
> 'Till half a patriot, half a coward grown,
> I fly from petty tyrants to the throne.
>
> $\qquad\qquad\qquad\qquad\qquad$ (4.265–66; ll.381–92)

Taken in historical context, these lines mark out a distinct political position. The antidote to the tyranny of "aristocratical" plutocrats whose vast wealth is founded upon commerce (especially foreign trade) is to contain them within a reinvigorated royal authority.

A more detailed exposition of the ideas behind *The Traveller* appears in chapter 19 of *The Vicar of Wakefield*, where Dr. Primrose argues vehemently against a "very well-drest gentleman" who has asked him home to a fine supper but who is soon discovered to be a politically radical butler masquerading as the absent master. The upstart servant merely parodies his master's "aristocratical" imposture. Primrose asserts that "external commerce" not only destroys home industry, and class identity, it also undermines sovereignty because it yields accumulations of wealth so vast that they cannot be expended on "necessaries and pleasures." Instead, this wealth is spent to purchase power competitive with the king's. And in the very next chapter, when Primrose is reunited with his wandering son, George, he hears that the poverty-stricken young man's adventures in quest of patronage have included a time as servant-companion to a rake who required him to fight as his substitute in a duel. The rake is none other than that same Squire Thornhill who has just seduced George's sister and will shortly imprison his father. All three fall prey to the squire's expression of superfluous wealth as power. The wealth actually belongs to the squire's uncle, Sir William Thornhill, whose omniscience extends to heights that might well be envied by a king, yet whose power, though miraculously benevolent, also derives from riches gained abroad. The two Thornhills are fantasy opposites who move, respectively, beneath and above royal notice.

The 1760s in England was a period of transient ministries within the government and radical action outside it. George III aggravated both the instability of his cabinets and the radicalism of the Wilkesites even if he did not cause them. But though the king proved to be politically inept, he stood for much that men of Goldsmith's stamp admired, and his defects were far less evident during the first few years of the reign than later. Six days after the succession, he issued a proclamation "for the encouragement of piety and virtue, and for the prevention of vice, profaneness and immorality."[15] In addition, he worked successfully to force the end of an ongoing, and largely triumphant, imperial war with France in which Pitt, as prime minister, had been enthusiastically backed by commercial interests in the City. George, the first notably "English" king in living memory, stood for traditional values and against the grasping machinations of clever politicians. He called the counterbalancing arrangement of Britain's constitution "the most beautiful combination ever framed,"[16] and eagerly sought to maintain, even to rejuvenate, the crown's operative role in the processes of rule.

The throne to which the poet would fly in *The Traveller*, like the overarching royal authority that Dr. Primrose views as a protection against the "aristocratical" tyranny of new wealth on the one hand and the intrusion of "liberty" men on the other, unmistakably idealizes Goldsmith's aspirations for the reign of George III. Dr. Primrose exclaims in a similar vein:

> It should be the duty of honest men to assist the weaker side of our constitution, that sacred power that has for some years been every day declining, and losing its due share of influence in the state. (4.98)

In such a context, attacks on prison conditions and arguments against capital punishment become tokens of a broad resentment against Whiggish petty tyrants who assume the forms of aristocracy but not its values:

> And thus, polluting honour in its source,
> Gave wealth to sway the mind with double force.
>
> (*The Traveller*, 4.267; ll.395–96)

Squire Thornhill stands for the lot of them. By their means,

> the natural ties that bind the rich and poor together are broken, and . . . [the] middle order of mankind may lose all its influence. . . . In such a state, therefore, all that the middle order has left, is to preserve the prerogative and privileges of the one principal governor with the most sacred circumspection. (4.101–2)

Goldsmith's later *Life of Bolingbroke* (1770) characterizes Henry St. John's *Idea of the Patriot King* as "that excellent piece" which "describes a monarch uninfluenced by party, leaning to the suggestions neither of whigs nor tories, but equally the friend and the father of all" (*Works*, 3.470). Goldsmith appears sincerely to have viewed George III in such a light. For him, reform participates in a large wish for authoritative intervention and supervision.

The idealization of George III has broad implications for an ideological understanding of *The Vicar of Wakefield*. Goldsmith clearly longed for reform of the body politic to come about through paternalist intervention by the throne, his view of which, again, aligns with that of Bolingbroke, who wrote that "the image of a free people" living in a "genuine" polity is "that of a patriarchal family, where the head and all the members are united by one common interest."[17] Thus Dr. Primrose in his roles as "priest" and "father of a family" can appropriately, if somewhat implausibly, reform the microcosmic, old-style prison into which he is thrown by Squire Thornhill. Prison serves as a condensed image of tyranny that is at once traditional and loaded with contemporary political significance. As E. P. Thompson observes, both the Whig "jealousy" of the crown and Walpole's lavish financial support of the throne as a partner sharing the spoils of government arose less from anxiety about an absolutist takeover than from "the more realistic fear that an enlightened monarch might find means to elevate himself, as the personification of an 'impartial,' rationalizing, bureaucratic State power, above and outside the predatory game [of party and court politics]. The appeal of such a patriot king would have been immense, not only among the lesser gentry, but among great ranges of the populace."[18]

In the short run, reformist adaptation might well have been part of the program of the kind of enlightened, patriot monarch whom Bolingbroke and Goldsmith envisioned, and whom George III hoped to be. Goldsmith's advocacy of the king as the agent of change is comprehensible not only in the English context but in the larger frame of European politics: a number of absolutist monarchs and princes on the continent did in fact reform their criminal laws on principles recommended by Beccaria and other intellectuals. In the long run, however, the rationalization of the state—its emergence as an impersonal network of laws, rules, parties, and bureaucratic procedures that intersperse authority throughout everyday life—would in part accomplish the containment of oligarchic depredation that Goldsmith sought. To the degree that such rationalization ultimately would come to epitomize bourgeois class interests, it also would serve the "middle order of mankind" which, as Primrose argues, subsists independently "between the very rich and the very rabble" and in which "are generally to be found all the arts, wisdom, and virtues of society" (4.101–2).

Finally, however, the procedures of the modern state could not effectively be assimilated to a royalist program like Goldsmith's because their authority could not be personified: their regulative power depends upon their impersonality. In the fully realized penitentiary, for example, impersonal authority is projected as the "principle of inspection" as Jeremy Bentham described it in his *Panopticon*.[19] Bentham's idealized plan revealed that the operational fact of the penitentiary is the *principle* of inspection itself, not the person of the inspector. The point is that the inspector-keeper is not really omniscient, or even really a person, but rather that the transparency of penitentiary architecture forces the prisoner to *imagine* him as such. Goldsmith envisioned the new penitentiary regime but misapprehended its means by attributing its power to the throne. Both the French connection and the politics of opposition enabled him to define prison conditions and abuses in the criminal law as crucial issues and brought about his advocacy of changes that had quite different implications than he could have foretold in the early 1760s. But Goldsmith's lack of foresight is not surprising. Reform found its initial representation within the existing boundaries of those political, conceptual, terminological, generic, or institutional species it eventually would alter, because it encoded emergent social practices in such mystified shapes that their significance was easily misunderstood by actors in a fundamentally tactical political context. In short, reform had a wide range of unforeseen consequences. The novel served as a laboratory where potential outcomes were enacted as textual experiments.

The novel provides a formally distinct arena where political and social contradictions become accessible to analysis. This is because works of art—perhaps the novel above all—attempt the unified representation of different social and cultural structures—the residual, the dominant, the emergent—simultaneously in a single frame of reference. In aesthetic works the very contrivance of formal coherence out of disparate materials allows us to glimpse—through what have been called "eloquent silences"—the process of generation and regeneration that drives all cultural formation.[20] Such works are peculiarly revealing as compared with the infinite sequences of historical process as a whole because of those breaks in tone, conflicts in representational method, and tensions among generic expectations that occur within their formal boundaries. Alterations in form, the emergence of new subject matters, or developments in technique, can enact broader cultural change. But works of art are not mere reflections. They clarify structures of feeling characteristic of a given historical moment and thereby predicate those available in the future. This is the specific sense in which they may serve as a medium of cultural emergence through which new images of society move into focus and become tangible.

III

The implicit logic of Goldsmith's reformist advocacy stands in contradiction to his politics and yields a fractured, paradoxical mode of narration. The ironies that mid-twentieth-century critics have found in *The Vicar of Wakefield* are generated not by flaws in the character of Dr. Primrose but by contradictions that mark reformist thought during the 1760s and that more generally characterize the transition to modern impersonal governance. At one level—that of political consciousness—Goldsmith undoubtedly was a monarchist with nostalgic longings for the old constitution; but the textual ideology of his novel—the import of its form—points categorically to the emergence of an all-present state order, not to the personal rule of a benevolent individual. Precisely because the king was a personification, he could not act during the 1760s as the embracing, neutral, guarding force Goldsmith so desired and so struggled to embody in a surrogate, Sir William Thornhill. Thus Sir William must make a personal appearance in order to set things right at the story's end; to do this he must unmask since, quite remarkably, he has acted in disguise as the family friend, Mr. Burchell, throughout much of the novel. Goldsmith's politics were rather old-fashioned, but both the institutional reformation advocated in chapter 27 and the narrative techniques that structure the text anticipate the all-embracing rule of rules, the neutral impersonality of modern government as epitomized in the penitentiary and in the transparency upon which the illusionism of the realist novel depends. The generic shift toward reformist argumentation that occurs in chapters 26 and 27 is a rupture that asks for investigation and alerts us to seek out meaning in the text's most fundamental procedures.

Primrose's surprise and revulsion at conditions in the old-style prison where he is taken make the reformist position seem inevitable. Although the narration is nominally personal and ostensibly reflects Primrose's personal response, the novel provides a context and point of view within which these observations take on the appearance of natural, intuitively obvious facts, not merely opinions. Primrose describes his prison in these terms:

> I expected upon my entrance to find nothing but lamentations, and various sounds of misery; but it was very different. The prisoners seemed all employed in one common design, that of forgetting thought in merriment or clamour. I was apprized of the usual perquisite required upon these occasions, and immediately complied with the demand, though the little money I had was very near being all exhausted. This was immediately sent away for liquor, and the whole prison soon filled with riot, laughter, and prophaneness. (4.141)

The "usual perquisite" is "garnish," a levy imposed upon new arrivals by the prisoners themselves in order to buy drinks all around. The vicar depicts his prison scene like a dedicated reformer and recoils at the unchecked "execrations, lewdness, and brutality" that reign in a jail where there is "no other resource for mirth, but what [can] be derived from ridicule or debauchery" (4.144–45).

Primrose soon establishes a protopenitentiary within his old-style jail. And in doing so he creates a social institution as yet unnamed (modern usage of the word "penitentiary" was new in the 1770s). He begins with sermons that inspire the prisoners to a consciousness of their situation and then consolidates thought into habit by establishing a disciplinary regime based on labor, fines, and rewards:

> Their time had hitherto been divided between famine and excess, tumultuous riot and bitter repining. Their only employment was quarrelling among each other, playing at cribbage, and cutting tobacco stoppers. From this last mode of idle industry I took the hint of setting such as chose to work at cutting pegs for tobacconists and shoemakers. . . . I did not stop here, but instituted fines for the punishment of immorality, and rewards for peculiar industry. Thus in less than a fortnight I had formed them into something social and humane, and had the pleasure of regarding myself as a legislator, who had brought men from their native ferocity into friendship and obedience. (4.149)

Here are sketched the elements that would figure in various permutations and with different emphases in penitentiary schemes of the 1770s and after. The one significant omission is solitary confinement, some anticipation of which occurs when Primrose finds every prisoner in this jail to have "a separate cell, where he was locked in for the night" (4.141). Thus, of his first night as a captive, the vicar can report: "After my usual meditations, and having praised my heavenly corrector, I laid myself down and slept with the utmost tranquility till morning" (4.143). In solitude, the vicar displays an ideally reflective submission. In fact, separate night cells were highly unusual in prison buildings prior to the 1770s, when this solution to the riotousness of the old prisons was proposed by some of the more moderate reformers. Goldsmith's unrealistic anticipation of the "separate cell" marks the ideological content of his account of Primrose's imprisonment.

The new penitentiaries would banish chance and fortune—the providential order of plot so central to the events and the social structure depicted in *The Vicar of Wakefield*—in favor of the earthly planning and certitude that Primrose strives for as a "legislator" who wishes,

> that legislative power would . . . direct the law rather to reformation than severity. . . . Then instead of our present prisons, which find or make men guilty, which enclose wretches for the commission of one crime, and return them, if returned alive, fitted for the perpetration of thousands; we should see . . . places of penitence and solitude, where the accused might be attended by such as could give them repentance if guilty, or new motives to virtue if innocent. And this, but not the increasing punishments, is the way to mend a state: nor can I avoid even questioning the validity of that right which social combinations have assumed of capitally punishing offences of a slight nature. (4.149)

In his small nation, the prison, the vicar first personally displaces—and then enacts laws to replace—the structures of authority that prevail elsewhere in the world of the novel and that have reduced him to his plight as a prisoner. He acts to retell the story by a different set of rules—those of the penitentiary.

Terminology makes the case. "Reform" assumes rationally ordered causal sequence and conceives human invention as capable of reconstructing reality. By contrast, religious rebirth proceeds from mysterious re-creation. Reformative confinement in the penitentiary does not deny religion's motive power, it rather appropriates spiritual symbolism for secular ends. A process that transcends but may include religious belief shapes reformist thought and comprehends its other aspects. In this sense, *The Vicar of Wakefield* partakes of a reformist discourse, conducted in the broadly shared vocabulary of sensationalist empiricism, that will unite in common purpose figures as diverse as dissenting Christian religionists like Jonas Hanway or John Howard and secular pagans like Jeremy Bentham. Certainly the unfolding of plot is understood by the vicar as a trope for the working out of providential will. And certainly religious belief and the figurations that accompany it are central to the novel's symbolic apparatus; Martin Battestin has shown, for example, the novel's pervasive repetition of the plot, style, and thought of the Book of Job.[21] In my account, however, the text discloses both providence and plot as attributes of a functional omniscience more akin to that of the secular state than to Jehovah's kingdom. This effect is demonstrated in the plot itself, when Sir William Thornhill emerges, however awkwardly, not just as an *agent* of the denouement but as the power who will determine it.

IV

The prison episode in *The Vicar of Wakefield* is an eruption or fracture that allows us to glimpse an ideology which is at once pervasively encoded throughout the novel and contradicted by the text's political rhetoric. Virtually the whole machinery of the new penitentiary is sketched out in chapter 27, and this apparatus in turn implies a peculiarly modern way of viewing character and conscience as impersonal narrative functions. In Sir George Onesiphorus Paul's later Gloucestershire system, for example, male and female felons were confined in penitentiaries under detailed rules setting forth regimes of work and diet appropriate to different stages of the sentence, which was analyzed into segments like the stages of a classic plot.[22] To manipulate identity by restructuring the fictions on which it is founded is the exact aim of the penitentiary as an institution. Yet in the novel's prison episode the impersonal principle of inspection, which animates both the penitentiary and the rational/purposive social order it epitomizes, is enacted as the story of a personal intervention by Dr. Primrose. This personification of social power is no less incongruous than the fictional pretence that the operations of reformative confinement might be carried out within the architectural framework of an old-style prison.

The incongruous attribution of regulative omniscience to personal agents in fact occurs throughout the novel. Overdetermined personifications of authority crowd the whole text. Dr. Primrose's authoritative role is especially important in the prison episode, as in the family setting, but elsewhere he competes with the all but God-like powers of Mr. Burchell/

Sir William Thornhill. Acting in the guise of Burchell, Sir William protects the family from the imposture of Squire Thornhill's dubious lady friends, who invite the Primrose girls to London in order to make them easy prey, and, when the squire lures the eldest into elopement, Burchell tracks her and hovers about trying to warn her off. Later, he is able to foil an abduction of the younger daughter staged by the squire. The motif of disguise itself becomes a figure for the idea that efficacious governance strives to work invisibly as a mode of control rather than through personal action. Burchell's true identity as Sir William is discovered not by himself but by accident, and the Olympian revelation inspires almost unbearable awe: "Never before had I seen any thing so truly majestic as the air he assumed upon this occasion" (4.167). The vicar also must compete with the perverted, aggressively personal, feudal authority of Squire Thornhill, whose defeat is adumbrated by the vicar's reform of the old-style prison—at once the instrument and symbol of "aristocratical" tyranny. These overdetermined personifications manifest a frustrated struggle to find technical narrative forms both correlative to the emergent penitentiary idea set forth in chapter 27 and consonant with the novel's expressed politics. A version of that struggle can also be seen in the choice of narrative mode. The text contains evidence of a reach toward the impersonal narrative procedures characteristic of later realist fiction and, analogously, of the penitentiary as idealized in Bentham's "principle of inspection." *The Vicar of Wakefield* is an intermediate sociocultural structure whose textual operations allow us to view emergence in process.

Ronald Paulson argues that Dr. Primrose combines attributes of a simple wise man like Parson Adams in *Joseph Andrews* with the ironic perspective of Fielding's omniscient narrators. Primrose's witty character includes an ironic streak, yet his limited personality and point of view make him subject to dramatic irony.[23] The vicar also includes authoritative qualities reminiscent of Dr. Harrison in Fielding's *Amelia* (1751). Indeed, the character of Dr. Harrison in that earlier novel provides a key to an appreciation of the technical development represented by *The Vicar of Wakefield*. The narrator in *Amelia*, though at times obtrusively omniscient, all but disappears during long stretches of the fiction, and many of his authoritative attributes—including considerable management of the action—are lodged in a character in the story, Dr. Harrison. Yet Dr. Harrison also proves fallible, and his mistakes have provoked considerable commentary by critics who rightly notice inconsistencies in the character. Properly viewed as products of Fielding's experimentation with narrative technique, however, these inconsistencies in Dr. Harrison can point us toward a fuller understanding of the problematic formal status of Goldsmith's narrator. *The Vicar of Wakefield* combines similar attributes in Dr. Primrose, a character who is at once the apparent narrator, the chief actor, the possessor of considerable foresight, and a laughably erroneous good soul.

The resulting compound differs markedly from previous first-person narration, because the speaker in Goldsmith's novel is framed by a coherent, controlling, putatively invisible omniscience. In *Amelia*, this omniscience had been personified as an intrusive third-person narrator, even though that narrator was often submerged and some of the attributes of authority were transferred to Dr. Harrison. In *The Vicar of Wakefield*, although omniscience must be inferred within the body of the narrative proper, we learn on the title page that Dr. Primrose's story is "a tale, supposed to be written by himself." Who, we may ask, is doing the supposing? Some covert impersonality is at work here, some tacit collaboration between an implied third-person perspective within which Primrose's supposed narration must be staged and an implied reader who seems to require omniscience and individualism at once. The reader is licensed to imagine an individual as the figure of narrative authority, much as Bentham's prisoner is invited to imagine the keeper-inspector of the penitentiary as a representation of the principle of inspection and omniscience itself. The text attempts to contain first-person narration within a covert, impersonal omniscience. This controlling presence is manifest in the rigidly symmetrical structure of the novel and in the blatantly contrived reversals of its plot. Such features are linked in turn to the overdetermined personifications discussed above: these personifications may be read as outcroppings of dysfunctionally manifested authority. These and other qualities of the novel cause it to seem more like a fable, parable, or fairy tale than a realist fiction. But, as Robert Rosenblum has observed of painting during this same period in Britain, some of the most striking formal developments in realist technique appear in tandem with their opposites—the visionary, the romantic, the fantastic, and the gothic.[24]

I say that the novel "attempts" the containment of the first-person point of view within a coherent third-person perspective because this is a contradictory aim that cannot be fully realized in first-person narration. Only later when full development of the third-person technique known as *style indirect libre* (free indirect discourse) enables the presentation of thought through seemingly untrammeled, all-seeing, impersonal narration does this become possible. Fielding has a place in the early history of free indirect discourse because of the scattered instances in which he employs this device "for rendering a character's thought in his own idiom while maintaining the third-person reference and the basic tense of narration."[25] It is a fundamental mechanism underlying the convention of transparency that distinguishes the later realist novel. Flaubert condensed the basic principle into a vivid formulation later echoed by Joyce: "The illusion (if there is one) comes . . . from the *impersonality* of the work. . . . The artist in his work must be like God in his creation—invisible and all-powerful: he must be everywhere felt, but never seen."[26] Free indirect discourse disperses authoritative presence into the very third-person grammar and syntax through which the illusion of thought is created. Transparency is the convention that both author and beholder are absent from a representation, the objects of which are rendered *as if* their externals were entirely visible and their internality fully accessible. Transparency treats the one presence within which all other presences are staged as if its embrace were invisible.

The Vicar of Wakefield, though written in the first person and not self-evidently part of the prehistory of free indirect discourse, nonetheless reaches toward this technique: in fact, certain passages can be understood as third-person narration reinscribed *as if* from the first-person perspective of the vicar. Dr. Primrose may not be an extraordinarily reflective character, and he is decidedly fallible, but he does have penetrating qualities as an observer. These qualities are less functions of his character than of the encrypted person of his narration. Collaterally, because of inconsistencies and contradictions in Goldsmith's technique, the implied omniscient narratorial presence not only is displaced into the first person, it is variously projected into the actions of characters who—like Burchell, Sir William, Squire Thornhill, and, in certain episodes, Primrose himself—seem to transcend typical human capacity or even to assume all but supernatural powers.

A simple test can reveal how the novel obliquely ventures upon the representation of thought from the impersonal, all-penetrating perspective that free indirect discourse makes possible. Roland Barthes proposes such a test during a discussion of personal and apersonal narration as systems or codes independent of superficial linguistic markers: "there are narratives or at least narrative episodes . . . which though written in the third person nevertheless have as their true instance the first person."[27] And he proceeds to rewrite the third-person pronouns of such a text in the first person. Run in reverse, his test yields fascinating results when applied to the passage in chapter 15 where Primrose, having intermittently assumed some attributes of a third-person narrator in describing the discovery of Mr. Burchell's letter-case, then shifts to a brief account of his own thoughts upon discovering that Burchell had written to prevent Squire Thornhill's

London women from taking the Primrose daughters to town. The following translation of this passage yields a convincing episode of third-person narration ranging in technique from neutral psychological description (first sentence), to a passing instance of free indirect discourse (marked with my italics), to a summation ambiguously poised between impersonal narratorial observation and another rendering of thought (last sentence). I insert the alternate pronouns in brackets:

> As for my [his] part, it appeared to me [him] one of the vilest instances of unprovoked ingratitude I [he] had met with. *Nor could I [he] account for it in any other manner than by imputing it to his [Burchell's] desire of detaining my [his] youngest daughter in the country, to have the more frequent opportunities of an interview.* In this manner we [they] all sat ruminating upon schemes of vengeance, when our [their] other little boy came running in to tell us [them] that Mr. Burchell was approaching at the other end of the field. It is easier to conceive than describe the complicated sensations which are felt from the pain of a recent injury, and the pleasure of approaching vengeance. (*Works*, 4.77–78)[28]

Primrose's private observations take on the perspective of impersonal narration, though hidden under the first person. The novel actually alerts us to the possibility of such interchanges of person when, quite early in the text, Mr. Burchell momentarily slips from the third person into the first during his account of Sir William Thornhill's life and works (4.30). Goethe describes this famous slip as the point at which, according to Herder, the audience of the novel must divide between those who view the work as "a production of Art" and those who, like children, naively confuse it with the "productions of Nature."[29] Interestingly, the intermediate mode of personal/apersonal narration that I am noticing here appeared contemporaneously with Adam Smith's identification of the psychic interchange of "I" and "he" as the fundamental mechanism establishing morality and character through the introjection of social norms as individual values. Smith named this internalized representation of the third person the "impartial spectator." *The Vicar of Wakefield* allows us to see the embodiment of the "impartial spectator" in literary culture, and to uncover the dispersed and secret assertions of omniscience and power in the private voice of the individual.[30]

Attention to *The Vicar of Wakefield*'s articulate politics, to its reformist episode in chapter 27, and to its "supposed" first-person narration shows certain ways in which it displays a new ideology. Goldsmith's individual politics brought him to idealize the personal powers of the monarch as if they represented a new system of impersonal, transparent order—an enabling anachronism that allowed him to delineate the essential character of the new penitentiary in considerable detail, without giving explicit voice to its overarching rationale. His novel, in epitomizing those details, and in producing narration with technical features that anticipate the impersonal omniscience of modern supervisory authority—whether in novelistic procedures or in governmental technology—defines a textual scene within which ideological contradictions become visible and through which we can witness the emergence of a new system of order beneath the surface evocations of divine providence and first-person narration. These contradictions have meaning. They have cognitive force.

V

We may return, at last, to my earlier question: why should an essay on prison reform be lodged in a novelistic context? My answer has two elements. First, the novel, even more than other literary forms, is sensitive to emergent institutional orders because it incorporates the dialogic transactions at work in society at any given historical moment. Second, the penitentiary as conceived during the later eighteenth century and institutionally established following the Penitentiary Act of 1779 is itself a narrative institution structured on principles analogous to, and within the same epistemology as, the realist novel. Penitentiaries have regimes, schedules, disciplines; their inmates progress or regress, and they have stories not to be told upon release or just prior to execution (like the subjects of *The Newgate Calendar*) but to be lived out in the penitentiary itself. Much of the history of penology subsequent to the establishment of penitentiaries in England during the last quarter of the eighteenth century can be described as an attempt to order the prison story generically with divergent classifications for each age, sex, and type of convict. This idea is central: the form prisons took when they were remade in correspondence to and collaboration with the period's new systems of political and moral consciousness was *narrative* form of a distinctively novelistic kind; this form, in turn, implied a whole new way of being in a transparent world.

Finally, one may ask why it now has become possible, even necessary, to read *The Vicar of Wakefield* as a document of ideological emergence. The work's previous critical reception can offer a clue. The idea that the text maintains two fundamentally disparate points of view—that of Primrose and that of some embracing ironist—became established only during the mid-twentieth-century after nearly two hundred years in which the novel had been prized for its simple clarity of representation. Only during the past generation has Primrose been viewed primarily as a figure with comic, even ridiculous, limitations or as an object of sustained satire.[31] My analysis works to explain these critical strategies as last-ditch efforts to maintain the novel's coherence and illusionism in face of ever-increasing evidence of its contradictions. My reading accepts these contradictions as meaningful rather than trying to reintegrate them into a more complex illusionism. Such a critical move becomes possible, I believe, only once the order of transparent realism and the mechanisms of neutral, rational/purposive social institutions that it reproduces have ceased to be accepted as inevitable, unremarked conventions and have begun to take on the awkwardness of residual formulations. These conventions can and do remain powerful forces in present-day culture and society, but their operations have fallen into the line of critical vision and have become subject to ever more corrosive analysis. Their dissolution has been in progress through most of the twentieth century. Free indirect discourse, for example, was recognized, described, and named by Romance philologists around the turn of that century, more than a hundred years after it came into pervasive use but precisely when the mode of realism it defined was undergoing radical revision in novelistic practice and when the destructive impact of world war and revolution forever altered the European social order.[32] By the 1920s and 1930s it was an avant-garde commonplace to treat realism as a historical development, and its contradictions, once visible, became increasingly unsupportable in literary and cultural theory even though the practice of everyday life and techniques of popular fiction continued to take many aspects of the convention for granted.[33] Those who remain unperplexed by theoretical concerns may live still within the residual convention of realism—either entirely undisturbed or engaged unselfconsciously in the business of keeping it in operation (this is where I would locate most ironist critics of *The Vicar of Wakefield*).

Today, it seems to me that self-conscious criticism of the novel has to deal with two irreconcilable facts. First, everyday life still proceeds for the most part within the conventions of transparency and realism, just as the penitentiary (in however decrepit a form) remains the ordinary last resort and essential symbolic projection of state power. And second, these conventions and institutions have been subjected to critiques which, though aimed at profound deconstruction, have yet to prove fatal. What characterizes our moment—our episteme as Michel Foucault would have called it—is the seemingly indefinite persistence of a parallax existence in which these conditions pertain practically but do not pertain intellectually. We live in a fractured state of illusion/disillusion of which I believe the theoretical eclecticism of this essay to be a product. The contradictions that we have observed in mid-eighteenth-century society inversely parallel the fissures in our own. Both societies are transitional. What was emergent two hundred years ago now is residual—but also different. The novel is now a commodity—part of the culture industry—and penitentiaries now serve as mere holding areas primarily populated by racial and cultural aliens. Signs appear that prisons, known now as "facilities," may soon he returned to operation by private industry like the unreformed eighteenth-century jails that went before them. Even the Enlightenment zeal to abolish capital punishment, a reform closely linked to the rise of the penitentiary, has waned: in California, for example, three justices of the state Supreme Court were unseated in 1986 because the public believed them opposed to the death penalty. In this context, then, I rationalize my own theoretical eclecticism as having, at least, the virtue of keeping fissures in the present mode of social and literary production in constant view by restaging them in multiple perspectives.

CHAPTER 8

Impersonal Violence

The Penetrating Gaze and the Field of Narration in *Caleb Williams*

With a Postscript on My Gross Anatomy Lab

My subject is the violence habituated within certain techniques of impersonal narration typical of realist prose fiction. I want to point to issues at once broad, complex, and by no means intuitively obvious. In developing them here, however, I shall concentrate mainly upon William Godwin's attempt, in his novel *Caleb Williams*, at a radical critique of the machinery of character and conscience as socially, legally, and governmentally constructed during the Enlightenment: a critique ultimately overwhelmed from within by the technology it assailed.

I

But I shall begin again, this time with three quotations, the first from Jonathan Swift's Hack in "A Digression on Madness." Both Swift's dichotomy between ordinary vision and the scientific gaze and his metaphor fusing female skin and foppish clothing—his feminization of the body under the knife of scientist inquiry—emerge as uncannily prophetic:

> The two Senses, to which all Objects first address themselves, are the Sight and the Touch; These never examine farther than the Colour, the Shape, the Size, and whatever other Qualities dwell, or are drawn by Art upon the Outward of Bodies; and then comes Reason officiously, with Tools for cutting, and opening, and mangling, and piercing, offering to demonstrate, that they are not of the same consistence quite thro'. . . . Therefore, in order to save the Charges of all such expensive Anatomy for the Time to come; I do here think fit to inform the Reader, that in such Conclusions as these, Reason is certainly in the Right; and that in most Corporeal Beings, which have fallen under my Cognizance, the *Outside* hath been infinitely preferable to the *In*: Whereof I have been farther

convinced from some late Experiments. Last Week I saw a Woman *flay'd*, and you will hardly believe, how much it altered her Person for the worse. Yesterday I ordered the Carcass of a *Beau* to be stript in my Presence; when we were all amazed to find so many unsuspected Faults under one Suit of Clothes: Then I laid open his *Brain*, his *Heart*, and his *Spleen*; But, I plainly perceived at every Operation, that the farther we proceeded, we found the Defects encrease upon us in Number and Bulk: from all which, I justly formed this Conclusion to my self; That whatever Philosopher or Projector can find out an Art to sodder and patch up the Flaws and Imperfections of Nature, will deserve much better of Mankind, and teach us a more useful Science, than that so much in present Esteem, of widening and exposing them.[1]

Swift's contempt for deluded rationalist projectors leads him to prefigure, from an opposite political perspective, a counter-Enlightenment rebel such as William Blake, and to offer a satiric anticipation of Godwin's political idealism. Swift's Houyhnhnms in fact distilled for Godwin an ideal of society governed by orderly thought and practice: that is to say, a society inhabited by Godwin's peculiar brand of individually autonomous rationalism, by benevolence, and by honesty, rather than by institutions and contractual rights.[2]

This counter-Enlightenment current surfaces, too, in poststructuralist thinking, for example, in Jacques Derrida's appreciation of the thought of Emmanuel Levinas, entitled "Violence and Metaphysics":

Incapable of respecting the Being and meaning of the other, phenomenology and ontology would be philosophies of violence . . . [connected with] the ancient clandestine friendship between light and power, and the ancient complicity between theoretical objectivity and technico-political possession. . . . The heliological *metaphor* only turns away our glance, providing an alibi for the historical violence of light: a displacement of technico-political oppression in the direction of philosophical discourse.[3]

The metaphor of "enlightenment," which we inherit from the eighteenth century, is one of those "heliological metaphors" that conceals the impersonal violence involved in the scientistic framing of objects, in effacing mysterious otherness by infiltrating autonomous bodies with knowledge, by "flaying" them with light's probing rays. When the form of knowledge known as realist narrative infiltrates the bodies and minds it represents, as it progressively does in the eighteenth-century novel, its "technico-political possession" dominates and mutilates (symbolically dissects and even castrates) these bodies whether the instrument is the anatomical knife in the impartial hands of Reason that exposes flaws in the carcass of Swift's Beau, or the penetrating gaze of clinical inquiry, or the novelistic depiction of thought. Caleb Williams is no more than a representative victim of enlightened inquiry analogous to the precisely specified female vagrants whose anatomized bodies are depicted in William Hunter's *Anatomy of the Human Gravid Uterus* (1774: Figures 8 and 9) or the more generalized male figures dismembered for Gautier d'Agoty's *Myologie complette en couleur et grandeur naturelle* (1746: Figures 10 and 11).

The third quotation comes from a preface that Godwin wrote nearly forty years after *Caleb Williams*'s publication. He thematizes the metaphor of dissection, also a favorite of his novelistic predecessors:

> I began my narrative . . . in the third person. But I speedily became dissatisfied. I then assumed the first person, making the hero of my tale his own historian. . . . [This] was infinitely the best adapted . . . to my vein of delineation, where the thing in which my imagination revelled the most freely, was the analysis of the private and internal operations of the mind, employing my metaphysical dissecting knife in tracing and laying bare the involutions of motive. . . . I rather amused myself with tracing a certain similitude between the story . . . and the tale of Bluebeard. . . . Falkland was my Bluebeard, who had perpetrated atrocious crimes. . . . Caleb Williams was the wife, who in spite of warning, persisted in his attempts to discover the forbidden secret; and, when he had succeeded, struggled fruitlessly to escape the consequences, as the wife of Bluebeard in washing the key of the ensanguined chamber, who, as often as she cleared the stain of blood from the one side, found it showing itself with frightful distinctness on the other.[4]

Later, I shall return to this belated preface by Godwin. For now, let me just point out that he views his assumption of Caleb's first-person voice as a metaphysical dissection and that he feminizes Caleb as the last in the sequence of Bluebeard's murdered wives. The context of this passage includes Godwin's review of the fictional analogues on which he depended and clearly places Caleb in a long line of novelistic cadavers whose authors were, as Godwin says, "employed upon the same mine as myself, however different was the vein they pursued: we were all of us engaged in exploring the entrails of mind and motive" (340). Hogarth already had conceived such exploration as the literal dissection of criminal innards illustrated in the final plate of his *Four Stages of Cruelty* (Figure 12) and had visually likened the process to a juridical trial, which is the scene of action more prevalent than any other in *Caleb Williams*.[5]

It is time to turn to certain framing propositions. A first set concerns the social and psychological significance of the emergence of the third-person narrative term known as *style indirect libre* (free indirect discourse), a technical innovation historically specific to the later eighteenth century that enables the presentation of thought through seemingly untrammeled, all-seeing, impersonal narration. As Dorrit Cohn says, free indirect discourse is a device "for rendering a character's thought in his own idiom while maintaining the third-person reference and the basic tense of narration."[6] It is the characteristic mechanism for securing the illusion of transparency that marks the realist novel from the later eighteenth century onward. Transparency is the convention that both author and beholder are absent from a representation, the objects of which are rendered as if their externals were entirely perceptible in a unified field of vision and their internality fully accessible. Flaubert condensed the basic principle into a vivid formulation: "The illusion (if there is one) comes . . . from the *impersonality* of the work. . . . The artist in his work must be like God in his creation—invisible and all-powerful: he must be everywhere felt, but never seen." Free indirect discourse disperses authoritative presence into the very third-person grammar and syntax through which the illusion of thought is created. The technique's prominence in narrative fiction correlates historically with the projection of impersonal authority in the penitentiary prison as epitomized by Jeremy Bentham's *Panopticon.* Bentham's idealized plan revealed that the operational fact of the penitentiary is what he called the "principle of inspection," not the person of the inspector. The point is that the inspector-keeper is not really omniscient, or even really a person, but rather that the transparency of penitentiary architecture forces the prisoner to *imagine* him as such. Reformation hinges upon the conviction that omniscience enfolds being.[7]

Both free indirect discourse and Bentham's "principle of inspection" correlate, further, with Adam Smith's identification of the sympathetic interchange of "I" and "other" as the fundamental psychic mechanism establishing conscience and character through the introjection of social norms as individual values. Thus, by a central irony, the sensation of sympathy founds an order of power. Smith, who named this internalized representation of the third person as the "impartial spectator," himself sometimes employed narrative devices very similar to free indirect discourse. He presents his construction as a natural universal, whereas I view it as a description of the dominant behavioral ideology or social system of post-Enlightenment culture. Later, in my analysis of *Caleb Williams,* I will show how Godwin attempted to restage the very mechanisms of this ideology to expose it as a system of domination.[8]

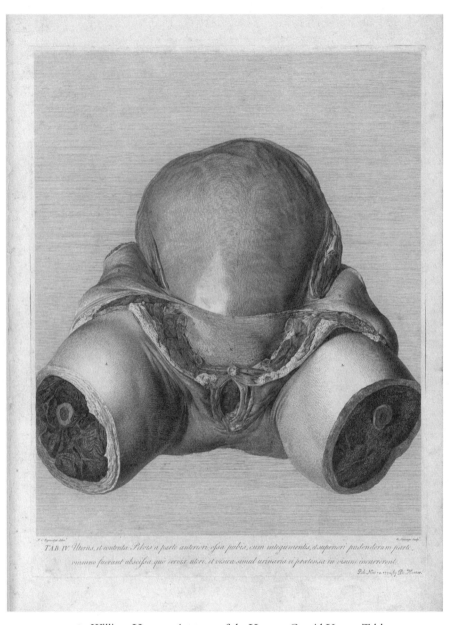

TAB IV. *Uterus, et contenta Pelvis a parte anteriori, ossa pubis, cum integumentis, et superiori pudendorum parte, omnino fuerant abscissa, quæ cervix uteri, et vesica simul urinaria ei prætensa in visum incurrerent.*

Pub. Nov. 12 1774 by Dr Hunter.

FIGURE 8. William Hunter, *Anatomy of the Human Gravid Uterus*, Table 4 (1774). Wellcome Images.

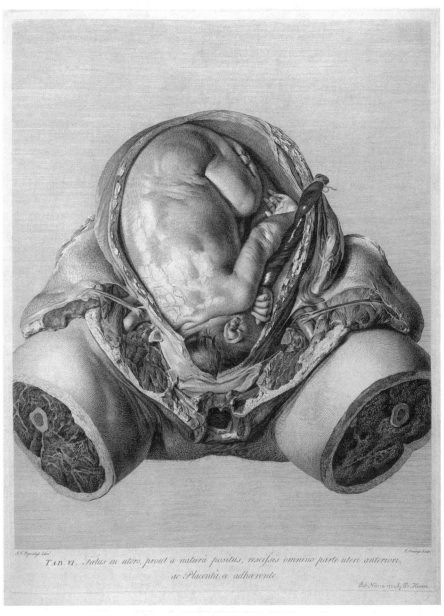

TAB. VI. *Fœtus in utero, prout a naturâ positus, rescissis omnino parte uteri anteriori, ac Placentâ ei adhærente.*

FIGURE 9. William Hunter, *Anatomy of the Human Gravid Uterus*, Table 6 (1774). Wellcome Images.

FIGURE 10. Gautier d'Agoty, *Myologie complette en couleur et grandeur naturelle*, Plate 4 (1746). Wellcome Images.

FIGURE 11. Gautier d'Agoty, *Myologie complette en couleur et grandeur naturelle*, Plate 7 (1746). Wellcome Images.

FIGURE 12. William Hogarth, *The Four Stages of Cruelty*, Plate 4 (1735). Harvard Art Museums/Fogg Museum, Gray Collection of Engravings Fund, G9035.

Smith's contemporary Goldsmith allows us to see the embodiment of the impartial spectator in literary culture, and to uncover the dispersed and secret assertions of omniscience in the seemingly private voice of the individual. *The Vicar of Wakefield*, although written during the 1760s in the first person and not self-evidently part of the prehistory of free indirect discourse, nonetheless reaches toward this technique. Certain passages in the novel can be understood as third-person narration reinscribed *as if* from the first-person perspective of the vicar.[9] The first-person subject emerges as a remarkably permeable web spun of individual sensation but *structured* by the impersonal geometry of sociopsychic organization. In hindsight, this fact has startling political implications for Goldsmith's case, since not merely his specific advocacy of penitentiary confinement but the dispersed, impersonal grounding of his narration cut across the grain of his articulate philosophy as a nostalgic country conservative with longings—à la Bolingbroke—for the concentration of authority in the highly individual person of a paternalistic king.

Godwin presents the obverse case: he is a utopian anarchist whose attack on personified authority in *Caleb Williams* is also staged within a field of narration that profoundly contradicts his enterprise. So compelling is the teleology of representation as configured in the realist novel that Godwin not only recast the ending of his story in conformity to its dynamic, but he proceeded thereafter to a wholesale rewriting of *Political Justice*. This rewriting and further insertions in *Caleb Williams* indicate that the novel became a conflictual scene within which Godwin's initial belief in radically individualistic virtue could not maintain itself. His thought remained in the current of rational dissent, but was enveloped within a delineation of moral being that emerged as increasingly hegemonic from the 1760s onward and that established a dialectic between a psychologized inner world of subjective reflection and an abstracted social order introjected through sympathetic identification with representative individuals. The gaze, and of course the spectatorship attendant upon it, are primary media within which this dialectic operates but the broader issues at stake concern the *vraisemblable*—the appearance of reality—within which post-Enlightenment culture constructs character and social relations.

Contemporary discussion of the gaze as a mechanism embraces ranges of generalization too vast and subtleties of distinction too refined for complete exposition here. But some opening to the topic is required by way of a second set of framing propositions. Especially relevant in this context are concerns about sexual domination brought forward in the work of Laura

Mulvey and other feminist film theorists, and questions about the history of the gaze raised by Michel Foucault.[10] They have assisted in historicizing the gaze as an ideologically laden cultural procedure that works to stabilize social forms by representing the political order as if it arose naturally from individual perception and psychology. This procedure establishes subjective character as a function acting at the conjuncture of a double or collateral gaze that stabilizes the Other within a fictionalized field of vision and knowledge, so as, finally and paradoxically, to introject its image as an impersonal gaze that fixes the subject within a moral, social, and political order. This gaze is figured metaphorically and ideologically as a neutral, natural perspicuity that spontaneously opens objects in its field to analytic yet painless dissection.

Foucault has outlined a history of the medical gaze that moves from a clinical phase, focused on the description of symptomatic surface, to an anatomical phase that opens the body's interior to analytic pathology. Loosely but suggestively correlative would be Norman Bryson's contrast between Renaissance painting, where the gaze both predicates bodily surfaces in the field of vision and situates the viewer's body at the point of comprehension, and later European painting in which the gaze is disembodied and analytically sequenced.[11] Foucault's chapter title, "Open Up a Few Corpses," like his discussion of Sade and the metaphorics of light in the conclusion to *The Birth of the Clinic*, points to the piercing quality of the gaze. As Bryson says, "The *regard* attempts to extract the enduring form from fleeting process; its epithets tend towards a certain violence (penetrating, piercing, fixing), and its overall purpose seems to be the discovery of a second . . . surface standing behind the first, the mask of appearances."[12] We recur, then, to the medical imagery Godwin himself used, because it carries the correct (if usually submerged) implication that the gaze is an instrument that violently, albeit precisely, cuts open the body in the act of mapping its functions. This gaze is charged with sexual energy because it penetrates and wounds the body, which it characteristically genders female.

Film studies, the history of science, and speculative art history offer richly elaborated theories of the gaze. Comparatively novel, however, is my correlation of contemporary ideas about the violence latent in the gaze with the eighteenth-century British school of benevolist moral thought— especially Adam Smith's—and with the narrative mode of free indirect discourse. The only current thinking I know about that explicitly links violence with sympathy appears in David Marshall's *The Surprising Effects of Sympathy* and in a few extraordinarily suggestive pages in Leo Bersani and

Ulysse Dutoit's *The Forms of Violence*. Bersani and Dutoit suggest, in the context of psychoanalysis rather than eighteenth-century moral theory, that "there is a certain risk in all sympathetic projections: [namely, that] the pleasure which accompanies them promotes a secret attachment to scenes of suffering or violence" because any form of sympathetic identification with suffering must be considered to contain a "trace of sexual pleasure, and that this pleasure is, inescapably, masochistic." Psychoanalysis provides a more detailed account, but, as Marshall suggests, the text of Smith's *Theory of Moral Sentiments* implies some linkage between the pleasures of sympathy and sadomasochistic identification.[13]

II

I need to insist, as I move to the main part of this essay, that my aim is not to produce a single unified reading of *Caleb Williams*. Instead, I consider *Caleb Williams* as a fractured text, conflictual and dynamic at its very core, a text most usefully imagined as a residue of intellectual and representational struggle, rather than as the embodiment of a single set of purposive intentions or the outcome of a teleological development in thought.[14] This struggle involves contestants that the rules of criticism—despite the presence of a book such as Ian Watt's *The Rise of the Novel*—have traditionally consigned to separate leagues: political thought and narrative technique. Godwin criticism abounds in treatments of both but not in studies of their interaction. If we look at the two together, especially under the rubric of violence, we can see that the variously revised texts of Godwin's treatise and novel exhibit at least two sets of interrelated symptoms having to do first with Godwin's political critique and, second, with the narrative field he constructs.

Before specifically treating the textualization of these symptoms in *Caleb Williams*, I must offer a brief plot summary. With the hero, we enter a story long after many important events have transpired. Caleb, a bookish young man of humble birth, becomes upon his parents' death secretary to Falkland, a melancholy aristocrat of broad accomplishment who once relished society but now is reclusive. After an incident in which Falkland threatens to trample Caleb when the secretary accidentally comes upon him moaning and hastily locking a mysterious trunk, the youth elicits the patron's story from his steward, Mr. Collins. We encounter this long narrative in Caleb's third-person retelling, itself lodged within the novel's retrospective first-person account of actions beginning with Caleb's entry into Falkland's household.

The polished Falkland had innocently fallen afoul of his neighbor, Mr. Tyrrel, a brutal country squire. After many perceived slights and real reprimands from Falkland, Tyrrel redirects his anger at his own dependent niece, the naïve Emily Melville. He punishes Emily's admiration of Falkland by forcing her engagement to an odious fiancé and then, upon her flight, casting her into a debtors' prison for not paying her keep during her residence in his house. Emily, of course, dies. Falkland's condemnation so infuriates Tyrrel that he beats him up before a county assembly. The same evening Tyrrel is secretly murdered. Falkland, having denied his guilt before an admiring public and having allowed a farmer and his son to be executed for the crime, retires into the solitary reflection that is disrupted by Caleb's arrival on the scene.

The curious Caleb, actuated by a magnetic sympathy and convinced of Falkland's deed, employs observation, innuendo, and sly questioning to reach the firm conviction of "guilty." When a household fire presents the chance, Caleb breaks open that mysterious trunk and is apprehended by Falkland, who confesses to the terrified secretary after extorting an oath of secrecy and bondage. Caleb flees, and is apprehended and indicted for theft upon planted evidence. After twice escaping prison in the manner of Jack Sheppard, and then joining and fleeing a well-governed band of thieves, he feels himself under universal surveillance because his story has been widely circulated by folktale and criminal broadside. He undertakes a series of disguises before being captured in London by a seemingly omniscient agent named Gines. He breaks the oath of secrecy but no magistrate will countenance his accusation and he is returned to prison. Released, and seemingly free when Falkland declines to appear against him, Caleb begins a new life in Wales, only to have it destroyed when Gines seeds the town with an old broadside. Debarred from exile and informed that Falkland intends England to be his lifelong prison, Caleb resolves to assail his patron with a full and circumstantial written narrative—that is, with the novel we are reading—and to accuse Falkland once more on his home ground. A dramatic postscript concludes the action. I want to defer that, however, in order to discuss the symptoms mentioned above and to notice how Godwin's staging of the novel manifests them.[15]

The first range of symptoms has to do with Godwin's sociopolitical critique and indicates that he initially arranged *Caleb Williams* as a contention between two systems of moral and political order, both of which he hoped to discredit because both were working hegemonically in the society of his day to maintain corrupting institutional forms. Roughly speaking, Falkland

and Caleb figure forth an opposition between the two: on the one hand, an aristocratic system preoccupied with class honor and actuated by shame; and on the other a contract system propelled by sympathy and actuated by guilt.[16] The preceding year, in the 1793 version of *Political Justice*, Godwin had powerfully argued instead for a society in which all institutions would be supplanted by autonomous private judgment equally exercised by all members. What he called "political justice" opposed party politics and questioned even republicanism, because he viewed all forms of government as giving "substance and permanence to our errors."[17] Rather, justice was for Godwin "a rule of conduct originating in the connection of one percipient being with another" and politics was "the adoption of any principle of morality and truth into the practice of a community."[18] Godwin strove to maintain this utopian ideal as an alternative to any institutional formation.

Godwin founds individual judgment on the human capacity to make reasoned comparisons among perceptions, which refer themselves in turn to sensations. A virtuous community assists the process by transmitting its forms through practice, education, discussion, and literature, but not through formal institutions, which by their nature lend authority to error. He insists upon the role of education in training autonomous judgment, and upon communal discussion in calibrating it to specific situations, but rejects its maintenance through mechanisms of shame or guilt. Both the old system based upon honor and the newer one based upon sympathetic introjection are political in the worst sense because they personify judgment as an enforcing third person rather than founding it upon the analogous but independent percipience of individuals. The one holds this spectator externally, the other introjects and holds it internally, but both situate individual morality in the regard—in the gaze—of others rather than in one's own integrity. Both deny what Rousseau called *amour de soi*: that crystalline openness of self that he equates with true sentiment, and which, as Mark Philp says in his study of *Political Justice*, constitutes in Godwin's view the "moral independence . . . required for genuine happiness and genuine concern for others."[19]

I divide into two clusters the second range of symptoms: that is, the ones having to do with formal narrative features. They indicate that Godwin fundamentally undermined his project from the beginning because narration as he undertook it reproduced the constructions of character he was assailing and precluded any stable delineation of autonomous private judgment of the kind he idealized.

The first cluster of symptoms points to a fundamental contradiction in narrative practice: even though, as Godwin indicated in his 1832 preface, he abandoned his initial conduct of narration in the third person in order, as he says, to make "the hero of my tale his own historian," the purpose, as Godwin says, was in fact to wield his "metaphysical dissecting knife . . . in exploring the entrails of mind and motive" (339–40). In truth, not only is the nominally first-person account of fact in *Caleb Williams* shot through with knowledge about past events and motives that no single individual could possibly possess, but also the field of narration is fractured by sentences that render thought in encoded free indirect discourse of the kind I have elsewhere pointed out in Goldsmith. By *encoded* I mean that the first-person form is maintained while the grammatical instance of communication—the speech act—is of the third person. Ann Banfield has argued that such discourse is historically produced and can take place only in written narration.[20] Godwin's entry into the grammar of omniscient presence, even or perhaps especially for purposes of fiction, replicates the very structure of domination he is assailing.

The second cluster of symptoms reveals that Godwin persistently frames his narration as a progression of images or tableaus that reproduce the violence of the gaze as a demand that the individual submit to external authority. Possibly because Godwin was straining to intensify conventional narration in order to propel his audience into awareness of a new kind of identity, or possibly because his virtually exclusive focus on two male characters throws the gender-laden phenomenology of realist narrative into prominence, he pushes toward the extreme instance of the European tendency (described by Bersani and Dutoit) "to isolate and to immobilize the violent act as the most significant moment in . . . plot development." In arguing that "a coherent narrative depends on stabilized images; [and that] stabilized images stimulate the mimetic impulse," they observe that "our views of the human capacity for empathetic representations of the world should therefore take into account the possibility that a mimetic relation to violence necessarily includes a sexually induced fascination with violence."[21]

I shall turn, then (working under the symptomatic rubrics just traced, and in the same order), to ways in which *Caleb Williams* both exhibits apprehensions about sympathetic identification and narrative violence and is captured by their spell.

Godwin obviously attacks the aristocratic code of honor, which always has been understood as his chief target, but the novel also works to indict the newer orthodoxy of sympathy. Caleb's transparent subjectivity makes plain that the sympathetic equation, no less than Falkland's aristocratic *amour-propre*, holds up the opaque mask of appearance that Rousseau condemned as merely artificial social form. But Caleb's sympathy is no neutral or innocent alternative; it is an irrational and exploitative by-product of political power, experienced as a real psychological state, though itself produced in masquerade. When he decides, as he says, to "place myself as a watch upon my patron," he confesses to "a strange sort of pleasure in it." This pleasure is directly aroused by Caleb's fear of authority: "To do what is forbidden always has its charms, because we have an indistinct apprehension of something arbitrary and tyrannical in the prohibition." The more domineering the object, the more intense the "enjoyment [and] the more the sensation was irresistible. . . . The more impenetrable Mr. Falkland was determined to be, the more uncontrolable was my curiosity" (107–8). This "magnetical sympathy," as Caleb calls it (112), propels him to the first climax of the action when Falkland, sitting as justice of the peace on a case analogous to his own, flees the scene, thus convincing the closely observant secretary of his patron's guilt. If Caleb's "involuntary exclamations" and the feeling that his "animal system had undergone a total revolution" were not sexually explicit enough, he cries "I had had no previous conception . . . that it was possible to love a murderer" (129–30). Once the fire and Caleb's burglary of Falkland's trunk have followed with a haste that smacks of allegory, he justifies his "monstrous" act by claiming that "there is something in it of unexplained and involuntary sympathy" (133). A more scathing depiction of the sympathetic construction of character would be hard to imagine.

Now, let us move to specific instances of the two clusters of formal symptoms previously outlined, treating first the novel's actuation of plot through immobilized tableaus and then the technical forms of its narration. The first third of the novel, containing Caleb's retelling of Mr. Collins's narrative, replicates in hyperconcentrated form Godwin's comprehensive organization of plot as a sequence of stabilized tableaus, many of them violent. This narrative explicitly inspires Caleb's sympathetic identification and establishes it as the motive force of the main action. In fewer than one hundred pages we encounter more than a dozen such tableaus: a duel narrowly averted during Falkland's grand tour of Italy; a stand-off between Falkland and Tyrrel at a country ball; a call upon Tyrrel meant by Falkland to substitute rational expostulation for the duel they seem headed toward (which visit ends with veiled mutual threats); Falkland's rescue of Emily from a fire during which he orders adjacent houses destroyed and can be seen to walk across a burning roof; Tyrrel and the fiancé's threat of Emily's dispoilage in a forced marriage; her flight in the manner of Clarissa; her wasting illness, imprisonment, and death; Falkland's verbal assault on Tyrrel and, of course, their final altercation ending in Tyrrel's murder; a hearing on Falkland's arraignment; and the execution of innocent parties. Caleb's fictional mimesis of this history recapitulates for readers the profound sympathetic engagement the young man is said to have experienced upon hearing Mr. Collins's version.

So compelling is the mechanism that establishes Caleb's destructive fascination with Falkland that it assumes control of the novel. In order to assure the reader's identification with his hero, Godwin establishes in this opening Collins/Caleb narration a paradigm of concentrated plot deployment that structures the balance of the work. He thus authorizes in *Caleb Williams* as a whole a pattern of identification that, in the early segments of the novel, he had used to unveil the awful dynamic of power underlying the sympathetic construction of character. Godwin's revisions show his defensive response to this fact. In the third edition, that of 1797, the interpolated fourth paragraph of chapter 1 specifies Caleb as a person whose fascination with sequences of cause and effect propagated "an invincible attachment to books of narrative and romance." "I panted," he says, "for the unravelling of an adventure, with an anxiety, perhaps almost equal to that of the man whose future happiness or misery depended on its issue. I read, I devoured compositions of this sort. They took possession of my soul; and the effects they produced, were frequently discernible in my external appearance and my health" (4). This paragraph attempts to reinscribe susceptibility to narrative as a pathological trait of Caleb's (not to mention as a vector of bodily penetration) and thus to exempt readers from any taint produced by their own engagement with Godwin's novel.

In the end, however, Godwin cannot novelistically produce a subject capable of sustaining the utopian autonomous private judgment he so forcefully advocated in the 1793 *Political Justice*. In many ways it appears that Godwin framed Caleb's third-person narration of Mr. Collins's story within the larger first-person context of the novel to act out the illusion of mastery conferred by the false sense of first-person autonomy based upon sympathetic introjection. This mastery is a juridical illusion, because the very power it confers to construct one's own version of another's subjectivity derives from the maintenance of an impartial spectator within a permeable self.[22]

Interestingly, the two passages in Caleb's third-person retelling of the Collins story that come closest to free indirect discourse (and hence to sympathetic illusionism) both thematize a sense of powerlessness on the part of the entered subject. These are our only points of access in the novel to reflections by Tyrrel and Falkland, who otherwise remain opaque precisely because they mark one pole in an opposition with transparency that Godwin in general maintains. The first occurs when Tyrrel, thwarted by Emily's flight and condemned by Falkland for persecuting tenant farmers, "recollected all the precautions he had used . . . and cursed that blind and malicious power which delighted to cross his most deep laid schemes":

> To what purpose had heaven given him a feeling of injury and an instinct to resent, while he could in no case make his resentment felt? It was only necessary to him to be the enemy of any person, to insure that person's being safe against the reach of misfortune. What insults, the most shocking and repeated, had he received from this paltry girl! And by whom was she now torn from his indignation? By that devil [Falkland] that haunted him at every moment, that crossed him at every step, that fixed at pleasure his arrows in his heart, and made mows and mockery at his insufferable tortures. (80)

After these reflections, Tyrrel immediately proceeds to his destruction of Emily by imprisonment.

The other passage comes after Tyrrel's furious public assault on Falkland, whom he knocks to the ground and kicks. Falkland's reflections appear in the text as follows:

> Every passion of [Falkland's] life was calculated to make him feel it . . . acutely. . . . [His] mind was full of uproar. . . . He wished for annihilation, to lie down in eternal oblivion, in an insensibility, which compared with what he experienced was scarcely less enviable than beatitude itself. Horror, detestation, revenge, inexpressible longings to shake off the evil, and a persuasion that in this case all effort was powerless, filled his soul even to bursting. (96)

These passages might be read as ironically intended signs of Caleb's delusion that he can enter Falkland's, or any other, mind. But in fact, information Caleb could not possibly possess, and encoded episodes that verge on free indirect discourse, both covertly invade—even capture—the first-person account that makes up the balance of the novel.

Key instances of such encoded first/third-person introspection occur, for example, during Caleb's earlier and later episodes of imprisonment. I present them in simultaneous translation into quasi-free indirect discourse by inserting into Caleb's first-person narration brackets that contain the third-person pronouns:[23]

> I [Caleb] recollected with astonishment my [his] puerile eagerness to be brought to the test and to have my [his] innocence examined. I [He] execrated it as the vilest and most insufferable pedantry. I [He] exclaimed in the bitterness of my [his] heart. . . . why should I [he] consign my [his] happiness to other men's arbitration? (182)

Or again later,

> My [His] resolution was not the calm sentiment of philosophy and reason. It was a gloomy and desperate purpose; the creature, not of hope, but of a mind austerely held to its design, that felt, as it were, satisfied with the naked effort, and prepared to give success or miscarriage to the winds. (278)

The surprising consequence of Godwin's representational strategy is that his thought appears to have been overtaken in some considerable measure by the allied force of the grammar that governs his field of narration and the propulsion derived from a plot suspensefully and climactically structured into images stabilized by the gaze of covert omniscience. Both mechanisms engender sympathetic identification by replicating the violence upon which they are predicated.

In the dramatic postscript that concludes the first edition (1793), Godwin rewrote the original climax he had intended for the novel, enacting not his initial plan for Caleb's defeat and probable destruction by the malice of Falkland but showing, rather, the capacity of the young man's sympathetic identification with the anguish of his haughty patron to inspire both Falkland's confession and his spontaneous death. The remorse that instantly descends upon Caleb follows inevitably in the system of sympathetic representation, like guilt after an exultantly violent sexual fantasy. The new ending closes with the novel's most famous lines: "I began these memoirs with the idea of vindicating my character. I have now no character that I wish to vindicate: but I will finish them that thy story [Falkland's] may be fully understood" (326).

Just about everyone agrees that the revised ending makes for a more powerful narrative than the unpublished original, which leaves Caleb scribbling away like the ravingly incoherent Clarissa after her rape. In that ending, the feminizing logic of the gaze was overtly thematic but there was no magical reversal, no fixated tableau where, in the manner of Bluebeard's wife, the victim becomes keeper of the perpetrator's violence. But paradoxically, the most successful readings of the novel (those of Myers and Philp, for example) do not respond to Caleb's lines about lack of character. In my account, this gap in response occurs because these lines reassert the structural logic of the novel in face of the overwhelming triumph of its narrative momentum. But the fame of Caleb's final lines also speaks a truth: the dissonant truth that the novel's conceptual order lives in contradiction with its mode of representation.

In my analysis, then, *Caleb Williams* is best understood as the textual residue of a struggle to define the price paid for that moral progress which other critics attribute to Caleb. Myers argues, for example, that he learns to appreciate the essential humanity of sympathetic understanding, while Philp maintains that he gains the kind of autonomous private judgment Godwin values above all else. This moral progress, like the narrative that produces it, is typically experienced as *real* when in fact it is merely *realistic* and, in truth, deeply fractured. *Caleb Williams* reveals the idea of moral progress to be historically specific and ideologically laden: a product of a certain kind of violently fixated narrative structuration implicit in sympathetic spectatorship.

No doubt one could construct a linear reading that found Caleb, as first-person narrator, to be distorting the real meaning of sympathetic identification. Certainly the first published version of 1793 left open the possibility of a radical reading that would leave Caleb in the delusionary state of *believing* that he at last had reached the highest ideal of humankind in his sympathetic union with Falkland, while in fact recording the truth that he has no character at all. Such a reading of the 1797 version, profoundly contradictory as it remains, is far more difficult to support. Godwin's strenuous efforts in the revised editions of 1796 and 1797 to incorporate passages toward the end of the novel that extol the impartial spectator and that found the idea of humanity itself on sympathetic identification make it quite clear that he is trying ex post facto to clarify the novel and to redeem it from the fractious struggle of its original production. What had been Caleb's investment in the new orthodoxy has become Godwin's investment. Godwin, as Mark Philp shows, clearly changed his mind in the course of his novel's initial composition. The remarkable fact is that he responded so powerfully to the narrative logic of sympathetic introjection that he also entirely rewrote *Political Justice* for its second and third editions to bring it, much more closely than before, into conformity with that main line of British moral thought from which he had so carefully established a distance in 1793. Disquisitions on sympathy and the impartial spectator figure importantly among these additions.

III

I close by returning, however briefly, to the body. The stringent economy of a short essay allows only a passing glance at the myriad ways Falkland and Caleb each employ the gaze as an instrument to waste away the body of the other. Falkland fades into a corpse well before his death and Caleb, after his long flight, must literally be strip-searched by Gines in order to be identified. At one point Caleb, dreaming that Falkland has sent an assassin, awakes to behold the "Amazonian" hag who cooks for the band of robbers that is hiding him. She wields a butcher's cleaver that sinks into the bedpost in an attempt to halve his skull. Her "glance" no less than her strength all but overwhelm him and, when he prevails in the struggle, she threatens to dash his entrails into his eyes (231). This same economy permits no more than a mention of Godwin's addition in 1796 of a new third paragraph in chapter 1 concerning the strength and flexibility of Caleb's youthful body, for the purpose, I believe, of counterbalancing the powerful feminization his field of narration had worked upon his hero.

Instead of accumulating further examples from the text, I turn in conclusion to a spellbinding recollection of the terrifying eighteenth-century machine placed on exhibit in London for five shillings per view during the year 1733 by the surgeon Abraham Chovet:

> [It was a] new figure of Anatomy which represents a woman chained down upon a table, suppos'd opened alive; wherein the circulation of the blood is made visible through glass veins and arteries; the circulation is also seen from the mother to the child, and from the child to the mother, with Histolick and Diastolick [*sic*] motion of the heart and the action of the lungs.

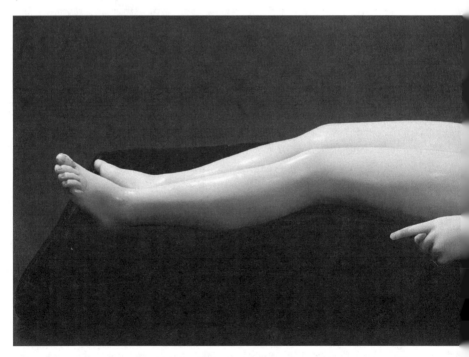

FIGURE 13. Anara Morandi Mazzolini, *Wax Female Figure with Parts Moveable to Reveal the Structure Beneath* (c. 1760). Wellcome Images.

No such automaton remains but amazing wax anatomical models made famous by Felice Fontana and others of the Florentine school do survive in Florence, Vienna, London, and elsewhere. Goethe and Sade were among the many eighteenth-century figures who visited them as part of the Grand Tour. Not only are they startlingly realistic but they are narrative figurations of the body, since their organs may be progressively displayed by the removal of layers that reveal a succession of tableaus which mimic dissection (Figures 13–17). A number of these models display a seductive sexuality that is new to anatomic figures and that may be considered a symptom of the early modern gendering of the gaze as a tool of scientific inquiry.[24]

I have been suggesting that we ourselves may take for granted another kind of anatomizing that survives from the eighteenth century because to some degree we still live within its canon. I refer, of course, to realism as a cultural practice.

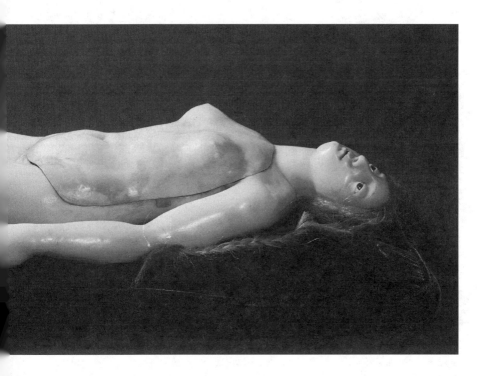

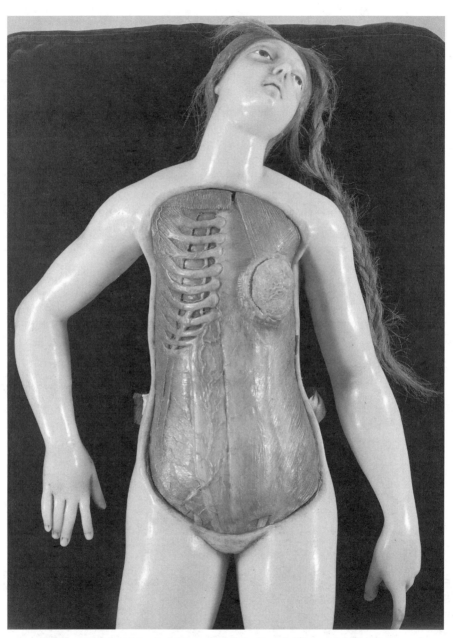

FIGURE 14. Anara Morandi Mazzolini, *Wax Female Figure with First Part Removed to Show Superficial Layers, Ribs, and Structures of the Breast* (c. 1760). Wellcome Images.

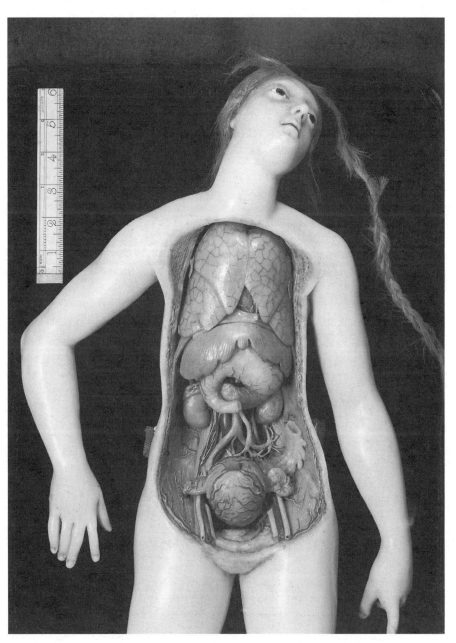

FIGURE 15. Anara Morandi Mazzolini, *Wax Female Figure, Parts Removed to Show the Stomach, Kidneys, Bladder* (c. 1760). Wellcome Images.

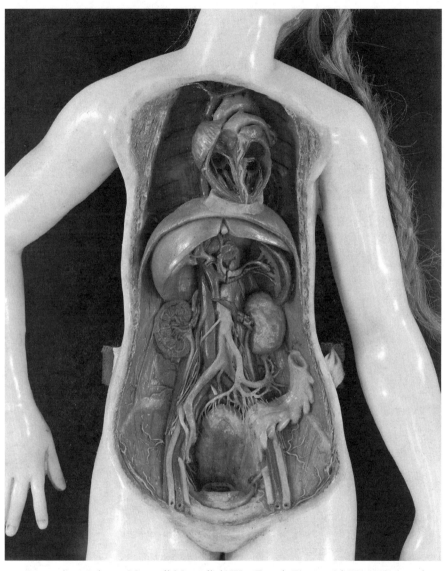

FIGURE 16. Anara Morandi Mazzolini, *Wax Female Figure with Uterus Removed and the Structure of the Heart Revealed* (c. 1760). Wellcome Images.

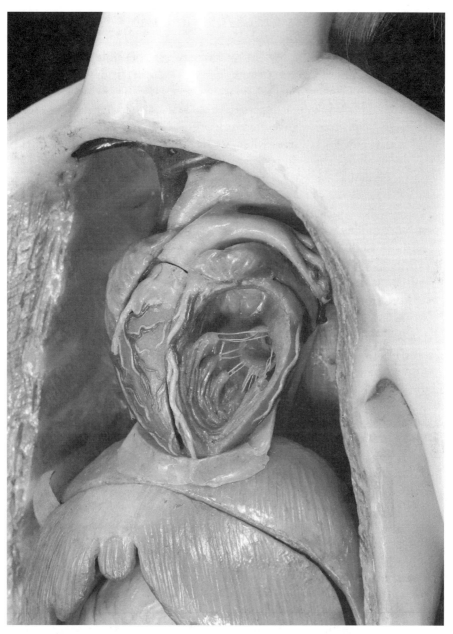

FIGURE 17. Anara Morandi Mazzolini, *Wax Female Figure, Close-up of Heart* (c. 1760). Wellcome Images.

A Postscript on My Gross Anatomy Lab

"Impersonal Violence" is my only published essay concerning eighteenth-century anatomical images (Chapter 8 in this volume). It draws upon ten years of research about their relationship to the gaze, to violence, to novelistic technique, and to pornography. This research inspired me, a professor of English and comparative literature, to take an introductory course in gross anatomy. I was a freak when, in the fall of 1995, I joined three first-year medical students—and a fifty-year-old woman dead of heart disease—on a team in the Stanford Medical School's beginning anatomy course. The late Dr. Lawrence H. Mathers, Dr. Robert A. Chase, and their cohort of fellow anatomists had accepted my promise (one I fulfilled) to undertake all work in the course side by side with regular first-year medical students. At the outset, I saw myself considering—as in "Impersonal Violence"—the cruelty that is explicit in much modern pornography and implicit in a scientific anatomical view of the dismembered body.

My purpose was to gain a richer understanding of early anatomical works and of the old culture of dissection that I already had been studying, not to lay the foundation for a career in medicine. I had been exploring the crossover between ways of visualizing the body in anatomical atlases and in pornography. Expensive books of both kinds were shelved together in private libraries during the eighteenth century, the period when, according to today's experts, modern pornography was invented.[1] The kind of strict, linear perspective associated with painting from the Renaissance onward fused in this period with new analytic ways of making mechanical and scientific diagrams. This fusion produced both a modern level of precision in works of anatomy and new erotic effects arising from close-up looks at the body that seemed to come from secret, hidden vantage points. Several images in "Impersonal Violence" clearly provoke such effects.

From the rise of modern anatomical studies in universities and academies in Italy during the sixteenth century to the era of increasingly rigorous professional education and certification during the nineteenth, the spectacle of dissection was visible to members of the public. They might have been patrons, artists, or even ticket-buying curiosity-seekers who had paid a high price, but they certainly did not have to be aspiring physicians to witness dissection.[2] The title page of Andreas Vesalius's *De humani corporis fabrica* (1543) shows a veritable mob straining to see the open female corpse in the foreground.[3] Apart from its formal architecture, the scene is more like a booth at a fair than like today's laboratories where first-year medical students learn anatomy. Much later, during the last half of the eighteenth century, William Hunter, who published the first complete atlas of the pregnant uterus, gave anatomical demonstrations at the Royal Academy in London for painters, sculptors, and paying members of the public. This contrasts with the more recent order, in which physicians walk through society with the aura of privileged initiates to a mysterious and frightening priesthood.[4]

Compulsory study in gross anatomy initiates the newly arrived into the professional tribe of physicians. Medical students begin to share the tribal aura immediately because of the placement of the gross anatomy course as a threshold at the beginning of their curriculum. Their daily encounter with cadavers throws a veil of mystery around them for family members and friends. Like the students, I quickly noticed that it took only two or three minutes before friends asked whether I was cutting up corpses. The timing of the question was precise, like the eruption of a geyser developing enough pressure to burst forth. Our special arena was the anatomy lab—closed to any visitor and to all cameras. Isolated, we sought to find life in death. The lab did not resemble the classic anatomical or surgical theater, much less the grizzly butchery shown in plate 4 of Hogarth's *Four Stages of Cruelty* (Figure 12 in Chapter 8). Instead, each of our teams of four dissected one of twenty corpses in a windowless, low-ceilinged, modern room, lined with powerful ventilators to draw away chemical fumes. Even the raised rails around the stainless steel tables that held the cadavers were perforated to allow the suction of air.

The anatomist is a ghost who returns from the dead upon each exit from the dissection room. I lived this daily ghost life. The anatomy theater is a private and privileged space analogous to arenas for initiation in some tribal cultures, where boys were brought to special men's houses for a period of isolation, arduous trials, and adventure, culminating in often-dangerous rites that included the cut of circumcision prior to passage to adulthood. The cut of dissection marks the threshold between life and death. One can learn anatomy at first hand only through the death of others. Our arduous trial lay not just in dissection and in our confrontation with dead bodies, nor in some twenty hours per week of formal yet sometimes grizzly lectures followed by supervised dissection, nor in breathing the pungent atmosphere of formalin, nor yet in double-gloving to protect the nerve endings of our fingers from this chemical. Rather, the challenge was to find bridges between these visceral experiences and the intellectual abstraction required by regular exams, which demanded the identification of anatomical structures pierced by tiny flagged pins.

The anatomy theater lies at the mysterious heart of medicine in the public fantasy and the professional imagination. To open a human body is to enter the realm where life and death cohabit: the didactic dissection of corpses traffics in death and disrepute. (The corpses for anatomical demonstrations used to be stolen from graveyards or cut down from gallows.) In the distant past, however, transgressions against the dead did not coincide with professional initiation. In contemporary medicine, anatomy works as a threshold experience for medical professionals, because they alone may violate such taboos as part of their training. The content of their knowledge depends, like their professional efficacy, on their violation of the taboo, on their access to the interior of the body and to death. Thus, the religious dimension remained under the surface in the modern medical school environment I experienced, but it did break through the scientific membrane when the faculty exhorted us at the start of the course to respect the spirits of those who had dedicated their bodies to science and to our education. A nonsectarian memorial service closed our term, in honor of the dead whose corpses now lay in scattered heaps, either at the foot of our dissection tables or at the sanitary disposal dump.

What did I learn in my anatomy course? For me, the most chilling experience in the dissection room was not cutting open the penis and testicles of the male cadaver at the next table, although friends asked about this and fellow males in the class worried about it (Figure 11 in Chapter 8). Rather—and perhaps not surprisingly for a historian of art and vision—my crisis came when one of my partners dove into the globe of an eye, extracting the iris, lens, and retina. Less viscerally and more academically, I saw that the Latin terms used to identify anatomical structures remain identical to those of the eighteenth century, a time when atlases on the pregnant uterus and the larger structures of the brain largely completed the subject. But I also saw that the role eighteenth-century anatomists had, of being educators who served not only physicians, but sculptors, painters, and a literate scientific public, has vanished. This sense has slipped away as the firsthand experience of anatomical dissection has become a guarded professional ritual, a marker of special knowledge, and a sign of the power over life and death. Modern professional medicine has deprived the larger public of firsthand visual experience of the body's interior and of its immense variability from person to person. In this manner, medicine has become less tangible to patients.[5] I count it a piece of great good fortune that my months of anatomical study allowed me to recover in a small way something of the eighteenth-century encounter with death and life.

CHAPTER 9

Rational Choice in Love

Les Liaisons dangereuses

One of the reigning methods for understanding conflict among states since World War II has been rational choice theory. Nowadays, this is a highly mathematical instrument that at its heart involves the contemplation of decision-making and action in the world as a game or series of games in which it is possible to have good, better, and best outcomes. One way to consider rational choice theory would be as a normative device for beating the odds—that is, as a system invented by human beings in order to transcend merely human common sense. An ensemble of elements marks rational choice theory: (1) neutral action orientation as opposed to the moral or ethical; (2) treatment of situations of choice in personal life, military strategy, or diplomacy as defined by gaming; (3) explicit, complex, mathematical reasoning as the basis for decision. Common sense, as we shall see, is the failure-prone heuristic that rational choice theory works to displace with methodically computed gaming moves. Can the human animal execute these moves with perfect dispassion? I argue here that both the flow of history and the precariousness of emotion—which is to say, the sheer weight of everything human and worldly that is left out by rational choice theory—suggest not.

I focus on a single work of literature. It is not directly concerned with war among states, though its author was in fact a soldier, an artillery officer, and an expert in fortifications. It deals with other kinds of war. This work, so apt in its juxtaposition of love and rational choice as strategy, is *Les Liaisons dangereuses* (1782), the scandalous novel by Choderlos de Laclos. At its turning point, the novel's two chief characters declare war, where, as in the novel, reasoned strategy, gaming, and the passions meet.[1]

My goal in this essay is, then, to consider the place of reason in the commonsense version of the term and, more specifically, of rational choice theory, as they play out in the realms of unreason. I bridge between the eighteenth and twentieth centuries as I pursue this goal. In order to narrow the field, I take love as my example. Within the unreasonable realm of the passions, love is, if not necessarily the most irrational, at least the most often subject to attempts at regulation by theoretical and practical reason. To contemplate the question of rational choice in love is to contemplate the interaction between the most systematic among methods of gaming, planning, and choice-making and the least systematic—that is, love as passion.

I

I will make two points before continuing. The first is to note that the modern opposition between statistical projections of circumstance and common sense does not align with eighteenth-century practice, in which, according to Lorraine Daston and her colleagues, the mathematicians concerned with probability felt free to adjust their mathematical findings to conform with commonsense reasoning.[2] The common sense of the general public could take precedence over specialized knowledge.

My second point requires a longer digression. It has to do with an important concern about the ways in which what we call "rational choice" might have been conceived in the eighteenth century. I have searched many databases and dictionaries to discover what I could about the terms "reason" and "choice" in the period. I have found that when it comes to "reason," in its general sense as a logical faculty, the term is continuous from the Renaissance to the present, but, in the eighteenth century, it did not cover what modern technical terminology in rational choice theory describes—not even in combination with the word "choice." Modern variants I have in mind include not just the idea of rational choice theory as a formal system for weighing alternatives, but also usages such as "markets are rational."[3]

There was, however, a highly significant discourse in the seventeenth and eighteenth centuries that does run partially parallel to our terminologies in rational choice theory and game theory—though it shares little of their mathematical basis. I refer to the period's richly textured theories of *interest* and *self-interest*. La Rochefoucauld defined the felt pervasiveness of interest at the time when he wrote, "Interest speaks all kinds of languages and plays all kinds of roles, even that of disinterestedness."[4] The best-known book on this topic is Albert O. Hirschman's *The Passions and the Interests*, which argues that increasingly interest, as applied to the objectives of collectivities, and self-interest, as applied to personal objectives, came to be viewed as powerful antidotes to the passions and as correctives to the ineffectuality of reason in governing human behavior. According to Hirschman, the interests became almost a mode of salvation because they allowed people to understand the social order in terms that broke free of the traditional dyad of reason versus passion and enabled a reframing of the actual behavior of human beings with regard to other actors and objects.[5]

To illustrate the extent to which, by the 1740s, interest was assumed to mediate between passion and reason, one need only quote a few words from Lovelace, the libertine villain of Samuel Richardson's *Clarissa*. He utterly rejects the received idea that interest has a moderating force. He parodies the sense, by then clichéd, that passion can be subordinated to interest. He says of Clarissa's friend Anna Howe that she tells the heroine, *"it is in my interest to be honest*—INTEREST, fools!—I thought these girls knew that my *interest* was ever subservient to my *pleasure."*[6] This conflation of interest and pleasure by Lovelace, in a novel intimately known to Laclos as he wrote *Les Liaisons dangereuses*, sums up the gesture taken by his heroine and hero, the Marquise de Merteuil and the Vicomte de Valmont.

Intérêt is a recurrent term in Laclos's novel and the word itself actually appears 49 times—occasionally in the ordinary sense of being attentive to something, but on several other occasions meaning engagement concerned with one's own benefit. Yet even as Laclos's Merteuil and Valmont echo the Lovelacean gesture by refusing the idea that interest rules their passions, they set out to manage the interests of others. They manipulate the mode of interest in defining a set of game-oriented aims of their own, and in this they approach the concerns and strategies, if not the outcomes, envisioned by rational-choice theorists. Later, I will explore how they deceive themselves into accepting heuristics that are not actually rational. At this juncture it is important to recognize that Valmont and Merteuil are very much aware of the notion of interest and strive to turn it to their own advantage—against the interests of their victims. Merteuil's stance becomes entirely explicit in her scandalous manifesto addressed to Valmont.[7] They willingly accept collateral damage to incidental players. They set out to be analysts or second-order observers of the action and to govern their own behavior by rational management. In many ways they illustrate a variant on La Rochefoucauld's statement that disinterestedness itself is permeated by interest: the very detachment that characterizes their scheming cannot in the end efface their passions.

Perhaps the eighteenth-century name most associated with the kind of manipulations in which our hero and heroine engage was that of Bernard Mandeville, who elevated self-interest to the role of an engine capable of producing positive material outcomes for the individual and society—and even positive moral outcomes for both. Mandeville insists that larger benefits, including the function of markets, derive from self-interested actions, the ethics and morality of which are irrelevant to the greater good. He illustrated this, for instance, with his fable of the sugar traders Decio and Alcander, who deceive each other to their mutual economic benefit. Hypocrisy became for Mandeville an essential social virtue—a system for comprehending self-interest as a mode of disinterestedness for the betterment of society.[8]

An early episode in *Les Liaisons dangereuses* seems tailored to illustrate the Mandevillean idea that self-interest can be served by hypocrisy. We will see later how this fits into the overall picture in Laclos's novel. Valmont finds a way to advance his seduction of Madame de Tourvel, a pure wife of large religious scruples. Knowing that her servant is watching, Valmont hypocritically saves some villagers from destitution with a handsome gift of money. They gather around him, saying "Let us fall at the feet of this image of God." To Valmont's surprise, he himself is overcome with "unwonted but delicious emotion" as tears gather in his eyes and, echoing Richardson's Pamela, he finds himself "astonished at the pleasure to be derived from doing good" (Letter 21). The villagers gain materially. Valmont gains emotionally. Hypocrisy serves the larger good. But it also advances Valmont's seduction of Madame de Tourvel.[9]

Valmont and Merteuil combine the kind of self-management that Mandeville treats as hypocrisy with the kind of rational manipulation that we now view as part of rational choice theory. As Hirschman says, the value of interest lay in its being self-centered while including elements of rational calculation.[10] Thus, Valmont and Merteuil are engaging in a diabolical parody of the role envisioned for interest and self-interest during the period. They define a set of interests contractually agreed upon between themselves and then use their reason to manipulate the perceived self-interests of others in order to gain outcomes favorable to themselves. The crucial underlying principle is that the combination of their interests and their reason can moderate their own passions to such an extent that they are able to play their games against others while remaining themselves immune to the passions, if not to pleasure.

II

I enjoy paradox and I am a skeptic, so I have asked myself what rational choice theory might have to say about unreason. One way to think about rational choice theory is as a way of managing unreason or even of mobilizing unreason to advance the cause of the rational management of choice. Some rational choice theorists, including Jon Elster, have gone so far as to explore the role of emotion in shaping or improving the functioning of choice—even rational choice—in the world. My interest here, rather, is to explore how rational choice can be undermined and how the positive force of self-interest can be rendered impossible or irrelevant by the play of emotion. Can the two ever act together? I shall turn later to Max Weber's theories, which suggest that they may.

Laclos's novel is paradigmatic because we see in it not just the age-old conflict between reasonable and emotional motives, but a story in which the two principal actors consciously manage their actions following a protoscientific version of strategic thinking devised by themselves. They take on the traits of second-order observers or analysts within the fiction of the novel. They comprehend the primary action from a superior position within the narrative. We as readers are placed as third-order observers who, thanks to the epistolary form, hover between engagement with the fictional world of the novel and a perspective outside. Valmont and Merteuil eventually approach this third-order position. While watching the players manipulate the system, we are forced into a hyperanalytic apprehension of the action, in which sheer technical fascination supplants our absorption in the emotional plight of the characters. The strong alliance created between the reader and the novel's two leading figures virtually forces us into the position of third-order rational-choice analysts. We become rational-choice theorists *avant la lettre*.[11]

It seems that Laclos may have been ahead of the game as a proto-rational-choice theorist. Although many speculations about probabilistic understanding in moral, ethical, and judicial affairs were undertaken during the eighteenth century (the Marquis de Condorcet, for instance, tried to apply probabilistic thinking to judicial practice), the sense that the calculus of probability might govern practical human decisions was not typical. Insurance brokers and annuity writers, for instance, were slow to bring into practice the findings of mathematicians—findings specifically about their fields of business. The idea that we might govern our lives strictly by rational, probabilistic gaming, as Valmont and Merteuil attempt, seems to have been radical for its time—even leaving out their corrupt premises.[12]

Thomas C. Schelling, who was adventurous among the first twentieth-century analysts, treats rational choice theory as intimately related to ir-rationality. Derek Parfit, in turn, invokes Schelling's somewhat improbable example of the rational use of irrationality: in this thought experiment, armed extortionists invade the house of a rich man and threaten to kill his children one by one until he hands over the gold he keeps in a safe. Since he realizes that surrendering the gold will not save his children or himself, the only rational choice available to the rich man is to self-induce a hysteric fit of despair in which he demands that the children all be killed immediately because there is no hope for any of them anyway. The invaders lose their leverage and flee.[13]

Relevant here is Daniel Kahneman, Paul Slovic, and Amos Tversky's *Judgment under Uncertainty*, which documents numerous experiments showing that human beings typically make irrational decisions because they are guided by commonsense heuristics that they believe to be reason-able. These include: (1) faith in cause-and-effect sequences; (2) naïve esti-mations of probability; (3) over-prediction based on limited experience; and (4) misperception of their own capacity to control events.[14] In this context, one may view rational choice and game theories as strategies that aim at overriding the unreason of ordinary experience by marking out sys-tematic methods of decision-making. But in repressing the very unreason they work to transcend, these theories risk becoming yet another of Kahne-man and Tversky's heuristics. After all, the rich madman in Schelling's and Parfit's example makes the seemingly rational choice to induce an epi-sode of irrationality to deceive the intruders. One is reminded of Carl von Clausewitz, the great nineteenth-century theorist who saw war as a tool for diplomacy.[15] And, one could link rational choice and game theory to the Cold War, which Schelling's book openly theorizes. Brinksmanship was a version of rational choice theory codified in the 1950s. I shall return below to a later instance of this sort of thinking: Richard Nixon and Henry Kiss-inger's so-called "madman strategy," the goal of which was to persuade the Russians to press North Vietnam for peace by convincing them that Nixon was obsessive enough to use nuclear bombs.[16]

III

Having sketched in this background, I turn now to consider how two different historical love-systems play out in novels: in one, love is strin-gently and explicitly rule-bound; in the other, love is detached from rational management. These are, broadly speaking, the classic absolutist system in which marriage is an economically, socially, and politically motivated contract independent of love, and, second, the more modern system in which marriage follows upon romantic love—that is, upon what may seem real but may be called a phantasmatic ecstatic interpenetration of the passions of two subjects.[17] This is the kind of love that provokes war in Laclos's novel.

In the first system—at least during Europe's aristocratic absolutist era toward the end of which Laclos's novel plays out—sex no less than marriage was managed through rule-bound love affairs that were themselves tightly coupled to the power hierarchy of community politics. The royal court staged the most extreme and stylized versions. Loves that played out at the margins of these rules, and may seem on the surface to be modern in character, like that of Madame de La Fayette's Princesse de Clèves, in fact were rigidly contained by protocol and subordinated within a single system of norms. La Fayette's novel dramatizes the force by which the absolutist system contained passion within the conventions of courtship and marriage, while stretching the membrane of its power to an extreme limit. Some remarkable passages in La Fayette's novel show the technical signs of this stress in the system by using the innovative technique of free indirect discourse to narrate thought. These appear in the text just as the Princesse struggles to contain her love for Nemours within the conventional chastity of thought and action that defines spousal duty to her husband.[18]

The romantic love system, by contrast with the contractual, runs in tandem with what Niklas Luhmann calls modern functional differentiation. Subject-centered romantic love goes hand-in-hand with the individual mobility required by modern societies, in which hierarchy is based on organizational function. Paradoxically, the untethered irrationality of modern romantic love enables functionally differentiated societies to operate, precisely because the love-system becomes relatively autonomous from other social systems. This love serves to cut individuals loose from formal social networks: they become free operators in both a modern marriage market and a functionally differentiated economic system. Individualism increases as large-scale family ties decrease; the demand for specialized skills and functions follows market demand and supplants traditional social networks.[19]

The subjective manifestation of this romantic love is of an absolute, profound, and irrefutable incapacity to make rational choices. At least in its idealized (or ideological) version, this self-surrender works in modernity like a secular version of the empowerment that Luther attributed to his surrender through faith to God's mercy. It enables bold, improvisatory actions in a mobile and unpredictable world and, as such, goes in tandem with Max Weber's sense of the professional "calling" as an enabling force. Love in the private realm and the professional calling in the economic domain are the engines of productivity.

Conflict between the old and new systems of love and marriage is the force that actuates the plot of a famous novel that shares the formal perfection of Laclos's work without its overt conceptual complexity. I have in mind Jane Austen's *Pride and Prejudice*. Austen puts all of the machinery of the managed-marriage system into play. The Bennet family will lose its wealth and social position without profitable marriages for their daughters. A highly placed and rich gentleman, Mr. Bingley, is the object of Mrs. Bennet's main strategy to profit from the marriage of Jane, her most beautiful daughter. The aristocratic Mr. Darcy—already destined to marry his socially well-placed cousin, even before the story begins—is the plot's candidate to marry the heroine, Elizabeth Bennet. I assign Darcy's candidacy structurally to the plot itself because no character—certainly not Darcy and Elizabeth themselves—conceives that they could be future partners until deep into the story. The planned marriage of Darcy to his cousin is an unmistakable marker that the absolutist system is operative. Elizabeth, on the other hand, is at the largest plausible social remove from Darcy within the plot's requirement that the two be able to meet socially. Ultimately, their pivotal encounter, at his noble house and its environs in Derbyshire, is depicted as an accident. In the immediate aftermath of her angry refusal when he first proposes after that chance encounter, Darcy serves up a litany of reasons against their union straight out of the lexicon of managed marriage. All of these reasons were overcome, he says, by his love. The only force to countervail managed marriage is an ecstatic love that can be assuaged solely in romantic marriage.

When Darcy's aunt, Lady Catherine de Bourgh, descends unannounced on the Bennet house, her purpose is to declare the impossibility of her nephew's marriage to Elizabeth on the ground that every kind of social decency forbids it, no less than does a preexisting lineal alliance with his cousin. Lady Catherine's clinching argument against the marriage centers on *interest*. She declares against a union between Elizabeth and Darcy, "Because honour, decorum, prudence, nay, interest forbid it. Yes, Miss Bennet, interest; for do not expect to be noticed by his family or friends, if you wilfully act against the inclinations of all."[20] But ecstatic love of course prevails over managed marriage and countless misunderstandings. A crucial passage in Austen's *Emma* underlines the point that true romantic love is without interest, when Mr. Knightley marvels at the luck of the wealthy, feckless Frank Churchill in securing the "disinterested love" of Jane Fairfax despite her many trials: "for Jane Fairfax's character vouches for her disinterestedness."[21]

In the romance of *Pride and Prejudice*, romantic love brings with it wealth far beyond the hopes of the petty manager—Mrs. Bennet—and also dashes the hopes of her spiritual double, Lady Catherine. Lest we miss the point, however, Elizabeth's friend Charlotte Lucas, having accepted marriage to the obsequious and officious Mr. Collins, who ultimately will inherit the Bennet property by entail, delivers a long statement to Elizabeth on the merits of rational marriage and the familial limitations that force her to yield to interest as an alternative to romance. Nor does Austen fail to show the dangers of love as passion, for the brilliantly intertwined plot of Elizabeth's sister Lydia's elopement with Darcy's prime enemy, Wickham, reveals the evil of passion run amok, precisely because it is not governed by the rigid frameworks of the managed system. This elopement also occasions Darcy's philanthropic rescue of Lydia, which proves his worth to Elizabeth.

IV

It may be helpful at this point to recall that the two main characters in Laclos's novel are the Marquise de Merteuil and the Vicomte de Valmont. She is a secretly libertine young widow, and he a younger, infamously licentious playboy. They have been long-term lovers and are now co-conspirators who may or may not resume their affair. His chief victim is a ravishingly chaste wife known as Madame, la Présidente de Tourvel. Merteuil writes a long letter in this epistolary novel about her realization as a young widow that she could rationally master both her own passions and the classic love system in order to gain independence, pleasure, and power for herself through choice. It is her manifesto (Letter 81). Presenting a public facade of unassailable virtue based on her reading of conventional moralists, she ranges through love affairs that allow her to shape the destiny of others by knowing their secrets, while guarding her own. By her own account, she learns how to do so from novelists and philosophers—the then-current purveyors of rational choice theories.

It is hard to have fun alone, however, and when the novel begins, Merteuil already is forming a fresh alliance with the Vicomte. They have been physically passionate in the past but have turned for a time to a more delicious intercourse as co-conspirators in a plot Merteuil has designed for revenge against a range of enemies, especially the Comte de Gercourt, a former lover of Merteuil. The seduction of the innocent fifteen-year-old Cécile de Volanges will be their means to this end. Madame de Tourvel is Valmont's concurrent object of passion, a venture in sexual conquest that fascinates Merteuil but lies to the side of her grand plan. Valmont's reward for executing these more than cynical conquests will be a return to Merteuil's bed. As we shall see, when he has succeeded and demands his reward, war breaks out between our conspirators. Our antihero is killed in a duel. Our antiheroine is disgraced by letters he makes public on his deathbed (including her infamous manifesto) and, in a surprising allegorical gesture, her face is ravaged by smallpox.

What destroys Merteuil and Valmont's rational management of the classic system of love separated from marriage? What leads them to war? They have been supremely successful players at a secret second-order game based on their rational analysis of the implicit rules and strategies of the first-order love system accepted by their society. They have executed their choices to perfection. They have gained the pleasures—admittedly vicious ones—of sex with and superiority over their dupes—along with the power socially to destroy others at will. All the while, they enjoy rank and prestige in a ritualized aristocratic society that continually threatened tedium for those of its members who lacked actual posts at court. Add the frisson that each knows enough about the other's crimes to bring prison or exile down on their heads, and you have a transgressive scene that brought scandal upon Laclos and his book in 1782, and left an air of danger around the novel until quite recent times.

The two players are destroyed because their game depends on an absolute rational detachment that they cannot maintain to the end, even with diverting respites for pleasure. No doubt, Valmont may along the way enjoy writing letters on the back of a young prostitute—a famous scene. Merteuil may savor a complex bed trick arranged to humiliate a military fop. Likewise, nowadays, a skilled poker player may savor reducing another person to nothing through a brilliantly executed bluff without for an instant losing the count and continuing to play the hand according to strict analysis.

Merteuil's infamous manifesto reveals in a detached manner both the social world she inhabited during marriage and the quest for power and pleasure that she pursued thereafter. It is no less similar if less sustained than the analytic manifestos from Valmont. Merteuil's manifesto assumes a degree of control and predictability of causation that may itself be understood as a delusion, or as a heuristic, in light of Kahneman and Tversky's findings. Merteuil's system for putting herself in charge as a woman is itself rule-bound and relies for its effectiveness on being lodged like a Chinese box within the broader system of predictable rules, reactions, and conventions that govern her milieu. In short, she depends on everyone else in her social order to perform the rules of their game perfectly, or, at least, to be manipulated into doing so by her skilled hands. The classical prose style of the novel—a French so disciplined, simple, and rigorous that it recalls Racine's severity—works to signal that the managed social system is in play. In historical reality, of course, the actors and the audience were in the midst of a revolution in love systems.

Merteuil lives the fiction that love can be managed through rational choice, that the most irrational of experiences can be staged as if they conformed to a clearly understood set of societal rules and thus brought into the domain of interest as governed by choice. Thus, when we initially learn that Merteuil and Valmont were lovers, and when they say they loved each other, we must understand that they actually speak of passion and are working within the paradoxical old system. Within this system, the more extreme the passion, the more strict the regulation it will evoke in terms of discretion, delimitation, and the understanding that it will have a self-contained and secret history or story. It is no accident that the genre called the secret history was a leading type of fiction in the seventeenth century, during the heyday of absolutist marriage.

We see these assumptions played out in *La Princesse de Clèves*, where the tragedy is actuated by the husband's knowledge of a secret and the heroine's profound reaction to his discovery. In this paradoxical system, every lover is always already a former lover just as every person is always a potential lover. The system also had attributes that led to its own internal acceleration and intensification. In its normal unfolding, with an affair between sophisticated lovers who knew and followed the rules, the system worked within the frame of conventional marriages. Merteuil and Valmont, who of course are not married, introduce a mutation by gaming a system that is itself a game: they join in an alliance to manipulate others in part to gain specific goals—such as humiliating an enemy—but largely for the displaced erotic pleasure of displaying their manipulations of the system to each other.

The old marriage system had a certain stability, but our players' gaming of its rules is intrinsically unstable, because, like all games, it may be imperfectly played by the dim-witted or inexperienced. Or imperfectly played by the impassioned. The gamesters Merteuil and Valmont make judgments on the basis of insufficient data, to mention another of Kahneman and Tversky's heuristics, assuming that they can predict the playing out of their maneuvers even though their private game is parasitical and therefore intrinsically unstable. This instability can be understood historically and sociologically as a function of changes in the love system as Luhmann accounts for it. They are gaming the game at the edge of the historical period in which the old set of rules pertained. The condition of possibility for their gaming might even be seen as itself the breakdown of that old system of managing marriage and love. That increasingly altered system had included strict protocols for the management of passion, protocols now being undermined by romantic love.

Valmont's ruthless management of the genesis and efflorescence of the Présidente's horribly destructive love ultimately positions him as a removed third-order actor playing out a script that has been given him by Merteuil. He has surrendered the second-order option of surveying the plot as a field open to his own improvisations. The moment he moves away from equality with Merteuil as a player of the second order, he is doomed. At the fatal climax of Valmont's affair—as his genuine love for the Présidente becomes evident to Merteuil—she literally scripts the words to be spoken repeatedly when he breaks up with his ecstatic lover: "It is not my fault" (Letter 141). His contract with Merteuil has trumped his passion for Tourvel. Both conspirators are fatally weakened at this point, when she must script him in order to trust him and he must in effect become a reader of his own actions. They now move toward fourth-order positions, as defined by an infinite regress of observation without the control that before had marked their definition of the action. In a sense, they join us in attempting the role of rational-choice theorists. As I have noted, the emotional impact of the horrible destruction of the Présidente is defused or short-circuited for readers by these layers of observation. Even in Michelle Pfeiffer's brilliant film performance, it is hard as a viewer to enter into full empathy with the Présidente.[22] At the end of the novel, this house of cards—this system of second-, third-, fourth-order observations—collapses and Valmont and Merteuil become mere first-order actors deprived of dispassionate observation and their tools of manipulation. They move out of their roles as classical rational-choice theorists into the position of ordinary actors. Their alliance of interest—their impregnable treaty—collapses. At this pivotal moment, Valmont sends a letter to Merteuil asking whether "there is still any community of interest between us?" She immediately replies, quoting the question back to him word-for-word, and then warns, "Beware, Vicomte! Once I reply to that question, my reply will be irrevocable" (Letters 140 and 141).

V

How Merteuil and Valmont have come to this impasse is perhaps best understood with reference to the theories of Max Weber and his four-tiered account of rational orientation. He suggests that self-interest is served by "goal-oriented rationality," that is, by an approach to action in which the ends justify the means. Self-interest may also be served by what he calls "value-oriented rationality," that is, by the sort of principled behavior that might, for example, cause a soldier to go into battle or a captain to go down with his ship. In our novel, Tourvel also fits this profile. In value-oriented rationality, for Weber, deep-seated emotional commitments are managed through rational consideration and can be quite methodical and systematic. Self-interest for Weber, which is part of a separate set of categories in his work, combines aspects of goal-oriented rationality and value-oriented rationality. We can view Merteuil and Valmont as having defined for themselves a set of artificially contrived values in which they are autonomous and able to exert extreme power over others by manipulating the values of the social system that surrounds them. In Weber's terms, their self-interest combines dimensions of value-oriented rationality and goal-oriented rationality.

Weber can help us to see that the embrace of values, even if those values include the pursuit of pleasure, can still be defined, maintained, and managed by systematic and rational methods. Valmont sums up such a rationalistic stance when he declares of Madame de Tourvel, early in the novel, that, "it has become necessary for me to have this woman, so as to save myself from the ridicule of being in love with her" (Letter 4). More broadly, since Merteuil and Valmont are characters in a novel, not real people, we may come to view them as instantiations of what Weber called "ideal types," which is to say that they are concrete indices of abstractions such as "goal-oriented rationality" and "value-oriented rationality." My story here, of course, is the story of Laclos's novel, in which the ability of the hero and heroine to engage in these orderly behaviors collapses. It does so in the face of an emotional crisis, which fits into Weber's four-tiered system, where affectual action and traditional action supplement the two rational kinds on which I have been focusing.[23]

So, considered in the frame of eighteenth-century theories that equate interest and rational calculation, and in the frame of Weber's modern theories, Valmont and Merteuil engage in rational games in order to achieve their goals through the shaping of irrational forces in others. But their failure can be understood more clearly in light of issues surrounding rational choice theory than, despite their value here, in light of eighteenth-century analyses of interest or even in view of Weber's.

The fatal flaw that brings down the game is that Valmont falls hopelessly into romantic love with the Présidente, Madame de Tourvel, just upon the completion of his most impossibly difficult, most extended, most ingenious, and most vicious seduction. This truly chaste woman submits after months of agony—for she has been relentlessly manipulated and does love him profoundly. She submits sexually when, in a clichéd strategy straight out of the plots of heroic drama or opera, he convinces her that he will kill himself if she does not. This variant on the Nixonian madman strategy clearly predates rational choice theory.

When Valmont seeks to collect his prize from Merteuil and describes his triumph in novelistic—even confessional—detail, she quickly sees in the romantic diction and style of his letter that he is in love with her rival (Letter 125 and following). Not in lust, not in the libertine quest to expand his repertory of passionate pleasure, but in ecstatic modern romantic love. In an ironic gesture, Laclos assigns an account of this kind of love to a young and romantic lover, the Chevalier Danceny. His letter to the Marquise declares: "only the voluptuary . . . working always according to plan, is able to regulate his progress and control his resources and foresee the outcome from a distance. True love does not allow considerations and calculations. It uses our feelings to distract us from our thoughts; its power is never so strong as when we are least aware of it; and it is by stealth and in silence that it entangles us in the web that is as invisible as it is indestructible" (Letter 148). Here we see that romantic love is itself a system. But Valmont is so enmeshed in the old game with Merteuil, and so unable to recognize the fate that has entangled him in love, that he accepts her challenge to break off the affair with Madame Tourvel *before* gaining his wages (for that is what Merteuil's sexual submission would be). He acts in this way, against his own interests, to prove that he is still bound by their game, not by love of the Présidente.

The break is to be accomplished brutally by Valmont's catechistic invocation, fully scripted by Merteuil, of the many reasons, ranging from boredom to continuing lust for another woman, that he must end his affair with his newly found, deeply felt love. Each reason is to be followed by the phrase, "It is not my fault" (Letter 141). The strategy is cruel, not least because it echoes religious incantations dear to the devout Madame de Tourvel. Counter to Valmont's own deep feelings of love, it is so successful that she believes him and actually dies of a broken heart. Stephen Frears's film transmutes Valmont's repeated phrase to "It is beyond my control," scripting a modern perspective that signals the surrender that Merteuil anticipates.[24]

Valmont is trapped by the binary logic of rational-choice games in which there is always a dominant position that wins over other possible but strategically inferior positions or choices. Jean-Pierre Dupuy has shown that this binary, which underlies so much of modern rational choice theory, is intrinsically flawed because it forecloses the multivariable realities produced by human bonds, especially the collective social order of affect. One can be in the dominant position, as Merteuil is and as Valmont seeks to be, but one can fail to realize options outside the game or, as we may say in historical terms, the emergence of new games with more variables. Laclos already is exploring the limitations of game-oriented choice.[25]

In the final pages of *Les Liaisons dangereuses*, the conditions of possibility for the game have vanished. Valmont is still in love with Tourvel and Merteuil knows it. Further, in a twist that recalls René Girard's plot of mimetic desire, Merteuil's old-style erotic relationship with Valmont morphs into jealous love. The more he presses for his wages, the more jealous she becomes of his love for her rival. The more he insists, the more, as Merteuil says, he resembles a husband, and she had long ago resolved never to have another of those. Dupuy notes that this letter shows Valmont to have lost the possibility of making the dominant move in his game with Merteuil. She writes, "Oh well, I shall do your reasoning for you. Either you have a rival or you don't. If you have one, you must set out to please, so as to be preferred to him; if you don't have one, you must still please so as to obviate the possibility of having one. In either case the same principle is to be followed" (Letter 152). Merteuil is describing the "sure thing principle" that rides in tandem with the dominant position in games.[26] But Merteuil, who was the perfect player when allied with Valmont, now makes the mistake implicit in the binary of dominant and inferior. She fails to see that there are options outside the parameters of their game. As the Marquis de Sade's Dolmancé declares, "the heart deceives, because it is never anything but the expression of the mind's miscalculations."[27]

This bitter standoff ends with Valmont's explicit challenge to Merteuil that she submit or go to war. She chooses war. It appears at first that the kind of war Merteuil has in mind is the kind of limited war that paralleled the managed love system and marriage arrangements in absolutist society. By the rules of her game, she might have submitted cynically. It surely would not be the first time for her to do so as part of a long-term strategy. Later, she could move against Valmont. In fact, Merteuil has actuated the entire plot of the novel by setting up a scheme of managed revenge against a former lover. But no. The game is over and the players are destroyed because they love one another in a way surprising and incalculable for them. Their private version of modern, absolute war breaks out. They make the irrational choice.

Luhmann describes the emotions as products of internal crises in psychic systems or, as we might say, consciousness. Psychic systems work to maintain their own coherence and continuity. They are, for Luhmann, fundamentally like Locke's "understanding." That is, they are self-governed by their own intrinsic capacities to absorb and process information and to sustain and reproduce the chains of cause and effect that their own internal coherence requires. Luhmann accounts for emotions as the immune function of psychic systems. That is, emotion emerges when systems of consciousness are overloaded or confused. Emotions, thus, are not "representations that refer to the environment but *internal* adaptations to *internal* problem situations in the psychic system that concern the ongoing production of the system's elements by the system's elements. Emotions are not necessarily formed in an occasional and spontaneous manner; one can be more or less disposed to an emotion-laden reaction."[28] Emotions are, instead, effects of process in the psychic system. For this reason, they are transient and unreliable. They also can be socially conditioned and, as one may infer here and from Luhmann's *Love as Passion*, historically conditioned. It is now possible to understand romantic love as an ecstatic interpenetration of the passions of two subjects.

Luhmann allows us to theorize the conditions under which rational choice, and even rational choice theory itself, may be highly mobile, historically.[29] How the passion of love is managed or becomes evident in different historical and cultural situations can vary phenomenologically. The example of *La Princesse de Clèves* illustrates a very powerful system for managing the passions—a system that normally contained them within social conventions and yet allowed the adventurous play of passion within the rigid structures of marriage. The breakdown occurs in La Fayette's novel because the Princesse's husband truly does love her and cannot recover from the blow of imagining that she loves someone else. She is doomed because neither her psychic system nor the social system she has internalized can process the overload. The breakdown that occurs in Laclos is located at a historical node between systems that renders impossible the management of passion either by accepting it in its modern version or by confining it in its classical version. Even Merteuil is infected by the demonic double of the modern version of passion, which erupts in her jealousy of Valmont and the Présidente. Toward the end of the novel she displays jealousy as a version of mimetic desire that contrasts with the revenge-motivated plot with which she actuates the whole drama at the beginning of the work.

Laclos shows Valmont and Merteuil, in my analysis, on the cusp between two systems for managing the sexual impulse. They are hyperrationalists and brilliant players at the end of an epoch. When environmental conditions change around them—including their own responses to these conditions— their rational system assumes qualities of a doomsday machine.

IV. Enlightenment Frameworks

Rhetoricality

On the Modernist Return of Rhetoric

With David E. Wellbery

Roman architects employed materials and methods of construction utterly alien to the Greeks. Instead of the static post and lintel system that stood behind virtually all Greek architecture, the Romans used concrete and brick to enclose space in dynamic membranes based upon circular and spherical forms: the arch, the dome, the vault. At the same time, the Romans brilliantly integrated into their immense structures the Hellenistic system of columnar orders—orders that seemed to manifest proportions fundamental to geometry, to the human body, and to nature itself. Using the orders as visual analogies to human scale, the Romans anchored vast edifices within the same perceptual framework as the observer. The Pantheon's gorgeously encrusted marble interior testifies that the Romans employed the orders in a full, coherent, and systematic way as part of a figurative vocabulary, as devices to communicate the relationship of human proportion to monumental space.

Greek and Roman societies were differently constituted yet bound together in a visual tradition that continued deep into the Middle Ages. Once powerfully reformulated during the Italian Renaissance, this same tradition defined European architecture until eclecticism, historicism, and exoticism emerged during the later Enlightenment and Romantic periods. From this point onward, Greek and Roman classicism came increasingly to be viewed as regional or historical styles—like the Egyptian, the Chinese, the Persian—from among which architectural choices might be made. Classicism ceased to be *the* style and became *a* style. Even though residual, and often highly prestigious, use of the orders continued in the nineteenth- and early twentieth-century official architecture associated with the École des Beaux

Arts, the introduction of new structural materials such as cast iron and, above all, the prodigious increase of scale that typifies buildings of the industrial era ultimately toppled the orders. Their isolated revival as token elements in today's so-called postmodern architecture merely calls attention to the fact of their demise. When classical architectural forms return on the contemporary scene, their mode of existence is fundamentally different—despite outward similarities of appearance—from that which characterized them in antiquity and in premodern Europe. Only a formalism blinded by its own abstractness could overlook this historical transformation.

In this essay, we shall make an analogous argument regarding rhetoric as a tradition of discursive architecture and adornment, which, like the Greco-Roman paradigms of spatial organization, dominated the production, interpretation, teaching, and transmission of speech and writing in Europe from antiquity to the Enlightenment and the Romantic period. Even more clearly than in postmodernist citations of classical architectural forms, one can observe today a *return* of rhetorical inquiry, a resurgence of intellectual interest in the issues treated by classical and postclassical theoreticians of rhetoric. But returns and repetitions, as Kierkegaard and Gilles Deleuze have shown, are not reproductions of the same.[1] A temporal hiatus separates and distinguishes them from their original instance or reference. The contemporary return of rhetoric presupposes, through its very structure as return, an end of rhetoric, a discontinuity within tradition, and an alteration that renders the second version of rhetoric, its modernist-postmodernist redaction, a new form of cultural practice and mode of analysis. To understand the significance of rhetoric today is to understand why and in what ways it is discontinuous with its past.[2]

Although classical rhetoric followed a historical course different in myriad details from that of architectural orders, the broad outlines correlate. The discipline of rhetoric—adapted through a wide range of reformulations to the specific requirements of Greek, Roman, Medieval, and Renaissance societies—dominated European education and discourse, whether public or private, for more than two thousand years. We can merely glance at the rhetorical conduct of thought and speech during this protracted epoch. We shall concentrate instead on the two-phased period—the phases styled here in drastic abbreviation as those of the Enlightenment and Romanticism—that brought about the end of classical rhetoric as the dominant system of education and communication. We locate the factors determining rhetoric's demise in a bundle of social and cultural transformations that occurred, roughly speaking, between the seventeenth and nineteenth centuries. The various factors that caused, or accompanied, the demise of rhetoric merged into two major historical trends: the first banished rhetoric from the domain of theoretical and practical discourse; the second, from that of imaginative or aesthetic discourse.

We begin by outlining the historical factors that contributed to the end of rhetoric. This historical construction then points us to a thesis delineating rhetoric's modernist return. The specific shape of this return—and thus the specific mode of existence of the new rhetoric—can be grasped only with reference to the end that preceded it. In fact, the rebirth of rhetoric can take place only when those factors that conditioned its cultural death are themselves eliminated. Modernism presents a cultural frame that, by contrast with those of the Enlightenment and Romanticism, is hospitable to, and even requires, a reinvigoration of the rhetorical. But, as compared with its classical antecedent, this rhetoric is radically altered. These alterations we explore in a concluding survey of the premises of some exemplary modern disciplines. The return of rhetoric is a return with a difference, a difference that resonates to the foundations of discursive practice.

I. The End of Rhetoric: A Historical Sketch

In tracing the demise of rhetoric, or rather in highlighting some of its essential features, we distinguish two large phases of historical development, the Enlightenment and Romanticism. These epochal concepts designate major tendencies in the post-Renaissance world of European culture that exploded the hegemony of the classical rhetorical tradition and created the historical gap following which a return or repetition of rhetoric—not its continuation—becomes possible. Our use of the terms "Enlightenment" and "Romanticism" should not be taken to imply a typology of cultural epochs nor to suggest an all-too-linear logic of succession. On the contrary, the various cultural developments we shall collect beneath these two familiar terms are complexly interlocked, and their effects are visible up to the present day. This point holds also for what we term the classical rhetorical tradition. Although we argue that this tradition effectively ceased, we of course notice that rhetoric maintained itself in numerous residual forms throughout the very centuries that emptied it of cultural centrality.

Classical rhetoric survives today in strangely contracted form as a subject taught in universities. It is contracted because so much of the terrain over which it held absolute sway during the two millennia between Aristotle and Bacon has now been appropriated by other disciplines: linguistics, information theory, stylistics, literary criticism, sociology, communications, marketing, public relations. From its earliest appearance in Grecian Sicily to its residual influence on secondary curricula of the nineteenth and twentieth centuries, the discipline of rhetoric attended to the compilation of instructional synopses often entitled "The Art of Rhetoric." At first, rhetoricians dealt with the performative units of discourse—with such parts of an orator's presentation as his exordium, his relation of facts, his argumentation, his digressive illustration of proof, his conclusion. Later, in imitation of poetics, they treated the local phenomena of sentence structure and style, describing the schemes of thought and the figures of speech that might be employed as devices of persuasion. Plato and Aristotle broadened the discipline to include the psychology, sociology, and ethics of communication and, above all, extended its descriptive typology to embrace the immense range of protological and quasilogical formulations that characterize language use in public spaces. Thus, to classical rhetoric eventually belonged the description and theorization of all aspects of discourse not comprehended by the more delimited formulations of grammar and logic, the other two divisions of the so-called trivium within which knowledge about discursive practice was distributed.

Rhetoric began as a codification of oratorical usage. It survived as an extraordinarily long-lived theory of verbal action in part because it worked to account for behavior in the vast, contingent realm of human dialogue. No less importantly, the early institutionalization of rhetoric within the educational curriculum assured that the ability to perform according to its principles in council chambers or legislatures, in legal disputes, or in public oratory aimed at praise and blame (later to include sermons in church) served as a marker of authority and social standing. The "overcoding" that Umberto Eco finds characteristic of rhetorical speech may signify, for instance, the seriousness of a topic, an occasion, or a cause.[3] But this overcoding points, above all, to the speaker's capacity to employ it. Rhetorical speech marks, and is marked by, social hierarchy.

Rhetorical speech adheres to power and property. Indeed, Cicero tells us that Aristotle traced the origin of codified rhetoric to a time, following the expulsion of the tyrants (467 BC), when confusion over the title to confiscated property formerly held by returning exiles led the claimants to employ the expert assistance of Corax and Tisias. These Sicilians no doubt wrote speeches for their clients to memorize but also devised general rules of practice that Corax set down in his, the first known, handbook or "art" of rhetoric.[4] As a specialized system of knowledge acquired, through

formal education, in order to maintain property and negotiate social interaction, the art of rhetoric discriminates among audiences according to rank,
education, and social character. The orator will address equals in the legisla-
ture or judges in the court of law differently from the crowd in the forum.

Rhetoric is an art of positionality in address. Audiences are characterized
by status, age, temperament, education, and so forth. Speakers are imper-
sonators who adapt themselves to occasions in order to gain or maintain
position. Thus the bond of classical rhetoric to speech itself, as opposed
to writing, betokens the place of rhetoric in the physically demonstrative
social systems that so powerfully institutionalized its doctrines: city-state
democracy and its republican redactions, as well as aristocracy. The cultural
hegemony of rhetoric as a practice of discourse, as a doctrine codifying
that practice, and as a vehicle of cultural memory, is grounded in the social structures of the premodern world. Conceived in its broadest terms,
then, the demise of rhetoric coincides with that long and arduous historical
process that is often termed modernization: the replacement of a symbolic-
religious organization of social and cultural life by rationalized forms, the
gradual shift from a stratificational differentiation of society to one that
operates along functional axes.[5]

The antirhetorical bent of modernization shows itself first of all in the
Enlightenment. The general feature of Enlightenment that contravenes inherited rhetorical tradition is the development, in various domains, of a
mode of discourse conceived as neutral, nonpositional, and transparent.
Nowhere is this tendency more apparent than in the emergence of science,
the most powerful innovation of the post-Renaissance world, a force that
has transformed with dizzying rapidity and thoroughness the shape of life
in Europe and, more recently, beyond. From its beginnings, science relied
on the convention of a putatively true and undistorted—that is, arhetorical—depiction of natural states of affairs. Bacon's *Novum organum*, one of
the foundational texts for modern scientific thinking, variously attacks the
practices of rhetoric. The critique of the *idoli fori*, the idols of the marketplace, betrays in particular this aspect of Bacon's program: his denunciation
of the illusions of a discourse that is measured only by its persuasive appeal
within the shifting contexts of popular whims, antagonisms, and power
ploys. His polemic mirrors central features of Plato's (or Socrates's) attack
on the Sophists, those purveyors of rhetorical tricks and marketeers of sem-
blance, power, and prestige. But whereas Plato establishes dialectical ascent
to the realm of suprasensible ideas as the alternative to rhetoric, Bacon en-
visions an arhetorical discourse that would ground itself in the empirical

givens of nature. "The true end, scope or office of knowledge," he writes in *Valerius terminus: Of the Interpretation of Nature*, "consist[s] not in any plausible, delectable, reverend or admired discourse, or any satisfactory arguments, but in effecting and working, and in discovery of particulars not revealed before." This adherence to observable givens leads to "the happy match between the mind of man and the nature of things."[6]

The new science envisioned by Bacon bespeaks a shift in the relationships of power that define discourse. Scientific discourse is no longer embedded within the array of relative power positions that characterizes a stratified or hierarchical social structure; it withdraws from this interpersonal fray and takes as its opposite nature itself, over which it endeavors to establish a total command.[7] The subject who holds this new form of power is no longer an individual leader or hegemonic group, but rather mankind in general, a neutral or abstracted subject, a role that can be represented by whoever attains the neutrality requisite for exercising it. Not until the twentieth century would this universal subject of inquiry be reparticularized as an amalgam of theoretical paradigms, scientific institutions, and sociopolitical positionality.

The withdrawal of scientific discourse from the rhetorical fray of feudal society is strikingly exemplified in the work of Bacon's Italian counterpart Galileo, the founder of the mathematical strand of scientific inquiry that dominates the modern world. Galileo's life has been mythologized as the heroic battle of the scientific spirit against religious dogma and oppression, the tragic encounter of the old world with the new. Although this has proved a persuasive legitimating myth, we know today that Galileo operated as a skillful strategist within a complex network of political and religious alliances. But this very strategic endeavor—realized, inevitably, through the tactics of rhetoric—allows us to measure the gulf that came to separate the rhetorical tradition from the discourse of modern science. In 1610, Galileo published, under the protection of his ruler, *Sidereus nuncius* (*The Starry Messenger*), in which he announced his construction of a telescope and reported on some of the research conducted with that instrument. The text contains two parts, a dedication to Galileo's patron, Cosimo II de Medici, and the actual account of the scientific observations. Here is a brief passage from the dedication:

> Indeed, the Maker of the stars himself has seemed by clear indications to direct that I assign to these new planets Your Highness's famous name in preference to all others. For just as these stars, like children worthy of their sire, never leave the side of Jupiter by any appreciable distance, so (as indeed who does not know?)

clemency, kindness of heart, gentleness of manner, splendor of royal blood, no-
bility in public affairs, and excellency of authority and rule have all fixed their
abode and habitation in Your Highness. And who, I ask once more, does not
know that all these virtues emanate from the benign star of Jupiter, next after
God as the source of all things good? Jupiter; Jupiter, I say, at the instant of Your
Highness's birth, having already emerged from the turbid mists of the horizon
and occupied the midst of the heavens, illuminating the eastern sky from his
own royal house, looked out from that exalted throne upon your auspicious
birth and poured forth all his splendor and majesty in order that your tender
body and your mind (already adorned by God with the most noble ornaments)
might imbibe with your first breath that universal influence and power.[8]

The dedication reflects and refers to a hierarchical situation—a vertical
chain of power positions—and treats this distribution of powers as its sole
and complete reality. Within this utterly social and particular frame (everything hinges on the proper name of Cosimo), the text situates itself and
performs its operation by employing all the strategies of classical epideictic
rhetoric. In order to praise it simulates a drama of praise enacted across a
chain of eloquent figurations that draw on astrology, classical mythology,
and Christianity, and that even refashion the stars (that is, the moons of
Jupiter whose discovery the report will announce) as tokens within this
game of suasion.

When we turn to the properly scientific portion of Galileo's text, however, we find no such rhetorical saturation, no overcoding of the discourse.
A new mode of address has emerged here that differs from the old in far
more than tone:

> The most easterly [star] was seven minutes from Jupiter and thirty seconds from
> its neighbor; the western one was two minutes away from Jupiter. The end stars
> were very bright and were larger than that in the middle, which appeared very
> small. The most easterly star appeared a little elevated toward the north from
> the straight line through the other planets and Jupiter. The fixed star previously
> mentioned was eight minutes from the western planet along the line drawn from
> it perpendicularly to the straight line through all the planets, as shown above.
>
> I have reported these relations of Jupiter and its companions with the fixed
> star so that anyone may comprehend that the progress of those planets, both in
> longitude and latitude, agrees exactly with the movements derived from plan-
> etary tables.[9]

In scientific reporting, the author (clearly a *writer* now since there is no
simulation of oral speech) and reader communicate without awareness of
differential social rank. On the contrary, their positions are mutually in-
terchangeable: the reader is addressed as the potential observer of what
the writer recounts as having himself observed. Perhaps we can even take

the telescope as the emblem of this derhetoricized situation. It is an instrument of vision, not of persuasion; it creates an abstract or asocial standpoint that can be assumed by anyone, and, as a matter of scientific convention, everyone who assumes that standpoint is functionally the "same" generalized observer, the same eye and I. Finally, the data the telescope supplies provide an absolute standard against which any discourse purporting to describe them can be checked and, if necessary, corrected. The *message* of *Sidereus nuncius* appears to come not from a personal speaker but from the stars themselves. Scientific discourse is arhetorical not merely because it is stylistically spare, unencumbered by the figures of eloquence, but more essentially because it incarnates a pragmatics that is entirely foreign to that of the hierarchized and relativized social field. Inevitably, therefore, once this discourse becomes culturally established, it draws in its wake a severe critique of the doctrine, practice, and institutions of rhetoric.

Such a critique gains full voice in Descartes, the founder, it is often said, of modern philosophy and a fascinated follower of Galileo's ups and downs. The autobiographical portion of the *Discourse on Method* unfolds a conversion narrative that frees the inquiring mind—the "I" of Descartes's text—from the errors and confusions of the past and opens up a futurity for the acquisition of certain knowledge. Part of the aberrant past Descartes repudiates is the institutionalization of knowledge as *eruditio* and the traditional form of schooling, which, among other things, rested on the teaching of rhetorical skills:

> I esteemed Eloquence most highly and I was enamoured of Poesy, but I thought that both were gifts of the mind rather than fruits of study. Those who have the strongest power of reasoning, and who most skillfully arrange their thoughts in order to render them clear and intelligible, have the best power of persuasion even if they can but speak the language of Lower Brittany and have never learned Rhetoric. And those who have the most delightful original ideas and who know how to express them with the maximum of style and suavity, would not fail to be the best poets even if the art of Poetry were unknown to them.[10]

Note here that Descartes rejects as useless and empty not only the doctrine and practice of rhetoric, but also the teaching of poetry as a rhetorical skill. His notion that poetic talent and imagination dwell solely within the inwardness of the subject anticipated by one hundred and fifty years the Romantic elimination of rhetoric as the basis of poetic theory. There is a reason for this historical prolepsis: the Cartesian cogito inaugurated the subject-centered philosophical and cultural discourse that would find its culmination in Romantic thought (Kant's transcendental synthesis of apperception,

Fichte's self-positing Absolute Ego, Hegel's notion of substance as subject). Perhaps we can grasp here the affinity between the Enlightenment and Romantic destructions of rhetoric. The cogito, the unshakable foundation of certainty, generates at once the impersonal or abstracted subject of science and the creative, self-forming subject of Romanticism. Once these subjective functions took command over the field of discourse and representation, rhetoric could no longer maintain its cultural predominance. Foundational subjectivity—be it the subject as *res cogitans* or as creative origin, as unique individual personality or as disinterested free agent within the political sphere—erodes the ideological premises of rhetoric.

The transformations we have been describing with reference to Galileo and Descartes had, by the mid-eighteenth century, extended beyond the reaches of speculative thought into the daily conduct of affairs temporal and spiritual. In England, for example, not only had legal theorists increasingly embraced probabilistic, broadly Cartesian thinking about questions of proof, but trial courts were also making practical changes, such as the admission of counsel for the defense, that presaged the development of those impersonal rules of evidence and consistently specified burdens of proof that distinguish modern criminal procedure. Previously, the English criminal trial had been what Sir Thomas Smith once called an "altercation." Accused and accuser confronted one another personally, without benefit of counsel for the prosecution or defense. Judges, unhampered by rules, freely intervened. The parties to the trial occupied rhetorical positions delineated in their own words according to whatever structuring principles they might choose to adopt. Evidence, too, was personal and rhetorically structured since direct testimony (including confession) was the chief basis of proof. Circumstantial evidence, including even inference based upon physical fact, was not fully probative. By the eighteenth century, legal theorists already had begun to embrace the kind of thinking that would lead nineteenth-century jurists actually to prefer circumstantial and inferential evidence over direct testimony. Increasingly, from the mid-eighteenth through the nineteenth centuries, English trials changed from personal, rhetorically governed exchanges to procedures in which plaintiff, defendant, judge, and counsel occupied impersonal, rule-governed positions. We still think of trials as places for high rhetoric, but the ancient forensic speech in fact holds little more than a residual place in the modern Anglo-American trial, almost as if to validate our exacting, impersonal trial procedures by the token inclusion of symbolic gestures that connect contemporary juridical practice with a venerable tradition. Precisely because they are rhetorical, the modern counsel's opening and closing statements (so significant in courtroom melodrama) are not structural features of the modern trial.[11]

Interestingly, as Alexander Welsh has shown, the discourses of law and natural religion embraced virtually identical forms of probabilistic thinking during the period when the changes just described were occurring in trial procedure. Matters of religion and of the spirit became subject to impersonal categories of proof. If, says Bishop Butler, we conduct every other aspect of our lives on the basis of probable inference, as in the wake of scientific empiricism perforce we must, why should we not found upon inference a belief in God as secure as our confidence in the existence of matter or of our own personal being? Is inference from circumstance not more persuasive than personal testimony of miraculous experience or scriptural revelation?[12]

These arhetorical tendencies in science, philosophy, religion, and law can be taken as emblematic of the Enlightenment as a whole. They bespeak a general movement toward representational neutrality that could be traced as well in such domains as theory of government, historiography, and psychology. In all these areas, especially across the eighteenth century, a model of critical communication emerged that stresses the neutrality and transparency of discourse and that, in consequence, throws off the rhetorical tradition. Discourse in the Enlightenment, we might say with Michel Foucault, took on a new existence. The effects of this massive cultural transformation can still be felt today. The thinkers of the Enlightenment, however, not only practiced this new discourse, but also developed its theory, a theory that in many cases coincided with the conception of Enlightenment itself. We have already mentioned Descartes, whose philosophy served as the foundation of the first major antirhetorical theory of language, the *Port-Royal Logic* of Arnauld and Nicole. In England, the temporal threshold is drawn somewhat later. Hobbes, the last great philosopher of absolutism, could still, despite his indebtedness to Descartes, compose an *Art of Rhetorick* whose every page reveals itself tributary to the classical tradition.[13]

This was no longer possible, however, for Locke. Not only does the founder of modern empiricism unleash, in the fourth book ("On Words") of his *Essay Concerning Human Understanding*, one of the most virulent antirhetorical tirades on record, he also presents there a "semiotics," or theory of language as sign, that is designed to eliminate the deceptions of rhetoric and to guarantee the transparency of discourse. Locke's was not the first but certainly one of the most influential in a long series of attempts to free language and thought from the confoundments of rhetoric. In Germany, the Enlightenment ideal of linguistic transparency, of a purely neutral representational medium, emerged in Leibniz's project of an *ars characteristica*, a philosophical calculus that would leave the deflections of human language behind in order to reproduce the language of things themselves. This dream, which in a variety of forms obsessed the entire eighteenth century, perhaps most fully exemplifies the removal of discourse from what we referred to above as the rhetorical fray. For, as Leibniz and later Herder well understood, such a perfected sign system would coincide exactly with the absolutely nonpositional mind of God.

Kant brought together the theory of Enlightenment and the theory of discourse. Enlightenment, in Kant's view, is a process of critical communication that unfolds within a free public sphere, a sphere of discourse separated from the particularist interests and pressures of political and religious institutions and authority. Here the subject speaks (more accurately, writes and publishes) as a "scholar," a free inquirer whose only guide is the light of impartial reason and whose addressee is the ideal person, "mankind." Within this sphere, ideas are circulated and submitted to criticism, to a kind of winnowing process that removes the chaff of error and in the end leaves nothing but the golden wheat of truth. Kant envisioned, in fact, a kind of intellectual market, but no longer the market of false opinion, varying whims, delusions, and conflicts in which the Sophists and rhetoricians were thought to perform their manipulations. Rather, this is the marketplace of Adam Smith, ordered by an invisible hand that inevitably makes the right selections, or, as in Kant, ordered by a transcendental reason that is everyone's and no one's: that is positionless and therefore arhetorical.[14]

The vehicle that carried Kant's public sphere toward its future of perpetual improvement was the institution of publishing, without which Enlightenment is unthinkable. One need only consider the great publishing enterprises of the period—foremost of all perhaps the *Encyclopédie* of d'Alembert and Diderot—or the expansion of literacy that occurred across the eighteenth century, with its proliferation not only of books but of learned and moral journals.[15] Practical and theoretical knowledge, not to speak of literature, were no longer tied to a situation of oratorical exchange, no longer simulated the scene of face-to-face contact. From midcentury on print established itself as the dominant medium of linguistic communication, reading became the passion of the age, and publishing statistics for the first time caught up with and surpassed the post-Gutenberg boom of the sixteenth century. This is another feature of the Enlightenment that caused rhetoric's demise, for rhetoric took its point of departure from the direct and oral encounters of classical civic life, and even as it maintained itself across the manuscript culture of the Middle Ages and into the first phase of modern print culture, it inevitably referred back to a face-to-face oratorical situation. All this disappeared with the Enlightenment, the first epoch to constitute itself as a culture of print. Rhetoric drowned in a sea of ink.

What the Enlightenment accomplished in the domains of theoretical and practical discourse, Romanticism achieved in the aesthetic domain. Only with Romanticism was rhetoric finally and thoroughly evacuated from the realm of imaginative expression. In fact, this very phrase—"imaginative expression"—reveals the impact of the Romantic revolution. Prior to the last decades of the eighteenth century, the concept of literature covered virtually all of writing; the breadth of its application was made possible by the overriding unity of rhetorical doctrine, which governed all of verbal production. With Romanticism, however, the concept of literature emerged that still today shapes the organization of disciplines within the university. Literature became imaginative literature, an autonomous field of discourse endowed with its unique inner laws and history.[16] Romanticism, in other words, set the paradigm for the postrhetorical production, interpretation, and historiography of literature, and in this sense brought on the second death of rhetoric.

One consequence of this cultural transformation is legible in Ernst Robert Curtius's elegiac monument, *European Literature and the Latin Middle Ages*.[17] The elaborate system of *topoi* this book describes did not fall into desuetude, as Curtius notes, until the last third of the eighteenth century. In other words, the evacuation from cultural memory of the *topoi*—those dense and finely branched semantic clusters that had since antiquity governed discursive invention—coincided exactly with the emergence of Romanticism. The Romantic destruction of rhetoric altered the temporal framework of literary production, replacing rememorative conservation (*traditio*) with an insistence on originality.

This shift can be delineated in other ways. One major Romantic innovation was the full articulation of the concept of "author" as the productive origin of the text, as the subjective source that, in bringing its unique position to expression, constitutes a "work" ineluctably its own. Subjectivity and not adherence to a generic type or reference to an esteemed predecessor or topical paradigm now gave a work its identity. This insistence on the principle of authorship—still today one of the most compelling assumptions of literary studies and the very organizing principle of our libraries—does not flow merely from the nature of things. As Foucault has suggested in a powerful essay, authorship is a function, one that varies both historically and among disciplines. Romanticism produced the author function in its modern form.[18]

Legal history makes this perfectly clear. The English Copyright Law of 1709 still did not protect the author against reproduction of his work. Its point of reference was the book itself, over which it gave the first publisher command for fourteen years (a limitation of previous practice) and the author for twenty-eight, the same duration as for a patent. The practice of royal privileges still remained common, and the universities held onto certain special exemptions. Only in 1774, after a tangled history of legal disputes, did the author receive an exclusive right over his work. In 1814 this authorial right was specified as holding for a period of twenty-eight years after first publication or, should the author outlive this duration, until the end of his life. In France, the old system of royal privileges and permissions held until the Revolution. Then, in its meeting of 19 July 1793, the National Assembly granted exclusive rights over reproduction to the authors themselves. This right held until ten years after the author's death. Finally, in the German-speaking countries the Universal Prussian National Law of 1794, which instituted from above so many of the reforms that in France had come into being with the Revolution, based the right of publication in a contract between author and publisher, with the publisher-seller, however, still the more important figure. Only in 1810, with the National Law of Baden, was the author finally accorded exclusive rights over "his" work. As these dates reveal, the years arrayed around the turn of the nineteenth century witnessed the full emergence of the author as the decisive factor in assigning proprietary status to printed language. This legal transformation is one institutional counterpart to the Romantic reconceptualization of literature.[19]

The same period revised educational practices bearing on literature. The Latin schools that had emerged across post-Renaissance Europe initiated their pupils into discourse by leading them through the rhetorical constructions of exemplary classical texts. This education culminated with imitative exercises in which the student produced speeches and poems in the manner of one of the great authorities. But by the end of the eighteenth century this rhetorical pedagogy was experienced as moribund. Reviewing a treatise on the cultivation of taste in the public schools, the young Goethe, destined to become one of the major figures of European Romanticism, wrote in 1772: "We, however, hate all the imitation that the author recommends at the end. We know there are many whose claim to fame is that they write like Cicero or Tacitus, but it always demonstrates a lack of genius when they fall into this misfortune."[20] Genius is the vital term here, the name of subjective originality and the antithesis of rhetorical *inventio*. Goethe's complaint was soon to see results as new methods of pedagogy entered the schools, methods that sought to disclose and cultivate the personal uniqueness of the pupils by teaching "free" expression. The medium of this expression was no longer the public oratorical performance in which the pupil demonstrated his mastery of standard techniques, but rather a written product that articulated his own individual point of view.[21] A similar change occurred in the universities. Whereas the study of the classical authors had traditionally meant memorizing, translating, and imitating the *loci classici*, the new discipline of philology encouraged an interpretive grasp of the animating authorial intention out of which the entire work was produced. These academic institutes of philology, the most famous of which was established by Christian Gottlob Heyne at the University of Göttingen during the 1770s, institutionalized Romantic hermeneutics as the methodology of modern literary understanding. Since then literary education has lent support to the antinomy between creative self-expression on the one hand and interpretation on the other.[22]

Of course, the Enlightenment had already begun to dismantle rhetorical doctrine as the organizing matrix of literary production. On the level of theory the late Enlightenment witnessed the birth of philosophical aesthetics, a discipline whose emergence marked a decisive cultural relocation of art and literature. Alexander Baumgarten's *Aesthetica* (1750–55), the foundational treatise of the new discipline, was still based on the traditional rhetorical triad of *inventio*, *dispositio*, and *elocutio*, but one nevertheless notes a shift in the significance of the terms. Aesthetics is not a theory of the production of effective or persuasive discourse; it is a theory of "sensate cognitions" and of the signs that convey them. Its frame of reference is not a notion of social interaction within a hierarchical space, but the soul conceived as a faculty of representation. Art retreats from the *cour et ville* of aristocratic society and takes up residence within the mental immanence of a universalized "mankind."[23] As Michael Fried has shown, a similar development took place in French painting and art criticism during the same period: the shift from a paradigm of "theatricality" to one of "absorption" amounted to a derhetorization, an abandonment of oratorical gesturality.[24] Finally, at the brink of Romanticism, Kant made the obsolescence of rhetoric explicit, banishing it in a famous paragraph of his *Critique of Judgment* not only from poetry but also from the legal courts, the chambers of government, and the pulpits of the church. His condemnation of rhetoric so thoroughly epitomizes the developments we have tried to sketch here that it is worth citing it at length:

> Rhetoric, in so far as this means the art of persuasion, i.e. of deceiving by a beautiful show (*ars oratoria*) and not mere elegance of speech (eloquence and style), is a dialectic which borrows from poetry only so much as is needful to win minds to the side of the orator before they have formed a judgment and to deprive them of their freedom; it cannot therefore be recommended either for the law courts or for the pulpit. For if we are dealing with civil law, with the rights of individual persons, or with lasting instruction and determination of people's minds to an accurate knowledge and a conscientious observance of their duty, it is unworthy of so important a business to allow a trace of any luxuriance of wit and imagination to appear, and still less any trace of the art of talking people over and of captivating them for the advantage of any chance person. For although this art may sometimes be directed to legitimate and praiseworthy designs, it becomes objectionable when in this way maxims and dispositions are spoiled in a subjective point of view, though the action may objectively be lawful. It is not enough to do what is right; we should practice it solely on the ground that it is right.[25]

Kant's *Critique of Judgment* not only assembles in this passage and elsewhere the accusatory motifs typical of all antirhetorical polemics (deception, unfreedom, luxuriant excess, demagogic manipulation), it also clearly reveals why rhetoric becomes irrelevant to the literary arts. For art, in Kant's view, has its source in genius, in the subjective instance of creativity that derives the rules of its productive action not from any cultural code, but from nature itself.[26] This attachment of art to expressive subjectivity led directly into the Romantic reconceptualization of the aesthetic, after which rhetoric lost its centrality to the production and interpretation of poetry. In Descartes initially, and then in Kant and the Romantics, we find this rule everywhere confirmed: the insistence on the originating power of subjectivity is incompatible with rhetorical doctrine. This is why Romanticism represents the final destruction of the classical rhetorical tradition.

Indicative literary genres appeared in tandem with characteristic refusals of rhetoric during the Enlightenment and Romantic stages even though the rhetorical model of production continued to prevail in officially sanctioned literature throughout the seventeenth and well into the eighteenth centuries. However, both the seeming inability of European writers to sustain the ancient tradition of epic poetry (except through translation and mock heroic) and, during the Enlightenment, a relative decline of lyric poetry in favor of satire and didactic-descriptive verse (those closest to prose among traditional forms) evince the incursion of prosaic rationalism.

The eighteenth-century emergence of the extra-official "new" novel is still more significant. The novel is the genre of writing par excellence. As Mikhail Bakhtin argues, all of the traditional literary genres, "or in any case their defining features, are considerably older than written language and the book, and to the present day they retain their ancient oral and auditory characteristics. Of all the major genres only the novel is younger than writing and the book: it alone is organically receptive to new forms of mute perception, that is, to reading."[27] Even if Bakhtin overstates the case—even if residues of orality may be found in certain earlier novels—the marked consolidation during the later eighteenth century of a novelistic technique such as free indirect discourse (*style indirect libre*), which has no counterpart outside of written narrative, validates for our period the point about reading and mute perception.[28] The novel's peculiar gravitation toward a neutral transparency of style (the opposite of rhetorical overcoding) participates in the genre's conventional pretense to reportorial accuracy of the kind possible only in writing. In other respects as well the eighteenth-century novel operates within the Enlightenment model of critical communication. The novels of Defoe, Richardson, and Fielding, for example, not only pretend to offer densely particular, virtually evidentiary accounts of the physical and mental circumstances that actuate their characters and motivate the causal sequences of their plots, but also attempt, with greater or lesser consistency, to frame the subjectivity of their characters within editorial (Defoe and Richardson) or narratorial (Fielding) objectivity. In point of both thematic exposition and narrative strategy, these novels force readers into the position of neutral observers arriving, probabilistically, at judgments based upon available facts and reasonable inferences. Although these novels in truth continue to echo plot forms and incidents traditional to the fantastical romances their prefaces ritually condemn, the concern expressed by these novelists to distinguish their enterprise from that of earlier prose fiction indicates from our point of view the urgent significance of the generic reformulation then in progress.

If the emergent novel demarcates a generic space within which the impersonality of the modern subject position may be exercised, the Romantic lyric exhibits the creative, self-forming aspect of the subject. Though the novel's opposite in so many other respects, the genre of the Romantic lyric not only shares the novel's use of natural, unadorned language, but also aggressively deprecates rhetorical speech as disingenuous. The earlier lyric tradition had displayed the ancient rhetorical forms of praise and blame, as well as the schemes and tropes designed to persuade a particular kind of person, in some specified situation, to act in some precise way. The Romantic lyric affirms individual personal identity by delineating a specific epiphanic moment in the history of a single speaking subject. Some of the most remarkable examples go so far as to efface entirely the scene of rhetorical speech by incorporating into the lyric another equally specific subject who uniquely shares the epiphany. Wordsworth's "Tintern Abbey" places his sister Dorothy in this empathetic role, while Coleridge's "This Lime Tree Bower My Prison" reflects upon a specific occasion when the absence of friends provoked meditations that might have been shared but would, of course, have been altered had the friends been present. Similar developments can be traced on the Continent, where, as in England, the model of folk poetry became the chief paradigm of lyric song. Already in the 1770s the young Goethe had begun to produce lyric texts that cleave to the inner movements of subjectivity and that redefine orality as the inner voice of emotion rather than as public-oriented oratorical communication. The lyrics of Goethe and his romantic successors are, in fact, a kind of verbal music that eventually could fuse seamlessly with the melodies of Schubert, Schumann, and Wolf.

Romanticism brought with it one final cultural transformation that worked to institutionalize the devolution of rhetoric. The rhetorical paradigm was international in character, tied to the Latin language, which dominated the higher schools and universities throughout Europe, and to the classical treatises and authorities that enjoyed universal recognition. Rhetoric was the foundation of an international intellectual community, the *res publica litteraria*, and the vehicle of a unified tradition. This quintessentially international character of classical rhetoric came to an end in the period of Romanticism because the Romantic destruction of rhetoric was linked to the rise of the modern nation-state. National identity was grounded in the linguistic identity of the *Volk*; the national languages replaced the international Latin koine, cutting off civic and cultural consciousness from its Roman roots. The universality of the *res publica litteraria* was shattered by the proliferation of vernacular reading publics, and the classical *traditio* ceded its preeminence to national historical traditions.[29] Perhaps the anxious territorialism so common today in university departments of literary study is a last desperate defense of the Romantic organization of the world of letters along national historical lines.

The linguistic character of the nation-state worked to bring on the end of rhetoric, but an equally important factor was the political structure—the form of sovereignty and political participation—that the nation-state developed. Within the context of national civic organization rhetorical performance was restricted to specialized legislative venues and ceremonial occasions. Citizenship came to reside in the relation of an individual to a collectively willed body of law; governmental participation and legal practice became professionalized and increasingly print-bound; and the scene of political action, which had previously possessed the concrete reality of a forum or court, was dispersed. The citizen, thoroughly privatized, was thus no longer distinguished by oratorical talent, as his Roman ancestor had been, and therefore no longer required rhetorical training. The nation-state is not a sphere of face-to-face encounter, but an ideal entity to which one relates abstractly through the internalization of its laws and concretely through its various bureaucratic apparatuses.

II. The Modernist Return of Rhetoric: A Thesis

Such were the manifold developments that, concurrently with the Enlightenment and Romanticism, brought the classical tradition of rhetoric to its end. Our procedure in sketching these developments has been to highlight individual cases and local events exemplifying the fact of rhetoric's demise. But these particular instances also have opened a view onto structural features of bourgeois culture that dethroned rhetoric from its position of supremacy much as the French Revolution dethroned the king as the symbol of traditional hierarchical order in European society. In other words, our historical narrative has led us to formulate a thesis specifying the constellation of forces that brought about rhetoric's end. Reversing the Kantian formula, we may call these ideological and institutional forces the *conditions of impossibility* of rhetoric: cultural presuppositions that, by relocating and reshaping discourse within society, rendered the traditional practice and doctrine of rhetoric obsolete. Five factors seem especially prominent:

1. Transparency and neutrality emerged as the leading values of theoretical and practical discourse—scientific discourse became anchored in objectivity.
2. The values of authorship and individual expression came to define the literary domain—imaginative discourse became anchored in subjectivity.
3. Liberal political discourse emerged as the language of communal exchange.

4. The oratorical model of communication was replaced by print and publishing—Europe was alphabetized.
5. The nation-state became the central political unit, and standardized national languages emerged as the linguistic sphere of reference for cultural production and understanding.

Where these conditions obtain, rhetoric can occupy only the place of a memory, an anachronistic and ritualized practice, or a dusty academic specialization. Once it becomes estranged from both cultural production and the most advanced forms of inquiry, associations of mendacity, empty scholasticism, and false artfulness attach themselves to its name. And this is what the Enlightenment and Romanticism accomplished: they altered the conditions of discursive action along the lines of the five tendencies listed here and thereby rendered irrelevant the rhetorical tradition that had for centuries been the organizing matrix of communication in Europe.

But rhetoric has returned. It has acquired renewed theoretical and practical importance, and more recently it has become an explicit focus of inquiry in a variety of domains. How is this possible? How can rhetoric return after having been so thoroughly displaced from our cultural horizon? We contend, centrally, that this repetition of the rhetorical tradition within modernism comes about when the five conditions of rhetoric's impossibility are themselves eliminated, when a new cultural and discursive space is fashioned that is no longer defined by objectivism, subjectivism, liberalism, literacy, and nationalism. The modernist cultural transformation, in other words, is accompanied by a return of rhetoric precisely because it explodes the cultural predominance of these five tendencies. From this perspective, modernism (construed as a broad sociocultural epoch) presents a reverse image of the antirhetorical cultural premises that increasingly organized the production of discourse from the seventeenth century onward:

1. From the paradoxes of Heisenberg and Gödel to the demotion of truth in the epistemology of Nelson Goodman, modernism has witnessed the crumbling of the ideal of scientific objectivity and the loss of faith in the neutrality of scientific and practical discourse. Modernism no longer possesses a reliable standard of representational transparency; even so-called observation sentences are recognized as theory-laden; and the history of science itself has come to be viewed less as a progressive discovery of the facts than as a series of constructions accomplished within the framework of governing conceptual paradigms.

2. Modernism has eroded as well the value of founding subjectivity, which, starting from Descartes and continuing through Romanticism, had contributed so powerfully to the decline of rhetoric. From Baudelaire's relegation of authorship to an anachronism and Mallarmé's elimination from poetic writing of the elocutionary subject to the automatic writing of the surrealists, the willed anonymity of Kafka, Beckett, and Blanchot, and the collective compositions of the Renga poets, modernist literary production has dismantled the values of individual authorship and creativity. Freudian psychoanalysis has decentered the subject, while disciplines such as linguistics and sociology have disclosed impersonal patterns and forces at work in human agency. Far from forming a world out of itself, the modernist subject, as Heidegger suggests, is "thrown" into the world, split by an alterity that can never be recuperated into a homogeneous and sovereign self-mastery. Rimbaud's line is emblematic of this condition: "Je est un autre."

3. Modernism, arising in tandem with mass society and its forms of exchange, explodes the liberal Enlightenment model of communication, in which individual rational subjects contribute disinterestedly to political debate within the public sphere. In both the modern political arena and the modern marketplace rhetorical manipulation becomes the rule. Advertising, marketing, propaganda, and public relations stir the cauldron of public opinion; politics, as Walter Benjamin noted, is aestheticized; and art, which Romanticism had enclosed within its own autonomous sphere, becomes one discursive force among others: impure, tendentious, a reflection on its own inadequacy.

4. Modernism is marked by the dethroning of print. Of course, the graphic word continues to infiltrate the other media at innumerable points, yet we no longer live in the world of newspaper and book. Print has given way to film and television, to phonographic reproduction and to the various forms of telecommunication. Literacy, far from being the sole access to culture, is merely one form of information processing, and a highly restricted one at that.

5. Finally, modernism has destroyed the model of a national language, which had served as the supervening form of Enlightenment and Romantic cultural production and self-understanding. The urbanistic marketplace of the twentieth century is irreducibly polyglottal; dialects, sociolects, and idiolects proliferate and clash; disciplines develop and dwell within their respective jargons. Translation is the universal state of affairs. This dispersion of the national language, the language of the people, is accompanied by an

unraveling of national tradition: modernism fosters an inrush of the archaic into the scene of culture, the shattering of the idea of national uniqueness and of an individual national history. The frame of national culture, which had displaced the internationalism of the rhetorical tradition, collapses.

These modernist cultural tendencies have created, then, the conditions for a renaissance of rhetoric, which today is asserting itself in all fields of intellectual endeavor and cultural production. But the new rhetoric is no longer that of the classical tradition; it is attuned to the specific structures of modernist culture; its fundamental categories are markedly new. Rhetoric today is neither a unified doctrine nor a coherent set of discursive practices. Rather, it is a transdisciplinary field of practice and intellectual concern, a field that draws on conceptual resources of a radically heterogeneous nature and does not assume the stable shape of a system or method of education. The rhetoric that, with the ruin of Enlightenment-Romantic culture, now increasingly asserts itself, shares with its classical predecessor little more than a name.

Our historical thesis leads us to this conclusion: *Modernism is an age not of rhetoric, but of rhetoricality*, the age, that is, of a generalized rhetoric that penetrates to the deepest levels of human experience. The classical rhetorical tradition rarified speech and fixed it within a gridwork of limitations: it was a rule-governed domain whose procedures themselves were delimited by the institutions that organized interaction and domination in traditional European society. Rhetoricality, by contrast, is bound to no specific set of institutions. It manifests the groundless, infinitely ramifying character of discourse in the modern world. For this reason, it allows for no explanatory metadiscourse that is not already itself rhetorical. Rhetoric is no longer the title of a doctrine and a practice, nor a form of cultural memory; it becomes instead something like the condition of our existence.

We have proposed that the modernist return of rhetoric be conceived in relation to a complex set of historical factors. The social, scientific, technological, and experiential formations of modern life have altered the conditions of discourse. These formations are coextensive with a cultural frame in which language becomes detached from the supports created for it by the Enlightenment and Romanticism. Rhetoricality names the new conditions of discourse in the modern world and, thus, the fundamental category of every inquiry that seeks to describe the nature of discursive action and exchange. Rhetoricality may be considered as a name for the underlying features both of modern practice and of the theories that seek to account for it. In the modernist phase these structural features, on the whole, had to be inferred from symptomatic social, cultural, and disciplinary phenomena. More recently, in the episode—or episteme—now designated by the term "postmodernism," new forms of rhetorical inquiry are emerging that explicitly recognize and analyze features we designate under the term "rhetoricality."

Nowhere is the modernist shift in the meaning of rhetoric—the shift from rhetoric to what we are calling rhetoricality—more forcefully evident than in Nietzsche, the paradigmatic philosopher of modernity and postmodernity. Acutely aware of the condition of language in mass culture, Nietzsche set the agenda for the modernist reconceptualization of rhetoric and opened that general field within which the diverse forms of rhetorical inquiry on the contemporary scene formulate their individual programs.

As a professor of classics at the University of Basel, the young Nietzsche offered a course in rhetoric, which, as Philippe Lacoue-Labarthe has shown, was of fundamental importance to his mature thought.[30] The early text by Nietzsche that sets the groundwork for all his thinking about language— "On Truth and Lies in an Extra-Moral Sense"—insists especially on the essential rhetoricity of language and on the human "drive to form metaphors" as the basis of our rendering of the world. The inherited concept of figures of speech here undergoes a decisive reinterpretation: the figures are no longer devices of an *elocutio* that adorns and presents the invented thoughts of the speaker, but mobile, shifting categories that are always at work in every encounter with the world. During this same early phase of his career Nietzsche developed the notion that truth itself is the product of a certain "pathos," that it is an affectively invested figure able to claim no legitimacy beyond the urgency with which it is affirmed. This conceptual move tears the underpinnings from the notion of an arhetorical language of observation: the truth claims of science, in Nietzsche's reading, are themselves merely one rhetoric among others.

The later Nietzsche promotes the category of "appearance" (*Schein*) to universal status: appearance is not the opposite of truth, but rather includes truth as one of its varieties. Nietzsche's insistence on the concept of power is similarly motivated: if all language is rhetorical, if even objectivity is the product of a certain strategy, then discourses are no longer to be measured in terms of their adequacy to an objective standard (which Nietzsche's perspectivism exposes as a myth) but rather to be analyzed in terms of their strategic placement within a clash of competing forces, themselves constituted in and through the very rhetorical dissimulations they employ. In this sense, Nietzsche's philosophy can be characterized as the thought of a generalized rhetoricality, of a play of transformation and dissimulation, that is the condition of possibility of truth and of subjectivity. Rhetoric returns in Nietzsche, not as a doctrine governing the production and analysis of texts, not as a procedure to be employed within specific situations toward determinable ends, but rather as a kind of immemorial process—an a priori that thought can never bring under its control precisely because thought itself is one of the effects of that process. Rhetoric loses in Nietzsche its instrumental character and becomes the name for the rootlessness of our being.[31]

III. Rhetoricality and Contemporary Styles of Knowledge: A Survey

The field of inquiry that Nietzsche's thought discloses is at once vast and diverse. Its conceptual repertoire resists synopsis, for its unity is as diffuse as modern knowledge itself. Thus, it would be impossible to provide a précis of modernist rhetoric such as that sketched out for the classical tradition with such precision and economy by Roland Barthes.[32] And even an encyclopedic account patterned after Heinrich Lausberg's compendious handbook of classical rhetoric would be incapable of absorbing contemporary rhetorical practice into a sharply delineated structure.[33] The best one can do at this point is to list some of the major disciplinary approaches to rhetorical questions and to chart their congruences and divergences.

The New Rhetoric of Science   One of the most fascinating areas of contemporary rhetorical inquiry—although it does not always go by that name—is concerned with the discourse of the sciences. As we have mentioned, the ideal of scientific objectivity, that is, of a neutral and standpoint-free language of description, came to an end in the twentieth century. The last gasp of this ideal was in all likelihood the neopositivist notion of the protocol sentence, a linguistic formulation that was thought to present in propositional form the raw data generated by experiment. But the notion did not hold up to scrutiny, and the ideal of neutrality was dismantled from within the neopositivist school itself. The paradigmatic instance of this turn in scientific metatheory is Thomas Kuhn's book *The Structure of Scientific Revolutions*, written as a contribution to the neopositivist-inspired *Encyclopedia of Unified Science*.[34] Despite the criticism and controversy the book has encountered since its publication, Kuhn's basic argument to the effect that scientific inquiry rests on research paradigms themselves not derivable from observed data or from axiomatic statements still enjoys a general consensus.

And Kuhn's historical approach has spawned an entire body of research bearing on the extrascientific forces at work in the formation of scientific knowledge. For example, in *Against Method* Paul Feyerabend, the prophetic voice of anti-objectivism, reviews with extreme care the scientific work of Galileo, discovering there not the untarnished presentation of facts, but a complex strategic-rhetorical operation of persuasion.[35] In a similar, if less jubilantly radical vein, Ian Hacking has shown how scientific instruments, far from being the neutral devices that Galileo's telescope appeared to be, in fact participate in the "creation of phenomena," in what we would like to call a scientific *inventio*.[36] Finally—and still remaining within the post-analytic tradition—according to Nelson Goodman's *Ways of Worldmaking*, no one world exists that we strive to represent as neutrally as possible, but rather there are a host of world-versions, themselves functions of divergent representational or symbolic systems.[37]

In this plurality of worlds, rhetoric, albeit in a nonclassical version, finds its place once again. At issue in this new form of metascientific analysis is the essential rhetoricality of the scientific enterprise: its procedures of legitimation; its institutional context; its dependence on overriding convictions or presuppositions on the part of its practitioners.[38] The same interest in rhetoricality also has penetrated the social and human sciences. Hayden White, for example, has elaborated a rhetoric of classical historiography that undermines any claims of impartiality and objectivity that discipline might proffer.[39] Likewise, Clifford Geertz has examined the production of anthropological knowledge as an intrinsically rhetorical operation and his explorations will soon be followed by others that explore the rhetoric of neighboring human sciences.[40] Perhaps above all, Foucault's work, with its insistence on both the institutional embeddedness and the cultural productivity of discourses, sets the standard for any inquiry that seeks to lay bare the rhetoricality of what we anachronistically call our positive knowledge.

Rhetoric and Modern Linguistics　The Romantic concept of language essentially banned rhetoric from the field of language study, replacing it with stylistics conceived as the analysis of individual or national expressive forms. Indeed, if we recall the work of the last great avatars of Romantic linguistics, the neo-idealists Charles Bally and Karl Vossler, it becomes clear that stylistics is not merely a branch of Romantic language study, but rather its culmination. With the Saussurean breakthrough, a return of rhetorical analysis became possible, and once again this return of the rhetorical tradition assumed the form of a differential repetition.

No doubt the privileged—the most famous and influential—site of this return is Roman Jakobson's 1956 article "Two Aspects of Language and Two Types of Aphasic Disturbances."[41] What Jakobson accomplished in this piece can be described as a reorganization of the rhetorical field, or, to be precise, of the rhetorical subfield traditionally denoted *elocutio*. By using the term "reorganization" we want to emphasize the idea of creative change and transformation, the idea of a reconstitution of the object of rhetorical study. How does this occur? Through the projection of the categorical pair paradigm/syntagm from post-Saussurean linguistic theory (Saussure himself used the term "association" rather than "paradigm") onto the domain of the rhetorical figures. And since the terms of this categorical pair are juxtaposed within structuralist theory as are "similarity" and "contiguity," the projection yields within the rhetorical domain a fundamental bifurcation into two semantic-figural processes, operating along the paths of similarity relations on the one hand and contiguity relations on the other. In Jakobson's terminology, these processes carry the names, familiar from the rhetorical tradition, of "metaphor" and "metonymy." Thus, a powerful homology emerges into view: in the domain of language "paradigmatic" is to "syntagmatic" as in the domain of semantic-discursive processes "metaphor" is to "metonymy."

Jakobson's homology has engendered various confusions, among them that the terms "metaphor" and "metonymy," as he uses them, are held to be equivalent to those same terms within the rhetorical tradition. This is clearly not the case. Within the traditional doctrine of *elocutio*, metaphor and metonymy are two figures among a host of others; they are, we might say, particularistically conceived, pertaining to individual instances of discourse. Jakobson means something quite different: for him the terms designate two (and, in his view, the only two) general processes of semantic production; they are class terms that subsume the entire field of the traditionally defined figures, dividing it into two basic groups. Thus, when Jakobson suggests that Romanticism and Symbolism are predominantly metaphorical, Realism predominantly metonymical, he is not saying that in these literary movements either metaphors or metonymies are exclusively used, but rather that the large-scale tendencies of semantic production within these movements follow the paths of similarity and contiguity respectively. What we find in Jakobson's inquiry, then, is a fundamental displacement that affects the traditional terminology of rhetoric, a generalization of certain items within that terminology and a wholesale abandonment of other items. Certain old rhetorical terms have come to designate general processes that are at work, in their juxtapositional interplay, across the entire field of discourse, that are anterior to any instrumental choices a writer might make, and that even govern such transindividual phenomena as the succession of period styles. Exactly this shift in the theoretical function and significance of concepts is what we are calling the move from rhetoric to rhetoricality.

Of course, post-Saussurean linguistics has spawned efforts to rethink in detail the utterly specific categories of traditional *elocutio*. Two examples of this research program are the *Rhétorique génerale* of the Belgian Groupe Mu, and Paolo Valesio's *Novantiqua*.[42] But even in these cases, where the inherited taxonomies of rhetorical theory are respected in their specificity, the displacement of tradition is nonetheless perceptible. For what such analyses show is that the traditional classifications of the tropes and figures are crude; terms such as "metaphor" or "synecdoche" designate not at all simple and homogeneous operations, but rather bundles of phonological, syntactical, and semantic processes so complex in their intertwining that they must be deemed inaccessible to the reflective manipulation of the speaker. What the rhetorical tradition conceived as a set of tactics available to the strategic intentions of the speaker has been displaced into that same unconscious knowledge in which linguistic theory locates our ability to speak and write. Rhetorical competence, to adapt Noam Chomsky's terminology, is a theoretical fiction, the product of a reconstructive process that deploys a reticulated repertoire of theoretical concepts. The object of study here, as in a different way in the case of Jakobson, is no longer rhetoric but rather rhetoricality.

Rhetoric and Psychoanalysis   Correlative with the modernist alteration of the object of study in linguistics from evident to unconscious patterns, from national syntax to universal structure, and from commonsensical to counterintuitive evaluation is Freud's inferential psychology of the unconscious. In psychoanalysis the mechanisms of an otherwise hidden mental world are revealed in the figurations of language. Verbal patterns, metaphors, replacements, and similar tropes that classical rhetoric might have described in terms of surface ornamentation and effect upon an audience become outward, consciously unintended manifestations of wishes and fears, desires and terrors that have been driven inward. Thus, in tandem with his discovery of the revelatory condensations and displacements operative in dreams, Freud also probed "figures" such as jokes, spoonerisms, and puns as symptoms of unconscious operations. Particular content may vary with each individual, but the structure of the unconscious—its ways of proceeding and the strategies of containment whereby it is held in check— is constant. The manifest content of dreams or slips of the tongue may be specific to the individual's history, but the mechanisms are impersonal and function without reference to subjective choice. The old figures of speech and thought are depersonalized and transformed into general conditions of existence rather than remaining, as in classical rhetoric, part of a lexicon or repertory from among which speakers make deliberate choices according to occasion. At least in retrospect, Lacan's famous dictum that the unconscious is structured like a language seems to follow inevitably from the juxtaposi- tion of Freud's treatises on dreams and jokes with Jakobson's specification of metaphor and metonymy as the basic mechanisms of discourse produc- tion, since these figures, as Jakobson notices, are the rhetorical equivalents of condensation and displacement—the fundamental processes of Freud's "dream work." Furthermore, the rhetoric employed in current psychoana- lytic theory is not limited to expressive phenomena. As Jean Laplanche has suggested, the very processes of ego formation are rhetorical in nature, fol- lowing paths of contiguity and similarity.[43] Indeed, psychoanalysis itself, as Nicolas Abraham and Marie Torok have argued, is a rhetorical enterprise, its terminology a figurative shell that refers to kernels of psychic meaning without being able to grasp them directly.[44] The metatheory that endeavors to chart psychic processes is imbued, in other words, with the dynamic of rhetoricality that characterizes those processes themselves.

Rhetoric and Mass Communication   As the forms of communication characteristic of mass society have been extended and consolidated, the classical liberal model in which individual free subjects contribute disinter- estedly to open, unconstrained political exchange has become no more than heuristic. Images and slogans replace the ideas and expository discourse by which exchange in the public sphere was defined. Although the basic technology of movable type was developed during the Renaissance, print as a medium (especially newspapers, periodicals, and cheap books) and the growth in literacy that it ultimately fostered were distinctive to the Enlight- enment and to the bourgeois culture of nineteenth- and earlier twentieth- century industrial Europe. But, while the graphic word continues to play a significant role in cultural life, the structure of literacy has undergone deci- sive alterations. Print has given way to film and television, to phonographic reproduction, and the digital inscription of language itself in computers. The collation of image and sound in the mechanical media, even where oral language is concerned, recalls but does not reconstitute the face-to-face speech and physiognomic and gestural performances of classical rhetoric. For images and sounds may now be synthesized: the voice, like that of our current telephone information "operators," may be no more than a mechanical function, the opposite of an impersonation.

Advertising, in particular, works by condensation and montage to shatter those sequences of cause and effect integral to the construction, representation, and comprehension of personal identity. Like other forms of mass communication, advertising rehabilitates—indeed renders virtually universal—a rhetoricality at once akin to and utterly divorced from classical persuasion. The fixed traits of celebrity replace the classical orator's varied impersonations. Metonymic substitution and juxtaposition supplant that imitation of the logical connectedness of philosophical discourse so central to Aristotle's conception of rhetoric. Thus, the forms of communication operative in contemporary life lie closer to the figurative formations described by Freud and Lacan than to the manifest processes of a traditional forum.

The depersonalizing tendencies of modern rhetoricality find illustration in the conjunction, so characteristic of mass society, of advertising and fashion. The mimicry endemic to the selection of clothing is now directed toward personality functions concocted and circulated by the media. In perhaps the ultimate extension of this principle, the names of celebrities known as designers are inscribed on clothing and other accessories in place of the personal monograms that once discreetly marked attire as individual. The designer, in turn, need not be alive, or even a real person, since the creative personality marked by the famous name is often itself produced artificially by a corporation—or at least by a corporate design team. The putatively individual name works metonymically to screen collectivity.

Collective effort on a huge scale is the reality of which individuality has become the imaginary or fantastic representation. This phenomenon, in which audiences are manipulated by the delusion that products are the result of individual creative effort, replaces the old forms of persuasion. And, incidentally, any real human beings who happen to occupy the position of metonymic celebrity—be they Calvin Klein or Ronald Reagan—become virtually mechanized ciphers acting out the script of their own renown, themselves as much manipulated as the audience they manipulate. The recent presence of a professional film actor in the White House merely made self-evident the contemporary truth that the performative force of presidential elocution lies not with the seeming individual who happens to be in office but with the impersonal corporate state.

Rhetoric and Pragmatics   Not only in the metatheory of science, linguistics, mass communication, and psychoanalysis are we the inheritors of Nietzsche's legacy, but also in what might be termed the sphere of everyday life. The concept of rhetoricality bespeaks the universality of the rhetorical condition, its nonrestriction to the specialized circumstances of formal communication and persuasion. It is a characteristic of modernism that the sphere of everyday life—the domain of utterly trivial activities and interchanges through which we daily pass—has increasingly become an object of scientific inquiry. To cite just two examples from philosophy, both the early Heidegger with his hermeneutics of *Dasein* in its *Alltäglichkeit* (everydayness) and the British school of ordinary language philosophy that developed out of the later Wittgenstein's work are oriented toward this most secularized and elusive of domains, the nexus of our normality. And it is no accident that what inquiry finds in this domain (Wittgenstein's concept of language game tells us as much) is a web of rhetorical operations. In other words, precisely that sea of invisible communicative transactions that the tradition of classical rhetoric did not and could not take into account becomes in the modernist environment a privileged object of study. Just as the modernist return of rhetoric displaces the rhetorical operations to an unconscious sphere in such fields as linguistics and psychoanalysis, so too in the area of what might be termed "pragmatic" studies modernist rhetoric finds its theme in the impersonal domain of what occurs among us, unnoticed and without deliberation or grandeur.

The displacement of rhetoric from the classical trivium to the dense tangle of our triviality can be illustrated through reference to a plethora of research programs that have emerged within various disciplines but nevertheless share a concern for the *pragmata* of everydayness. What else, for example, is ethnomethodology (despite its insistence on a phenomenological grounding) but a sociological rhetoric of normal doings? Within the disciplinary limits of sociology, one could also refer to the illustrious example of Erving Goffman, whose major works bear titles like *Forms of Talk* and *The Presentation of Self in Everyday Life*.[45] Linguistics also has addressed itself with increasing sophistication to this domain. One thinks in this connection of the recent boom in pragmatic studies, an example of which is Dan Sperber and Deirdre Wilson's book *Relevance*, a study of "communication and cognition" that endeavors to formalize the

rules of conversational exchange and that develops along its way a reconceptualization of such rhetorical tactics as metaphor and irony. Indeed,
Sperber and Wilson's argument in this portion of their study exactly confirms our thesis regarding the shift from rhetoric to rhetoricality insofar
as it demonstrates that metaphor and the other tropes "are simply creative
exploitations of a perfectly general dimension of language use."[46] That is
to say, the figures of language can no longer be treated as a specialized
domain, as a limited set of elocutionary options. Rather, they make up the
very fiber of every communicative transaction.

One could further document the new rhetoric of everyday life through
reference to other fields. For instance, cognitive science and artificial intelligence stand, in our view, to inherit and radically reformulate the heuristics of classical rhetoric. Marvin Minsky's "frames," for example, or Roger
Shank's "scripts" are schemata of practical knowledge that can be regarded
as redactions of the classical theory of topoi.[47] Even asking for ketchup at a
hamburger joint can prove to be a rhetorical operation of astonishing complexity, accomplished by recalling and modifying a "restaurant frame" or
schema of typical restaurant behavior to which no single eatery conforms in
every detail. George Lakoff and Mark Johnson's book *Metaphors We Live By*
demonstrates even in its title that from the perspective of cognitive science
rhetoricality has become the condition of modern life.[48]

Rhetoric and Literary Criticism   During the period when classical rhetoric governed the analysis and production of discourse, the aspects of the
discipline now called literary criticism not comprehended by rhetorical categories were treated under the subheading "poetics." Later, after the Enlightenment and Romantic demolitions of rhetoric, criticism of literature
could be found in association with the new, often nationalistic, disciplines
of aesthetics, philology, and positivistic history. Traditions derived from
these disciplines have enjoyed surprising longevity among Western literary
scholars, as have survivals and revivals of the ancient rhetorical scholia. The
Anglo-American movement known as "new criticism," springing initially
from William Empson, I. A. Richards, and Allen Tate, may be considered,
for example, as a nostalgic attempt to fuse the organicist presumptions of
Romantic aesthetics with the formal, figural analysis characteristic of classical rhetoric. Also nostalgically present in the new criticism was the presump-
tion of a shared community of literate and tasteful gentlemen who, though
writing for publication, took the forms of conversation as their stylistic
ideal. Their obsession with the figures of irony, paradox, and ambiguity de-

rives at once from the contradictions inherent in their project and from their virtually oratorical impersonation of the detached stance of the disinterested man of letters.

The revivalist aspect of new criticism—so deeply entrenched in British and American academic departments of literature—may help to account for the shock that greeted the arrival of structuralist and poststructuralist methods from Europe during the late 1960s and early 1970s. These methods, based upon characteristic modernist developments in linguistics and philosophy, worked from utterly different principles. Consider, for example, the difference between the contained, localized irony of the new critic and the deep-structural irony of Derrida or de Man. In these writers, irony is no longer a figure of speech or an educated habit of mind; it is the fundamental condition of language production. Since there is no such thing as a first, original, or direct statement, they view every utterance as intrinsically figural, unstable, and haunted by implications that militate against its overt claims. Poetry is no longer a privileged kind of discourse but a specific case illustrating the general instance of language itself. In the structuralist—and now poststructuralist—frame of reference, every human endeavor, including fundamental social and cultural institutions, must be understood as discursively constituted and therefore subject to the foundational irony disclosed by analyses such as Derrida's. As the rhetoricality of culture becomes ever more apparent, both survivals of classical rhetorical analysis and revivalist methods like the new criticism appear terribly restricted in scope. It is not surprising, therefore, that prestructuralist Anglo-American critics who attempted large typologies of discourse, such as Kenneth Burke and Northrop Frye, have fared better than many others.

Burke's work presents an especially forceful illustration of our argument bearing on rhetoricality. Even where the focus of his ruminations is a specific literary text, as for example in his famous analysis of Keats's "Ode on a Graecian Urn" or his speculations on Goethe's *Faust*,[49] Burke characteristically directs his inquiry not at meaning in a hermeneutic sense, nor at the cooperation of formal and thematic components in the manner of the new criticism, but rather at the text's symbolic labor, its suasive operations. Thus, his analyses are rhetorical in their basic orientation; it is indicative that two of his books carry the term "rhetoric" in their titles.[50] Although Burke himself named his method "dramatism," a term that signals his abiding concern for the place of language in human action and interaction, the rhetorical thrust of his wide-ranging inquiry is evident on every page. Much of Burke's vocabulary can be taken as the lexicon for a modernist rhetoric: terministic screen, entitlement, representative anecdote, strategies of motivation, master tropes, scene-act ratio, god-term, temporizing of essence. Moreover, Burke's work illustrates many features we take to be characteristic of rhetorical inquiry under the conditions of modernity. It is resolutely interdisciplinary, drawing on sociology, anthropology, psychoanalysis, philosophy, and poetics; it is recursive in structure, applying its categories to itself as a strategy of argument and inquiry; its range of objects (one might better say: occasions) crosses disciplinary boundaries and includes philosophical schools, political tracts, everyday life, ritual and religion, economic and foreign policy, literary works, and bodily practices, to mention just a few. Its final ground is an anthropology that comes close to the Nietzschean definition of man as the imperfect animal, as a being whose only nature is the unremitting nonnaturalness of his symbolic-rhetorical self-constitution.[51]

Rhetoricality pervades even methods that, viewed superficially, might seem to continue formalistic traditions. Julia Kristeva's concept of "intertextuality" for instance, could easily be misunderstood as a reinscription of the old rhetoric.[52] But whereas the new critics considered the formal boundaries of the poem, story, or other verbal construct to delimit a universe with its own rules and self-referentiality, Kristeva's intertextuality reveals how every seemingly closed, evidently personal or otherwise situational utterance actually consists of all-but-infinite interlocking networks of reference, quotation, and paraquotation. Every text merges without boundary into every other, just as for Bakhtin—Kristeva's font of inspiration during the period when she worked out her ideas about intertextuality—every word abides in, and itself contains, countless intersecting ideological contexts. For Bakhtin every utterance is many utterances; every speaker is many speakers; and every seemingly rhetorical context encodes many other occasions. Bakhtin's works, deeply influenced by those of Nietzsche, could be read as virtual treatises on the nature and functioning of rhetoricality.

Why, then, does contemporary literary research continue to draw on the terminology of the inherited rhetorical tradition? Is there not a fundamental continuity that knits past and present together? Especially in literary studies, a field often deeply troubled by the rifts of history and by the fear of cultural oblivion, one encounters projects that anxiously work to reconstitute for the present a unity of tradition and doctrine that no longer exists. This suggests that in those cases where the rhetorical tradition is invoked, what is really being accomplished is the satisfaction of a nostalgia or the legitimation of one's enterprise of inquiry through a venerable genealogy. Of course, overriding constants may be posited in order to construct a history of rhetoric from, say, Aristotle to the present, and thus to attribute contemporary value to ancient rhetorical theory in the manner of the Chicago neo-Aristotelians.[53] But such continuities will be largely terminological or so abstract (e.g., rhetoric has always been concerned with language in action) that their cognitive value will be minimal. In either case, the categorical displacements that have occurred behind the apparent stability of signifiers such as "metaphor" or "irony" will be suppressed. Rhetorical study has been able to vitalize literary research today precisely because it is no longer what it used to be. To get clear on this point, moreover, seems to us a prerequisite for the continued vitality of that research. Once rhetoricality is understood as the fundamental condition under which any contemporary literary criticism must proceed, the discipline itself will be transformed because its boundaries will be redrawn.

In general, then, what are we to conclude about the shape of rhetoric today, following its return? This question elicits a double answer, both parts of which point to the decisive transformations that rhetoric has undergone. First, the very object of rhetorical analyses and theories has changed. We are dealing no longer with a specialized technique of instrumental communication, but rather with a general condition of human experience and action. We have designated as "rhetoricality" this new category—the category that opens the field of modern rhetorical research. Second, there can be no single contemporary rhetorical theory: rhetoricality cannot be the object of a homogeneous discipline. Modernist (and postmodernist) rhetorical study is irreducibly multidisciplinary; one cannot study rhetoric *tout court*, but only linguistic, sociological, psychoanalytic, cognitive, communicational, medial, or literary rhetorics.

Note that these two aspects of rhetoric in its modernist return fit together: for if rhetoricality is our condition and if it names the irreducible, a priori character of rhetorical processes, then it also implies the impossibility of a single governing discourse that could know that condition. No single theory can detach itself from the limits set to knowledge and representation by rhetoricality; and every version of theory bearing on rhetoricality itself partakes of the rhetorical processes it endeavors to map. Rhetoric, we mentioned at the outset, originated in disputes regarding property, and has been concerned throughout its tradition with ensuring the identification of the proper. But rhetoricality designates the thoroughgoing impropriety of language and action and therefore cannot be captured in the net of a single form of knowledge. This is not to say that the different disciplines that address themselves to questions of rhetoric are entirely insulated from one another. On the contrary, interdisciplinary translations are not only possible but necessary. Such translations, however, fruitful and provocative as they are, can never culminate in a totalizing theory of rhetoric such as the classical tradition possessed. Modern rhetorical research must be an open-ended series of translations and transformations. It is irrevocably dispersed because of the nature of its foundational category. Rhetoricality, then, also designates the partial and provisional character of every attempt to know it.

Notes

Introduction

1. The article *"Philosophe"* in the *Encyclopédie*, ed. Denis Diderot and Jean-Baptiste le Rond d'Alembert, vol. 12 (1765), was based on an earlier essay from about 1730, probably by César Chesneau Dumarsais (1676–1756). The version in the *Encyclopédie* is compressed and concerned less with religion than the original. See Herbert Dieckmann, *"Le Philosophe": Texts and Interpretation* (St. Louis: Washington University, 1948). My thanks to Dan Edelstein for this background. See Edelstein's book, *The Enlightenment: A Genealogy* (Chicago: University of Chicago Press, 2010). For Immanuel Kant, see *Critique of Pure Reason*, trans. and ed. Paul Guyer and Allen W. Wood (Cambridge: Cambridge University Press, 1998), 100–101; and "Answer to the Question: What Is Enlightenment?" in *Basic Writings of Kant*, ed. Allen W. Wood (New York: Modern Library, 2001), 133–41.

2. Anthony Giddens, West Memorial Lectures (lecture, Stanford University, Stanford, California, April 1988). A written version of these extempore lectures has appeared as *The Consequences of Modernity* (Stanford, CA: Stanford University Press, 1990). The basic idea to which I refer here is developed, much less explicitly than in the lectures themselves, on 10–17 and 36–45.

I find Daniel Brewer's approach to the issues of the kind raised in this introduction to be congenial. He argues for the "situated" nature of Enlightenment knowledge in *The Enlightenment Past: Reconstructing Eighteenth-Century French Thought* (Cambridge: Cambridge University Press, 2008), esp. 15–16 and 41–43.

3. A ghostly scaffolding for this collection earlier appeared in "Rhetoricality," a piece I wrote with David E. Wellbery to launch our thematic volume *The Ends of Rhetoric: History, Theory, Practice* (Stanford, CA: Stanford University Press, 1990), 3–39. The essay appears in this collection as Chapter 10. We argued that the eighteenth century witnessed the decline of conditions of possibility that had underpinned the system of classical rhetoric—a system that had governed the production and comprehension of discourse for some two millennia. We considered, further, how the very forces that had brought an end to classical forms of speech, writing,

and interpretation themselves eroded as twentieth-century modernity took hold. This enfeeblement of the Enlightenment's antirhetorical force field—the removal of what we called the conditions of *impossibility* that had damped down rhetorical practice within the Enlightenment proper—allowed the resurgence of rhetoric in new, at times hardly recognizable forms, which we called *rhetoricality*. The treatment of the Enlightenment in this introduction points toward the analogous structure of formation and return.

4. John Bender, *Imagining the Penitentiary: Fiction and the Architecture of Mind in Eighteenth-Century England* (Chicago: University of Chicago Press, 1987). For detailed citations on free indirect discourse, see Note 25 in Chapter 7 and Note 6 in Chapter 8.

5. David Hume, *A Treatise of Human Nature*, 2nd ed., ed. L. A. Selby-Bigge and P. H. Nidditch (Oxford: Clarendon Press, 1978), 215.

6. Steven Shapin and Simon Schaffer, *Leviathan and the Air-Pump: Hobbes, Boyle, and the Experimental Life* (Princeton, NJ: Princeton University Press, 1985).

7. The crucial work by Horkheimer and Adorno is *Dialectic of Enlightenment*, which was written in 1944, late in World War II, and published in 1947. The title itself implies the truth that the view of Enlightenment in this book is not entirely negative, but its memorable characterization of instrumental reason as the destructive product of Enlightenment tends to override more subtle aspects of the book. See *Dialectic of Enlightenment*, ed. Gunzelin Schmid Noerr, trans. Edmund Jephcott (Stanford, CA: Stanford University Press, 2002). Habermas did not finish his thesis with Horkheimer, but left the Frankfurt School in disagreement with his mentor prior to completing his Habilitation at the University of Marburg.

Ernst Cassirer's contemporaneous book, *The Myth of the State*, reached similar conclusions about totalitarianism by viewing the growth and potential of reason across history as crucially positive but threatened by a persistence of ancient forms of irrationality that may erupt at any historical moment into mythic thinking that defies reason and truth—like that of the mass psychology of fascism. Cassirer's *The Myth of the State* (New Haven, CT: Yale University Press, 1946) was written in English during World War II and published posthumously the year after his death.

8. See Jürgen Habermas, *The Structural Transformation of the Public Sphere: An Inquiry into a Category of Bourgeois Society*, trans. Thomas Burger with the assistance of Frederick Lawrence (Cambridge, MA: MIT Press, 1989). The book was first published in German in 1962, three years after Koselleck's negative account of Enlightenment critique. A misleading French translation appeared in 1988: for instance, it introduced the doubtful rendering of Habermas's term *Öffentlichkeit* into *l'espace public* ("public sphere") thus turning a sociological term for a kind of interaction among people into one for a set of spatial relationships. Fortunately for me, this translation appeared too late to mislead me in *Imagining the Penitentiary*. For later development of Habermas's ideas, see *The Philosophical Discourse of Modernity: Twelve Lectures*, trans. Frederick Lawrence (Cambridge, MA: MIT Press, 1987).

For an account of *Dialectic of Enlightenment* by Habermas and Thomas Y. Levin, see "Entwinement of Myth and Enlightenment: Re-Reading *Dialectic of Enlightenment*," *New German Critique* 26 (1982): 13–30.

Reinhart Koselleck, *Critique and Crisis: Enlightenment and the Pathogenesis of Modern Society* (Cambridge, MA: MIT Press, 1988). The work was published in German in 1959, three years before Habermas's *Strukturwandel der Öffentlichkeit*.

9. On audience-oriented subjectivity, its origins in the bourgeois family, and its illustration in the novel, see Habermas, *Structural Transformation*, 47–51.

10. Albert O. Hirschman, *The Passions and the Interests: Political Arguments for Capitalism Before Its Triumph* (Princeton, NJ: Princeton University Press, 1977).

11. "Wikipedia: Five Pillars," *Wikipedia*, last modified 27 August 2011, accessed 28 August 2011, http://en.wikipedia.org/wiki/Wikipedia:Five_pillars.

12. See also Robin Valenza, *Literature, Language, and the Rise of the Intellectual Disciplines in Britain, 1680–1820* (Cambridge: Cambridge University Press, 2009).

13. George Herbert Mead, *Mind, Self, and Society*, ed. Charles W. Morris (Chicago: University of Chicago Press, 1934); Alvin W. Gouldner, *Enter Plato: Classical Greece and the Origins of Social Theory* (New York: Basic Books, 1965); Erving Goffman, *The Presentation of Self in Everyday Life* (Garden City, NJ: Doubleday, 1959). A founding work on "mind reading" is Simon Baron-Cohen, *Mindblindness: An Essay on Autism and Theory of Mind* (Cambridge, MA: MIT Press, 1995), followed by many papers from the same author. See also Shaun Nichols and Stephen P. Stich, *Mindreading: An Integrated Account of Pretence, Self-Awareness, and Understanding Other Minds* (Oxford: Clarendon Press, 2003). Accounts of mirror neurons came in the 1990s from Vittorio Gallese, Giacomo Rizzolatti, and others in their research group. For convenient accounts with references, see Gallese's article "Mirror Neurons," in *The Oxford Companion to Consciousness*, ed. Tim Bayne et al. (Oxford: Oxford University Press, 2009), 445–47. See also Giacomo Rizzolatti, Leonardo Fogassi, and Vittorio Gallese, "Mirrors in the Mind," *Scientific American* 295.5 (November 2006): 54–61; Giacomo Rizzolatti and Corrado Sinigaglia, *Mirrors in the Brain: How Our Minds Share Actions, Emotions, and Experience*, trans. Frances Anderson (Oxford: Oxford University Press, 2008).

14. On the "*Philosophe*" article, see above, Note 1. The translation here is from Denis Diderot et al., *Encyclopedia: Selections*, ed. and trans. Nelly S. Hoyt and Thomas Cassirer (Indianapolis: Bobbs-Merrill, 1965), 285.

15. Hume, *Treatise*, 180.

16. Jean Baudrillard, *Simulacra and Simulation*, trans. Sheila Faria Glase (Ann Arbor: University of Michigan Press, 1995).

Jean-François Lyotard argued in *La condition postmoderne: Rapport sur le savoir* (Paris: Minuit, 1979) that the fragmentation and dispersal of the subject in postmodernism—its perceptions, its reasoning, and its moral stance—allow chiefly the realm of aesthetic experience both as the medium within which individual awareness unfolds and also as the tissue that binds, however loosely, the political and moral discourses that govern our lives. Habermas attacked this kind of thinking as self-contradictory because it uses the tools of reason to articulate a metacritical position for itself outside the phenomena it supposes to describe. More significantly, Habermas argues that, even in the absence of a traditional humanistic subject, the rules that define and govern rational discussion concerning the politics of society and its future remain functional and necessary. See Jean-François Lyotard, *The Postmodern Condition: A Report on Knowledge*, trans. Geoff Bennington and Brian

Massumi (Minneapolis: University of Minnesota Press, 1984); Jürgen Habermas, "Modernity versus Postmodernity," *New German Critique* 22 (1981): 3–14.

On Lyotard and Habermas, see Richard Rorty, "Habermas and Lyotard on Postmodernity," in *Habermas and Modernity*, ed. Richard J. Bernstein (Cambridge, MA: MIT Press, 1985), 161–75; and Gary Aylesworth, "Postmodernism," *The Stanford Encyclopedia of Philosophy*, ed. Edward N. Zalta, first published 30 September 2005, last accessed 28 August 2011, http://plato.stanford.edu/archives/win2010/entries/postmodernism/. Aylesworth writes: "As Lyotard argues, aesthetic judgment is the appropriate model for the problem of justice in postmodern experience because we are confronted with a plurality of games and rules without a concept under which to unify them. Judgment must therefore be reflective rather than determining. Furthermore, judgment must be aesthetic insofar as it does not produce denotative knowledge about a determinable state of affairs, but refers to the way our faculties interact with each other as we move from one mode of phrasing to another, i.e. the denotative, the prescriptive, the performative, the political, the cognitive, the artistic, etc. In Kantian terms, this interaction registers as an aesthetic feeling."

17. See, for instance, Scott's *Heart of Midlothian* (1818). Edmond de Goncourt (1822–96) and Jules de Goncourt (1830–70) wrote continually about the eighteenth century, including a book on Marie Antoinette and, for instance, *French Eighteenth-Century Painters: Watteau, Boucher, Chardin, La Tour, Greuze, Fragonard* (Oxford: Phaidon, 1981). The Wallace Collection of eighteenth-century painting, furniture, and decorative arts was assembled by Richard Seymour-Conway, 4th Marquess of Hertford (1800–70). It passed to his son Sir Richard Wallace, whose estate conferred it upon the British nation. The Wallace Collection opened in Hertford House on Manchester Square in London in 1900. On Tchaikovsky and Mozart, see Richard Taruskin, *Defining Russia Musically* (Princeton, NJ: Princeton University Press, 2001), 291–307. On Marie Antoinette, see Terry Castle, *The Apparitional Lesbian: Female Homosexuality and Modern Culture* (New York: Columbia University Press, 1993), chap. 6, 107–49; and "Phantasmagoria and the Metaphorics of Modern Reverie," in *The Female Thermometer* (New York: Oxford University Press, 1995), 140–67.

18. Koselleck, *Critique and Crisis*.

19. Michel Foucault, "What Is Enlightenment?" in *Ethics: Subjectivity and Truth*, ed. Paul Rabinow, trans. Robert Hurley et al. (New York: The New Press, 1997), 303 and 315.

20. Bender, *Imagining the Penitentiary*. On Foucault's place in my thinking, see the preface, xv.

21. John Bender and Michael Marrinan, *The Culture of Diagram* (Stanford, CA: Stanford University Press, 2010), 211.

22. On hierarchical vs. functional differentiation, see Niklas Luhmann, *The Differentiation of Society*, trans. Stephen Holmes and Charles Larmore (New York: Columbia University Press, 1982). Also, *Essays on Self-Reference* (New York: Columbia University Press, 1990); and *Social Systems*, trans. John Bednarz, Jr., and Dirk Baecker (Stanford, CA: Stanford University Press, 1995).

23. See *The Re:Enlightenment Project*, eds. Clifford Siskin, Kevin Brine, et al., last accessed 28 August 2011, www.reenlightenment.org; and also Clifford Siskin

and William Warner, "This Is Enlightenment: An Invitation in the Form of an Argument," in *This Is Enlightenment* (Chicago: University of Chicago Press, 2010), 1–33.

24. In *The Culture of Diagram*, esp. 10 and 19–52, Marrinan and I appropriate the concept of the "working object" from Lorraine Daston and Peter Galison in order to redefine the significance of cross-references in Diderot and d'Alembert's *Encyclopédie* and to redescribe the structure and operation of the plates in that compendium.

25. Hume, *Treatise*, 264–70.

26. Ibid., 210–11.

27. Cited in *The Culture of Diagram*, 110 (trans. by Marrinan). Samuel Richardson made a closely similar point in discussing *Clarissa*: "I could wish that the *Air* of Genuineness had been kept up, tho' I want not the letters to be *thought* genuine; only so far kept up, I mean, as that they would not prefatically be owned *not* to be genuine: and this for fear of weakening their Influence where any of them are aimed to be exemplary; as well as to avoid hurting that kind of Historical Faith which Fiction itself is generally read with, tho' we know it to be Fiction"; quoted from Richardson to William Warburton, 19 April 1748, *Selected Letters of Samuel Richardson*, ed. John Carroll (Oxford: Clarendon Press, 1964), 85.

Chapter One

This chapter was originally published as "Novel Knowledge: Judgment, Experience, Experiment," in *This Is Enlightenment*, ed. Clifford Siskin and William Warner (Chicago: University of Chicago Press, 2010), 284–300. © University of Chicago. All rights reserved.

1. Émile Zola, *The Experimental Novel, and Other Essays*, trans. Belle M. Sherman (New York: Haskell House, 1964), 20–21, 3.

2. Len Gougeon, "Holmes's Emerson and the Conservative Critique of Realism," *South Atlantic Review* 59.1 (1994): 107–25 (111–14).

3. Henry David Thoreau, *Walden; or, Life in the Woods*, ed. Norma Holmes Pearson (New York: Rinehart, 1959), 41. The episodes in *Walden* titled "Economy" and "The Bean-Field" specifically recall Crusoe's experiments with crops.

4. William Godwin, *Caleb Williams*, ed. David McCracken (London: Oxford University Press, 1970), 1.

5. Henry Fielding, *Tom Jones*, ed. John Bender and Simon Stern, World's Classics (Oxford: Oxford University Press, 1996), 352.

6. Charlotte Lennox, *The Female Quixote, or, The Adventures of Arabella*, ed. Margaret Dalziel and intro. Margaret Anne Doody (Oxford: Oxford University Press, 1989), 372, 379, 377. Lennox was in direct correspondence with Richardson and Johnson during the composition of the novel. The claim that Johnson may have written the final chapter, from which these quotations are drawn, is skeptically addressed by Margaret Doody in the appendix, 419–28. On the standing of fiction as a mode of inquiry leading to fact or truth, see John Bender, "Enlightenment Fiction and the Scientific Hypothesis," *Representations* 61 (1998): 6–28, republished in this volume as Chapter 2.

7. Dictionary citations come from the various editions of the *Dictionnaire de l'Académie française*, on the ARTFL database, last accessed 28 August 2011, http://artfl-project.uchicago.edu/. English citations are from the *Oxford English Dictionary*

Online, last accessed 28 August 2011, www.oed.com/. For Helvétius, see *De l'Esprit* (Paris: Durand, 1758), 11.

8. David Hume, *A Treatise of Human Nature*, 2nd ed., ed. L. A. Selby-Bigge and P. H. Nidditch (Oxford: Clarendon Press, 1978), 105. I have dropped Hume's italics. See the analytical index in this edition of the *Treatise* under "experience," "experiment," "knowledge," "judgment," and "probability."

9. For instances of Thoreau's many uses of "experiment" and "experience," see, for instance, *Walden*, 1, 6, 41, 44–45, 52, 135, 171, 251.

10. Peter Robert Dear, *Discipline and Experience: The Mathematical Way in the Scientific Revolution*, Science and Its Conceptual Foundations (Chicago: University of Chicago Press, 1995), 12–13, 246. Bacon is taken as background in Dear's book and receives light treatment because the focus is on developments across the seventeenth century.

11. Francis Bacon, *Novum organum*, in *The Works of Francis Bacon*, ed. J. Spedding, R. L. Ellis, and D. D. Heath, 7 vols. (London, 1857–59), vol. 4 (1858), 81 (bk. 1, aphorism 82).

12. Hume, *Treatise*, xviii–xix.

13. The influence of Lockean empiricism on Laurence Sterne's *The Life and Opinions of Tristram Shandy, Gentleman* (1759–67) has often been cited as a more common example of the relationship of the new epistemology to novelistic experimentation. See, for example, John Traugott, *Tristram Shandy's World: Sterne's Philosophical Rhetoric* (Berkeley: University of California Press, 1954); and Arthur H. Cash, "The Lockean Psychology of Tristram Shandy," *English Literary History* 22.2 (1955): 125–35. Also, more recently, Christina Lupton, "Tristram Shandy, David Hume and Epistemological Fiction," *Philosophy and Literature* 27.1 (2003): 98–115. For an examination of the "equivocal" nature of Locke's influence on Sterne, see W. G. Day, "Locke May Not Be the Key," in *Laurence Sterne: Riddles and Mysteries*, ed. Valerie Grosvenor Myer (London: Vision, 1984), 75–83.

14. Fielding, *Tom Jones*, 107.

15. Hume, *Treatise*, xix.

16. Steven Shapin and Simon Schaffer, *Leviathan and the Air-Pump: Hobbes, Boyle, and the Experimental Life* (Princeton, NJ: Princeton University Press, 1985), chaps. 2 and 6. On factuality, see also Steven Shapin, "The House of Experiment in Seventeenth-Century England," *Isis* 79.3 (September 1988): 373–404; Mary Poovey, *A History of the Modern Fact: Problems of Knowledge in the Sciences of Wealth and Society* (Chicago: University of Chicago Press, 1998), chaps. 3 and 4; and Lorraine Daston, "Description by Omission: Nature Enlightened and Obscured," in *Regimes of Description: In the Archive of the Eighteenth Century*, ed. John Bender and Michael Marrinan (Stanford, CA: Stanford University Press, 1995), 11–24.

17. Attempts at replication raised their own specters because the literal replication of the equipment that produced the original findings was dependent on highly skilled professionals. On the central role of technical glassmaking to Newton's success in his optical experiments, see Simon Schaffer, "Glass Works: Newton's Prisms and the Uses of Experiment," in *The Uses of Experiment: Studies in the Natural Sciences*, ed. David Gooding, T. J. Pinch, and Simon Schaffer (Cambridge: Cambridge University Press, 1989).

18. The "Rules of Reasoning" is discussed by Ernan McMullin, "Empiricism and the Scientific Revolution," in *Art, Science, and History in the Renaissance*, ed. Charles Southward Singleton (Baltimore: Johns Hopkins University Press, 1967), 331–69; and by Richard S. Westfall, *Never at Rest: A Biography of Isaac Newton* (Cambridge: Cambridge University Press, 1991), 801. For the text of the "Rules of Reasoning," see Isaac Newton, *The Principia: Mathematical Principles of Natural Philosophy*, ed. I. Bernard Cohen and Anne Miller Whitman (Berkeley: University of California Press, 1999), 794–96.

19. Daniel Defoe, *Robinson Crusoe: And Other Writings*, ed. James Runcieman Sutherland (New York: New York University Press, 1977), 294–301. The authorship of this piece has not generally been disputed, nor is Defoe's authorship necessary to my argument. For doubts about Defoe's authorship, see George Starr, "Why Defoe Probably Did Not Write *The Apparition of Mrs. Veal*," *Eighteenth-Century Fiction* 15.3–4 (2003): 421–50. For a rebuttal, see James Walton, "On the Attribution of 'Mrs. Veal,'" *Notes and Queries* 54 (2007): 60–62.

20. Samuel Richardson to William Warburton, 19 April 1748, in Samuel Richardson, *Selected Letters of Samuel Richardson*, ed. John Carroll (Oxford: Oxford University Press, 1964), 85.

21. Catherine Gallagher, "The Rise of Fictionality," in *The Novel*, vol. 1, *History, Geography, and Culture*, ed. Franco Moretti (Princeton, NJ: Princeton University Press, 2006), 336–63. Gallagher, in turn, cites Felix Martinez-Bonati, "The Act of Writing Fiction," *New Literary History: A Journal of Theory and Interpretation* 11.3 (1980): 425–34.

22. Ian P. Watt, *The Rise of the Novel: Studies in Defoe, Richardson, and Fielding* (Berkeley: University of California Press, 1957), 256–57, 288–97.

23. John Locke, *An Essay Concerning Human Understanding*, ed. P. H. Nidditch (Oxford: Clarendon Press, 1975), 645.

24. Hume, *Treatise*, 82, 87.

25. Samuel Richardson, *Clarissa: or, The History of a Young Lady*, ed. John Butt, 4 vols. (London: J. M. Dent, [1932], 1979 printing), 1.295–96.

26. Daniel Defoe, *Robinson Crusoe*, ed. John J. Richetti, Penguin Classics (London: Penguin Books, 2001), 83–84.

27. Ibid., 83–84. The citations may also be found by searching "experience" in *Robinson Crusoe* at http://collections.chadwyck.com.

28. John Bender, *Imagining the Penitentiary: Fiction and the Architecture of Mind in Eighteenth-Century England* (Chicago: University of Chicago Press, 1987), 55–56.

29. Richardson, *Clarissa*, 3.216.

30. Jonathan Swift, *Gulliver's Travels*, ed. Claude Rawson (Oxford: Oxford University Press, 2005), 81–82. The citations may also be found by searching "experience" in *Gulliver's Travels* at http://collections.chadwyck.com.

31. John Bender, "Enlightenment Fiction"; and "The Novel as Modern Myth," in *Defoe's Footprints: Essays in Honour of Maximillian E. Novak*, ed. Robert M. Maniquis and Carl Fisher (Toronto: University of Toronto Press, 2009). Both of these essays are republished in this volume, as Chapters 2 and 5.

32. Locke, *Essay*, 525, 654–55. I have dropped some of Locke's italics.

33. Dear, *Discipline and Experience*, 23.

34. On Condorcet, see Gerd Gigerenzer, Zeno Swijtink, Theodore Porter, Lorraine Daston, et al., eds., *The Empire of Chance: How Probability Changed Science and Everyday Life*, Ideas in Context (Cambridge: Cambridge University Press, 1989), 17; see also Antoine-Nicolas de Condorcet, *Sketch for a Historical Picture of the Progress of the Human Mind*, trans. June Barraclough (Westport, CT: Hyperion Press, 1955).

35. See Jesse Molesworth, *Chance and the Eighteenth-Century Novel: Realism, Probability, Magic* (Cambridge: Cambridge University Press, 2010).

36. Gigerenzer et al., *The Empire of Chance*, chap. 1.

37. Lennox, *Female Quixote*, 372, 378.

38. John J. Richetti, *Philosophical Writing: Locke, Berkeley, Hume* (Cambridge, MA: Harvard University Press, 1983), 89. John Richetti read an early draft of this essay and suggested the idea, noted earlier, that Gulliver is inconsistent in his judgments.

39. Hume, *Treatise*, 180.

Chapter Two

This chapter was originally published as "Enlightenment Fiction and the Scientific Hypothesis," in *Representations* 61 (1998): 6–28. © Regents of the University of California. I thank Mary Poovey for insightful comments that were crucial in the revision of this essay for publication. Her book *A History of the Modern Fact: Problems of Knowledge in the Sciences of Wealth and Society* (Chicago: University of Chicago Press, 1998) is a major statement in the field of this essay's concern. I also wish to thank Elizabeth Heckendorn Cook, Lorraine Daston, H. U. Gumbrecht, Lynn Hunt, Margaret Jacob, Michael McKeon, J. B. Shank, Clifford Siskin, Dorothea von Mücke, and William B. Warner for important assistance.

1. Denis Diderot and Jean le Rond D'Alembert, *Encyclopédie, ou dictionnaire raisonné des sciences, des arts et des métiers, par une société de gens de lettres*, which appeared serially beginning in 1751, with ten of the seventeen volumes delayed until 1765; the plates appeared from 1762 to 1772; the four-volume supplement, under different editorship but employing a number of the original contributors, in 1776–77 under the title *Supplément à l'encyclopédie, ou dictionnaire raisonné des sciences, des arts et des métiers, par une société de gens de lettres* (Amsterdam, 1776–77); and the independent, two-volume analytic tables of contents, sometimes with additional content, in 1780. The dates I assign to articles are the publication dates of the volumes in which they appear. Quotations from the *Encyclopédie* are translated from the text in the facsimile edition published by Pergamon Press (Elmsford, NY, 1969).

Throughout this essay, the word "science" carries its customary modern English meaning of "natural science." Although this usage is anachronistic, it is common and allows me to suggest affinities between Enlightenment and modern science. Relationships between the eighteenth-century English novel and science are not commonly discussed. Ian Watt alludes to Isaac Newton just once in *The Rise of the Novel: Studies in Defoe, Richardson, and Fielding* (Berkeley: University of California Press, 1957), 24, linking him with John Locke in a discussion of the reorientation of temporality during the later seventeenth century. Changing ideas about factuality and truth in the novel are the concerns of Barbara J. Shapiro's *Probability and Certainty in Seventeenth-Century England* (Princeton, NJ: Princeton University

Press, 1983), a book that addresses shifts in the definition of knowledge during the Scientific Revolution. Lennard J. Davis's *Factual Fictions: The Origins of the English Novel* (New York: Columbia University Press, 1983) is not concerned with science but relates ideas about factuality in emergent newspaper culture and the law to the rise of the novel. More recently, Michael McKeon, in *The Origins of the English Novel, 1600–1740* (Baltimore: Johns Hopkins University Press, 1987), and J. Paul Hunter, in *Before Novels: The Cultural Contexts of Eighteenth-Century English Fiction* (New York: Norton, 1990), have opened questions about truth claims in the Scientific Revolution and in the early novel, but the terms "hypothesis" and "fiction" in their technical, philosophic usages appear in neither book. J. Paul Hunter's "Robert Boyle and the Epistemology of the Novel," *Eighteenth-Century Fiction* 2.4 (1990): 275–91, focuses on the relationship between the novel and works by Boyle such as *Occasional Reflections* (1665) that involve meditation on observed fact. I consider the novel in relation to David Hume's and Jeremy Bentham's philosophic treatments of fiction in *Imagining the Penitentiary: Fiction and the Architecture of Mind in Eighteenth-Century England* (Chicago: University of Chicago Press, 1987), as does Leo Damrosch in *Fictions of Reality in the Age of Hume and Johnson* (Madison: University of Wisconsin Press, 1989). Robert Markley treats a number of related issues in their religious context in *Fallen Languages: Crises of Representation in Newtonian England, 1660–1740* (Ithaca, NY: Cornell University Press, 1993). In Wolfgang Iser's fascinating book *The Fictive and the Imaginary: Charting Literary Anthropology* (Baltimore: Johns Hopkins University Press, 1993), Newton is twice mentioned and his statement against hypothesis is quoted but only in the context that places Newton at the end of the Renaissance tradition of viewing fiction negatively. Iser never discusses the term "hypothesis." And so little does the novel figure in Iser's book that Samuel Richardson is not mentioned at all, while Daniel Defoe and Henry Fielding each appear only once, in contexts that have nothing to do with the genre of the novel per se. Most recently, Everett Zimmerman's *The Boundaries of Fiction: History and the Eighteenth-Century Novel* (Ithaca, NY: Cornell University Press, 1996) does not deal with science but does treat some other issues that come up in the present essay. Ilse Vickers, *Defoe and the New Sciences* (Cambridge: Cambridge University Press, 1996), chiefly treats the novelist's relationship to Francis Bacon and, very interestingly, to Robert Boyle.

2. Discussion of the issues surrounding these and related terms occurs throughout two recent guides that have been helpful in the preparation of this essay: *The Philosophy of Science*, ed. Richard Boyd, Philip Gasper, and J. D. Trout (Cambridge, MA: MIT Press, 1991), and *Companion to the History of Modern Science*, ed. R. C. Olby et al. (London: Routledge, 1990). In the latter I note especially articles on "Realism," by W. H. Newton-Smith; "The Development of the Philosophy of Science, 1600–1900," by Ernan McMullin; and "The Development of the Philosophy of Science since 1900," by M. J. S. Hodge and G. N. Cantor. Articles that treat such issues in the former volume are too numerous to list, but they include "Confirmation, Semantics, and the Interpretation of Scientific Theories," by Richard Boyd, and "The Confutation of Convergent Realism," by Larry Laudan.

3. See Virginia P. Dawson, "The Limits of Observation and the Hypotheses of Georges-Louis Buffon and Charles Bonnet," in *Beyond the History of Science*, ed.

Elizabeth Garber (Bethlehem, PA: Lehigh University Press, 1990), 107–25. A crucial text is Denis Diderot's *Pensées sur l'interpretation de la nature* (1754); see the helpful introduction to this work in Denis Diderot, *Oeuvres*, ed. Laurent Versini, 5 vols. (Paris: R. Laffont, 1994), 1.555–57. Parts of this and other scientific works of Diderot are translated in Jean Stewart and Jonathan Kemp, *Diderot, Interpreter of Nature* (London: Lawrence and Wishart, 1937). *Les Bijoux indiscrets* appears in vol. 2 of Diderot, *Oeuvres*; important in this context are the chapters on "The State of the Academy of Science of Banza" and "Mangogul's Dream; or, A journey to the Land of Hypotheses," in Denis Diderot, *The Indiscreet Jewels*, trans. Sophie Hawkes (New York: Marsilio Publishers, 1993), where these appear as chaps. 9 and 32. On Thomas Reid, see Larry Laudan, *Science and Hypothesis: Historical Essays on Scientific Methodology* (Dordrecht: D. Reidel, 1981), chap. 7.

4. The standard text on this process is Gerd Buchdahl, *Metaphysics and the Philosophy of Science, The Classical Origins: Descartes to Kant* (Cambridge, MA: MIT Press, 1969). See also Shapiro, *Probability and Certainty*, and, on the shift in rhetoric from syllogistic to probabilistic argumentation, Wilbur Samuel Howell, *Eighteenth-Century British Logic and Rhetoric* (Princeton, NJ: Princeton University Press, 1971).

5. See Jürgen Habermas, *The Structural Transformation of the Public Sphere: An Inquiry into a Category of Bourgeois Society*, trans. Thomas Burger with the assistance of Frederick Lawrence (Cambridge, MA: MIT Press, 1989). For commentary on Habermas's ideas about the "public sphere," see Craig Calhoun, ed., *Habermas and the Public Sphere* (Cambridge, MA: MIT Press, 1992). Central to Habermas's definition of life in the public sphere is the exchange of ideas through an active print culture. Thus, Boyle's experiments, while directly witnessed by a select few, gained public presence through their circulation in print. I share many of the doubts that have been voiced about Habermas's account of the rise and fall of the public sphere, as well as about his insistence that consensus must be founded upon rational discourse. His terms still have value, I believe, even when shorn of their ideological freight.

On the public circulation of debates about science and public experiments, see especially Larry Stewart, *The Rise of Public Science: Rhetoric, Technology, and Natural Philosophy in Newtonian Britain, 1660–1750* (Cambridge: Cambridge University Press, 1992). But see also, among other essays in David Goodring, Trevor Pinch, and Simon Schaffer, eds., *The Uses of Experiment: Studies in the Natural Sciences* (Cambridge: Cambridge University Press, 1989), Simon Schaffer's "Glass Works: Newton's Prisms and the Uses of Experiment," 67–104.

6. See Alexander Welsh, *Strong Representations: Narrative and Circumstantial Evidence in England* (Baltimore: Johns Hopkins University Press, 1992). In order to avoid repeated notes, I group here some standard texts that have helped to inform me about early modern science and that touch on many issues raised in this essay. Barry Gower, *The Scientific Method: An Historical and Philosophical Guide* (London: Routledge, 1997); Steven Shapin, *The Scientific Revolution* (Chicago: University of Chicago Press, 1996); Margaret C. Jacob, *Scientific Culture and the Making of the Industrial West* (Oxford: Oxford University Press, 1997); Margaret C. Jacob, *The Cultural Meaning of the Scientific Revolution* (Philadelphia: Temple University Press, 1988); Thomas L. Hankins, *Science and the Enlightenment* (Cambridge: Cambridge

University Press, 1985); A. Rupert Hall, *The Revolution in Science, 1500–1750* (London: Longman, 1983); A. Rupert Hall, *From Galileo to Newton* (New York: Dover, 1981); Ryan D. Tweny, Michael E. Doherty, and Clifford R. Mynatt, *On Scientific Thinking* (New York: Columbia University Press, 1981); and Ralph M. Blake, Curt J. Ducasse, and Edward H. Madden, *Theories of Scientific Method: The Renaissance through the Nineteenth Century* (Seattle: University of Washington Press, 1960).

7. *Webster's New Collegiate Dictionary* (Springfield, MA: G. & C. Merriam, 1979), s.v. "enlightenment." Steven Shapin and Simon Schaffer, *Leviathan and the Air-Pump: Hobbes, Boyle, and the Experimental Life* (Princeton, NJ: Princeton University Press, 1985), chaps. 2 and 6. Hunter suggests the relevance of this book to the study of the novel in his article, "Robert Boyle and the Epistemology of the Novel."

8. Samuel Johnson's *Dictionary of the English Language* (1755) is cited from Harrison's edition (London, 1786). See also the important anonymous articles in the *Encyclopédie* on "Probability" and "Verisimilitude" (both dating from 1765).

9. David Hume, *A Treatise of Human Nature*, 2nd ed., ed. L. A. Selby-Bigge and P. H. Nidditch (Oxford: Clarendon Press, 1978), 630.

10. On this huge issue in Hume of causation and induction, especially his skeptical analysis of the bases of induction, see Buchdahl, *Metaphysics and the Philosophy of Science*, chap. 6. See also John Biro, "Hume's New Science of Mind," and Alexander Rosenberg, "Hume and the Philosophy of Science," in *The Cambridge Companion to Hume*, ed. David Fate Norton (Cambridge: Cambridge University Press, 1993), 33–64 and 65–89.

11. Hume, *Treatise*, 181–82.

12. Samuel Richardson to William Warburton, 19 April 1748, in *Selected Letters of Samuel Richardson*, ed. John Carroll (Oxford: Clarendon Press, 1964), 85.

13. See Buchdahl, *Metaphysics and the Philosophy of Science*, chap. 6. For eighteenth-century summations, see the 1765 article on "Induction" in the *Encyclopédie* and Johnson's *Dictionary*, where "induction" is defined as "when, from several particular propositions, we infer one general." Johnson quotes Newton's *Opticks*: "Although the arguing from experiments and observations by *induction* be no demonstration of general conclusions, yet it is the best way of arguing which the nature of things admits of, and may be looked upon as so much the stronger by how much the *induction* is more general; and if no exception occur from phaenomena, the conclusion may be general." For twentieth-century discussions of induction by Karl Popper, Hilary Putnam, and W. V. O. Quine, among others, see also Boyd, Gasper, and Trout, *Philosophy of Science*.

14. Henry Fielding, *Tom Jones*, ed. John Bender and Simon Stern, with introduction by John Bender (Oxford: Oxford University Press, 1996), bk. 5, chap. 4, 194. On the novel's connections with materialist philosophy in the period, see Margaret C. Jacob, "The Materialist World of Pornography," in *The Invention of Pornography: Obscenity and the Origins of Modernity, 1500–1800*, ed. Lynn Hunt (New York: Zone Books, 1993), 157–202; she cites in particular John Cleland, whose *Memoirs of a Woman of Pleasure* was published in the same year as *Tom Jones*.

15. Samuel Richardson, *Clarissa: Preface, Hints of Prefaces, and Postscript*, ed. R. F. Brissenden (Los Angeles: William Andrews Clark Memorial Library, Univer-

sity of California, 1964), 5. For a discussion of the juridical context of this passage, see Welsh, *Strong Representations*, 69–70. See also Bender, *Imagining the Penitentiary*, chap. 6.

16. See McKeon, *Origins of the English Novel*, 25–64.

17. Isaac Newton, "General Scholium," in *Mathematical Principles of Natural Philosophy and His System of the World*, trans. Andrew Motte, ed. and revised by Florian Cajori (Berkeley: University of California Press, 1934), 543–47. For a convenient account of the meaning of the phrase *hypotheses non fingo*, see Derek Gjertsen, *The Newton Handbook* (London: Routledge & Kegan Paul, 1986), 266; Alexandre Koyré persuasively argued that *fingo* meant "feign" in *Newtonian Studies* (Cambridge, MA: Harvard University Press, 1965). For an excellent account of the background and context of Newton's thought on hypotheses, see Ernan McMullin, "Empiricism and the Scientific Revolution," in *Art, Science, and History in the Renaissance*, ed. Charles Southward Singleton (Baltimore: Johns Hopkins University Press, 1967). On the very fine distinction between hypotheses and induction involving "imaginative constructs" in Newton's evolving practice, see I. Bernard Cohen, *Franklin and Newton: An Inquiry into Speculative Newtonian Experimental Science* (Philadelphia: American Philosophical Society, 1956), chaps. 1 and 4–6; and I. Bernard Cohen, *The Newtonian Revolution* (Cambridge: Cambridge University Press, 1980), chaps. 1 and 3. The complex question of the relationship of Newton's scientific work to his religious belief is a major theme in Richard S. Westfall, *Never at Rest: A Biography of Isaac Newton* (Cambridge: Cambridge University Press, 1980); see also Betty Jo Teeter Dobbs, *The Janus Faces of Genius: The Role of Alchemy in Newton's Thought* (Cambridge: Cambridge University Press, 1991), and Markley, *Fallen Languages*.

18. The text of the preface to Daniel Defoe's *Robinson Crusoe* is modernized from J. Donald Crowley's edition (Oxford: Oxford University Press, 1972); Daniel Defoe's "Author's Preface" to *The Farther Adventures of Robinson Crusoe* is cited, with my italics, from George A. Aitken's edition (London: J. M. Dent, 1899). The most convenient place to find the prefaces and Charles Gildon's pamphlet is in Ioan M. Williams, ed., *Novel and Romance, 1700–1800: A Documentary Record* (London: Routledge & Kegan Paul, 1970), 56–70. The issue of parable and allegory is central to Defoe's debate with Gildon; in the "General Scholium" Newton discusses both the heuristic value of allegories describing God's powers and their limitations as fictions when considered as scientific explanations of cause. See H. G. Alexander, ed., *The Leibniz–Clarke Correspondence* (Manchester, UK: Manchester University Press, 1956), esp. 24. The correspondence was published in 1717 in English, then in various languages and editions throughout the century. For a bibliography and summary account, see Gjertsen, *Newton Handbook*, 300–304.

19. Newton, *Mathematical Principles*, 400. The "Rules of Reasoning" are discussed by McMullin in "Empiricism and the Scientific Revolution" and by Westfall in *Never at Rest*, 801. The *Principia* underwent many revisions, the chief of which are clarified in Gjertsen, *Newton Handbook*, 466. As Gjertsen points out, Newton retreated from applying the term "hypothesis" to his method, even though he had frequently used hypotheses before. For Cajori's full listing of the chief instances, see Newton, *Mathematical Principles*, 671–76. The interesting notion of "approximate

truth" is still alive in the philosophy of science; it arises in a number of articles in Boyd, Gasper, and Trout, *The Philosophy of Science*.

20. Daniel Defoe, *Serious Reflections during the Life and Surprising Adventures of Robinson Crusoe*, ed. George A. Aitken (London, 1895), 98–99. Discussed by McKeon, *Origins of the English Novel*, 120–21. Interestingly, the context of Defoe's statement is a long chapter titled, "Of the Immorality of Conversation, and the Vulgar Errors of Behaviour," the drift of which is that conversation is inherently corrupting and productive of error and falsification. This is the opposite of the more modern Enlightenment ideal of conversation as productive of knowledge advanced in Addison's *Spectator* and paradigmatic for Habermas.

21. Newton, *Mathematical Principles*, 542.

22. Hans Vaihinger, *The Philosophy of "As if": A System of the Theoretical, Practical, and Religious Fictions of Mankind*, trans. C. K. Ogden (London: Routledge & K. Paul, 1935). Vaihinger works through every category of "fiction" in this book (see 15–77 for a summary). He defines hypotheses as strictly separate from fictions of all kinds, and especially poetic fictions, because of their verifiability (81–90). I show how difficult it proved to maintain this distinction in the eighteenth century, and I believe that discussions in the philosophy of science show that it remains so now. Vaihinger, a neo-Kantian, makes interesting arguments for the value of fictions in the conduct of practical reason.

23. Wesley Trimpi, "The Ancient Hypothesis of Fiction: An Essay on the Origins of Literary Theory," *Traditio* 27 (1971): 54–55. On the changing idea of "hypothesis" in Copernicus, Boyle, and others, see McMullin, "Empiricism and the Scientific Revolution."

24. Wesley Trimpi, *Muses of One Mind: The Literary Analysis of Experience and Its Continuity* (Princeton, NJ: Princeton University Press, 1983), 30, where he quotes Quintilian 5.10.95–96; see *Muses of One Mind*, 50–51 for hypothesis as plot outline and 25 for Trimpi's basic definitions. See also George Kennedy, ed., *The Cambridge History of Literary Criticism*, vol. 1, *Classical Criticism* (Cambridge: Cambridge University Press, 1989), 198 and 207 on hypothesis, plus numerous entries on fictionality. As A. Rupert Hall notes in *Isaac Newton, Adventurer in Thought* (Oxford: Blackwell, 1992), 15, rhetoric was the chief study at Cambridge during the first year; see also Westfall, *Never at Rest*, chap. 3, who cites Newton's notes on Aristotle, including the *Nicomachean Ethics*. Quintilian stood at the heart of grammar school and university education, both of which were focused on disputation according to ancient principles. The curriculum at Newton's grammar school in Grantham is not specifically known but, for a detailed account of study both at St. Paul's in London and at Cambridge, see Harris Francis Fletcher, *The Intellectual Development of John Milton*, 2 vols. (Urbana: University of Illinois Press, 1956 and 1961).

25. Joseph Priestley, quoted in Simon Schaffer, "Natural Philosophy and Public Spectacle in the Eighteenth Century," *History of Science* 21.1 (1983): 1. Schaffer cites Joseph Priestley, "Lectures on History and General Policy," in *The Theological and Miscellaneous Works of Joseph Priestley*, ed. J. T. Rutt (London: Printed by G. Smallfield, 1817–31), 24.27–28.

26. Voltaire, *Lettres philosophiques*, ed. Raymond Naves (Paris: Garnier, 1988), 232; this quotation is from Voltaire's 1739 revision of the opening of the letter (my

translation). The reference to Père Louis-Bertrand Castel is from a letter of March 1738, cited in Jean Ehrard, *L'idée de nature en France* (Paris: S.E.V.P.E.N., 1963), 1.121. I am indebted to J. B. Shank for these references. Many more similar uses of the word *roman* appear in the on-line ARTFL database of French texts of the period maintained at the University of Chicago. This usage of the word *roman* to mean "an account without verisimilitude or demonstration" became well established from the 1730s onward: it appears in the fifth edition (1798) of the *Dictionnaire de L'Académie française* but not in the first edition (1694). The *Encyclopédie* article "*Roman*" (1765) by Louis de Jaucourt does not reflect this usage, though it does credit Madame de La Fayette with initiating a new taste for "truthful painting" in the novel and the English (especially Richardson and Fielding) with making the genre "useful." The final paragraph stresses the emotional power of the new novel in contrast to the abstract sciences of Plato, Aristotle, and Euclid. In the table showing the "System of Human Knowledge" at the beginning of the *Encyclopédie*, the novel appears under the category "imagination" and the subheading "narrative."

27. The long article on "Phenomenon" by D. F. in the *Supplément* contains a more skeptical view of hypotheses; the article has not been attributed. The standard work attributing articles is the *Inventory of Diderot's "Encyclopédie"* by Richard Schwab, Walter E. Rex, and John Lough, which appeared as vols. 80, 83, 85, 91–93 of Theodore Besterman, ed., *Studies on Voltaire and the Eighteenth Century* (Geneva and Oxford: Institut et musée de Voltaire and Voltaire Foundation, 1971–72). See also Jacques Proust, *Diderot et "L'Encyclopédie"* 3rd ed. (Paris: A. Michel, 1995), and John Lough, *Essays on the "Encyclopédie" of Diderot and d'Alembert* (London: Oxford University Press, 1968). For biographies of the authors, including Jean-François Marmontel and Abbé de La Chapelle, see Frank A. Kafker and Serena L. Kafker, *The Encyclopedists as Individuals: A Biographical Dictionary of the Authors of the "Encyclopédie"* (Oxford: Voltaire Foundation at the Taylor Institution, 1988). I am grateful to Mark Olsen and Jack Iverson at the ARTFL project for their views on the authorship of the articles cited in this essay.

28. Nelson Goodman, *Ways of Worldmaking* (Indianapolis: Hackett, 1978).

29. See Buchdahl, *Metaphysics and the Philosophy of Science*; and the article on "Realism" by W. H. Newton-Smith in R. C. Olby et al., *Companion to the History of Modern Science*, 181–95; or, for instance, Ian Hacking, *Representing and Intervening: Introductory Topics in the Philosophy of Natural Science* (Cambridge: Cambridge University Press, 1983).

30. Diderot, *Oeuvres*, 1.563. My translation, with reference to that in Stewart and Kemp, *Diderot, Interpreter of Nature*, 43.

31. See Bender, *Imagining the Penitentiary*, 36–37, and 269n49.

32. Gabrielle Émilie Le Tonnelier de Breteuil du Châtelet, *Institutions de physique* (Paris: Prault fils, 1740), 87, my italics and translation, cited in Phillip R. Sloan, "L'hypothéisme de Buffon: Sa place dans la philosophie des sciences du dix-huitième siècle," in *Buffon 88: Actes du Colloque international pour le bicentenaire de la mort de Buffon*, ed. Jean Gayon (Paris: J. Vrin, 1992), 212.

33. These questions thread obsessively through the large number of prefaces and pamphlets about the novel conveniently collected in Williams, *Novel and Romance*. For narratological perspectives on fictionality, see Jean-Marie Schaeffer,

"Fiction, feinte et narration," *Critique* 481–82 (1987): 555–76; and Marie-Laure Ryan, *Possible Worlds, Artificial Intelligence, and Narrative Theory* (Bloomington: Indiana University Press, 1991).

34. Catherine Gallagher, *Nobody's Story: The Vanishing Acts of Women Writers in the Marketplace, 1670–1820* (Berkeley: University of California Press, 1994), esp. chap. 4.

35. Quoted from Williams, *Novel and Romance*, 281.

36. Martin C. Battestin, "*Tom Jones*: The Argument of Design," in *The Augustan Milieu: Essays Presented to Louis A. Landa*, ed. Henry Knight Miller, Eric Rothstein, and G. S. Rousseau (Oxford: Clarendon Press, 1970), 307.

37. Laurence Sterne, *The Life and Opinions of Tristram Shandy, Gentleman*, ed. Ian Watt (Boston: Houghton Mifflin, 1965), 114–16.

38. The quotations come from Horace Walpole, *The Castle of Otranto*, ed. W. S. Lewis (Oxford: Oxford University Press, 1964), 4, 5, and 7–8.

39. Friedrich A. Kittler, *Aufschreibesysteme 1800/1900* (Munich: Fink, 1985); published in English as *Discourse Networks, 1800/1900*, trans. Michael Metteer and Chris Cullens, with foreword by David E. Wellbery (Stanford, CA: Stanford University Press, 1990). It is worth noting that the efflorescence of fiction that Walpole advocates comes in the same year as the publication of Thomas Reid's *An Inquiry into the Human Mind on the Principles of Common Sense* (1764), though Reid's formal attack on hypotheses is not fully developed until his *Essays on the Intellectual Powers of Man* (1785). On Reid, see Laudan, *Science and Hypothesis*, chap. 7, and Keith Lehrer, *Thomas Reid* (London: Routledge, 1989).

40. Welsh, *Strong Representations*, ix–x.

41. Jean-Jacques Rousseau, *Discours sur l'origine et les fondements de l'inégalité parmi les hommes*; my translation, with reference to Lester G. Crocker, ed., *The Social Contract and Discourse on the Origin of Inequality* (New York: Pocket Books, 1967), 177; and Jean-Jacques Rousseau, *The First and Second Discourses*, trans. Roger D. Masters and Judith R. Masters (New York: St. Martin's Press, 1964), 103.

42. See Dawson, "Limits of Observation." A convenient collection of early reviews of the *Histoire naturelle* appears in John Lyon and Philip R. Sloan, ed. and trans., *From Natural History to the History of Nature: Readings from Buffon and His Critics* (Notre Dame, IN: University of Notre Dame Press, 1981), 213–45.

43. Georges-Louis Buffon, *Histoire et théorie de la terre* (1749), quoted by Sloan in "L'hypothéisme de Buffon," 218, my translation. Sloan's essay offers a compact account of Buffon's place in Madame du Châtelet's circle and of his work presenting the calculus of Newton in French.

44. Buffon's "Initial Discourse" is cited here from Lyon and Sloan, *From Natural History to the History of Nature*, 122–23.

45. I refer to the section of Buffon's *Natural History* entitled "Of Reproduction in General"; see *Selections from "Natural History General and Particular"* (New York: Arno Press, 1977), 17–38, which reproduces pages from the English edition of 1780–85, printed for W. Creech, Edinburgh.

46. I thank Mary Poovey for summarizing the arguments of the present essay along the lines given in this paragraph.

47. John Dunlop, *The History of Fiction: Being a Critical Account of the Most Cel-*

ebrated Prose Works of Fiction, from the Earliest Greek Romances to the Novels of the Present Age, 3 vols. (Edinburgh: Printed for Longman, Hurst, Rees, Orme, and Brown, 1814). William B. Warner suggested the importance of John Dunlop's work and its title. The use of the term "fiction" to mean "novel" already had some currency, for instance in the passage from Anna Laetitia Barbauld and her brother cited earlier; for a still earlier usage, see Samuel Johnson, *The Rambler* 4 (Saturday, 31 March 1750), in *The Yale Edition of the Works of Samuel Johnson*, vol. 3, ed. W. J. Bate and Albrecht B. Strauss (New Haven, CT: Yale University Press, 1969), 19–25.

Chapter Three

This chapter was originally published as "Matters of Fact: Virtual Witnessing and the Public in Hogarth's Narratives," in *Hogarth: Representing "Nature's Machines,"* ed. David Bindman, Frédéric Ogée, and Peter Wagner (Manchester: Manchester University Press, 2001), 49–70. By permission of Manchester University Press.

1. Jean Rouquet, *Lettres de Monsieur ** à un de ses amis à Paris, pour lui expliquer les Estampes de Monsieur Hogarth* (London: R. Dodsley, 1746). See also John Trusler, *Hogarth Moralized, Being a Complete Edition of Hogarth's Works* (London: S. Hooper and Mrs. Hogarth, 1768); John Ireland, *Hogarth Illustrated* (London: J. & J. Boydell, 1791); Georg Christoph Lichtenberg, *Lichtenberg's Commentaries on Hogarth's Engravings*, trans. Innes and Gustav Herdan (London: Cresset, 1966), which originally were essays published between 1794 and 1799 in the *Göttinger Taschenkalender*. Paulson discusses these commentaries in *The Beautiful, Novel, and Strange: Aesthetics and Heterodoxy* (Baltimore: Johns Hopkins University Press, 1996), chap. 10, "The Novelizing of Hogarth." *Hogarth: His Life, Art and Times*, 2 vols. (New Haven, CT: Yale University Press, 1971) was rewritten as *Hogarth*, 3 vols. (New Brunswick, NJ: Rutgers University Press, 1991–93); *Hogarth's Graphic Works*, 2 vols. (New Haven, CT: Yale University Press, 1965) was revised in 1970 and reworked as *Hogarth's Graphic Works*, 3rd ed. rev. (London: The Print Room, 1989). The later versions will be cited hereafter as, respectively, *Hogarth* and *HGW*.

2. *Oxford English Dictionary*, s.v. "facticity," accessed 22 February 2011, www.oed.com/view/Entry/67485?redirectedFrom=facticity#eid. It follows, then, that the usual English sense of "factitious" and the usual French sense of *facticité* to refer to the specious, the artificial, and the inauthentic are not in play here. One sense in the *Oxford English Dictionary*, dating from 1678 and used by Hartley, Gibbon, Bentham, and Mill, plays interestingly on my sense: "Got up, made up for a particular occasion or purpose; arising from custom, habit, or design; not natural or spontaneous; artificial, conventional." Space does not allow much exploration here of the extent to which what we may call the everyday, commonsense experience of the world is also customary, habitual, and, in some sense, not natural. This is precisely the point Heidegger pursued.

3. See Martin Heidegger, *Being and Time*, trans. John Macquarrie and Edward Robinson (New York: Harper, 1962); Jürgen Habermas, *The Structural Transformation of the Public Sphere: An Inquiry into a Category of Bourgeois Society*, trans. Thomas Burger with the assistance of Frederick Lawrence (Cambridge, MA: MIT Press, 1989); and *The Philosophical Discourse of Modernity*, trans. Frederick G. Lawrence (Cambridge, MA: MIT Press, 1987), esp. chap. 6. See also *Habermas and The Pub-*

lic Sphere, ed. Craig Calhoun (Cambridge, MA: MIT Press, 1992). For articles on "facticity" and other matters philosophical, I have relied in part on *A Companion to Continental Philosophy*, ed. Simon Critchley and William R. Schroeder (Oxford: Blackwell, 1998); on *Encylopédie philosophique universelle*, ed. André Jacob, vol. 2, *Les Notions philosophiques*, ed. Sylvain Auroux (Paris: Presses Universitaires de France, 1989); and on *Historisches Wörterbuch der Philosophie*, ed. Joachim Ritter (Darmstadt: Wissenschaftliche Buchgesellschaft, 1971–95), vol. 2. I thank H. U. Gumbrecht and Richard Rorty for their advice on the implications of the term "facticity" in Heidegger and on the relationship between Heidegger's and Habermas's thought on related issues (they have, of course, no responsibility for the outcome here).

4. See John Bender, *Imagining the Penitentiary: Fiction and the Architecture of Mind in Eighteenth-Century England* (Chicago: University of Chicago Press, 1987). On satire, see Ronald Paulson, *Satire and the Novel in Eighteenth-Century England* (New Haven, CT: Yale University Press, 1967), and David Bindman, *Hogarth and His Times* (Berkeley: University of California Press, 1997), 33–40. For Ian Watt's influential definition of "formal realism," see *The Rise of the Novel* (Berkeley: University of California Press, 1957), 32. On factuality, see Mary Poovey, *A History of the Modern Fact: Problems of Knowledge in the Sciences of Wealth and Society* (Chicago: University of Chicago Press, 1998), esp. chaps. 3 and 4. With regard to the ideas presented here, one way to paraphrase Norman Bryson's important book on still life, *Looking at the Overlooked* (Cambridge, MA: Harvard University Press, 1990), would be to say that still life is about the efficacy of the idea of the object.

5. These disruptions recall theater settings, which are relevant especially because of Hogarth's connections with John Gay and Henry Fielding. Yet, distortions in perspective of the kinds found in scenery by the Bibienas to which Hogarth refers in his series of paintings of *The Beggar's Opera* and elsewhere do not necessarily register as such in the theater. In prints, such distortions are evident. The theatrical context of Hogarth's cycles is rich indeed. See, for instance, *Hogarth*, 1.238–41 and 2.19–20. For careful discussion of the overlap of frames of reference in the cycles, including the theatrical frame, see Peter Wagner, *Reading Iconotexts: From Swift to the French Revolution* (London: Reaktion Books, 1995), esp. chap. 3; and "Hogarthian Frames: The 'New' Eighteenth-Century Aesthetics," in *Das 18. Jahrhundert*, ed. Monika Fludernik et al. (Trier: Wissenschaftlicher Verlag, 1998), 277–302. See also Claude Fierobe, "Monde du théâtre, théâtre du monde dans l'oeuvre gravé de William Hogarth," *Bulletin de la Société d'études anglo-américaines des XVIIe et XVIIIe siècles* 33 (1991): 61–75; Mary Klinger Lindberg, "Stylistic Strategies in William Hogarth's Theatrical Satires," in *The Question of Style in Philosophy and the Arts*, ed. Caroline van Eck et al. (Cambridge: Cambridge University Press, 1995), 50–69; Carl A. Peterson, "Figure and Actor: Theater and Theatricality in the Narrative Art of William Hogarth," *Bulletin* (Allen Memorial Art Museum) 48.2 (1995): 3–24.

6. The first phrases are my translation from Rouquet's "Description du tableau de M. Hogarth qui représente la marche des gardes à leur rendez-vous de Finchley," bound with his *Lettres de Monsieur ****, 2; the last phrase is as translated by Paulson in *The Beautiful, Novel, and Strange*, 258. The original reads: "Le premier & le plus grand défaut que je trouve au Tableau de Mr. Hogarth, c'est qu'il est tout neuf, & qu'il ressemble encore trop aux objets qu'il représente; si ceci vous paroit un

paradoxe, gardez vous de l'avouër: ce Tableau dis-je a le défaut d'être encore tout brillant de cette ignoble fraîcheur, qu'on découvre dans la nature, & qu'on ne voit jamais dans les Cabinets bien célébres."

7. Steven Shapin and Simon Schaffer, *Leviathan and the Air-Pump: Hobbes, Boyle, and the Experimental Life* (Princeton, NJ: Princeton University Press, 1985), 61–62. Further citations appear parenthetically in the text. See also the article on "Description" (and its supplements) and the plates to the *Encyclopédie*, by which I mean the *Encyclopédie, ou dictionnaire raisonné des sciences, des arts et des métiers, par une société de gens de lettres*, which appeared serially beginning in 1751, with ten of the seventeen volumes delayed until 1765; the plates appeared from 1762 to 1772; the four-volume supplement, under different editorship but employing a number of the original contributors, in 1776–77; and the independent, two-volume analytic tables of contents, sometimes with additional content, in 1780.

8. The question of alignment with the rules of perspective versus that with appearances to the eye was at the heart of the controversy about representation in which the "Satire on False Perspective" was situated. Joseph Highmore was on the side of mathematical precision, while Hogarth and Joshua Kirby argued for flexible visualization in Kirby's *Dr. Brook Taylor's Method of Perspective Made Easy* (Ipswich: W. Craighton, 1754), which teaches how "to produce representations consistent with the inconsistencies of seeing in the lived world of perceptual experience." I quote Jenn Fishman's unpublished essay, "Some Satires on False Perspective: Hogarth, Kirby and the Problem of Drawing What You See," given at meetings of the American Society for Eighteenth-Century Studies, Milwaukee, 25 March 1999. Paulson treats the "Satire on False Perspective" in *Hogarth*, 3.356. Paulson discusses perspective jokes in the cycles or "modern moral subjects" and notes that Hogarth "plays with [the] sense of spectator identification." He interprets these jokes rather specifically but does observe that "the sort of punning brought about by naïve perspective in effect replaces the Renaissance man as the proper spectator with the 'common observation' of the ordinary viewer," *Hogarth*, 3.61. See also Paulson's *Popular and Polite Art in the Age of Hogarth and Fielding* (Notre Dame, IN: University of Notre Dame Press, 1979), chap. 4. In *Looking at the Overlooked*, 71, Bryson notes that "although [still life] techniques assume a mastery of perspective . . . nevertheless perspective's jewel—the vanishing point—is always absent" in the genre. The double essence of still life is at once to familiarize and defamiliarize. One way to imagine facticity in Hogarth is as a localized wrenching of the object from its larger perspective context in the scene represented. This effect is often heightened in the cycles by the exaggerated, theatrical perspective of the scenes of action. See also Svetlana Alpers, *The Art of Describing: Dutch Art in the Seventeenth Century* (Chicago: University of Chicago Press, 1983), esp. 35.

9. David Hume, *A Treatise of Human Nature*, 2nd ed., ed. L. A. Selby-Bigge and P. H. Nidditch (Oxford: Clarendon Press, 1978), 215. Further citations will appear parenthetically in the text.

10. See John Bender, "Enlightenment Fiction and the Scientific Hypothesis," *Representations* 61 (1998): 6–28, and introduction by John Bender in Henry Fielding, *Tom Jones*, ed. John Bender and Simon Stern (Oxford: Oxford University Press,

1996), ix–xxiv. Republished as Chapters 2 and 6 of the present volume. See also George A. Starr, *Defoe and Casuistry* (Princeton, NJ: Princeton University Press, 1971). For full analysis of difficulties with the traditional assumption of alignment between Hogarth and Fielding, see Frédéric Ogée, "Fielding et Hogarth: les limites des correspondances," *Bulletin de la Société d'études anglo-américaines des XVIIe et XVIIIe siècles* 40 (1995): 143–62.

11. See John Brewer, *The Pleasures of the Imagination* (London: HarperCollins, 1997); *The Birth of a Consumer Society: The Commercialization of Eighteenth-Century England*, ed. Neil McKendrick, John Brewer, and J. H. Plumb (Bloomington: Indiana University Press, 1982); *Consumption and the World of Goods*, ed. John Brewer and Roy Porter (London: Routledge, 1993); *The Consumption of Culture, 1600–1800: Image, Object, Text*, ed. Ann Bermingham and John Brewer (London: Routledge, 1995); Deidre Lynch, *The Economy of Character: Novels, Market Culture, and the Business of Inner Meaning* (Chicago: University of Chicago Press, 1998).

12. Hogarth authorized inexpensive copies of *Harlot* by Giles King and most probably authorized those of *Rake* by Thomas Bakewell. Additional, unauthorized copies also circulated. See *HGW*, 76–77, 89–91, and plates 126/1 and 126/2. On Hogarth's audience, see Bindman, *Hogarth and His Times*, 29–32.

13. David H. Solkin, *Painting for Money: The Visual Arts and the Public Sphere in Eighteenth-Century England* (New Haven, CT: Yale University Press, 1993), esp. 1–26; Adam Smith, *The Theory of Moral Sentiments*, ed. D. D. Raphael and A. L. Macfie (Oxford: Clarendon Press, 1976).

14. Elizabeth Deeds Ermath, *Realism and Consensus in the English Novel* (Princeton, NJ: Princeton University Press, 1983), 16–24, argues that "realism" based on linear perspective makes for "a potential equality among viewpoints" (20); her meaning of "consensus" refers to the arbitrary fixity of position and putatively impartial quality of the perspective system. She also argues that the "realist consensus is in some ways a profoundly self-reflexive device, because it calls attention to the act of rationalization itself rather than to the objects used to specify that act" (21). These ideas are largely consonant with the analysis here. I focus, however, not on the consistency of perspective but on disruptions of it and the ways in which these disruptions actuate not consensus per se but the process of consensus-making. On the moral and social conventions of this process, see Shapin and Schaffer, *Leviathan and the Air-Pump*, 72–79, and Steven Shapin, *A Social History of Truth: Civility and Science in Seventeenth-Century England* (Chicago: University of Chicago Press, 1994).

15. E. P. Thompson, "Eighteenth-Century English Society: Class Struggle without Class?" *Social History* 3 (1978): 133–165; "Patrician Society; Plebeian Culture," *Journal of Social History* 7 (1974): 382–405; and "The Moral Economy of the English Crowd in the Eighteenth Century," *Past and Present* 50 (1971): 76–136. See also Paulson, *Popular and Polite Art*, esp. chaps. 1–3.

16. *Hogarth*, 2.xiv.

17. Donald W. Livingston, *Hume's Philosophy of Common Life* (Chicago: University of Chicago Press, 1984).

18. Facticity, therefore, differs from but is intertwined with the subjectless phenomenon of strict description as analyzed by Gérard Genette. See *Figures of Literary*

Discourse, trans. Alan Sheridan (New York: Columbia University Press, 1982), esp. 133–43.

19. Michael Fried, *Absorption and Theatricality: Painting and Beholder in the Age of Diderot* (Berkeley: University of California Press, 1980).

20. See, for instance, Norman Bryson, *Word and Image: French Painting of the Ancien Régime* (Cambridge: Cambridge University Press, 1981), 147–50. On Hogarth and Greuze, see François Rastier, "Comportement et signification," in *Langages* 10 (1968): 78–79. Rastier describes Greuze's and Hogarth's use of eyelids to communicate attitudes, with particular attention to *A Rake's Progress*.

21. See Bender, *Imagining the Penitentiary*, chaps. 6 and 7; and Bender, "Enlightenment Fiction and the Scientific Hypothesis."

22. Larry R. Stewart, *The Rise of Public Science: Rhetoric, Technology and Natural Philosophy in Newtonian Britain* (Cambridge: Cambridge University Press, 1992).

23. The debate centers on Habermas, *The Structural Transformation of the Public Sphere*, which argues, broadly, that the actuality of this public was transient and, in its fully functional form, confined to the first half of the eighteenth century, while the ideal has continued to its present form in Habermas's scheme. This debate recurs in the essays published in Calhoun, *Habermas and The Public Sphere*.

24. Bindman, *Hogarth and His Times*, 31–32. See Paulson, *Hogarth*, 2.4–7; and *HGW*, 84–85. For a precise discussion of the implications of *A Midnight Modern Conversation* for an understanding of Hogarth's position on social exchange, see Frédéric Ogée, "L'onction extrême: une lecture de *A Midnight Modern Conversation* (1733) de William Hogarth," *Études Anglaises* 45.1 (1992): 56–65. Arguably, with regard to content, the degree of consensus among the Shaftesburian elite that Solkin describes in *Painting for Money* was already in decline by the 1730s (perhaps the Addisonian idealization taken up by Habermas never strictly existed) but I am arguing here that Hogarth's cycles work precisely to extend, experientially, the practices that governed interactions among this elite to a much wider public.

25. *Hogarth*, 1.306. In *The Spectator* 10 (12 March 1711), Addison estimates his readership at 60,000.

26. See John Locke, *An Essay Concerning Human Understanding*, ed. Peter H. Nidditch (Oxford: Oxford University Press, 1975), 43 and 162–63. See also *Hogarth*, 1.329–34. Paulson's pages, which form the peroration to vol. 1 of his book, refer also to Hogarth's paintings of *The Beggar's Opera* and place them, with *A Harlot's Progress*, in the context of the young Hogarth's own experience in debtors' prison with his family. See also Jonathan Crary, *Techniques of the Observer* (Cambridge, MA: MIT Press, 1990), 38–50.

Chapter Four

This chapter was originally published as "Hume's Learned and Conversible Worlds," in *Just Being Difficult?*, ed. Jonathan Culler and Kevin Lamb (Stanford, CA: Stanford University Press, 2003), 29–42. © 2003 by the Board of Trustees of the Leland Stanford Junior University. All rights reserved.

1. Samuel Johnson, *The Idler*, no. 70 in *The Yale Edition of the Works of Samuel Johnson*, vol. 2, *The Idler and the Adventurer*, ed. W. J. Bate, John M. Bullitt, and L. F. Powell (New Haven, CT: Yale University Press, 1963), 219.

2. David Hume, *Essays Moral, Political, and Literary*, ed. Eugene F. Miller (Indianapolis: Liberty Classics, 1985), 534–35. The modern spelling of "conversible" is "conversable." We adopt Hume's spelling, which was permissible in Samuel Johnson's *Dictionary*.

3. John Locke, *An Essay Concerning Human Understanding*, ed. Peter H. Nidditch (Oxford: Clarendon Press, 1975), 10. Indeed, Locke's student Anthony Ashley Cooper, the third Earl of Shaftesbury, took up this cry, trying to develop a truly conversational philosophy.

4. For consistency's sake, throughout the essay we use the term "science" in the customary modern sense to refer to natural and/or physical sciences. This definition dates from the nineteenth century; these fields of study would in the eighteenth century still have been called "natural philosophy."

5. Larry Stewart pursues the distinction between "deeds" and "words" in seventeenth-century science in great and illuminating detail in *The Rise of Public Science: Rhetoric, Technology, and Natural Philosophy in Newtonian Britain, 1660–1750* (New York: Cambridge University Press, 1992).

6. As Stewart has shown, Newton's mechanical principles were illustrated by way of "mathematical analog[ies]" in traveling science shows, in which, for example, (naked) strong men were used to demonstrate how simple machines that took advantage of Newton's discoveries offered mechanical advantages, enabling more weight to be lifted, moved, balanced, and so on (ibid., 125–26).

7. Quoted by Simon Schaffer in "Natural Philosophy and Public Spectacle in the Eighteenth Century," *History of Science* 21 (1983): 1. Schaffer cites Joseph Priestley, "Lectures on History and General Policy," in *The Theological and Miscellaneous Works of Joseph Priestley*, ed. J. T. Rutt (London: Hackney, 1817–31), 24.27–28.

8. Mary Poovey, *A History of the Modern Fact: Problems of Knowledge in the Sciences of Wealth and Society* (Chicago: University of Chicago Press, 1998), xviii.

9. David Hume, *A Treatise of Human Nature*, 2nd ed., ed. L. A. Selby-Bigge and P. H. Nidditch (Oxford: Clarendon Press, 1978), xi.

10. Ibid., 623 (our italics).

11. David Hume, *An Enquiry Concerning Human Understanding*, ed. Tom L. Beauchamp (Oxford: Oxford University Press, 1999), 83 (our italics).

12. We cannot take credit for this slur; it comes from Thomas Hugh Grose, Hume's nineteenth-century editor, on whose work most modern editions of Hume are based. M. A. Box calls attention to Grose's remark that Hume's late-life retraction of the *Treatise* was the "posthumous utterance of a splenetic invalid" (M. A. Box, *The Suasive Art of David Hume* [Princeton, NJ: Princeton University Press, 1990], 63).

13. "Hume's Account of Necessity," *Common Sense: or the Englishman's Journal* (5 July 1740): 1–2; reprinted in James Fieser's *Early Responses to Hume's Metaphysical and Epistemological Writings* (Bristol, UK: Thoemmes Press, 2000), 89.

14. Ernest Campbell Mossner, "The First Answer to Hume's *Treatise*: An Unnoticed Letter of 1740," *Journal of the History of Ideas* 12.2 (1951): 293.

15. *Bibliothèque raisonnée des ouvrages des savans de l'Europe* 24 (April–May–June 1740): 328. Translated in Ernest C. Mossner's "Continental Reception of Hume's *Treatise*, 1739–1741," *Mind* 56 (1947): 36; and in Box, *Suasive Art of David Hume*, 74.

16. George Berkeley, *Philosophical Commentaries*, ed. A. A. Luce and T. E. Jessop,

vol. 1 of *The Works of George Berkeley, Bishop of Cloyne* (London: Thomas Newlson and Sons, 1948), 22.

17. See Thomas Reid, *An Inquiry into the Human Mind, on the Principles of Common Sense* (Edinburgh, 1764), esp. secs. 1.5–1.8, 2.6.

18. See, for example, J. L. Austin's remarks on the ordinary-language conceptions that underlie scientist models of the world in his *Philosophical Papers*, 2nd ed., ed. J. O. Urmson and G. J. Warnock (London: Oxford University Press, 1970), 185.

19. Even the vernacular language of scientific disciplines looks very different from parlance outside the discipline: a mathematician's statement "that's intuitively obvious," or "that's trivial," means that an observation does not have to be proven explicitly in mathematical terms. Such an utterance would decidedly *not* indicate that a nonmathematician would find the observation obvious; rather, it indicates that others inside the discipline would know how to find the solution without having it worked out for them.

20. See the introduction to his first *Enquiry*, the first paragraph of which denies the possibility that moral philosophy could be easy to understand at all times and the second paragraph of which professes that he may have achieved accessibility anyway.

21. Gerald Graff, "Scholars and Sound Bites: The Myth of Academic Difficulty," *PMLA* 115.5 (October 2000): 1044.

22. "*An Enquiry Concerning the Principles of Morals*," *Monthly Review* (January 1752): 1; reprinted in Fieser, *Early Responses*, 11–12.

23. There is, in fact, currently a closet industry of traveling rhetoric teachers (latter-day sophists?), mainly university-trained in humanistic disciplines, who teach scientists to communicate their work to outside readers.

24. Stephen W. Hawking, *A Brief History of Time*, 10th anniversary ed. (New York: Bantam, 1996), 191. This book was a runaway best seller. A former postdoctoral student of Hawking's has pointed out that Hawking has "sold more books on physics than Madonna has on sex" (vii).

25. To take advantage of what a separate language can offer analysis, in recent years analytic philosophers and linguists alike have increasingly moved toward mathematical representations of their work. For example, in using symbolic logic, practitioners of these disciplines have adopted notational forms that deliberately move away from natural language formulations. Aristotelian logic, grammatical analysis, and mathematics all come together under this shared symbolic system.

26. Hume, *Treatise*, 264 and 269.

27. This quotation comes from *The Spectator*, no. 10, first published 12 March 1711.

Chapter Five

This chapter was originally published as "The Novel as Modern Myth," in *Defoe's Footprints: Essays in Honour of Maximillian E. Novak*, ed. Robert M. Maniquis and Carl Fisher (Toronto: University of Toronto Press, 2009), 223–37. © John Bender.

1. Ian Watt, *The Rise of the Novel: Studies in Defoe, Richardson, and Fielding* (Berkeley: University of California Press, 1957). On the early popular adaptations of *Frankenstein* for the theater, see Richard Holmes, *The Age of Wonder: How the*

Romantic Generation Discovered the Beauty and Terror of Science (New York: Vintage Books, 2008), 334–35.

2. Mary Wollstonecraft Shelley, *The Frankenstein Notebooks*, ed. Charles E. Robinson, 2 vols. (New York: Garland, 1996).

3. [Edgar Allan Poe], review of *The Life and Surprising Adventures of Robinson Crusoe*, by Daniel Defoe, *Southern Literary Messenger* (January 1836).

4. Claude Lévi-Strauss, "The Structural Study of Myth," in *Structural Anthropology*, trans. Claire Jacobson and Brooke Grundfest Schoepf (New York: Basic Books, 1963), 206–31.

5. John Richetti, preface to *Robinson Crusoe*, by Daniel Defoe (London: Penguin Books, 2001).

6. Bronislaw Malinowski, *Myth and Primitive Psychology* (London: K. Paul, Trench, Trubner & Co., 1926), 18–19, quoted by Ian Watt in *"Robinson Crusoe* as a Myth," *Essays in Criticism* 1.2 (1951): 96.

7. Raymond Williams, *Keywords: A Vocabulary of Culture and Society* (New York: Oxford University Press, 1985), 212.

8. Roland Barthes, *Mythologies* (Paris: Éditions du Seuil, 1957).

9. Steven Shapin and Simon Schaffer, *Leviathan and the Air-Pump: Hobbes, Boyle, and the Experimental Life* (Princeton, NJ: Princeton University Press, 1985).

10. Daniel Defoe, *Robinson Crusoe* (Oxford: Oxford University Press, 1981), 153–54.

11. William Nestrick, "Coming to Life: *Frankenstein* and the Nature of Film Narrative," in *The Endurance of Frankenstein: Essays on Mary Shelley's Novel*, ed. George Levine and U. C. Knoepflmacher (Berkeley: University of California Press, 1979), 290–315.

12. Walter Benjamin, "The Work of Art in the Age of Mechanical Reproduction," in *Illuminations*, ed. Hannah Arendt (New York: Schocken Books, 1969).

13. Terry Castle, *The Apparitional Lesbian: Female Homosexuality and Modern Culture* (New York: Columbia University Press, 1993), and *The Female Thermometer: Eighteenth-Century Culture and the Invention of the Uncanny* (New York: Oxford University Press, 1995).

14. Alexander Welsh, *Strong Representations: Narrative and Circumstantial Evidence in England* (Baltimore: Johns Hopkins University Press, 1992).

15. William Beatty Warner, *Licensing Entertainment: The Elevation of Novel Reading in Britain, 1684–1750* (Berkeley: University of California Press, 1992).

16. Horace Walpole, preface to the 1st ed., *The Castle of Otranto*, ed. W. S. Lewis (London: Oxford University Press, 1964), 4; the quotation about "mortal agents" is taken from the preface to the 2nd ed., in Lewis, 7–8.

17. Paula R. Backscheider, *Daniel Defoe: His Life* (Baltimore: Johns Hopkins University Press, 1989).

18. Jesse Molesworth, *Chance and the Eighteenth-Century Novel: Realism, Probability, Magic* (Cambridge: Cambridge University Press, 2010).

19. See Leslie A. Fiedler, *Love and Death in the American Novel*, rev. ed. (New York: Dell, 1969), chaps. 6 and 12.

20. Watt, *"Robinson Crusoe* as a Myth," 96.

Chapter Six

This chapter was originally published as "Introduction," in Henry Fielding, *Tom Jones*, ed. John Bender and Simon Stern, Oxford World's Classics (Oxford: Oxford University Press, 1996), ix–xxxiv. By permission of Oxford University Press. www. oup.com. Although the approach combines that of an introduction with aspects of a scholarly essay, I decided to keep the original in its integral form except to introduce light annotation. References to *Tom Jones* will be cited parenthetically in the text by book and chapter.

　1.　For a full account of Fielding's life and works, see Ronald Paulson, *Henry Fielding: A Critical Biography* (Oxford: Blackwell, 2000). For a valuable sampling of responses to Fielding's works, see Ronald Paulson and Thomas Lockwood, eds., *Henry Fielding: The Critical Heritage* (London: Routledge and Kegan Paul, 1969).

　2.　Samuel Johnson, "Addison," ed. James L. Battersby, in *The Lives of the Poets*, ed. John H. Biddendorf, vols. 21–23 of *The Yale Edition of the Works of Samuel Johnson*, ed. Robert DeMaria, Jr. (New Haven, CT: Yale University Press, 2010), 2.596–679.

　3.　Henry Fielding, preface to *Joseph Andrews*, ed. Martin C. Battestin (Oxford: Clarendon Press, 1967), 4 and 10.

　4.　Samuel Johnson, *The Rambler* 4 (31 March 1750), in *The Yale Edition of the Works of Samuel Johnson*, vol. 3, ed. W. J. Bate and Albrecht B. Strauss (New Haven, CT: Yale University Press, 1969), 19–25.

　5.　All quotations in this paragraph are from Paulson and Lockwood, *Critical Heritage*. Catherine Talbot to Elizabeth Carter, 22 May 1749, 166; Elizabeth Carter to Catherine Talbot, 20 June 1749, 169; Samuel Richardson to Astraea and Minerva Hill, 4 August 1749, 174–75; Astraea and Minerva Hill to Samuel Richardson, 27 July 1749, 172–74; Orbilius [pseud.], *An Examen of the History of Tom Jones, a Foundling. . . . In Two Letters to a Friend, Proper to be bound with the Foundling*, 1750 [December 1749], 187–212; [Francis Coventry], from *An Essay on the New Species of Writing Founded by Mr. Fielding: with a Word or Two upon the Modern State of Criticism*, 1751, 261–69.

　6.　Jürgen Habermas gives a very influential account of the values outlined in this paragraph and below in *The Structural Transformation of the Public Sphere: An Inquiry into a Category of Bourgeois Society*, trans. Thomas Burger with the assistance of Frederick Lawrence (Cambridge, MA: MIT Press, 1989).

　7.　[Joseph Addison], *The Spectator* 10 (12 March 1711), ed. Donald F. Bond, vol. 1 (Oxford, Clarendon Press, 1965), 44–47.

　8.　These quotations and those in the subsequent paragraph are drawn from Sir Alexander Drawcansir [Henry Fielding], *The Covent-Garden Journal* 3 (11 January 1752), ed. Gerard Edward Jensen, vol. 1 (New York: Russell & Russell, 1964), 147–53.

　9.　David Hume, *A Treatise of Human Nature*, 2nd ed., ed. L. A. Selby-Bigge and P. H. Nidditch (Oxford: Clarendon Press, 1978), xix.

　10.　[Fielding], *Covent-Garden Journal* 66 (14 October 1752), ed. Jensen, vol. 2, 110–14.

　11.　Hume, *Treatise*, 182.

12. Ibid.

13. James Beattie, "From *On Fable and Romance*, 1783," excerpted in Ioan M. Williams, ed., *Novel and Romance, 1700–1800* (London: Routledge & Kegan Paul, 1970), 327; see also the passage on *Tom Jones* in Arthur Murphy, "Essay," 25 March 1762, excerpted from "An Essay on the Life and Genius of Henry Fielding, Esq.," in *The Works of Henry Fielding, Esq.: with the Life of the Author* (1762), excerpted in Paulson and Lockwood, *Critical Heritage*, 404–32.

14. Samuel Taylor Coleridge, *Table Talk*, ed. Carl Woodring, vols. 13 and 14 of *The Collected Works of Samuel Taylor Coleridge*, ed. Kathleen Coburn (Princeton, NJ: Princeton University Press, 1990), 2.295.

15. Henry Fielding, "An Essay on the Knowledge of the Characters of Men," in *Miscellanies by Henry Fielding, Esq.*, ed. Henry Knight Miller, vol. 1 (Oxford: Clarendon Press, 1972), 153–78.

16. See Paulson and Lockwood, *Critical Heritage*, Lady Mary Wortley Montagu, recalled by Lady Louisa Stuart (undated) in "Introductory Anecdotes," *Letters and Works of Lady Mary Wortley Montagu*, 359.

17. James Boswell, *Boswell's Life of Johnson* (London: Oxford University Press, 1953), 389.

18. Fielding, "Characters of Men," 155.

Chapter Seven

This chapter was originally published as "Prison Reform and the Sentence of Narration in *The Vicar of Wakefield*," in *The New Eighteenth Century: Theory, Politics, English Literature*, ed. Felicity Nussbaum and Laura Brown (London: Methuen, 1987), 168–88. Permission granted by Routledge. This essay considers Goldsmith in light of ideas worked out in my book *Imagining the Penitentiary: Fiction and the Architecture of Mind in Eighteenth-Century England* (Chicago: University of Chicago Press, 1987). A few of the theoretical statements here are adapted from the book, but my treatment of *The Vicar of Wakefield* is new.

1. Roland Barthes, *Mythologies*, trans. Annette Lavers (New York: Hill and Wang, 1972), 45.

2. Arthur Friedman, ed., *The Collected Works of Oliver Goldsmith*, 5 vols. (Oxford: Clarendon Press, 1966), 5.292. Subsequent references (whether in notes or parenthetically in the text) are to this edition. On the critical fortunes of the novel, see G. S. Rousseau, *Goldsmith: the Critical Heritage* (London: Routledge & Kegan Paul, 1974), esp. 9–13, and the critics cited there. Goldsmith, in his Advertisement to the novel, was the first to note the "faults" of the work and to defend any "absurdity" it might contain as subordinate to the "beauties" of the whole (4.14). Mr. Burchell takes up the theme in chapter 15 (4.79).

3. Mikhail Bakhtin, *The Dialogic Imagination: Four Essays*, ed. Michael Holquist, trans. Caryl Emerson and Michael Holquist (Austin: University of Texas Press, 1981), 33. On Bakhtin's communicational, or semiotic, definition of "behavioral ideology" as abiding in the continuous formation and reformation of systems of meaning through linguistic and social communication, see Bakhtin and Valentin Voloshinov, *Marxism and the Philosophy of Language*, trans. Ladislav Matejka and I. R. Titunik (New York: Seminar Press, 1973), esp. 91; and "Discourse in Life and Discourse

in Art (Concerning Sociological Poetics)," in *Freudianism: A Marxist Critique*, ed. Neal H. Bruss, trans. I. R. Titunik (New York: Academic Press, 1976), app. 1, 93–116.

4. See Anthony Giddens, *A Contemporary Critique of Historical Materialism* (Berkeley: University of California Press, 1981), esp. 1–25. My summary formulation closely paraphrases Erik Olin Wright's in "Giddens' Critique of Marxism," *New Left Review* 138 (1983): 12.

5. Raymond Williams, *Marxism and Literature* (Oxford: Oxford University Press, 1977), 126. I also draw upon Louis Althusser, *Lenin and Philosophy*, trans. Ben Brewster (New York: Monthly Review Press, 1971); Terry Eagleton, *Criticism and Ideology* (London: Verso Editions, 1978), chap. 2, 44–63, and "Ideology, Fiction, Narrative," *Social Text* 2 (1979): 62–80; Rosalind Coward and John Ellis, *Language and Materialism: Developments in Semiology and the Theory of the Subject* (London: Routledge & Kegan Paul, 1977), 77–78; and Tom Bottomore, ed., *A Dictionary of Marxist Thought* (Cambridge, MA: Harvard University Press, 1983), 219–23. I cannot, however, accept the a priori aspects of some versions of Marxism that privilege the economic bases of production by granting them ultimate causal, or at least explanatory, force. I adopt, rather, a sympathetic but skeptical stance akin to that of Anthony Giddens.

6. Morris Golden, "Goldsmith, *The Vicar of Wakefield*, and the Periodicals," *JEGP* 76 (1977): 525–36.

7. Cesare Beccaria, *On Crimes and Punishments*, ed. and trans. Henry Paolucci (Indianapolis: Bobbs-Merrill, 1963), 9. This work was translated into French by the Abbé Morellet; the first English translation appeared in 1767. On Beccaria's life, work, ideas, and influence, see Marcello Maestro, *Cesare Beccaria and the Origins of Penal Reform* (Philadelphia: Temple University Press, 1973).

8. On the French influence, see Pat Rogers, "The Dialectic of *The Traveller*," in *The Art of Oliver Goldsmith*, ed. Andrew Swarbrick (London: Vision Press, 1984), 115–16 and citations; Arthur Lytton Sells, *Les Sources françaises de Goldsmith* (Paris: Édouard Champion, 1924); R. S. Crane and H. J. Smith, "A French Influence on Goldsmith's *Citizen of the World*," *MP* 19 (1921–22): 83–92; R. S. Crane and J. H. Warner, "Goldsmith and Voltaire's *Essai sur les Moeurs*," *MLN* 38 (1923): 65–76; and R. S. Crane and Arthur Friedman, "Goldsmith and the *Encyclopédie*," *TLS* (11 May 1933): 331.

9. For detailed accounts of eighteenth-century prisons, see John Howard, *The State of the Prisons* (Warrington: William Eyres, 1777); reprinted in *Prisons and Lazarettos*, ed. Ralph W. England, Jr., 2 vols. (Montclair, NJ: Patterson Smith, 1973). Informative modern works on eighteenth-century prison reform include Leon Radzinowicz, *A History of English Criminal Law and Its Administration from 1750*, vol. 1 *The Movement for Reform, 1750–1833* (New York: Macmillan, 1948), 165–493; Michel Foucault, *Discipline and Punish: The Birth of the Prison*, trans. Alan Sheridan (London: Allen Lane, 1977), chaps. 2–3; Michael Ignatieff, *A Just Measure of Pain: The Penitentiary in the Industrial Revolution, 1750–1850* (New York: Pantheon, 1978), 15–113, and his "State, Civil Society, and Total Institutions: A Critique of Recent Social Histories of Punishment," in *Crime and Justice, An Annual Review of Research*, vol. 3, ed. Michael Tonry and Norval Morris (Chicago: University of Chicago Press, 1981), 153–92; Seán McConville, *A History of English Prison Administration*, vol. 1

(London: Routledge & Kegan Paul, 1981), 49–134; Robin Evans, *The Fabrication of Virtue: English Prison Architecture, 1750–1840* (Cambridge: Cambridge University Press, 1981), 1–236; and J. M. Beattie, *Crime and the Courts in England, 1660–1880* (Princeton, NJ: Princeton University Press, 1986), chaps. 9–10.

10. On Goldsmith and Chambers, see Ralph M. Wardle, *Oliver Goldsmith* (Lawrence: University of Kansas Press, 1957), 189; and John Ginger, *The Notable Man: The Life and Times of Oliver Goldsmith* (London: Hamish Hamilton, 1977), 243–46. On Johnson and Chambers, see E. L. McAdam, Jr., *Dr. Johnson and the English Law* (Syracuse: Syracuse University Press, 1951), 65–122.

11. See Friedman, who says the novel was composed between 1760 or 1761 and 1762 (*Works*, 4.3–4); and Ginger, who argues that Goldsmith was working on the novel as late as 1764 and that chapters 19 and 27 were "written during or after 1763" (appendix to *The Notable Man*, 363–70).

12. Grant T. Webster, "Smollett's Microcosms: A Satiric Device in the Novel," *Satire Newsletter* 5 (1967): 34–37.

13. On the Rockingham Whigs, see John B. Owen, *The Eighteenth Century, 1714–1815* (New York: Norton, 1976), 179–85, 282–90; and Frank O'Gorman, *The Rise of Party in England: The Rockingham Whigs, 1760–82* (London: George Allen and Unwin, 1975). On the issue of social class during the period, see E. P. Thompson, "Eighteenth-Century English Society: Class Struggle Without Class?" *Social History* 3 (1978): 133–65.

14. This phrase comes from "Of the Pride and Luxury of the Middling Class of People," which appeared in *The Bee* 7, 17 November 1759, (*Works*, 1.486–87). The phrase, "middle order of mankind," comes from *The Vicar of Wakefield, Works*, 4.102. On Goldsmith's politics, see R. W. Seitz, "The Irish Background of Goldsmith's Social and Political Thought," *PMLA* 52 (1937): 405–11, and "Some of Goldsmith's Second Thoughts on English History," *MP* 35 (1937–38): 279–88; Howard J. Bell, Jr., "'The Deserted Village' and Goldsmith's Social Doctrines," *PMLA* 59 (1944): 747–72; Sven Bäckman, *The Singular Tale: A Study of "The Vicar of Wakefield" and Its Literary Background* (Lund: G. W. K. Gleerup, 1971), 66–67, 184–87; Robert H. Hopkins, "Social Stratification and the Obsequious Curve: Goldsmith and Rowlandson," in *Studies in the Eighteenth Century* 3, ed. R. F. Brissenden and J. C. Eade (Toronto: University of Toronto Press, 1976), 55–71; and Donald Davie, "Notes on Goldsmith's Politics," in Swarbrick, *The Art of Oliver Goldsmith*, 79–89. For a related discussion, see Raymond Williams, *The Country and the City* (New York: Oxford University Press, 1973), 74–79.

15. Owen, *The Eighteenth Century*, 169.

16. Quoted in Roy Porter, *English Society in the Eighteenth Century* (Harmondsworth, UK: Penguin, 1982), 130.

17. Quoted in Isaac Kramnick, *Bolingbroke and His Circle: The Politics of Nostalgia in the Age of Walpole* (Cambridge, MA: Harvard University Press, 1968), 79, 230–35.

18. Thompson, "Eighteenth-Century English Society," 140.

19. *The Works of Jeremy Bentham*, 11 vols., ed. John Bowring (Edinburgh: William Tait, 1838–43), 4.40, 44–46. For a full account of Bentham's panopticon, see Evans, *The Fabrication of Virtue*, chap. 5.

20. I refer in part to Pierre Macherey, *A Theory of Literary Production*, trans. Geoffrey Wall (London: Routledge & Kegan Paul, 1978), esp. 59–60. For a considerable treatment of the subject, including discussion of Macherey, see Fredric Jameson, *The Political Unconscious: Narrative as a Socially Symbolic Act* (Ithaca, NY: Cornell University Press, 1981), chap. 1; and Eagleton, *Criticism and Ideology*, chap. 3, esp. 89 and 100–101. I adopt Raymond Williams's idea of cultural "emergence" and his term "structure of feeling" (*Marxism and Literature*).

21. Martin Battestin, *The Providence of Wit: Aspects of Form in Augustan Literature and the Arts* (Oxford: Clarendon Press, 1974), chap. 7.

22. J. R. S. Whiting, *Prison Reform in Gloucestershire, 1776–1820: A Study of the Work of Sir George Onesiphorus Paul, Bart.* (London: Phillimore, 1975), apps. A and B.

23. Ronald Paulson, *Satire and the Novel in Eighteenth-Century England* (New Haven, CT: Yale University Press, 1967), 269–75. My consideration of narrative technique and several other aspects of Goldsmith's novel has been influenced in part by Marshall Brown, *Preromanticism* (Stanford, CA: Stanford University Press, 1991).

24. Frederick Cummings et al., *Romantic Art in Britain: Paintings and Drawings, 1760–1860* (Philadelphia: Philadelphia Museum of Art, 1968), 12.

25. Dorrit Cohn, *Transparent Minds: Narrative Modes for Presenting Consciousness in Fiction* (Princeton, NJ: Princeton University Press, 1978), 100. See also Käte Hamburger, *The Logic of Literature*, trans. Marilynn J. Rose (Bloomington: Indiana University Press, 1973); Roy Pascal, *The Dual Voice* (Manchester, UK: Manchester University Press, 1977); and Ann Banfield, *Unspeakable Sentences: Narration and Representation in the Language of Fiction* (Boston: Routledge & Kegan Paul, 1982).

26. Gustave Flaubert, *The Letters of Gustave Flaubert, 1830–1857*, ed. and trans. Francis Steegmuller, 2 vols. (Cambridge, MA: Harvard University Press, 1980–82), 1.230; James Joyce, *A Portrait of the Artist as a Young Man* (New York: Viking, 1956), 214–15.

27. Roland Barthes, "Introduction to the Structural Analysis of Narratives," in *Image-Music-Text*, ed. and trans. Stephen Heath (New York: Hill and Wang, 1977), 112–13; reprinted in *A Barthes Reader*, ed. Susan Sontag (New York: Hill and Wang, 1982), 283–84.

28. Other passages that might be similarly "translated" include the last paragraph of chap. 13 (4.71) and the opening of the first paragraph of chap. 8 (4.45).

29. The passage from Goethe's *Dichtung und Wahrheit* is reprinted in Rousseau, *Goldsmith: The Critical Heritage*, 308–11.

30. Adam Smith, *The Theory of Moral Sentiments*, ed. D. D. Raphael and A. L. Macfie (Oxford: Clarendon Press, 1976), esp. 82–85.

31. See Rousseau, *Goldsmith: The Critical Heritage*, 9–13 and citations. The most extreme exposition of the satiric view is by Robert H. Hopkins, *The True Genius of Oliver Goldsmith* (Baltimore: Johns Hopkins University Press, 1969), chap. 5.

32. See Pascal, *The Dual Voice*, 2–32.

33. See, for example, the epigraph to this essay; also, Coward and Ellis, *Language and Materialism*, chap. 4.

Chapter Eight

This chapter was originally published as "Impersonal Violence: The Penetrating Gaze and the Field of Narration in *Caleb Williams*," in *Vision and Textuality*, ed. Stephen Melville and Bill Readings (London: Macmillan, 1995), 256–81. Reprinted by permission of the publisher.

1. Jonathan Swift, *A Tale of a Tub*, 2nd ed., ed. A. C. Guthkelch and D. Nichol Smith (Oxford: Clarendon Press, 1958), 173–74.

2. See Don Locke, *A Fantasy of Reason: The Life and Thought of William Godwin* (London: Routledge & Kegan Paul, 1980), 8; and Peter Marshall, *William Godwin* (New Haven, CT: Yale University Press, 1984), 48. Both Blake and Godwin in their different ways anticipate Max Horkheimer and Theodor Adorno's attack on the instrumental perversion of reason in their *Dialectic of Enlightenment*, trans. John Cumming (New York: Herder & Herder, 1972).

3. Jacques Derrida, *Writing and Difference*, trans. Alan Bass (Chicago: University of Chicago Press, 1978), 91–92. Other quotations from this essay might be added: "Heidegger still would have questioned and reduced theoretism from within, and in the name of, a Greco-Platonic tradition under the surveillance of the agency of the glance and the metaphor of light. That is, by the spatial pair inside-outside . . . which gives life to the opposition of subject and object" (88); or again,

> After having spoken of taste, touch, and smell, Hegel . . . writes in the *Aesthetics*: "*Sight*, on the other hand, possesses a purely ideal relation to objects by means of light, a material which is at the same time immaterial, and which suffers on its part the objects to continue in their free self-subsistence." . . . This neutralization of desire is what makes sight excellent for Hegel. But for Levinas, this neutralization is also . . . the first violence. . . . Violence, then, would be the solitude of a mute glance, of a face without speech, *the abstraction* of seeing. According to Levinas the glance *by itself*, contrary to what one may be led to believe, does not *respect* the other. (99)

4. William Godwin, *Caleb Williams*, ed. David McCracken (Oxford: Oxford University Press, 1970), 339–41. All subsequent citations are to this edition and appear parenthetically in the text. Godwin's retrospective description of the composition of *Caleb Williams* appears in his preface to the Standard Novels edition (1832) of his novel *Fleetwood*.

5. Ronald Paulson, *Hogarth's Graphic Works*, 3rd rev. ed. (London: The Print Room, 1989), plates 190–190a and, for commentary, 148–52. The corpse is not visibly castrated but in neither the preparatory drawing nor the final plate does the corpse appear with genitals. Sean Shesgreen refers to "intimations of cannibalism" in the drawing. See Sean Shesgreen, ed., *Engravings by Hogarth* (New York: Dover Publications, 1973), plate 80.

6. See Dorrit Cohn, *Transparent Minds: Narrative Modes for Presenting Consciousness in Fiction* (Princeton, NJ: Princeton University Press, 1978), 100; Käte Hamburger, *The Logic of Literature*, trans. Marilynn J. Rose (Bloomington: Indiana University Press, 1973); Roy Pascal, *The Dual Voice* (Manchester, UK: Manchester University Press, 1977); and Ann Banfield, *Unspeakable Sentences: Narration and*

Representation in the Language of Fiction (Boston: Routledge & Kegan Paul, 1982). Bakhtin/Voloshinov says of this technical narrative device:

> Some . . . shift had to have occurred within socioverbal intercourse . . . for that essentially new manner of perceiving another person's words, which found expression in [free indirect discourse], to have been established. . . . The inner subjective personality with its own self-awareness does not exist as a material fact . . . but it exists as an ideologeme. . . . *A word is not an expression of inner personality; rather, inner personality is an expressed or inwardly impelled word.*

Compressed from Mikhail M. Bakhtin and Valentin N. Voloshinov, *Marxism and the Philosophy of Language*, trans. Ladislav Matejka and L. R. Titunik (New York: Seminar Press, 1973), 143 and 152–53.

7. The quotation from Flaubert comes from *The Letters of Gustave Flaubert, 1830–1857*, ed. and trans. Francis Steegmuller, 2 vols. (Cambridge, MA: Harvard University Press, 1980–82), 1.230. On Bentham and the correlation with free indirect discourse, see John Bender, *Imagining the Penitentiary: Fiction and the Architecture of Mind in Eighteenth-Century England* (Chicago: University of Chicago Press, 1987), chap. 7.

8. On Smith and free indirect discourse, see Bender, *Imagining the Penitentiary*.

9. See "Prison Reform and the Sentence of Narration in *The Vicar of Wakefield*," Chapter 7 in this volume; originally published in *The New Eighteenth Century: Theory, Politics, English Literature*, ed. Felicity Nussbaum and Laura Brown (London: Methuen, 1987), 168–88; on the reinscription of certain kinds of first-person narration as quasi-free indirect discourse, see esp. 184–85.

10. See Laura Mulvey, "Visual Pleasure and Narrative Cinema," and "Afterthoughts on 'Visual Pleasure and Narrative Cinema,'" in *Feminism and Film Theory*, ed. Constance Penley (New York: Routledge, 1988), 57–68 and 69–79. For a convenient summary of theories of the "gaze" in feminist film theory, see Tania Modleski, *The Women Who Knew Too Much: Hitchcock and Feminist Theory* (New York: Methuen, 1988), 1–15. See also Constance Penley, *The Future of an Illusion: Film, Feminism, and Psychoanalysis* (Minneapolis: University of Minnesota Press, 1989), 41–54; and Mary Ann Doane, *The Desire to Desire: The Woman's Film of the 1940s* (Bloomington: Indiana University Press, 1987), 38–69. The main text by Michel Foucault is *The Birth of the Clinic: An Archaeology of Medical Perception*, trans. A. M. Sheridan Smith (New York: Vintage Books, 1975), esp. chaps. 7 and 8.

Although rarely mentioned in recent discussions, the chapter on "the gaze" (*le regard*) in Sartre's *Being and Nothingness* (part 3, chap. 1, sect. 4) marked out much of the philosophical terrain. Jacques Lacan has been very influential, especially in film theory. See, for example, *The Four Fundamental Concepts of Psycho-Analysis*, ed. Jacques-Alain Miller and trans. Alan Sheridan (New York: W. W. Norton, 1973), 67–105. For a current development of the Lacanian theory of the gaze, see Slavoj Žižek, "Pornography, Nostalgia, Montage: A Triad of the Gaze," in *Looking Awry: An Introduction to Jacques Lacan Through Popular Culture* (Cambridge, MA: MIT Press, 1991), 107–22.

11. See Foucault, *The Birth of the Clinic*, chaps. 7 and 8; and Norman Bryson, *Vision and Painting: The Logic of the Gaze* (New Haven, CT: Yale University Press, 1983). Svetlana Alpers, in *The Art of Describing* (Chicago: University of Chicago Press, 1983), treats this opposition as a contrast between southern and northern Eu-

ropean ways of seeing. For a discussion of the possibility of alternate gazes that do not participate in violence and domination, see Edward Snow, "Theorizing the Male Gaze: Some Problems," *Representations* 25 (1989): 30–41.

A point often submerged in discussions of the gaze is that its analytic and sequential character (in contrast to the "glance" or the "*coup d'oeil* ") makes it a narrative mode. Indeed, one of Foucault's central points is that the clinical gaze organizes its findings through linguistic description.

12. Bryson, *Vision and Painting*, 93.

13. Leo Bersani and Ulysse Dutoit, *The Forms of Violence: Narrative in Assyrian Art and Modern Culture* (New York: Schocken, 1985), 38 and 40–56. See also, by the same authors, "Merde Alors," in *Pier Paolo Pasolini: The Poetics of Heresy*, ed. Beverly Allen (Saratoga, CA: Anima Libri, 1982), 82–95. I read David Marshall's *The Surprising Effects of Sympathy* (Chicago: University of Chicago Press, 1988) after this chapter was written, but his argument linking violence to sympathy anticipates mine.

14. Every critic I have encountered on the novel attempts a unified reading, even those who, like Mitzi Myers in a marvelous essay, "Godwin's Changing Conception of *Caleb Williams*," *SER* 12 (1972): 591–628, and Mark Philp in his book *Godwin's "Political Justice"* (London: Duckworth, 1986) stress the rapid shifts that occurred in Godwin's thought between 1793 and 1798. These five years include the original publication of both treatise and novel as well as considerable revision. Kenneth W. Graham takes up questions about the novel's unity and about the influence of *Caleb Williams* on the revision of *Political Justice* in *The Politics of Narrative: Ideology and Social Change in William Godwin's "Caleb Williams"* (New York: AMS Press, 1990), a book that appeared after this chapter was written.

15. In what follows, for the sake of economy, I interweave manifest facts and accepted interpretations of Godwin's views with my own inferences. Limits of space cause me to focus upon my main assertions rather than upon the textual evidence that underlies my understanding of the novel.

16. On Godwin's attitude toward contract-governed society, see Ian Balfour, "Promises, Promises: Social and Other Contracts in the English Jacobins (Godwin/Inchbald)," in *New Romanticisms: Theory and Critical Practice*, ed. David Clark and Donald Goellnicht (Toronto: University of Toronto Press, 1994), 225–50. See also Leo Damrosch, *Fictions of Reality in the Age of Hume and Johnson* (Madison: University of Wisconsin Press, 1989), chap. 7. The contrast between shame and guilt as cultural orientations and modes of social control is compactly developed by Alvin W. Gouldner in *Enter Plato: Classical Greece and the Origins of Social Theory* (New York: Basic Books, 1965), 81–87. See also, Bender, *Imagining the Penitentiary*, 221.

17. Godwin's *Political Justice* (1793), bk. 1, chap. 4. See William Godwin, *Enquiry Concerning Political Justice and Its Influence on Morals and Happiness*, ed. F. E. L. Priestley, 3 vols. (Toronto: University of Toronto Press, 1946), 3.247. This edition is cited hereafter as "Priestley."

18. Godwin's *Political Justice* (1793), bk. 1, chap. 2 and bk. 1, chap. 4. See Priestley, 1.126 and 2.239.

19. Philp, *Godwin's "Political Justice,"* 47.

20. Banfield, *Unspeakable Sentences*, esp. 180, 227, and 257. For examples of "en-

coded" free indirect discourse, see the analysis below as well as Chapter 7 in this volume.

21. Bersani and Dutoit, *The Forms of Violence*, 52 and 38. See also 41 on the idea that capacity to stir "imaginative sympathy," often described (e.g. by E. H. Gombrich) as an innovation of Greek narrative art and associated with realism, aimed to excite audiences "out of themselves and into new identities as a result of high narrative skills."

22. *Caleb Williams* reveals this truth in numerous episodes that I cannot discuss here, but an elaborate paragraph about the standing as testimony in court of Caleb's version of the Collins narration makes it clear that such issues are alive in the text (106).

23. Roland Barthes proposes a similar test during a discussion of personal and apersonal narration as systems or codes independent of superficial linguistic markers: "there are narratives or at least narrative episodes . . . which though written in the third person nevertheless have as their true instance the first person." He then proceeds to rewrite the third-person pronouns of such a text in the first person. Run in reverse, his test reveals how first-person narration can venture obliquely upon the representation of thought from the impersonal, all-penetrating perspective that free indirect discourse makes possible. See Roland Barthes, "Introduction to the Structural Analysis of Narratives," in *Image-Music-Text*, ed. and trans. Stephen Heath (New York: Hill & Wang, 1977), 112–13; reprinted in *A Barthes Reader*, ed. Susan Sontag (New York: Hill & Wang, 1982), 283–84.

24. The description of Chovet's automaton is quoted in Thomas N. Haviland and Lawrence Charles Parish, "A Brief Account of the Use of Wax Models in the Study of Medicine," *Journal of the History of Medicine* 25 (1970): 62. On the Florentine models and the Grand Tour, see Sander L. Gilman, *Sexuality: An Illustrated History* (New York: John Wiley, 1989), 184–90. On the models more generally, see Ludmilla Jordanova, "Gender, Generation and Science: William Hunter's Obstetrical Atlas," in *William Hunter and the Eighteenth-Century Medical World*, ed. W. F. Bynum and Roy Porter (Cambridge: Cambridge University Press, 1985), 385–412; and Ludmilla Jordanova, "Natural Facts: A Historical Perspective on Science and Sexuality," in *Nature, Culture, and Gender*, ed. Carol P. MacCormack and Marilyn Strathern (Cambridge: Cambridge University Press, 1980), 42–69; also Barbara Maria Stafford, *Body Criticism: Imaging the Unseen in Enlightenment Art and Medicine* (Cambridge, MA: MIT Press, 1991), 21. More terrifying, even, than Chovet's machine would have been the "models" constructed from dissected corpses between 1766 and 1771 by Honoré Fragonard at the École Vétérinaire in Alfort. On Fragonard, see Annie Le Brun, *Petits et Grands Théâtres du Marquis de Sade* (Paris: Paris Art Centre, 1989), 69, 77, and 79.

Postscript to Chapter 8

A prior version of this Postscript was published as "From Theater to Laboratory," *Journal of the American Medical Association* 9 (6 March 2002): 1179. © American Medical Association. All rights reserved.

1. *The Invention of Pornography: Obscenity and the Origins of Modernity, 1500–1800*, ed. Lynn Hunt (New York: Zone Books, 1993).

2. Andrea Carlino, *Books of the Body: Anatomical Ritual and Renaissance Learning*, trans. John Tedeschi and Anne C. Tedeschi (Chicago: University of Chicago Press, 1999); Jonathan Sawday, *The Body Emblazoned: Dissection and the Human Body in Renaissance Culture* (New York: Routledge, 1996); Ruth Richardson, *Death, Dissection and the Destitute*, 2nd ed. (Chicago: University of Chicago Press, 2000).

3. Andreas Vesalius, *De humani corporis fabrica* (Basel, Switzerland: Johannes Oporinus, 1543).

4. William Hunter, *Anatomia uteri humani gravidi* (Birmingham, UK: John Baskerville, 1774).

5. Television and internet sites now offer access to anatomical information and surgical operations (which are conducted through live dissection). These sources do command audiences, but I would argue that they are not central experiences and that they do not change the basic mythology I describe here.

Chapter Nine

A prior version of this essay appeared under the editorship of David Palumbo-Liu in *Occasion: Interdisciplinary Study in the Humanities*, http://occasion.stanford.edu/node/11.

1. The power of Laclos's novel to fascinate has been the engine driving a huge critical output. Relatively recent works that I have found useful include Georges Poisson, *Choderlos de Laclos, ou L'Obstination* (Paris: Bernard Grasset, 1985), chap. 14; René Pomeau, *Laclos, ou le Paradoxe* (Paris: Éditions Hachette, 1993); Laurent Versini, *"Le Roman le plus intelligent"*: Les Liaisons dangereuses *de Laclos* (Paris: Honoré Champion Éditeur, 1998); and, esp., Joan DeJean, *Literary Fortifications: Rousseau, Laclos, Sade* (Princeton, NJ: Princeton University Press, 1984).

Patrick W. Byrne's "The Science of Man: Observations and Experiments in *Les Liaisons dangereuses*," *Essays in French Literature* 40 (2003): 1–37, is relevant to the concerns of this collection and, specifically, to those of my essay "Novel Knowledge." I unfortunately did not know about Byrne's essay when my own was written. "Novel Knowledge" appears as Chapter 1 in this volume.

2. See Gerd Gigerenzer, Zeno Swijtink, Theodore Porter, Lorraine Daston, et al., eds., *The Empire of Chance: How Probability Changed Science and Everyday Life* (Cambridge: Cambridge University Press, 1989), chap. 1. In *Classical Probability in the Enlightenment* (Princeton, NJ: Princeton University Press, 1988), xi, Daston describes the period's attempts at "a model of rational decision, action, and belief under conditions of uncertainty." See also Theodore M. Porter, "The Quantification of Uncertainty after 1700: Statistics Socially Constructed," in *Acting under Uncertainty: Multidiscliplinary Conceptions*, ed. George M. von Furstenberg (Boston: Kluwer Academic Publishers, 1990), 45–75; and Jesse M. Molesworth, *Chance and the Eighteenth-Century Novel: Realism, Probability, Magic* (Cambridge: Cambridge University Press, 2010), esp. 1–94.

3. Writers often mentioned as early precursors to rational choice theory include Niccolò Machiavelli, Thomas Hobbes, David Hume, Cesare Beccaria, and Jeremy Bentham. The closest to the mathematical side, which so centrally figures in rational choice theory, is Bentham's "felicific calculus" for understanding the operation of pleasure and pain in personal and social formations. See Ross Harrison,

Bentham (London: Routledge & Kegan Paul, 1983) for a convenient exposition of Bentham's ideas.

For a survey touching most of these precursors, see Stephen G. Engelmann, *Imagining Interest in Political Thought: Origins of Economic Rationality* (Durham, NC: Duke University Press, 2003), esp. chaps. 2 and 4, devoted to Bentham. In a chapter on "Self-Interest and Reason," in *Self-Interest before Adam Smith* (Cambridge: Cambridge University Press, 2003), 91, Pierre Force quotes Amartya Sen on standard economic theory's two definitions of rational behavior. "'One is to see rationality as internal *consistency* of choice, and the other is to identify rationality with *maximization of self-interest.*'" Sen observes that, "'in terms of historical lineage, the self-interest interpretation of rationality goes back a long way, and it has been one of the central features of mainline economic theorizing for several centuries.'" Force cites Sen, *On Ethics and Economics* (Oxford: Blackwell, 1987), 12.

4. François de la Rochefoucauld, *Collected Maxims and Other Reflections*, trans. E. H. and A. M. Blackmore and Francine Giguère (Oxford: Oxford University Press, 2007), 14–15, maxim 39. Translation modified by author. Dr. Yota Batsaki pointed me to this quotation. I am deeply indebted to Dr. Batsaki, whose original work on "interest" in seventeenth- and eighteenth-century literature allowed me to see connections between the period's well-established debate and ways of thinking we associate with rational choice theory. See, for instance, Batsaki, "Clarissa; or, Rake Versus Usurer," *Representations* 93 (2006): 22–24, and Batsaki, "Fictions of Interest: Enlightenment Economies of the Individual" (unpublished book manuscript).

5. Albert O. Hirschman, *The Passions and the Interests: Political Arguments for Capitalism before Its Triumph* (Princeton, NJ: Princeton University Press, 1977). See also, *Moral Sentiments and Material Interests: The Foundations of Cooperation in Economic Life*, ed. Herbert Gintis, Samuel Bowles, Robert T. Boyd, and Ernst Fehr (Cambridge, MA: MIT Press, 2005); Engelmann, *Imagining Interest*; Stephen Holmes, "The Secret History of Self-Interest," in *Beyond Self-Interest*, ed. Jane J. Mansbridge (Chicago: University of Chicago Press, 1990), 267–86; Jonathan Kramnick, *Actions and Objects from Hobbes to Richardson* (Stanford, CA: Stanford University Press, 2010). Dr. Batsaki pointed out some of these references.

6. Samuel Richardson, *Clarissa*, 7 vols. (London: S. Richardson, A. Millar, et al., 1748), vol. 4, letter 24 (Sunday, May 21). In the modern version of the first edition edited by Angus Ross (Harmondsworth, UK: Penguin Books, 1985), this is letter 198, 632–38.

7. Choderlos de Laclos, *Oeuvres complètes*, ed. Maurice Allem (Paris: Bibliothèque de la Pléiade, Éditions Gallimard, 1951), letter 81. I use this edition because the ARTFL database text of *Les Liaisons dangereuses* is based on it. See http://artflx .uchicago.edu/cgi-bin/philologic/navigate.pl?frantext0509.1026. The more recent authoritative edition is *Oeuvres complètes*, ed. Laurent Versini (Paris: Éditions Gallimard, 1979). I use the translation by P. W. K. Stone (London: Penguin Books, 1961). References hereafter are by letter number in the text and are to these editions.

8. Bernard Mandeville, *The Fable of the Bees*, 2 vols., ed. F. B. Kaye (Oxford: Oxford University Press, 1924). The long history of revision and additive publication of this work between 1705 and 1733 is covered in Kaye's prefatory note to the Oxford edition. For Decio and Alcander, see *Fable of the Bees*, 1.61–63. For expert placement

of Mandeville's ideas in context, see Laurence Dickey, "Pride, Hypocrisy, and Civility in Mandeville's Social and Historical Theory," *Critical Review* 4.3 (1990): 387–431.

9. Note that Mandeville was opposed to charity on the ground that the difficult and dirty work society requires must be accomplished through the desperation of the working poor. Laclos may have written this layer of irony into Valmont's episode of charity. See "An Essay on Charity, and Charity-Schools" in *Fable of the Bees*, 1.253–322.

10. See Albert O. Hirschman, "The Concept of Interest: From Euphemism to Tautology," in *Rival Views of Market Society and Other Recent Essays* (New York: Viking, 1986), 36. I owe this reference pointing up the rationality embedded in interest to Dr. Batsaki.

11. During this adventure, I have consulted several basic works on the classical theory of games and rational choice. Among them were John von Neumann and Oskar Morgenstern, *Theory of Games and Economic Behavior*, 60th anniversary edition (Princeton, NJ: Princeton University Press, 2004); Morton D. Davis, *Game Theory: A Nontechnical Introduction* (New York: Basic Books, 1983); J. C. C. McKinsey, *Introduction to the Theory of Games* (New York: McGraw-Hill, 1952); Thomas C. Schelling, *The Strategy of Conflict* (Cambridge, MA: Harvard University Press, 1960); and Derek Parfit, *Reasons and Persons* (Oxford: Oxford University Press, 1984). On the interaction of reason and emotion, works by Elster and John C. Harsanyi have been crucial. See Jon Elster, ed., *Rational Choice* (Oxford: Basil Blackwell, 1986); Elster, *Solomonic Judgements: Studies in the Limitations of Rationality* (Cambridge: Cambridge University Press, 1989); Elster, *Alchemies of the Mind: Rationality and the Emotions* (Cambridge: Cambridge University Press, 1999), esp. chap. 4.3; and John C. Harsanyi, *Rational Behavior and Bargaining Equilibrium in Games and Social Situations* (Cambridge: Cambridge University Press, 1977). For a trenchant "Primer in Game Theory," see Avner Greif, *Institutions and the Path to the Modern Economy* (Cambridge: Cambridge University Press, 2006), app. A.

12. Jean-Antoine-Nicolas de Caritat, Marquis de Condorcet, *Foundations of Social Choice and Political Theory*, trans. and ed. Iain McLean and Fiona Hewitt (Cheltenham, UK: Edward Elgar, 1994), esp. 13. See also Daston et al., *The Empire of Chance*, chap. 1; and Molesworth, *Chance and the Eighteenth-Century Novel*.

13. Parfit, *Reasons and Persons*, 12–13, citing Schelling, *The Strategy of Conflict*. This strategy was hardly unknown in the past, even though Schelling's and Parfit's analyses may be new. See, for instance, George Frederic Handel's 1725 opera, *Rodelinda*, act 2. I note below that Valmont's intimate strategy in the seduction of Tourvel comes from heroic tragedy and opera. For commentary on Schelling from a literary perspective, esp. Schelling's theories about "mixed games," see Philip Fisher, *The Vehement Passions* (Princeton, NJ: Princeton University Press, 2002), 125–31. Schelling discusses "mixed games" in "The Reciprocal Fear of Surprise Attack," *The Strategy of Conflict*, chap. 9.

14. Daniel Kahneman, Paul Slovic, and Amos Tversky, eds., *Judgment under Uncertainty: Heuristics and Biases* (Cambridge: Cambridge University Press, 1982), esp. chap. 4. See also Tversky and Kahneman, "Extensional versus Intuitive Reasoning: The Conjunction Fallacy in Probability Judgment," *Psychological Review* 90 (1983): 293–315.

15. Carl von Clausewitz, *On War*, ed. and trans. Michael Howard and Peter Paret (Princeton, NJ: Princeton University Press, 1984).

16. Brinksmanship was a term used by Secretary of State John Foster Dulles following World War II. On the theory, see Schelling, *Strategy of Conflict*, 16 and 199–203. On the madman strategy, see Robert D. Schulzinger, *U.S. Diplomacy since 1900*, 5th ed. (Oxford: Oxford University Press, 2002), 303.

17. Niklas Luhmann, *Love as Passion: The Codification of Intimacy*, trans. Jeremy Gaines and Doris L. Jones (Cambridge, MA: Harvard University Press, 1986), esp. chap. 16. The term "ecstatic interpenetration" is derived from Luhmann by H. U. Gumbrecht.

18. I have in mind, for instance, Madame de La Fayette, *La Princesse de Clèves*, preface and notes by Bernard Pingaud (Paris: Gallimard, 1972), 235–36. See also *La Princesse de Clèves*, trans. Terence Cave (Oxford: Oxford University Press, 1992), 90–91. For a discussion of early instances of free indirect discourse, including those in *La Princesse de Clèves*, see Marshall Brown, *The Gothic Text* (Stanford, CA: Stanford University Press, 2005), chap. 4. I have had productive exchanges about the text with Nicholas Paige. His recent article on *La Princesse de Clèves* is not specifically on this issue but valuably relocates the work in the history of the novel: "Lafayette's Impossible Princess: On (Not) Making Literary History," *PMLA* 125.4 (2010): 1061–77.

19. See Niklas Luhmann, *The Differentiation of Society*, trans. Stephen Holmes and Charles Larmore (New York: Columbia University Press, 1982); and Luhmann's *Essays on Self-Reference* (New York: Columbia University Press, 1990), chap. 10, "The World Society as a Social System," esp. 177–79.

20. Jane Austen, *Pride and Prejudice* (1813), vol. 2 of R. W. Chapman, ed., *The Novels of Jane Austen*, 3rd. ed. (London: Oxford University Press, 1932), 351–59, esp. 355.

21. Jane Austen, *Emma* (1815), vol. 4 of R. W. Chapman, ed., *The Novels of Jane Austen*, 3rd. ed. (London: Oxford University Press, 1934), 428.

22. Stephen Frears, with a screenplay by Christopher Hampton, *Dangerous Liaisons* (Lorimar, NFH, and Warner Brothers, 1988). Michelle Pfeiffer is the Présidente, Glenn Close the Marquise de Merteuil, John Malkovich the Vicomte de Valmont, Uma Thurman Cécile de Volanges, and Keanu Reeves the Chevalier Danceny. This film also has Valmont say, quite early, that seduction is his "profession," a term that does not appear in the novel, and one that anachronistically assigns Valmont a "calling" in Weber's sense. This idea is much too bourgeois for Valmont.

23. Weber's four-tiered system of orientations toward "social action" specifies types: the two rational ones discussed here, plus "affectual" and "traditional" action. Weber also specifies a three-tiered parallel system in which self-interest joins custom and usage as "regular behaviors." An important resonance exists between rational motivations in the first system and self-interest in the second. Note that all of these forms represent "ideal types" for Weber: they are devices for analysis, not necessarily detailed descriptions. Weber's system is not consonant with rational choice theory but it illuminates the problems I am discussing from a different angle. See Weber, *Economy and Society: An Outline of Interpretive Sociology* (New York: Bedminster Press, 1968), 24–29; *The Theory of Social and Economic Organization*, trans. A. M. Henderson and Talcott Parsons (New York: Oxford University Press, 1947), 115–20.

For Weber's key terms, see also Richard Swedberg, *The Max Weber Dictionary: Key Words and Central Concepts* (Stanford, CA: Stanford University Press, 2005).

24. Jayne Lewis noted this shift from the novel to the film at a conference when I presented this paper in 2006 at the William Andrews Clark Memorial Library.

25. Jean-Pierre Dupuy, "Quand la stratégie dominante se révèle irrationnelle," in *Décision, prospective, auto-organisation: Mélanges en l'honneur de Jacques Lesourne*, ed. J. Thépot, F. Roubelat, et al. (Paris: Dunod, 2000). Dupuy and I both spoke at the conference at which this paper first was delivered. During the question period, he declared that a paper of his own, like mine, employed a quotation from letter 152 of the novel.

26. See Paul Slovic, Baruch Fischhoff, and Sarah Lichtenstein, "Facts Versus Fears: Understanding Perceived Risk," in *Judgment under Uncertainty*, ed. Kahneman et al., 480–81.

27. Marquis de Sade, *The Complete "Justine," "Philosophy in the Bedroom," and Other Writings*, trans. Richard Seaver and Austryn Wainhouse (New York: Grove Press, 1965), 342. My thanks to Hannah Walser for this reference.

28. Niklas Luhmann, *Social Systems*, trans. John Bednarz, Jr., with Dirk Baecker (Stanford, CA: Stanford University Press, 1995), 274. H. U. Gumbrecht pointed me to this discussion by Luhmann. See, "Mozart's Presences: Can We Describe the Pleasures of Listening?" published as "Mozarts 'Präsenzen': Ist es möglich, Hörvergnügen zu beschreiben," in *Mozarts Klavier- und Kammermusik*, ed. Matthias Schmidt (Laaber: Laaber 2006), 483–98. My understanding of Luhmann is indebted as well to David E. Wellbery, "Aesthetic Media: The Structure of Aesthetic Theory before Kant," in *Regimes of Description: In the Archive of the Eighteenth Century*, ed. John Bender and Michael Marrinan (Stanford, CA: Stanford University Press, 2005), 199–211. Luhmann focuses on "intimate, interhuman interpenetration" in *Social Systems*, 224–29.

John Bednarz, Jr., noted, in responding to a draft of this essay, that the social modes for managing love that I discuss here are not, strictly, social systems in Luhmann's terms, but are, rather, what he calls symbolically generalized media of communication. Since there is no social system without such generalized modes of communication (for economics the mode is money) the boundary is fuzzy. For the sake of simplicity I use the term "system" in this essay. John Bednarz, Jr., e-mail message to the author, February 8, 2010.

29. See Greif, *Institutions and the Path to the Modern Economy*.

Chapter Ten

This chapter was originally published as "Rhetoricality: On the Modernist Return of Rhetoric," in *The Ends of Rhetoric: History, Theory, Practice*, ed. John Bender and David E. Wellbery (Stanford, CA: Stanford University Press, 1990), 3–39. © 1990 by the Board of Trustees of the Leland Stanford Junior University. All rights reserved.

1. Søren Kierkegaard, *Repetition*, trans. Walter Lowrie (New York: Harper & Row, 1941); Gilles Deleuze, *Différence et répétition* (Paris: Presses Universitaires de France, 1968).

2. Throughout this essay we generally use the terms "modernism" and "postmodernism" in conjunction or synonymously. This usage seems appropriate here

in view of the large-scale historical articulation we attempt. Of course, we realize that a more fine-grained analysis would distinguish between these terms. For our purposes, however, it seems most practical to consider postmodernism as the radicalization of tendencies already present in modernism. After this essay had been composed we learned of Renato Barilli, *Rhetoric*, trans. Giuliana Menozzi (Minneapolis: University of Minnesota Press, 1989), which develops a construction of the history of rhetoric that in several respects runs parallel to our own.

3. Umberto Eco, *A Theory of Semiotics* (Bloomington: Indiana University Press, 1976), 134, 276–88.

4. Aristotle, *Rhetorica*, with an English translation by John Henry Freese, Loeb Classical Library vol. 193 (Cambridge, MA: Harvard University Press, 1975), xii–xiii. On the important role of the Sophists, see Barilli, *Rhetoric*, chap. 1.

5. On the shift from stratificational to functional differentiation, see Niklas Luhmann, *The Differentiation of Society*, trans. Stephen Holmes and Charles Larmore (New York: Columbia University Press, 1982).

6. *The Works of Francis Bacon*, ed. Basil Montagu (London: W. Pickering, 1825), 1.281 and 254.

7. Max Horkheimer and Theodor W. Adorno, *Dialectic of Enlightenment*, trans. John Cumming (New York: Seabury, 1972), chap. 1.

8. Galileo Galilei, *Discoveries and Opinions of Galileo*, trans. Stillman Drake (New York: Doubleday Anchor, 1957), 24–25.

9. Ibid., 56. In the first paragraph Galileo refers to a diagram that precedes this passage.

10. *The Philosophical Works of Descartes*, trans. Elizabeth S. Haldane and G. R. T. Ross (New York: Dover, 1955), 1.85.

11. See John Bender, *Imagining the Penitentiary: Fiction and the Architecture of Mind in Eighteenth-Century England* (Chicago: University of Chicago Press, 1987), chap. 6; John H. Langbein, "The Criminal Trial before the Lawyers," *University of Chicago Law Review* 45 (1978): 280–81, and "Shaping the Eighteenth-Century Criminal Trial: A View from the Ryder Sources," *University of Chicago Law Review* 50 (1983): 55–83; Alexander Welsh, "The Evidence of Things Not Seen: Justice Stephen and Bishop Butler," *Representations* 22 (1988): 60–88.

12. Welsh, "Evidence of Things Not Seen," 69–70, 74–75. On probabilistic thinking, see also Ian Hacking, *The Emergence of Probability* (Cambridge: Cambridge University Press, 1975); Barbara J. Shapiro, *Probability and Certainty in Seventeenth-Century England: A Study of the Relationships between Natural Science, Religion, History, Law, and Literature* (Princeton, NJ: Princeton University Press, 1983); Douglas Lane Patey, *Probability and Literary Form: Philosophical Theory and Literary Practice in the Augustan Age* (Cambridge: Cambridge University Press, 1984), 3–74.

13. Antoine Arnauld and Pierre Nicole, *The Art of Thinking; Port-Royal Logic*, trans. James Dickoff and Patricia James (Indianapolis: Bobbs-Merrill, 1964); Thomas Hobbes, *The Art of Rhetorick; with a Discourse of the Laws of England* (London: Printed for William Crooke, 1681).

14. Immanuel Kant, "What Is Enlightenment?" in Immanuel Kant, *On History*, ed. and trans. Lewis White Beck (Indianapolis: Bobbs-Merrill, 1957), 3–10. It

is notable in this connection that the most powerful and influential antirhetoric on the current scene, the transcendental pragmatics of Habermas, is a redaction of this Enlightenment model. See Jürgen Habermas, *Communication and the Evolution of Society*, trans. Thomas McCarthy (Boston: Beacon, 1979), 1–64.

15. Robert Darnton, *The Business of Enlightenment: A Publishing History of the Encyclopédie, 1775–1800* (Cambridge, MA: Harvard University Press, 1979), 23.

16. See René Wellek, "The Name and Nature of Comparative Literature," in his *Discriminations: Further Concepts of Criticism* (New Haven, CT: Yale University Press, 1970), 1–36.

17. Ernst Robert Curtius, *European Literature and the Latin Middle Ages*, trans. Willard R. Trask (New York: Pantheon, 1953).

18. Michel Foucault, "What Is an Author?" in *The Foucault Reader*, ed. Paul Rabinow (New York: Pantheon, 1984), 101–20.

19. We have taken these data from Heinrich Bosse's excellent study *Autorschaft ist Werkherrschaft: Über die Entstehung des Urheberrechts aus dem Geist der Goethezeit* (Paderborn: F. Schöningh, 1981), 8–9. See also Mark Rose, "The Author as Proprietor: *Donaldson v. Becket* and the Genealogy of Modern Authorship," *Representations* 23 (1988): 51–85.

20. Johann Wolfgang von Goethe, *Sämtliche Werke nach Epochen seines Schaffens*, ed. Karl Richter with Herbert G. Göpfert, Norbert Miller, and Gerhard Sauder, vol. 1, pt. 2 (Munich: Hanser, 1987), 364, our translation.

21. Heinrich Bosse, "Dichter Kann man nicht bilden. Zur Veränderung der Schulrhetorik nach 1770," *Jahrbuch für Internationale Germanistik* 2 (1976): 81–125.

22. Robert S. Leventhal, "The Emergence of Philological Discourse in the German States, 1770–1810," *Isis* 77 (June 1986): 243–60.

23. David E. Wellbery, *Lessing's Laocoön* (Cambridge: Cambridge University Press, 1984), chap. 2.

24. Michael Fried, *Absorption and Theatricality* (Berkeley: University of California Press, 1980).

25. Immanuel Kant, *Critique of Judgment*, trans. J. H. Bernard (New York: Harper, 1951), 171.

26. Ibid., 150–51.

27. Mikhail Bakhtin, *The Dialogic Imagination: Four Essays*, ed. Michael Holquist, trans. Caryl Emerson and Michael Holquist (Austin: University of Texas Press, 1981), 3.

28. On free indirect discourse, see Dorrit C. Cohn, *Transparent Minds: Narrative Modes for Presenting Consciousness in Fiction* (Princeton, NJ: Princeton University Press, 1978). For arguments on the specifically written character of free indirect discourse, see Ann Banfield, *Unspeakable Sentences: Narration and Representation in the Language of Fiction* (Boston: Routledge & Kegan Paul, 1982).

29. See Manfred Fuhrmann, *Rhetorik und öffentliche Rede* (Konstanz: Universitätsverlag, 1983).

30. Philippe Lacoue-Labarthe, "Le détour," *Poétique* 5 (1971): 53–76. For a further development of the interpretation of Nietzsche sketched in the following paragraphs, see David E. Wellbery, "Nietzsche–Art–Postmodernism," *Stanford Italian Review* 6 (1986): 77–104.

31. Of course, the classical rhetoric we have been speaking of here descends from Plato and Aristotle through Quintilian and the Neoplatonists to a medieval and Renaissance tradition that remained vital into the Enlightenment. One could also construct a pre-Nietzschean history of rhetoric beginning with the Sophists and including such figures as Machiavelli and Vico. The aspect of Nietzsche's thought that we have sought to capture here with the notion of rhetoricality, in other words, has certain precursors. The fact remains, however, that only under the social and cultural conditions of modernity could the category of rhetoricality assume the operative force disclosed by Nietzsche.

32. Roland Barthes, "The Old Rhetoric: An Aide-mémoire," in his *The Semiotic Challenge* (New York: Hill and Wang, 1988), 11–93.

33. Heinrich Lausberg, *Handbuch der literarischen Rhetorik, Eine Grundlegung der Literaturwissenschaft*, 2 vols. (Munich: Hueber, 1960).

34. Thomas S. Kuhn, *The Structure of Scientific Revolutions* (Chicago: University of Chicago Press, 1962).

35. Paul K. Feyerabend, *Against Method: Outline of an Anarchistic Theory of Knowledge*, rev. ed. (London: Verso, 1988).

36. Ian Hacking, *Representing and Intervening: Introductory Topics in the Philosophy of Natural Science* (Cambridge: Cambridge University Press, 1983).

37. Nelson Goodman, *Ways of Worldmaking* (Indianapolis: Hackett, 1978).

38. See Peter Galison, *How Experiments End* (Chicago: University of Chicago Press, 1987); Bruno Latour, *Science in Action* (Cambridge, MA: Harvard University Press, 1987).

39. Hayden White, *Metahistory: The Historical Imagination in Nineteenth-Century Europe* (Baltimore: Johns Hopkins University Press, 1973).

40. Clifford Geertz, *Works and Lives: The Anthropologist as Author* (Stanford, CA: Stanford University Press, 1988). The University of Wisconsin Press published a series of books on rhetoric in various disciplines. See, e.g., Donald (Deirdre) N. McCloskey, *The Rhetoric of Economics* (Madison: University of Wisconsin Press, 1985).

41. Roman Jakobson, "Two Aspects of Language and Two Types of Aphasic Disturbances," in his *Fundamentals of Language* (The Hague: Mouton, 1956), reprinted in Roman Jakobson, *Language in Literature*, ed. Krystyna Pomorska and Stephen Rudy (Cambridge, MA: Harvard University Press, 1987), 95–119.

42. Jacques Dubois et al., *A General Rhetoric*, trans. Paul B. Burrell and Edgar M. Slotkin (Baltimore: Johns Hopkins University Press, 1981); Paolo Valesio, *Novantiqua: Rhetorics as a Contemporary Theory* (Bloomington: Indiana University Press, 1980).

43. Jean Laplanche, *Life and Death in Psychoanalysis* (Baltimore: Johns Hopkins University Press, 1976).

44. Nicolas Abraham and Marie Torok, *L'écorce et le noyau* (Paris: Aubier-Flammarion, 1978), esp. 203–28.

45. Erving Goffman, *Forms of Talk* (Philadelphia: University of Pennsylvania Press, 1981), and *The Presentation of Self in Everyday Life* (New York: Anchor, 1959).

46. Dan Sperber and Deirdre Wilson, *Relevance: Communication and Cognition* (Cambridge, MA: Harvard University Press, 1986), 237.

47. Marvin Minsky, "A Framework for Representing Knowledge," in *The Psy-*

chology of Computer Vision, ed. Patrick Henry Winston (New York: McGraw-Hill, 1975); Roger Shank, "The Structure of Episodes in Memory," in *Representation and Understanding*, ed. Daniel G. Bobrow and Allen Collins (New York: Academic Press, 1975).

48. George Lakoff and Mark Johnson, *Metaphors We Live By* (Chicago: University of Chicago Press, 1980).

49. Kenneth Burke, "Symbolic Action in a Poem by Keats," in his *A Grammar of Motives* (Berkeley: University of California Press, 1969), 447–64; Kenneth Burke, "Goethe's *Faust*, Part I," in his *Language as Symbolic Action* (Berkeley: University of California Press, 1966), 139–62.

50. Kenneth Burke, *A Rhetoric of Motives* (Berkeley: University of California Press, 1969), and *The Rhetoric of Religion: Studies in Logology* (Berkeley: University of California Press, 1970).

51. Burke's own "definition of man" (explicated in the essay by that title) reads: "Man is the symbol-using (symbol-making, symbol-misusing) animal, inventor of the negative (or moralized by the negative), separated from his natural condition by instruments of his own making, goaded by the spirit of hierarchy (or moved by the sense of order), and rotten with perfection" (*Language as Symbolic Action*, 16).

52. Julia Kristeva, *Desire and Language*, ed. Leon S. Roudiez, trans. Thomas Gora et al. (New York: Columbia University Press, 1980).

53. See R. S. Crane et al., *Critics and Criticism, Ancient and Modern* (Chicago: University of Chicago Press, 1952).

Index

Note: Page numbers in italic type indicate illustrations.

Abraham, Nicolas, 229
Absorption: painting and, 73, 76, 216; realist fiction and, 102, 103
Academic writing, 80, 85, 88
Accessibility: of knowledge, 12, 22, 80-82, 87, 120, 213; of philosophy, 83–89; of science, 82, 90 (*see also* Demonstrations, scientific)
Act of Union (1707), 115
Addison, Joseph, 9, 66, 91, 112, 120–21, 124, 127
Adorno, Theodor, 8; *Dialectic of Enlightenment* (with Max Horkheimer), 8, 238*n*7, 265*n*2
Advertising, 230
Aesthetics, 216–17
Aikin, John, 50
Air pump, 60, *62*, 67, 69
d'Alembert, Jean le Rond, 11, 38, 47. See also *Encyclopédie* (Diderot and d'Alembert)
Allegory, 44, 45, 46, 59, 73, 110
Allen, Ralph, 120
American novel, 107
Amour de soi, 167
Analytic philosophy, 258*n*25
Anarchism, 163, 167

Anatomy, 7–8, *158–62*, 164, 174–75, *174–79*, 180–82, 268*n*24
Anne, Queen, 115
Anthropology, 226
Apparitions and the apparitional, 103–8
Appearance (for Nietzsche), 224
Architecture, historical transformations in, 203–4
Aristocracy, 120, 139, 141, 167, 168, 189
Aristotle, 25, 45, 50, 105, 122, 126, 206, 230
Arnauld, Antoine, *Port-Royal Logic* (with Pierre Nicole), 212
Ars characteristica, 213
Artificial intelligence, 232
Audience and readers: eighteenth-century, 63, 120; experience of, related to causality and induction, 28, 31; and the experience of reading, 103; for Fielding's work, 120, 122–24, 130; for Hogarth's work, 77–78; Hume and, 83–91; ideal, 76–78; identification of, with works of literature, 50, 103; and language, 79–91; for *Les Liaisons dangereuses*, 187; and morality, 110; of novels, 150; as the public, 10; rhetoric and, 207;

for *The Vicar of Wakefield*, 148. See
   also Public sphere
Austen, Jane, 31, 35, 106; *Emma*, 191;
   Pride and Prejudice, 190–91
Authorship, 214–15, 220
Aylesworth, Gary, 239*n*16

Backscheider, Paula, 106–7
Bacon, Francis, 21, 26, 102, 207–8; *The
   Advancement of Learning*, 26; *The New
   Atlantis*, 26; *Novum organum*, 207
Baden, National Law of (1810), 215
Bakhtin, Mikhail, 134, 218, 234, 266*n*6
Bally, Charles, 226
Banfield, Ann, 168
Barbauld, Anna Laetitia, 50
Barthes, Roland, 101, 102, 133, 149, 225,
   268*n*23
Battestin, Martin, 50, 126, 146
Baudelaire, Charles, 222
Baudrillard, Jean, 13
Baumgarten, Alexander, 216
Beattie, James, 127–28
Beccaria, Cesare, 269*n*3; *On Crimes and
   Punishments*, 135–38, 142
Beckett, Samuel, 222
Bednarz, John, Jr., 273*n*28
Behn, Aphra, 110
Beliefs (for Hume), 83
Bender, John: *The Culture of Diagram*
   (with Michael Marrinan), 15–17;
   The Ends of Rhetoric (with David
   Wellbery), 237*n*3; *Imagining the
   Penitentiary*, 5, 9, 15, 58, 238*n*8, 245*n*1
Benjamin, Walter, 104, 108, 222
Bentham, Jeremy, 5, 146, 147, 269*n*3;
   Panopticon, 142, 157
Bentley, Richard, 96
Berkeley, George, 86
Bernard, Claude, 21
Bersani, Leo, 164–65, 168, 268*n*21
Bible, the, 114
Bindman, David, 59
Blackstone, William, *Commentaries on
   the Laws of England*, 136
Blair, Hugh, 86

Blake, William, 155
Blanchot, Maurice, 222
Boccaccio, Giovanni, 100
Body, the, 173–75. *See also* Anatomy
Bolingbroke, Henry St. John, First
   Viscount, 141
Book of Job, 146
Bourgeoisie, 142
Bow Street Runners, 111
Boyle, Robert, 28, 60, 62, 63, 66–67,
   69, 76, 82
Brine, Kevin, 16
Brinksmanship, 188
Brown, Charles Brockden, 107
Bryson, Norman, 164, 254*n*8
Buffon, Georges-Louis, 49, 53–55;
   Natural History, 53–54
Burke, Kenneth, 233–34, 277*n*51
Butler, Joseph, 212
Byron, George Gordon, Lord, *Don
   Juan*, 14

Calculus, philosophical (in Liebniz), 213
Canon, literary, 97, 99–100, 121. *See also*
   Literature, with capital "L"
Capital punishment, 153
Carlyle, Thomas, *Sartor Resartus*, 14
Carroll, Lewis, *Alice in Wonderland*, 95
Carter, Elizabeth, 118
Cartesianism, 39, 43, 46, 47
Cases (as narrative sequences), 49, 63
Cassirer, Ernst, 101; *The Myth of the
   State*, 238*n*7
Castel, Louis-Bertrand, 46
Castle, Terry, 104–5
Causality: Newton and divine, 43,
   45; plot and, 7, 40; and the reader's
   experience, 28, 31; realism and, 7,
   105; skepticism about, 32, 41, 48, 53;
   strong representation and, 52
Cervantes, Miguel de, *Don Quixote*,
   100, 113–14
Chambers, Robert, 136–37
Champion, The (newspaper), 112, 117
Characterization: in *Clarissa*, 109;
   Godwin and, 7; in new novels, 40,

110; in *Otranto*, 106; of protagonist in *Caleb Williams*, 156, 174; in *Tom Jones*, 131

Chase, Robert A., 180

Châtelet, Émilie du, 48, 53

Chaucer, Geoffrey, 100

Chomsky, Noam, 228

Chovet, Abraham, 174

Christianity, 110

Church of England, 116

Cicero, 206

Circumstantiality, 42, 52, 66, 132, 211

Citizens, of nation-states, 220. *See also* Ideal citizens

Clarke, Samuel, 44

Clausewitz, Carl von, 188

Coffeehouses, 9, 39, 66, 77, 81, 119

Cogito, 210–11

Cognitive science, 12, 232

Cohn, Dorrit, 156–57

Cold War, 188

Coleridge, Samuel Taylor, 128; "This Lime Tree Bower My Prison," 219

Colet, Louise, 107

Comedy, 114, 124, 125

Common life, language and, 79–91. *See also* Everyday life

Common sense, 36, 87, 183, 184, 188

Communication: eighteenth-century practices of, 65–66, 119–20, 212; everyday practices of, 231–32; modernist practices of, 222. *See also* Conversation; Public discourse

Condensation (in Freud, Lacan, and Jakobson), 229

Condorcet, Marie-Jean-Antoine-Nicolas Caritat, Marquis de, 14, 35, 187

Conscience, 134, 146, 157

Consensus, 39, 63, 65–67, 71, 76, 119, 255n14

Conversation: characteristics of eighteenth-century, 8–9, 119; consensus as goal of, 63; language pertaining to, 79–91; negative view of, 249n20; social networks and, 12. *See also* Public discourse

Copernicus, 45

Copyright Law (1709), 215

Corax, 206

Counter-Enlightenment, 155

Covent-Garden Journal, 121, 125

Coventry, Francis, 118

Critique and criticism: as Enlightenment characteristic, 3, 11, 119; Enlightenment subject to, 14–15; literary criticism, 232–35; of literature, 121–22; the novel and, 218

Curtius, Ernst Robert, *European Literature and the Latin Middle Ages*, 214

Damrosch, Leo, 245n1

Dance, George, 137

Dangerous Liaisons (film), 197, 272n22

Dante Alighieri, *The Divine Comedy*, 100

Daston, Lorraine, 36, 184

Davis, Lennard J., 245n1

Dawson, Virginia, 53

Dear, Peter, 35; *Discipline and Experience*, 26

De Bolla, Peter, 16

Declaration of Independence, 3

Defoe, Daniel, 40, 43–45, 49, 50, 60, 110, 111, 117, 218; *The Farther Adventures of Robinson Crusoe*, 43; *Robinson Crusoe*, 22, 25, 32–33, 35, 43–44, 95–100, 103–8, 111; *Serious Reflections*, 44; *A True Relation of the Apparition of One Mrs. Veal*, 30, 243n19

Deleuze, Gilles, 204

De Man, Paul, 233

Demi-illusion, 17–18

Demonstrations, scientific, 46, 66, 77, 81–82, 257n6

Derrida, Jacques, 155, 233, 265n3

Descartes, René, 46, 82, 210, 212, 217. *See also* Cartesianism

Description, 66, 71

Details, as indication of factuality, 40, 67, 69

Diagrams: anatomical, 180; Boyle's illustrations and, 60

Diderot, Denis, 3, 11, 17, 38, 47–48, 53, 55, 117; *The Indiscreet Jewels*, 39. See also *Encyclopédie* (Diderot and d'Alembert)

Digital media, 11–14

Disciplinarity: emergence of, 12, 38; language and, 38, 80, 81; rhetoric and, 235–36

Disinterestedness: interests and, 184–86; love and, 191; in public discourse, 6, 9, 10. *See also* Impartiality; Impersonality; Objectivity

Displacement (in Freud, Lacan, and Jakobson), 229

Dissection, 154–56, 164, 168, 175, 180–82, 268n24

Doody, Margaret, 241n6

Double vision. *See* Dual perspective

Dramatism, 233

Dreams, 228–29

Dual perspective: in contemporary culture, 152–53; in Hogarth's work, 60; Hume and, 68; in literature and art, 17–18, 30–31, 41, 148; of the mind, 17; of philosophy, 6; in science, 49

Dunlop, John, *The History of Fiction*, 55

Dupuy, Jean-Pierre, 197

Durkheim, Émile, 101, 102

Dutoit, Ulysse, 165, 168, 268n21

Eco, Umberto, 206

École des Beaux Arts, 203–4

Education, 97; and judgment, 167; and public discourse, 120; rhetoric as subject in, 204–6, 215–16, 249n24; Romantic influence on, 215–16; trivium in, 206

Elocutio, 227–28

Elster, Jon, 187

Emotions. *See* Passions and emotions

Empiricism: as Enlightenment characteristic, 17, 39; and language, 86; legitimation of, 82; the novel and, 21

Empson, William, 232

Encyclopedia of Unified Science, 225

Encyclopédie (Diderot and d'Alembert), 11, 13, 38, 39, 46–47, 60, 103, 213, 244n1

Enlightenment: challenges to, 14–15; characteristics of, 3, 40; counter-, 155; critique as characteristic of, 3, 11, 119; critique of, 8; empiricism in, 17, 39; ends of, 4, 15; Habermas's interpretation of, 8–11; ideal of knowledge/learning, 11; and the novel, 40; paradoxical character of, 17; persistence of, 4, 11, 15–18; pragmatism as characteristic of, 17; and the public sphere, 8–10, 213; and rhetoric, 204, 207–14

Epic poetry, 114–15, 126, 127, 217

Ermath, Elizabeth Deeds, 255n14

Error, as characteristic of human nature, 125

Essay on the New Species of Writing Founded by Mr. Fielding, An, 118

Ethnomethodology, 231

European Economic Community, 16

Everyday life: and probability, 107; and realist epistemology, 152; study of, 231–32. *See also* Common life, language and

Evidence: consensus formation and, 63, 67; as Enlightenment characteristic, 14; history and, 51; legal, 55, 105, 211; narrative presentation of, 52; the novel and, 28, 30, 35, 40, 42, 52, 63; role of, in truth and knowledge, 40–41, 71, 83

Experience: and character, 125; experiment in relation to, 6, 26; knowledge in relation to, 31–33; meanings of, 24–25; the novel and, 22–24, 103; realism as means of organizing, 4–5, 107; theory vs., 33

Experiment: contrived nature of, 29, 31; experience in relation to, 6, 26; and factuality, 66; knowledge as outgrowth of, 25–26, 66; the novel and, 21–24, 27–28, 31–35; science and, 82; temporal factors in, 33

Experimentum crucis, 29, 30

Extraordinary, the, 106–7. *See also* Fantasy and the marvelous

Eyewitness testimony, 105

Facebook, 16

Face-to-face interaction, 12

Facticity: dual perspective and, 60; in Hogarth's work, 57–78; meanings of, 57–58, 69, 252n2; realism in relation to, 58–59; and reflexivity, 58, 69, 73

Factuality: crisis of, 44; in eighteenth century, 63, 66; experiment and, 66; fictionality in relation to, 42–43, 46–56, 60; the novel's abandonment of, 49; overdetermination as sign of, 67, 69, 71; science and, 82; sense perception unsuited for, 83

Fantasy and the marvelous, 34–35, 51, 54, 126. *See also* Extraordinary

Fashion, 230

Faulkner, William, 107

Feminism, 97

Feminization of male protagonist in *Caleb Williams*, 156, 174

Feyerabend, Paul, *Against Method*, 226

Fichte, Johann Gottlieb, 211

Fictionality and fiction: aversion to/ denial of, 43–49, 60; in *Encyclopédie*, 46–47; and epistemology, 46–47; factuality in relation to, 42–43, 46–56, 60; hypotheses in relation to, 6, 40–41, 43–49, 53, 55; as means of organizing experience, 4; the novel and, 43–44, 51, 55, 123–24; science in relation to, 6, 26, 29, 38, 43–49, 52, 55, 82

Fielding, Henry, 31, 35, 40, 42, 50–51, 63, 103, 105, 109–32, 136, 139, 148–49, 218; *Amelia*, 109, 147; "An Essay on the Knowledge of the Characters of Men," 131, 132; *Jonathan Wild*, 112; *Joseph Andrews*, 113–15, 117,

147; *Miscellanies*, 115; *A Proposal for Making all Effectual Provision for the Poor*, 136; *Shamela*, 113; *Tom Jones*, 10, 22, 27–28, 42, 50, 109–11, 114–32; *The Tragedy of Tragedies*, 111

Fielding, John, 111

Fielding, Sarah, *David Simple*, 121

Film, apparitional quality of, 104, 106, 108

Firstness, 96, 97

First-person narration, 148–51, 156, 268n23

Fishman, Jenn, 254n8

Flameng, L., after W. P. Frith, "The End," from *The Road to Ruin*, 73, 75

Flaubert, Gustave, 107, 149, 157

Folk poetry, 219

Folktales, 101

Fontana, Felice, 175

Forensic evidence, 105

Foucault, Michel, 15, 152, 164, 215, 226

Fragonard, Honoré, 268n24

Frame stories, 97–98

France, 140, 215

Frankfurt School, 8

Frazer, James, 101, 102

Frears, Stephen, 197

Free indirect discourse, 5; in *Caleb Williams*, 168, 170–72; defined, 7, 102; Fielding and, 148–49; in the Gothic novel, 106; and illusionism, 76; and impersonality, 149–50; and modernity, 7, 102; as phenomenon of writing, 218; in *La Princesse de Clèves*, 189; prisons in relation to, 157; reflective awareness of, 152; significance of, 156–57, 266n6; *The Vicar of Wakefield* and, 149–50, 163

French Revolution, 14

Freud, Sigmund, 12, 101, 104, 222, 228–30

Fried, Michael, 73, 76, 216

Frith, W. P., "The End," from *The Road to Ruin* (Flameng engraving after), 73, 75

Frye, Northrop, 101, 233

Galileo Galilei, 208–10, 226; *Sidereus nuncius* (*The Starry Messenger*), 208–10

Gallagher, Catherine, 31, 49

Gambling, 107

Game theory. *See* Rational choice theory

Gautier D'Agoty, Jacques Fabien: *Myologie complette en couleur et grandeur*, 156; *Myologie complette en couleur et grandeur*, Plate 4, *160*; *Myologie complette en couleur et grandeur*, Plate 7, *161*

Gay, John, 139

Gaze, the, 163–64, 168, 173–74

Geertz, Clifford, 226

Generality (in science), 29

Genius, 216

George III, 138, 140–42

German idealism, 14

Giddens, Anthony, 4, 134, 262*n*5

Gildon, Charles, 44

Girard, René, 197

Glorious Revolution, 115

God, 31, 43–45, 124, 190, 212, 213. *See also* Providence

Gödel, Kurt, 221

Godwin, William, 156; *Caleb Williams*, 7, 15, 22, 154–74; *Political Justice*, 163, 167, 173

Goethe, Johann Wolfgang von, 150, 175, 215–16, 219; *Faust*, 100, 233

Goffman, Erving: *Forms of Talk*, 231; *The Presentation of Self in Everyday Life*, 12, 231

Goldsmith, Oliver, 136–39, 150–51, 163; *The Citizen of the World*, 136; *History of England*, 133; *Life of Bolingbroke*, 141; "The Revolution in Low Life," 139; *The Traveller*, 139, 140; *The Vicar of Wakefield*, 7, 15, 133–53, 163

Gombrich, E. H., 268*n*21

Goncourt brothers, 14

Goodman, Nelson, 47, 221, 226

Gothic novel: apparitional quality of, 104–5, 107; and modernity, 106;

probability in, 106–7; realism and, 7, 35, 106–7

Gouldner, Alvin W., 12

Government: Godwin's critique of, 167; impersonality of, 134, 143, 146–47; in 1760s, 140–43; tactical, 134. *See also* Politics

Goya, Francisco, *Caprichos*, 14

Graff, Gerald, 88, 90

Graham, Kenneth W., 267*n*14

Greuze, Jean-Baptiste, 76

Grimm, Jacob and Wilhelm, 101

Groupe Mu, *Rhétorique génerale*, 228

Habermas, Jürgen, 6, 8–11, 16, 39, 58, 63, 67, 238*n*7, 239*n*16, 246*n*5, 275*n*14; *The Structural Transformation of the Public Sphere*, 8–9, 67, 121, 238*n*8, 256*n*23

Habit, 125

Hacking, Ian, 35, 226

Hanway, Jonas, 138, 146

Hawking, Stephen, 90, 258*n*24

Hawthorne, Nathaniel, 107

Haywood, Eliza, 110, 117

Hegel, G.W.F., 211

Heidegger, Martin, 6, 57–58, 67, 96, 222, 231

Heisenberg, Werner, 221

Helvétius, Claude Adrien, 24

Herder, Johann Gottfried von, 101, 150, 213

Hermeneutics, 216

Heuristics, 188, 194

Heyne, Christian Gottlob, 216

Highmore, Joseph, 254*n*8

Hirschman, Albert O., 184–86; *The Passions and the Interests*, 10–11, 184–85

History and historiography, 33, 126, 226, 234–35

Hobbes, Thomas, 212, 269*n*3

Hogarth, William, 6, 57–78; *The Four Stages of Cruelty*, 77, 156; *The Four Stages of Cruelty*, Plate 4, *162*, 181; *A Harlot's Progress*, 57, 59, 64, 77–78; *A Harlot's Progress*, Plate 2, 69, *70*, 71; *A Harlot's Progress*, Plate 5, 71, *72*, 76;

Industry and Idleness, 76; *March to Finchley*, 59; *Marriage A-la-Mode*, 77; *A Midnight Modern Conversation*, 77; *A Rake's Progress*, 57, 59, 64, 71, 77, 78; *A Rake's Progress*, "The Rake in Bedlam," 73, *74*, 76; "Satire on False Perspective," 59–60, *61*, 254*n*8
Holmes, Oliver Wendell, 22
Homer, 114
Hooke, Robert, 29
Horace, 122
Horkheimer, Max, 8; *Dialectic of Enlightenment* (with Theodor Adorno), 8, 238*n*7, 265*n*2
Howard, John, 146
Hoyle, Edmond, 36, 107
Humanistic studies: in the public sphere, 81, 83; science vs., 80, 81, 84, 86–87
Humanity. *See* Man, definition of
Hume, David, 3, 5, 105, 117; on causality, 32, 41, 48; critical responses to, 85–89; *An Enquiry Concerning Human Understanding*, 84, 87–89; *An Enquiry Concerning the Principles of Morals*, 84, 87–89; on experience, 25, 32, 125; on experiment and moral philosophy, 27–28, 68; and induction, 6, 83; and judgment, 24; and language, 79–91; and morality, 27–28, 68, 83, 119; on purpose of philosophy, 6; and rational choice theory, 269*n*3; on reason and knowledge, 13, 28–30, 37, 41, 48, 68, 83, 86, 90, 126; and sense perception, 83, 105; and skepticism, 17, 68, 85; *A Treatise of Human Nature*, 13, 17, 25, 27, 60, 68, 78, 80, 83–91, 122–23, 126
Hunter, J. Paul, 245*n*1
Hunter, William, 181; *Anatomy of the Human Gravid Uterus*, 156; *Anatomy of the Human Gravid Uterus*, Table 4, *158*; *Anatomy of the Human Gravid Uterus*, Table 6, *159*
Hyperrealism, 6, 40, 66, 69, 71, 76
Hypocrisy, 186

Hypotheses: aversion to, 39, 43–45, 53–54; criteria for judging, 41; *Encyclopédie* article on, 39, 47; fictionality in relation to, 6, 40–41, 43–49, 53, 55; induction vs., 39, 42–45; Newton and, 43–46; paradoxical character of, 41, 48, 52, 55; role of, 41–42, 47, 53–54; truth in relation to, 48

Iconology, 65
Ideal citizens: Enlightenment and, 3; readers as, 10, 124; traits of, 6
Ideal types, 195, 272*n*23
Identification, reader's experience of, 50, 103
Ideology: meaning of, 134; novels and, 134; *The Vicar of Wakefield* and, 141, 143, 146, 150–51
Illusionism, 58–60, 69, 76
Imagination: realism averse to, 22; suspicion of, 41
Impartiality: of audience for art, 64; epistemological, 40, 119; imagination and, 76; and morality, 119; psychological, 12, 150, 157. *See also* Disinterestedness; Impersonality; Objectivity; Transparency
"Impartial spectator," 12, 64, 119, 123, 150, 157, 163, 173
Impersonality: advertising and fashion and, 230; free indirect discourse and, 149–50; in Hogarth's work, 76; the novel and, 76, 102, 218; of prisons, 142–44, 157; of realism, 147, 157; of science, 76, 119, 210; of the state, 141–44, 146–47; and violence, 155. *See also* Disinterestedness; Impartiality; Objectivity; Transparency
Indexing, in digital media, 11
Individuals. *See* Self and subjectivity
Induction: circular character of, 28; Hume and, 6, 83; hypothesis vs., 39, 42–45; meanings of, 247*n*13; the novel and, 28, 31; problem of, 30; and reflexivity, 3; in science, 29; validity of, 6

Inspection, as penal principle, 142, 146, 147, 157
Instantia crucis, 29
Interdisciplinarity. *See* Transdisciplinarity
Interests, 10, 121–22, 184–86, 190–91. *See also* Self-interest
Interpretation, 216
Intertextuality, 234
Ironic credulity, 31
Irony, 34–35, 233
Irrationality, 187–90
Iser, Wolfgang, 245*n*1

Jacobites, 115; "Tom Jones's Journey through England and the Jacobite Invasion of 1745," *129*
Jakobson, Roman, 229; "Two Aspects of Language and Two Types of Aphasic Disturbances," 227
James II, 115
Jaucourt, Louis de, 103, 250*n*26
Johnson, Samuel, 24, 40, 79, 112, 117, 118, 122, 123, 132, 136, 241*n*6
Joyce, James, 149
Judgment: as aesthetic, 239*n*16; Fielding's work and, 124, 126, 132; individual vs. communal, 167, 170; meanings of, 24; probability and, 35; and realism of assessment, 31, 34, 37; significance of, 13
Justice (in Godwin), 167

Kafka, Franz, 222
Kahneman, Daniel, *Judgment under Uncertainty* (with Paul Slovic and Amos Tversky), 188, 193, 194
Kant, Immanuel, 14, 210, 213; *Critique of Judgment*, 216–17; *Critique of Pure Reason*, 3; "What Is Enlightenment?," 3, 15, 39, 119
Keats, John, "Ode on a Graecian Urn," 233
Kierkegaard, Søren, 204
King, Giles, *A Harlot's Progress*, 73
Kirby, Joshua, 254*n*8

Kissinger, Henry, 188
Kittler, Friedrich, 52
Knowledge: accessibility of, 12, 22, 80–82, 87, 120, 213; conversation as means to, 119; digital media and, 11; in eighteenth century, 25–26; Enlightenment ideal of, 11; experience in relation to, 31–33; experiment as source of, 25–26, 66; Hume on, 13, 28–30, 37, 41, 48, 68, 83, 90; impartial, 40; language as related to, 79–91; Locke on, 31–32, 35–37, 242*n*13; and modernity, 27; the novel and, 5, 25, 31–37, 49, 242*n*13; organization of, 11–12; probability in relation to, 13–14, 35; public discourse as means to, 47; realism and, 5–8; scale of, 11; social production of, 66; theory in relation to, 33; transformations of, 11–12. *See also* Reason
Koselleck, Reinhart, 15; *Critique and Crisis*, 8, 238*n*8
Kristeva, Julia, 234
Kuhn, Thomas, *The Structure of Scientific Revolutions*, 225–26

Lacan, Jacques, 229, 230, 266*n*10
La Chapelle, Jean-Baptiste de, 47
Laclos, Pierre Choderlos de, *Les Liaisons dangereuses*, 10–11, 95, 183–99
Lacoue-Labarthe, Philippe, 224
La Fayette, Madame de, 103; *La Princesse de Clèves*, 189, 193, 198–99
Language: of everyday life, 231–32; general and specialized, 79–91; and ideology, 135; of literary classics, 100; modernism and, 222; national, 219, 222; plain, in novels, 100; psycho-analysis and, 228–29; rhetoric and, 226–28; transparency of, 212–13, 220
Laplanche, Jean, 229
La Rochefoucauld, François de, 184, 185
Latin, 215, 219
Lausberg, Heinrich, 225
Law: and authorship, 215; evidence in,

55, 105, 211; Fielding and, 111, 136; Goldsmith and, 136; legal reasoning, 42; and rhetoric, 211–12
Leibniz, Gottfried Wilhelm, 44, 213
Leibnizianism, 46, 53
Lennox, Charlotte, *The Female Quixote*, 23–24, 31, 36, 49–50, 55, 241*n*6
Levinas, Emmanuel, 155
Lévi-Strauss, Claude, 99, 102, 103
Liberalism, 220
Licensing Act (1737), 111
Linguistics, 226–28, 231
Literacy, 119, 213, 222, 229
Literary criticism, 232–35
Literature, with capital "L," 97, 99–100, 114–15, 214, 217–19. *See also* Canon, literary
Livingston, Donald, 68
Locke, John, 5, 125; *An Essay Concerning Human Understanding*, 78, 212; and judgment, 24; on knowledge, 31–32, 35–37, 242*n*13; and language, 84, 86; on politics, 16; and popular engagement with philosophy, 80; and rhetoric, 212; and understanding, 198
Longinus, 122
Luhmann, Niklas, 189, 194, 198; *Love as Passion*, 198
Lukács, Georg, 101
Luther, Martin, 189–90
Luxborough, Henrietta, 117
Lyotard, Jean-François, 13; *La condition postmoderne*, 239*n*16
Lyric poetry, 217–19

Machiavelli, Niccolò, 269*n*3, 276*n*31
Machines and machinery, 97, 100, 106, 108
Madman strategy, 188, 196
Malinowski, Bronislaw, 100–101, 103, 108
Mallarmé, Stéphane, 222
Man, definition of, 234, 277*n*51
Mandeville, Bernard, 186
Manley, Delarivier, 110, 117

Marie Antoinette, 14
Markley, Robert, 245*n*1
Marmontel, Jean-François, 17–18, 46–47
Marriage, 188–94
Marrinan, Michael, *The Culture of Diagram* (with John Bender), 15–17
Marshall, David, 164–65, 267*n*13
Marvelous, the. *See* Fantasy and the marvelous
Marxism, 262*n*5
Mary II, Queen, 115
Mass communication, 229–31
Mathematical probability, 35–36, 107, 184
Mathematics: language of, 80, 82, 86–87; philosophy and linguistics in relation to, 258*n*25; science in relation to, 40, 82
Mathers, Lawrence H., 180
Mazzolini, Anara Morandi: *Wax Female Figure, Close-up of Heart*, *179*; *Wax Female Figure, Parts Removed to Show the Stomach, Kidneys, Bladder*, *177*; *Wax Female Figure with First Part Removed to Show Superficial Layers, Ribs, and Structures of the Breast*, *176*; *Wax Female Figure with Parts Moveable to Reveal the Structure Beneath*, *174*; *Wax Female Figure with Uterus Removed and the Structure of the Heart Revealed*, *178*
McKeon, Michael, 42, 42–43, 49, 245*n*1
Mead, George Herbert, 12
Media: digital, 11–14; mass, 229–31; and reality, 106; visual, 222, 229
Medici, Cosimo II de, 208–9
Melville, Herman, 107
Metanovels, 105, 107
Metaphor, 227, 229
Metarealism, 104
Metonymy, 227, 229
Metropolitan Police (London), 111
Milton, John, 100, 126–27; *Paradise Lost*, 114
Minsky, Marvin, 232

Mirror neurons, 12, 16

Modernity: free indirect discourse and, 7, 102; the Gothic novel and, 106; knowledge and method and, 27; love in, 189–94, 196–98; postmodernism in relation to, 273*n*2; public and private in, 7; reality and simulation in, 106; rhetoric in, 204, 220–36; the state in, 141–44, 146–47, 219–21; *Tom Jones* and, 116

Modernization, 207

Molesworth, Jesse, 107

Monarchy (in *The Vicar of Wakefield*), 141–42

Monstrosity, 97

Montagu, Mary Wortley, 132

Montesquieu, Charles-Louis de Secondat, Baron de la Brède et de, 135–36; *Persian Letters*, 136; *The Spirit of the Laws*, 136

Monthly Review (magazine), 118

Morality: *Caleb Williams* and, 172–73; and conscience, 134, 157; consensus and, 71, 76; establishment of, 150; Fielding's work and, 124–25; Hogarth's work and, 64, 66, 71; Hume and, 27–28, 68, 83, 119; impartiality and, 119; and individual-social relationship, 7, 119, 150, 157, 167; justice and, 167; the novel and, 110, 118; readers and, 110; reflexivity and, 64

Moral philosophy, 27–28, 84

More, Thomas, *Utopia*, 26

Mulvey, Laura, 163–64

Murphy, Arthur, 127

Music, 219

Myers, Mitzi, 172–73, 267*n*14

Myths, 95–108; firstness of, 96; literature contrasted with, 100–101, 108; meanings of, 100–102; novels as, 95, 107–8; structural quality of, 108; style of, 96, 98–99

Narration and narrators: in *Caleb Williams*, 165, 167–74; causality

and, 52; in *Clarissa*, 109–10; and experiment, 27–28; and fictionality, 45; in Fielding's work, 110, 113–14, 122–24, 130, 147; first-person, 148–51, 156, 268*n*23; hypothesis and, 45; impersonal, 102; and induction, 29–31; and judgment, 34, 36, 42, 63; pedagogical function of, 10; and reality, 105; and reflexivity, 63; in science, 76; social manifestations of, 4; subjectivity and, 5; third-person, 54, 76, 127, 148–51, 268*n*23; in *The Vicar of Wakefield*, 143–44, 147–50, 163. *See also* Free indirect discourse

National identity, 219, 223

Nation-state. *See* State, modern

Naturalism, 21

Natural philosophy, 21, 23, 43, 84, 257*n*4

Nazism, 8–11

Neo-Aristotelians, 235

Neopositivism, 225

Nestrick, William, 104

New criticism, 232–33

Newgate Prison, London, 137

New media, 11–14

New novel: emergence of, 218; and the Enlightenment, 40; and experiment, 27; fictionality of, 24, 29, 49–50; and probability, 37; and science, 21, 34. *See also* Novel, the

Newspapers: the extraordinary and fantastical in, 105, 107; writing style of, 102

Newton, Isaac, 3, 29, 42–47, 82, 83, 249*n*24, 257*n*6; "General Scholium," 43, 46; *Principia*, 29, 43–44, 84; "Rules of Reasoning in Philosophy," 44

Newtonianism, 39

Nicole, Pierre, *Port-Royal Logic* (with Antoine Arnauld), 212

Nietzsche, Friedrich, 224–25, 231, 234, 276*n*31

Nixon, Richard, 188, 196

Novel, the: American novel, 107; Bakhtin on, 134; crisis of, 49; critical character of, 218; criticisms of, 23–24, 117–19; Enlightenment and, 40; and experience, 22–24; and experiment, 21–24, 27–28, 31–35; and fictionality, 43–44, 51, 55, 123–24; ideological character of, 134; and impersonality, 218; and induction, 28, 31; and knowledge, 5–6, 25, 31–37, 49, 242*n*13; and legal reasoning, 42; the literary canon and, 100; as Literature, 114–15; metanovels, 105, 107; and morality, 110, 118; as myth, 95–108; popularity of, 117–18; and possibility, 50–51; and probability, 35, 42–43, 50–52, 105, 126; and proof, 42; and the public sphere, 60, 63, 122; reader's experience of, 103; as representation of society and culture, 134–35, 142–44, 151–52; science in relation to, 4, 22, 27, 30, 51–52, 54–55, 244*n*1; virtual witnessing in, 28, 30, 40; and written vs. oral culture, 218. *See also* New novel

Objectivity: the novel and, 40; public discourse as means to, 39; science and, 48, 221, 225. *See also* Disinterestedness; Impartiality; Impersonality
Observation: Hogarth's work and, 73; science and, 53–54
Oligarchy (in *The Vicar of Wakefield*), 138–39, 142
Omniscience: in *Caleb Williams*, 168; in Fielding's work, 147; penitentiary design and, 142, 146, 157; in *The Vicar of Wakefield*, 140, 148, 149–51, 163
Orders, architectural, 203–4
Ordinary-language philosophy, 87, 89, 231. *See also* Accessibility
Originality, 214, 217
Overdetermination, as sign of factuality, 67, 69, 71

Painting, and the gaze, 164. *See also* Perspective
Parables, 44
Parfit, Derek, 188
Particularity, 29
Passions and emotions, 10, 184–85, 187, 198. *See also* Love
Paul, George Onesiphorus, 146
Paulson, Ronald, 59, 64–65, 77–78, 147, 254*n*8; *Hogarth: His Life, Art and Times*, 57; *Hogarth's Graphic Works*, 57
Penitentiaries. *See* Prisons
Penitentiary Act (1779), 135, 137, 151
Perspective, 59–60, 71, 164, 180, 254*n*8, 255*n*14
Pfeiffer, Michelle, 194
Phantasms, 104–5
Philosophes, 3, 9, 13
Philosophy: accessibility of, 83–89; common life vs., 91; and language, 79–80, 83–89, 258*n*25; and rhetoric, 210–11
Philp, Mark, 167, 172–73, 267*n*14
Piranesi, Giovanni Batista, 137
Pitt, William, 140
Plato, 206, 207
Plot: in *Caleb Williams*, 169–72; causality and, 7, 40; in *Tom Jones*, 28, 127–28, 130–32; in *The Vicar of Wakefield*, 146
Poe, Edgar Allan, 97–98, 100
Politics: Godwin and, 163, 165–67; liberalism in, 220; the nation-state and, 219–20; oppositional, 138–39; and prison reform, 138, 141; *The Vicar of Wakefield* and, 133–34, 138–53, 163. *See also* Government
Pope, Alexander, 59, 112; *Dunciad*, 97
Pornography, 180
Possibility: historiography and, 126; the novel and, 50–51
Postmodernism: architecture in, 204; and Enlightenment, 15; modernism in relation to, 273*n*2; rhetoric in, 204, 224; subjectivity in, 239*n*16

Poststructuralism, 155, 233
Pragmatics, 231–32
Pragmatism, 17
Priestley, Joseph, 46, 82, 83
Print culture, 63, 82, 90–91, 116–17, 213–14, 221, 222, 229
Prisons: contemporary, 153; free indirect discourse in relation to, 157; impersonality of, 142–44, 157; politics and, 138; pre-reform character of, 137; and realist novel structure, 151; reform of, 135–38, 141–51
Private sphere, 7
Probability: and common sense, 184; in eighteenth century, 187; emergence of, in nineteenth-century epistemology, 55; the Gothic novel and, 106–7; knowledge in relation to, 13–14, 35; mathematical, 35–36, 107, 184; meanings of, 35; the novel and, 35, 42–43, 50–52, 105, 126; reality and, 107; religion and, 212; science and, 51–52; truth in relation to, 54; verisimilitude and, 40–41
Prolixity, as sign of factuality, 66, 69, 71, 73
Proof, the novel and, 42
Propp, Vladimir, 99
Providence, 130, 146
Psychoanalysis, 105, 222, 228–29
Psychology, individual. *See* Self and subjectivity
Public discourse: consensus as goal of, 39, 63, 65–66, 119; disinterestedness in, 6, 9, 10; knowledge and, 47; transparency of, 212–13, 220. *See also* Conversation
Public sphere, 79–91; eighteenth-century, 64–65, 71, 119–21; Enlightenment principles and, 8–10, 213; fact and evidence in, 63; Habermas and, 8–10, 39, 58, 63, 246*n*5, 256*n*23; Hogarth's work and, 60, 63–65, 77; humanistic studies and, 81, 83; Hume and, 83–91;

ideal, 64–65, 77; impartiality of, 121; and language, 79–91; meritocratic character of, 120; modernity and, 7; the novel and, 60, 63, 122; science and, 39–40, 48, 60, 63, 77, 81–82; and women, 120–121. *See also* Audience and readers; Common sense
Publishing, 213. *See also* Print culture
Punishment, proportionality of, 136

Quintilian, 45

Rational choice theory, 183–99, 269*n*3
Rationality. *See* Reason and rationality
Rationalization: of love and sexuality, 188–99, 273*n*28; of prisons, 145; of the state, 141–42
Readers. *See* Audience and readers
Reagan, Ronald, 230
Realism: apparitional quality of, 104–5; characteristics of, 105; and consensus, 255*n*14; criticisms of, 21–22; epistemological, 47–48; facticity in relation to, 58–59; the Gothic novel and, 7, 35, 106–7; impersonality of, 147, 157; and knowledge, 6–8; as means of organizing experience, 4–5, 107; meta-, 104; and metonymy, 227; paradox of, 100; persistence of, 152; proponents of, 23–24; reflective awareness of, 152; *Robinson Crusoe*, *Frankenstein*, and *Dracula* as, 104; science in relation to, 22; style of, 100, 102; transparency of, 97–98, 100, 134, 157; and violence, 155. *See also* Factuality
Realism of assessment, 31, 34–37, 97
Reality: apparitional quality of, 108; indistinguishability of, 106; in modernity, 106; probability and, 107; representation of, 55, 58, 66–67, 69, 105
Reason and rationality: destructive uses of, 8, 238*n*7, 265*n*2; eighteenth-century meaning of, 184; fallibility

of, 13; goal-oriented, 195; Hume on, 13, 28–30, 37, 41, 48, 68, 83, 90; love and, 189–91; passions vs., 10, 185; and unreason, 187–90; value-oriented, 195; and violence, 155; Weber on, 195–96, 272*n*23. *See also* Knowledge; Rational choice theory

Reflexivity: and action, 67–68; cognitive science and, 12; and disinterestedness, 9; facticity and, 58, 69, 73; Habermas and, 67; Heidegger and, 67; in Hogarth's work, 69, 73, 78; and induction, 9; and morality, 64; in *Tom Jones*, 127

Reform, prison, 135–38

Reid, Thomas, 30, 39, 49, 87, 251*n*39

Religion: and anatomical dissection, 182; and prison reform, 137–38, 145–46; probability and, 212

Renga poets, 222

Replicability, 29

Representation: absorptive mode of, 73, 76; impersonal, 76; and language use, 90; of reality, 55, 58, 66–67, 69; of specialized knowledge, 80, 82, 88, 90; strong, 52, 55; and truth, 43, 44, 46, 48, 49, 55

Reynolds-Johnson Club, 137

Rhetoric: audience for, 207; and contemporary styles of knowledge, 225–36; decline of classical, 4, 204–21, 237*n*3; and disciplinarity, 235–36; in educational curriculum, 204–6, 215–16, 249*n*24; Enlightenment and, 207–14; and everyday life, 231–32; hypothesis in classical, 45; international character of, 219; Kant's criticism of, 216–17; law and, 211–12; linguistics and, 226–28; literary criticism and, 232–35; literature and, 217–19; and mass communication, 229–31; modernism and, 204, 220–25; Nietzsche and, 224–25; object of study for, 235; oral character of, 206–7, 211–12, 214; in painting-spectator

relationship, 73; persistence of, 205–6; postmodernism and, 224; psychoanalysis and, 228–29; purpose and value of, 206; and rhetoricality, 223–36, 276*n*31; Romanticism and, 214–20; science and, 66, 69, 76, 82, 207–11, 221, 224–26, 258*n*23; and social stratification, 206–7; topics in, 206; truth and reality promoted with, 66, 69, 76

Rhetoricality, 223–36, 276*n*31

Richards, I. A., 232

Richardson, Samuel, 24, 30–31, 40, 42, 103, 106, 109–11, 113, 117, 118, 126, 132, 218, 241*n*6; *Clarissa*, 32, 33, 41, 103, 109–10, 114, 117, 185, 241*n*24; *Familiar Letters*, 117; *Pamela*, 9, 10, 106, 109, 111, 112–13, 117

Richetti, John, 36–37, 100

Rights, 15

Rimbaud, Arthur, 222

"Robert Boyle's Air-Pump," 60, *62*, 69

Robinson, Charles, 97

Rockingham group, 138

Rococo art, 14

Roman, 46, 249*n*26

Romanticism, 14, 101, 204, 210–11, 214–20, 227

Rosenblum, Robert, 148

Rough-hewn quality of writing, 96, 98–100

Rouquet, Jean, 57, 59, 65

Rousseau, Jean-Jacques, 14, 52–53, 103, 117, 167, 168; *Confessions*, 103; *Julie*, 103

Royal Academy, London, 181

Royal Society, London, 66

Rules. *See* Rationalization

Sade, Marquis de, 164, 175, 197

Sadomasochism, 165

Salons, 9, 66, 77, 119

Satire, 59, 73, 218

Saussure, Ferdinand de, 226, 227

Schaffer, Simon, 6, 10, 28, 30, 40, 49, 66, 71, 102

Schelling, Thomas C., 188
Schlegel, August Wilhelm von, 100
Schubert, Franz, 219
Schumann, Robert, 219
Science: accessibility of, 82, 90;
    Enlightenment and, 207; fictionality
    in relation to, 6, 26, 29, 38,
    43–49, 52, 55, 82; the gaze and, 175;
    humanistic studies vs., 80, 81, 84,
    86–87; hypotheses' role in, 41–42,
    47; impersonality of, 76, 119, 210;
    induction in, 29; and language,
    80, 82, 89–90; meanings of, 244*n*1,
    257*n*4; the novel in relation to,
    4, 22, 27, 30, 51–52, 54–55, 244*n*1;
    and objectivity, 48, 221, 225; and
    observation, 53–54; and power,
    208–9; and probability, 51–52; and
    the public sphere, 39–40, 48, 60, 63,
    77, 81–82; realism in relation to, 22;
    rhetoric and, 66, 69, 76, 82, 207–11,
    221, 224–26, 258*n*23; speculative vs.
    inductive, 39, 53–54; and violence,
    155; and virtual witnessing, 6,
    10, 28–29, 40, 66–67, 77. *See also*
    Demonstrations, scientific
Scientific method, 26, 37
Scientific Revolution, 6, 21, 23, 27, 30,
    34, 39, 45, 49
Scotland, 115
Scott, Walter, 14, 106, 115
Secret history, 193
Self and subjectivity: Cartesian,
    210–11; of criminals, 137–38, 146; and
    decline of rhetoric, 210–11, 217, 219;
    free indirect discourse and, 7, 102,
    106, 156–57; the gaze and, 163–64;
    modernist, 222; and morality, 7, 119,
    150, 157, 167; the novel and, 21–22,
    50, 102; personality formation, 12;
    postmodern, 239*n*16; Romantic, 211,
    219; Adam Smith on, 7, 102, 119, 150,
    157; in *Tom Jones*, 124
Self-expression, 216, 220
Self-interest, 10–11, 184–87, 195–96,
    269*n*3, 272*n*23. *See also* Interests

Sen, Amartya, 270*n*3
Sense perception, 83, 105
Settlement Act (1701), 115–16
Sexuality: anatomy and, 175, 180; the
    gaze and, 163–64; violence and, 165,
    168
Shaftesbury, Anthony Ashley Cooper,
    Earl of, 257*n*3
Shakespeare, William, 97, 99, 100
Shank, Roger, 232
Shapin, Steven, 6, 10, 28, 30, 40, 49,
    66, 71, 102
Shapiro, Barbara J., 244*n*1
Shelley, Mary, *Frankenstein*, 95–100,
    103–8
Shelley, Percy, 97
Shenstone, William, 117
Sheppard, Jack, 166
Simulacra, 13
Siskin, Clifford, 16
Skepticism: as Enlightenment
    characteristic, 15; Hume and, 17, 68,
    85; the novel and, 21
Slovic, Paul, *Judgment under
    Uncertainty* (with Daniel Kahneman
    and Amos Tversky), 188
Smith, Adam, 7, 8–10, 16, 102, 117, 119,
    150, 157, 164; *The Theory of Moral
    Sentiments*, 5, 12, 64, 76
Smith, Thomas, 211
Smollett, Tobias, 137
Social networks, 12, 16
Social stratification, rhetoric and,
    206–7
Sociology, 231
Solitary confinement, 145
Solkin, David, 64, 77
Sophists, 207, 276*n*31
Specialization, language and, 81–88
Spectator, The (magazine), 9, 66, 78, 112,
    120–21, 126–27
Speculation, 53–54
Spence, Joseph, 97
Spenser, Edmund, 100
Sperber, Dan, 231–32
Standard Novels series, 96

State, modern, 141–44, 146–47, 219–21
Statistics. *See* Probability
Steele, Richard, 66, 112, 120
Sterne, Laurence, 106; *The Life and Opinions of Tristram Shandy, Gentleman*, 50–51, 55, 242*n*13
Stevenson, Robert Louis, *Dr. Jekyll and Mr. Hyde*, 95
Stewart, Larry, 77, 257*n*6
St. John, Henry. *See* Bolingbroke, Henry St. John, First Viscount
Stoker, Bram, *Dracula*, 95–100, 103–8
Structuralism, 233
Stuart, Prince Charles Edward, 115
Style: Addisonian, 112; architectural, 203–4; literary, 99; mythic, 96, 98–99; realist, 100, 102; transparency of, 97–98, 100, 102
Subjectivity. *See* Self and subjectivity
Supernatural, the, 97, 105, 107
Supranatural, the, 97
Surface, 132
Surrealism, 222
Surrogate observation. *See* Virtual witnessing
Suspension of disbelief, 18
Swift, Jonathan, 59, 112; "A Digression on Madness," 154–55; *Gulliver's Travels*, 33–35, 95
Symbolism, 227
Sympathy, 164–65, 167–73, 268*n*21

Tactical government, 134
Talbot, Catherine, 118
Tate, Allen, 232
Tchaikovsky, Pyotr, 14
Telescope, 210
Terror (emotion in novels), 97
Thackeray, William Makepeace, *Vanity Fair*, 14
Theory: Buffon and, 53–54; experience vs., 33
Things, 97, 100
Third-person narration, 54, 76, 127, 148–51, 268*n*23. *See also* Free indirect discourse

Thompson, E. P., 65, 141
Thoreau, Henry David, *Walden*, 22, 25
Tisias, 206
"Tom Jones's Journey through England and the Jacobite Invasion of 1745," 129
Topoi, 214
Tories, 116
Torok, Marie, 229
Tragedy, 114
Transdisciplinarity, 223
Transference (in psychoanalysis), 105
Translation, 88, 90, 100, 222
Transparency: of discourse, 212–13, 220; free indirect discourse and, 149; of prison architecture, 142, 157; of realism, 97–98, 100, 134, 157; of style, 97–98, 100, 102. *See also* Apparitions and the apparitional; Impartiality; Impersonality
Trimpi, Wesley, 45, 49
Trivium, 206
True Patriot, The (journal), 115, 117
Truth: hypotheses and, 48; probability in relation to, 54; representation and, 43, 44, 46, 48, 49, 55; status of, in modernity, 221, 224; verisimilitude in relation to, 12–13, 40–41, 54
Tversky, Amos, *Judgment under Uncertainty* (with Daniel Kahneman and Paul Slovic), 188, 193, 194
Twitter, 12, 16

Unconscious, the, 228–29
United States, 16
United States Constitution, 3
Universal Prussian National Law (1794), 215
Unreason, 187–90
Urban legends, 101
Utilitarianism, 14

Vaihinger, Hans, 45, 49, 249*n*22
Valenza, Robin, 12
Valesio, Paolo, *Novantiqua*, 228
Verisimilitude: crisis of, 44; Fielding

on, 50; probability and, 40–41;
scientific rhetoric and, 66; truth in
relation to, 12–13, 40–41, 54
Vertue, George, 64, 77–78
Vesalius, Andreas, *De humani corporis
fabrica*, 180
Vickers, Ilse, 245*n*1
Vico, Giambattista, 276*n*31
Vietnam War, 188
Violence: *Caleb Williams* and, 165–74;
the gaze and, 164, 168; realism and,
155; science and, 155; sexuality and,
165, 168; sympathy and, 164–65,
168–70, 172–73
Virgil, 114
Virtual witnessing, 5; in Hogarth's
work, 69, 71, 73, 76–77; in the novel,
28, 30, 40; scientific reasoning and,
6, 10, 28–29, 40, 66–67, 77
Visual media, 222, 229
Voloshinov, Valentin, 266*n*6
Voltaire, 46
Vossler, Karl, 226

Wallace Collection, 14, 240*n*17
Walpole, Horace, 54, 55, 106–7; *The
Castle of Otranto*, 35, 51–52, 106
Walpole, Robert, 111, 112, 141

Warner, William, 16, 106
Watt, Ian, 31, 34, 36, 97, 107–8, 165,
244*n*1
Weber, Max, 187, 190, 195, 272*n*23
Wellbery, David, 4; *The Ends of Rhetoric*
(with John Bender), 237*n*3
Welsh, Alexander, 52, 55, 105, 212
Whigs, 116, 138–39, 141
White, Hayden, 226
Whitman, Walt, 22
Wikipedia, 11, 16
Wilkesites, 140
William of Orange, 115–16
Williams, Raymond, 101, 135
Wilson, Deirdre, 231 32
Wittgenstein, Ludwig, 231
Wolf, Hugo, 219
Wolff, Christian, 53
Women, in the public sphere, 120–21
Wordsworth, William, "Tintern
Abbey," 219
Worldmaking, 47, 226
Writing to the moment, 109, 126

Zimmerman, Everett, 245*n*1
Zola, Émile, 21–23, 33; "Le roman
expérimental," 21

DATE DUE

PRINTED IN U.S.A.